David Conner

Also By Robert Shogan

*Hard Bargain: How FDR Twisted Churchill's Arm, Evaded the Law,
and Changed the Role of the American Presidency*

Riddle of Power: Presidential Leadership from Truman to Bush

None of the Above:
Why Presidents Fail and What Can Be Done About It

Promises to Keep: Carter's First 100 Days

A Question of Judgment:
The Fortas Case and the Struggle for the Supreme Court

The Detroit Race Riot: A Study in Violence (with Tom Craig)

The Fate of the Union

The Fate
of the Union

··

*America's Rocky Road
to Political Stalemate*

Robert Shogan

Westview Press
A Member of the Perseus Books Group

Copyright © 1998 by Robert Shogan

Published in 1998 in the United States of America by Westview Press, 5500 Central Avenue, Boulder, Colorado 80301-2877, and in the United Kingdom by Westview Press, 12 Hid's Copse Road, Cumnor Hill, Oxford OX2 9JJ

Library of Congress Cataloging-in-Publication Data
Shogan, Robert.
    The Fate of the Union : America's rocky road to political stalemate /
Robert Shogan.
        p.   cm.
    ISBN 0-8133-6750-6
    1. United States—Politics and government—1993–   . 2. United
States—Politics and government—1989–1993. 3. Presidents—United
States—Election—1996. 4. Political parties—United States—Public
opinion. 5. Clinton, Bill, 1946–   . 6. Dole, Robert J., 1923–   .
I. Title.
E885.S54   1998
320.973'09'049—dc21   97-13511
                                                                      CIP

The paper used in this publication meets the requirements of the American National Standard for Permanence of Paper for Printed Library Materials Z39.48-1984.

10   9   8   7   6   5   4   3   2   1

For Ellen

Contents

Author's Note

This book owes an initial debt to Tom Johnson, president of CNN, who suggested it and then helped to find its first home, at Turner Publishing. When Turner Publishing shut down after the merger between Turner Broadcasting and Time Warner, the book found a new home at Westview Press, thanks to Executive Editor Leo Wiegman. Along the way, I have incurred numerous additional debts, notably to the editors of the *Los Angeles Times,* whose flexibility with work schedules allowed me to carry the work through to completion. In particular I want to thank Jack Nelson, Dick Cooper, Doyle McManus, Don Frederick, David Lauter, and Drex Heikes at the *Times;* Michael Reagan, Alan Axelrod, and Greg Williamson of Turner Publishing; my friend Tom Allen; and my agent, Carl Brandt. I am grateful for the encouragement and patience of my two daughters, Cynthia and Amelia. My deepest obligation in this endeavor, as in most other aspects of my life, is to my wife, Ellen Shogan, for her research and editing skills, but mostly for her love and support.

Robert Shogan

The Fate of the Union

1

Born to Fail

ON HIS 1948 WHISTLE-STOP TOUR, Harry Truman, the icon of political underdogs, recalled an epitaph from a Tombstone, Arizona, cemetery and made it his battle cry: "He done his damnedest." Hopelessly behind in the closing days of his 1996 challenge to Bill Clinton, underdog Bob Dole made certain that no one would say anything less of him. The Republican nominee campaigned late into the night, forgoing food and sleep, and literally talked himself hoarse. "I trust the people," he rasped in West Covina, California, nearing the end of his self-imposed ordeal. "Look at my record," Dole demanded. "I look for your active help for the next forty-eight hours. Thank you very much and God bless America."

It was not much of a message. But even when his voice was hale and hearty, Bob Dole had little of consequence to say to the voters. Ambitious and forceful, a masterful legislator, and a shrewd judge of other politicians, he had miscalculated his own ability to adjust to the bizarre process of running for president. He had waged a brain-dead campaign.

Amidst the dying embers of his candidacy, Republican Dole often talked admiringly of Democrat Truman and his improbable 1948 victory over Thomas E. Dewey. That campaign had become part of the folklore of American politics. Never mind that the science of polling today has advanced far beyond its stage in 1948, when pollsters quit taking surveys weeks before the election. The photo of the victorious Truman holding aloft the *Chicago Tribune* with its monumentally inaccurate banner headline had been stamped in the minds of front-runners and long shots alike.

"Here's a man," Dole said of Truman, as his campaign raced on toward his own rendezvous with defeat, "who's a plainspoken man, and he never gave up. He was way behind in the polls. The *Chicago Tribune* said 'Dewey Wins.' The truth of the matter is that Truman won. And won by just hanging on his message. Defying the odds. Hanging in there."

Like Truman, though, Dole usually avoided fooling himself. He knew he was no Truman, and 1996 was not 1948. Indeed, many believed that this competition between Bob Dole and Bill Clinton had been over before it officially started after the August conventions. Certainly, since the second debate between the two candidates, when Dole finally launched his long-awaited and much heralded assault on Clinton's character—and far from damaging Clinton, only hurt himself—even Dole's strongest supporters found it difficult to maintain any hope for his chances. It was not some misguided faith in victory that drove Dole on in the campaign's dying hours; rather, it was pride.

Having played out his underdog role with dignity, Dole now had to consider his place in history. Losing was bad, no matter what, but how bad was a matter of degree. Dole knew what a landslide loss could mean to him and to his party. He was just coming of age in 1936 when that year's Republican candidate, Alf Landon, from Dole's own state of Kansas, had been overwhelmed by Franklin Roosevelt, carrying only the two tiny New England states of Maine and Vermont. Before that election, Maine's proud citizens had fancied their state to be a sort of bellwether, a notion embodied in the saying "As Maine goes, so goes the nation." After the 1936 election, wags put a different twist on the old adage: "As Maine goes, so goes Vermont." And Landon, who had been one of the most respected leaders in either party, became a laughingstock. If Dole could avoid that fate by talking through the night, he would never stop talking until every vote had been cast.

In contrast to his challenger, the incumbent president had started off the race with every advantage and had made the most of them all. Yet he, too, battled on until the final moments before the balloting. As with Dole, pride also drove Clinton. He had entered office in 1992 as a minority president, winning the popular vote by only a plurality, and that arithmetic had added to the obstacles that soured his first two years in the White House. Winning a majority of the popular vote, along with a hefty total of the electoral vote, would bring him a measure of vindication.

Yet as Clinton well knew, the significance of such achievements tended to be limited and short-lived. Two Republican presidents—Richard Nixon in 1972 and Ronald Reagan in 1984—had won huge victories, each capturing substantial popular-vote majorities and carrying forty-nine states. They subsequently learned that their landslides offered no protection against the scandals that rocked their second terms—Nixon's tenure foreshortened by Watergate; Reagan's reputation indelibly stained by Iran-Contra.

The dismal endings to those two presidencies confronted Clinton with a more pertinent question than the size of his own victory margin. This had to do with the battle between the two parties for control of Congress, the only issue of consequence that remained to be settled in the campaign. Yet in this competition, even the president could not be sure which outcome would best serve his own interests. Nominally, of course, he wanted the Democrats to recapture both the House and Senate. Still, he could not forget that the seizure of Capitol Hill by the Republicans in the 1994 midterm elections had worked to his political advantage.

"The best thing that happened to us is that we lost the Congress," Harold Ickes, one of Clinton's senior political advisers, told me a year after the 1994 earthquake that had shaken the congressional Democrats out of the power they had held for nearly half a century. "If we had won the Congress by a narrow majority, we would have had to struggle to get anything done. But when the Republicans took over, it became Bill Clinton against the Radical Republicans. They defined him better than he could have defined himself."

Then, chastened by their defeat in the great battle of the budget, the Republicans had become conciliatory. To help their own reelection chances, the GOP majorities on Capitol Hill had agreed to a series of compromises with the Democrat in the White House, which produced achievements that aided both parties in the 1996 campaign.

Looking ahead to his expected second term, though, Clinton had to wonder whether he would still be able to afford the luxury of such a collaboration. His first term concluded in a wave of allegations of assorted misconduct, which had somehow been obscured by the election campaign but still revived memories of Watergate and Iran-Contra. In the postelection Congress, lame-duck Clinton could find himself in trouble. And the notion of Republicans in control on Capitol Hill, free to conduct wide-ranging inquiries into the charges against him, was enough to spoil the taste of success already on his lips on election eve.

In the face of these uncertainties, even as the long campaign ground to a conclusion, Clinton seemed unable to decide which party he wanted in command of Congress. Instead, on his last day of campaigning, he brooded aloud about the shortcomings of the political system. Just after midnight, Clinton recalled at a rally in Bangor that when he had come to Washington to begin his presidency, he had been painfully weary of partisanship and all "that name-calling, liberal this, conservative that, Democrat, Republican." This election, he declared, was "an election of enormous consequence with a very clear choice. It's more important than the people involved and far more important than the political parties involved."

Yet whatever the importance of the election was, neither Dole nor Clinton had been able to explain it to the voters, a reality reflected in the evidence of a hundred or more public opinion polls expressing the apathy of the electorate. The campaign had boiled down to a contest between a challenger who could not explain himself and an incumbent whose explanations never ceased. It was fitting that at the end, the former should be mainly concerned with shielding his ego, while the latter could not make up his mind about the most important choice left for the electorate.

As for the voters, they had long ago tuned out. A Pew Research Center poll in July showed that more than 70 percent rated the campaign as dull, and about that same percentage assumed that Clinton would win. Dole's efforts to justify his candidacy earned a grade of D+, but Clinton did only slightly better with a gentleman's C. The validity of these soundings was borne out by the depressed turnout on election day. It was the lowest in more than seventy years, since Calvin Coolidge was returned to the White House in 1924. This modern record nadir in turnout came at a record-high price. The two political parties, combined, contrived to raise and spend the greatest sum lavished on an American election in history—close to $1 billion, much of it collected in possible violation of the law.

This dreary campaign was tailored to the convulsive pattern of events that had yanked the nation in every direction—except forward—throughout the final decade of the twentieth century. This fretful period began with the Gulf War, a triumph of American arms—and nearly bloodless for the forces of the United States—that vaulted Commander in Chief George Bush to levels of approval previously unvisited by any of his predecessors. Despite the bankruptcy of his economic policies, Bush's popularity made his reelection in the forthcoming 1992 campaign seem all but certain. As a consequence, the most prominent leaders of the Democratic party, quailing before Bush's polls, gave up on their chances of winning the presidency in 1992.

But severe recession and Bush's inability to respond to it eroded the esteem he had gained from the war, whose outcome left the nation's fundamental problems at home and abroad unresolved. And Bush's betrayal of his ill-conceived campaign pledge not to levy new taxes further undermined his prospects.

With the way back to the White House now opened to them, Democratic leaders deemed Governor Bill Clinton of Arkansas the most presentable of the slim field of candidates who had sought the nomination in the face of Bush's apparent invincibility. Once in power, though, Clinton stumbled repeatedly over obstacles created by the schizoid campaign he had conducted, in which he had cast himself simultaneously as the champion of a more conservative Democratic credo and as a paladin of the party's traditional activism. The public's thunderously voiced disillusionment in the 1994 election overturned entrenched Democratic majorities in the House and Senate, placing the Republicans in full charge of Capitol Hill for the first time since Ike's landslide victory in 1957.

Just as Clinton was widely faulted for possessing no firm convictions at all, the Republicans made themselves victims of their own convictions, by presuming these sentiments were shared by the electorate. Under the leadership of their new Speaker of the House, Newt Gingrich, the Republicans immediately set about promulgating a counterrevolution aimed at undoing as many as they could of the changes that Democrats had made in the federal government and American society over the previous sixty years.

By the time the Republican revolution was little more than a year old, it had collapsed in humiliating defeat, having inflicted immeasurable damage on the cause of conservatism and the Republican party, and having done for Bill Clinton, as Harold Ickes tacitly acknowledged, what he could never have done for himself—making his reelection all but inevitable.

Harnessed to the Republican majorities on Capitol Hill in an uneasy alliance, Clinton began his second term with no clear objective except to get through it. And even that minimalist goal was called into question when his scandal-ridden presidency was rocked by its worst scandal yet, stemming from charges that Clinton had obstructed justice in order to cover up a sexual dalliance with a White House intern. The results of subsequent opinion polls indicated that even though most Americans disbelieved Clinton's denial of the allegations, a majority were satisfied for him to continue in the White House, which suggested the extent to which this president had lowered the standards for the office he held.

As drastic as the shifts and swings of the past decade were, they represented not an aberration but rather a culmination of distortions and disruptions that haunted the American political system, particularly the presidency, in the last half of the twentieth century. All this was not the result of happenstance. At the root of the problem, as this book will show, is a political and governing system that was designed not to work.

The presidential election in which Clinton competed against Dole was the fifty-second in the history of the United States. The first was held in 1789 on the first Wednesday in February, when the presidential electors met, each in their own states, and cast their ballots. Although the outcome seemed certain, the votes were not counted until the new Congress assembled a quorum and convened in New York, nearly two months later. And it was not until April 14 that the secretary of Congress called upon George Washington to inform him that he had been elected the first president of the United States of America without a single opposing vote, adding the wishes of the Senate president pro tem that "so auspicious a mark of public confidence will meet your approbation."

With this simple ceremony, the American way of politics and governing formally began. More than two centuries later, near the close of another millennium, on November 5, 1996, what was remarkable and often forgotten was how little the fundamental system of governance under which Washington was chosen had changed. The overriding reality of the 1996 election campaign was that whoever emerged as the winner would have to contend against most of the same eighteenth-century restraints that had been imposed on the Father of His Country.

In many ways this suited Americans fine, because they had always feared and resented the idea of a government strong and efficient enough to intervene in their lives. But in modern times, as society became more complex and government expanded to meet its challenges, Americans had also learned to value the benefits that government brought to them. The tension between these two widely held attitudes—aversion to government and dependence on it—created the turmoil we are living through.

As Americans struggle to adjust to this dichotomy, they have to contend with one group of people that insists nothing is really wrong with the system and another that claims to have a simple cure for what is wrong, which they label a reform. But earlier, such panaceas have been tried and found wanting because they did not alter the fundamental governmental structure established by the framers of the Constitution. Indeed, these schemes often make matters worse by creating unforeseen new distortions in the political system and by raising false expectations.

Of the ten presidents who followed Franklin Roosevelt, the founder of the modern presidency, five have been Democrats and five Republicans. Three, including Clinton, had been governors, six had served in the Congress, and one had been a general. They came to the Oval Office from almost every section of the country—the West Coast, the Southwest, the Deep South, the Midwest, and New England—and have differed markedly in temperament and philosophy. Each initially had his own approach to meeting the responsibilities of the presidency. Yet ultimately, all of them created many of the same problems for themselves and their fellow citizens. Their combined experience makes plain that the chronic weaknesses of the presidency and of the political system overshadow differences in the characteristics of our presidents.

Bearing out this diagnosis is a series of other signs of ill health in the political system that have coincided with the troubles of the presidency. Voter turnout in congressional as well as presidential elections has dipped with almost every election, as has popular trust in political institutions and confidence in their ability to deal with national problems. Allegiance to political parties has fallen so steeply that the two-party system is in danger of disintegrating into a "no-party system." Instead of the long-sought partisan realignment that would establish a new majority coalition as a successor to the New Deal alliance forged by Franklin Roosevelt, the spasms of the political system have produced a permanent floating dealignment in which citizens, shifting their loyalties from time to time from one minority cohort to another, are doomed to stalemate, isolation, and frustration.

This condition is all the more disturbing because it followed a period of dramatic change aimed at making the system more open and equitable. The franchise was extended by constitutional amendment to eighteen-year-olds and by congressional action to black citizens in the South, who for a century had been denied free access to the polling booths. Supreme Court decisions brought an end to the grossest distortions of malapportionment and established the principle of one person, one vote as the rule of law. Regulation of campaign financing was greatly bolstered, establishing limits on spending and contributions, requiring broad public disclosure of both, and providing federal subsidies for presidential candidates. Agitation mainly within the Democratic party led to an overhaul of presidential-nomination procedures for both parties, spurring proliferation of direct primaries and a quantum increase in the number of voters directly participating in the selection of candidates for the White House. Yet these changes not only failed to overcome the problems of the political system but in some ways even aggravated them, adding to public disillusionment.

Underlying all this is the structure of the Constitution, which ensures what amounts to a gap between politics and government. The purpose of politics is to express the often conflicting concerns of the voters. The role of government is to resolve these concerns equitably. To put it in the simplest terms, politics defines what people want; government decides what they get. For democracy to work, government must respond to politics. This is where political parties come in. They are the best means available for connecting politics and government, by providing voters with meaningful choices between policies and candidates, and for holding government accountable to the electorate.

But under the Constitution, the parties were born to fail. The Founding Fathers were dead set against them. Hamilton warned that the spirit of "faction," a term then used interchangeably with party, "is apt to mingle its poison in the deliberations of all bodies of men." Jefferson declared: "If I could not go to heaven except with a party, I would not go at all." So much for heaven. Here on earth, the Constitution makes the task of parties next to impossible by ordaining a permanent antagonism between the executive and legislative branches that transcends party allegiance. By curbing the authority of parties in government, the Constitution undermines the influence of parties in politics and, in effect, institutionalizes the gap between politics and government.

The hamstringing of parties stems from the outlook of the framers of the Constitution, vexed by a series of dilemmas. Apprehensive of the power of government, they nevertheless felt they must bolster the tottering regime that had barely survived the struggle for independence. Committed by their rhetoric to the generous principle of popular sovereignty, they had learned by hard experience to mistrust human nature and doubt the wisdom of the masses. Fearful of monarchy and dictatorship, they also dreaded the tyranny of the majority. It was Madison, architect of the Constitution, who best defined the fundamental conundrum. "If men were angels, no government would be necessary," he wrote. "If angels were to govern men, neither external nor internal controls on government would be necessary." Since divine intervention could not be counted on, Madison crafted the system of checks and balances, which sought protection against the tyranny of either the president or the Congress by assuring that these two branches of government would almost always be at each other's throats. And for good measure, he created the judiciary as yet another counterweight to the other two branches. "The key to Madison's thinking," wrote James MacGregor Burns in his magisterial *The Deadlock of Democracy*, "is his central aim to stop people from turning easily to government for help."

The genius of Madison's scheme is that it relied for its effectiveness on the presumption of human frailty, which so dominated the thinking of the framers. Madison not only counted on the tendency of politicians to put their own self-interest above that of the larger good but did what he could to encourage that inclination. "Ambition must be made to counteract ambition," Madison wrote of the relationship between the Congress and the president. "The interest of the man must be connected with the Constitutional rights of the place." Madison transformed that vision of unending conflict into reality by giving the president and the Congress separate constituencies and separate terms of office, by granting the Congress the power to pass laws but establishing for the president the authority to veto them, and by enabling the chief executive to make appointments but reserving for the Senate the authority to reject them.

This combination of inherent restraints worked so well that it hamstrung Madison himself when he became president, moving him to complain to his colleague Thomas Jefferson that the rebellious Congress he faced had become "unhinged." It generated conflict and stalemate between the executive and the legislature not only when each was controlled by a different party but also when both were controlled by the same party.

"I've watched the Congress, man and boy for forty years," Lyndon B. Johnson recalled at the peak of his presidential powers. "And I've never yet seen a Congress that didn't ultimately take the measure of the president it was dealing with."

During the country's infancy and adolescence, with a frontier to conquer and exploit, the defects of the political system mattered little. But as the nation matured, its problems multiplied, forcing the weaknesses of the governing system to the fore. In the mid-nineteenth century, slavery provided the system with its most serious test and produced its first major failure.

By 1850, opposition to slavery, based not only on moral grounds but also on economic self-interest, was growing stronger and broader. This created the potential for an alliance of Northern businessmen and wage earners, Western farming interests, and small Southern freeholders committed to the prohibition of slavery in the new territories and its ultimate abolition in the South, a position that could have been moderated with proposals for economic compensation for slave owners and tariff concessions to the South. Such a coalition could have dominated national politics and presented the Southern plantation owners with an offer they could hardly afford to refuse.

But the two major parties of the day, the Whigs and Democrats, temporized, both weakened by sectional conflicts and squabbles between their congressional leaders and their presidents. The Whigs ultimately collapsed and were supplanted by the Republican party in 1856. The Democrats, under the irresolute stewardship of Presidents Pierce and Buchanan, watched the country drift into the Civil War and then saw their presidential candidates repudiated for the next twenty years.

After the war, the swift growth of industry and the cities presented unprecedented opportunities for graft and corruption. The great tycoons of the Gilded Age, determined to promote their burgeoning enterprises, were eager to reward the bosses of either party, whichever happened to be in charge, for special favors. This practical bipartisanship was summed up by Jay Gould, who controlled, among other things, the Erie Railroad: "In a Republican district I was a Republican, in a Democratic district I was a Democrat," Gould recalled of his political dealings. "In a doubtful district I was doubtful, but I was always Erie."

At the national level, from the late nineteenth century through the opening decades of the twentieth, the Republican party identified with the interests of business and the policy of laissez faire. The Democrats, their Southern base sheltered by their support for white supremacy, claimed to speak for the less privileged and for activism in government. But for the most part, the parties displayed their differences more in the generalities of campaign rhetoric than in specific proposals that offered the electorate clear alternatives to deal with the nation's problems.

Clashes between presidents and the factions within their own parties and Congress often overshadowed conflicts between the parties. Despite brief flurries of reforming zeal, neither party, when it controlled the presidency, was able to muster consistent support for programs to deal with the inequities of industrialization and the power of the economic oligarchs.

The party leaders who dominated the presidential-nominating process preferred candidates who would not make trouble and whom they could control. To break their power, reformers promoted the idea of direct primaries, which in theory would allow voters themselves a greater say in the selection of their party's candidates. The idea found support around the country, and by 1916, twenty-six states had adopted one form of primary or another. But the number was misleading. While in some states voters could choose directly between presidential candidates or delegates pledged to them, in others the primaries were merely advisory. Most delegates to the nominating conventions remained under the thumb of a state and local party boss. Presidential candidates soon lost interest, and so did the voters. After the 1928 Republican presidential primary, a North Dakota study commission noted that none of the candidates on the ballot had substantial support and concluded that "the election was a farce which cost the taxpayers $133,635."

Actually, the primaries had been oversold at any price. Like most reforms, the primary was only a superficial remedy, which did not attempt to cure the basic defects in the relationship between politics and government.

A far greater force for political change than the primaries was the nation's fundamental economic problems, which produced the Great Depression and led to the aggrandizement of federal power under Franklin Roosevelt. In his twelve years in the White House, Roosevelt maximized the possibilities for presidential leadership under the pressure of twentieth-century crisis. But he also suffered under the obstacles imposed by eighteenth-century strictures. Indeed, Roosevelt's recognition of those restraints conditioned his initial approach to presidential politics.

Campaigning against Herbert Hoover in 1932, FDR gave no indication of the bold programs he would recommend, if, in fact, he had yet thought them through himself. Addressing a campaign rally in Pittsburgh, the Democratic standard-bearer pledged to slash government spending and balance the budget. Returning to that city in 1936, seeking reelection after four years of record government outlays, he asked his top speechwriter, Samuel Rosenman, what he should say about the promise he had made in 1932. "Deny you were ever in Pittsburgh," Rosenman suggested.

Even as he fashioned the dramatic innovations of the New Deal, Roosevelt relied more on instinct than ideology and behaved in the American political tradition, playing ideas and advisers against each other. The implausible coalition he forged of Southern whites, Northern blue-collar workers, blacks, and Jews carried him to an enormous victory in 1936. But the election's aftermath demonstrated the limited impact of presidential success on the will of Congress. The lawmakers rejected FDR's scheme to pack the Supreme Court in his favor, the first in a series of setbacks on Capitol Hill, where the Democratic leadership was dominated by conservative Southerners. In full retreat on the domestic front when the United States entered World War II, FDR promptly announced the replacement of "Dr. New Deal" with "Dr. Win the War," thus sparing himself further embarrassment.

A deft maneuverer, Roosevelt was blessed with a buoyant temperament and a flair for theatrics. But his achievements could not be separated from the crises that shaped his presidency. Once the immediate threat to the nation's institutions subsided, business leaders and other conservative interests threw their weight against him. His supporters, who had helped him push through the landmark social and economic reforms of the New Deal, got bogged down in the institutional obstacle course created by the Constitution, particularly the bipartisan conservative opposition in Congress. The New Deal ran out of steam before it could get at the underlying causes of the depression. The outbreak of war mobilized support for the president personally, helping him gain unprecedented third and fourth terms. The wartime boom improved the lot of the voters who made up the New Deal coalition, but at the same time, it eased the pressures that had bound them together. Nothing in the system in which he had been reared inclined Roosevelt to provide his allies with a unifying, long-range agenda. More and more during his tenure, he relied on the symbolic force of his personality to hold his alliance together. No wonder, then, that after his death, that coalition began to crumble; and his successors have been struggling either to preserve it or to replace it ever since.

They failed because a combination of interlocking events and circumstances, in which nearly every factor seems to be both cause and consequence, widened the gap between politics and government. On one side of the gap, among the voters, sweeping social and economic changes eroded old political loyalties, producing what the sociologist Morris Janowitz has described as the "disarticulation" of our society. Meanwhile, on the other side of the gap, the government struggled against growing demands and rising expectations. And the parties, which ought to serve voters and their government, steadily lost authority and relevance.

For the past half century, Americans have been on the move in several directions at once—from the Northeast and Midwest to the South and West, from the cities and rural areas to the burgeoning metropolitan suburbs, and from old-line manufacturing plants into high-tech and service industries. The influx of immigrants of all colors and creeds exacerbates ethnic and racial tensions. Mounting economic and social pressures threaten the stability of the nuclear family. Fewer voters think of themselves as belonging to one group—Catholics or union members or Southerners. Instead, they now place themselves in categories that are either too broad or too narrow to meld into the customary political coalitions—consumers or commuters, for example, or gun owners or condominium owners.

Take the case of Dave Brown. He is a hypothetical example, but his circumstances are real enough. Brown is a skilled auto worker who earns more than $40,000 a year. His union endorsed Clinton in the 1996 election, but Brown voted for Ross Perot—mostly to protest Clinton's trade policies. Brown's real wages have not increased in nearly ten years, and he puts part of the blame on the North American Free Trade Agreement (NAFTA), which Clinton took pride in pushing through Congress.

Brown has other political conflicts over his job. On the one hand, he knows that the government pollution standards backed by Democrats, which the Republican Congress has been trying to cut back, add to his company's production costs and could take a bite out of his own paycheck. On the other hand, though, Brown likes to fish, and one weekend, he discovered that the lake he usually visits had been poisoned by chemical waste. All this leaves Brown uncertain where he stands on the environment.

Brown likes to hunt, too, and he belongs to a rifle club. Recently, he sent the club $10 to help lobby against gun control, which is more than he has ever contributed to a political party or candidate. All told, more than 20 million Americans like Brown belong to special-interest organizations, and an additional 20 million give money to such groups, far more than contribute to the two political parties. These citizens are walking multiple conflicts of self-interest, whose support the two major parties are having an increasingly hard time trying to gain.

Much has already been written about the Clinton presidency and about the nine post-FDR presidencies that have preceded his. But history is cumulative. The circumstances of each quadrennial have piled onto the next, melding the past into the present and outlining the shape of the future. This book explores the Clinton presidency as a continuum, first placing it in the context of his modern predecessors, then relating it to the events that led to his election and shaped his first term. Its aim is to illuminate the path down which our politics is headed.

The narrative that follows will show how social and economic change has transformed the anachronistic system bequeathed to us by the Founders into a political wasteland that is barren of ideas and remote from the concerns of the electorate, a breeding ground for cynicism and corruption.

In this misbegotten structure, innovations in technology and refinements in political techniques have undercut the traditional means of political influence. The preeminent technological force is, of course, television, which, with its capacity to reach mass audiences, has spurred competing media to expand their own reach and intensify their impact. The net result is media domination of political communication. "Men still talk to each other," the scholars Joseph Bensman and Bernard Rosenberg have pointed out in *America as a Mass Society*, "but what we say to each other is very often no more than an extension of facts and feelings relayed to us by the mass media."

The media have also enhanced the impact of polling, just as this branch of political science has come of age technologically. No pollster ever asked Dave Brown what he thinks about anything. But every week, Brown hears about some public opinion survey on television or in his newspaper, and what he hears shapes his views about politicians and issues.

Just as important, the polls influence the views of politicians about what the voters believe. The old-time politician, who took the pulse of his constituents by walking along Main Street, has been ousted by the scientific sample and its massive reinforcement by the press. While public pollsters like Gallup have increased their indirect influence on politics and government, private pollsters, armed with their computers, have been playing a greater direct role in shaping the strategies of the politicians whom they serve.

The combined impact of the new technology and the social and economic ferment of the postwar era have produced a new breed of candidates for offices across the spectrum of the political ladder, from alderman to president. Once in power, these self-selected politicians keep their distance from the parties that in the past helped provide some measure of accountability. Nowhere is this trend more evident that at the White House, where it has led to the personalization of the presidency. Unable and unwilling to depend on their parties, presidents have increasingly charted their own courses, relied on their own instincts, and tried to fulfill their own ambitions, as they strive to cope with the mounting burdens on the federal government in general and on the White House in particular.

Despite Clinton's claim that the era of big government is over, the importance of Washington's role in our lives has been enhanced by the sobering onset of the era of limits on national wealth and power and the need to establish new priorities for the uses of federal power and resources. Fresh anxieties have emerged to destabilize the political environment, as natural riches long taken for granted dwindle and global competition intensifies. Americans accustomed to pushing ahead toward broader and brighter horizons now worry mostly about preserving what they already have.

All this makes the president's job harder than ever—without a corresponding increase in power. In dealing with the Congress, the president remains what he always has been, a more or less coequal adversary. This is a problem for the president, even when his own party controls the Congress. But, of course, the problem is much bigger when a majority of Congress belongs to the opposition party—the state of institutional belligerency that, during the past two decades, has become the norm. During the sixteen years encompassing the beginning of Ronald Reagan's presidency to the end of Bill Clinton's first term, one party controlled the White House and both houses of Congress for only two years, the first two of Clinton's presidency.

Even when a majority of the Congress owes nominal allegiance to the same party as the president, the separate constituencies and divergent interests of the legislators make it difficult for the president to rely on them for support. "No member of that legislative majority has the constitutional duty, or the practical political need, to vote for each element of the president's program," Lloyd Cutler pointed out from bitter firsthand experience as President Carter's former counsel, when Congress as well as the White House was in Democratic hands. "Neither the president nor the leaders of the legislative majority have the means to punish him if he does not. In the famous phrase of Joe Jacobs, the fight manager, 'It's every man for theirself.'" And this anarchic condition has been aggravated over the years by the steady deterioration of parties and the rise of individual legislators who have learned to depend on their own resources and establish their own agendas.

Just as presidents have been victims of the changed political environment, they have also been guilty of widening the gap between politics and government. To gain support, they have made promises they could not keep and have lived to regret them, as Ronald Reagan did with his economic program, which pledged both tax cuts and a balanced budget. After persuading their party's legislators to face political risks, they have deserted them, as Clinton did when he abandoned the House Democrats during the budget battle. Impatient with their parties, they have ignored them, except as instruments to assure renomination, as Richard Nixon did in 1972. Stalemated at home, they have sought prestige by thrusting themselves into the drama of foreign affairs, as George Bush did in the Persian Gulf.

And by manipulating the power of the mass media, they have broadened the impact of the personalized presidency. Presidents have always enjoyed prestige, but in the past, they were regarded from a distance, as abstract representations of their office and their actions. The modern media, particularly television, have thrust them into our family rooms and inflated their personas out of all proportion. By transmitting their personalities into the gap that parties once were expected to fill, presidents have greatly enhanced their powers of persuasion; but by often focusing on superficialities and irrelevancies, they have clouded public debate.

In our celebrity-centered culture, the president has become the preeminent celebrity. Public fascination with his whims, moods, and incidental behavior, which the media stimulates and which the president exploits, fosters a pervasive mystique that further confuses values and judgments in an already distorted system. Thus it was that the public's attitude toward the office once cloaked with the dignity of General Washington reached a point, during the incumbency of Bill Clinton, where the chief executive would be questioned on national television about what kind of underwear he wore and, more remarkably, would answer the question without blinking an eye.

After he was wounded by a would-be assassin early in his presidency, Reagan's approval rating soared in the opinion polls, reflecting admiration for the good-humored grace with which he handled the ordeal. This was a natural reaction from a duly concerned and sympathetic public. But it was a measure of the potency of the personalized presidency that the positive public response spilled over into the totally unrelated debate over Reagan's economic policies, further hindering the efforts of the president's Democratic opponents to challenge his proposals.

Some might argue that Reagan was a special case because of his Hollywood-honed skills as a performer, but no one ever accused Gerald Ford of being charismatic. Yet during the first fourteen days of Ford's presidency, Barbara Tuchman noted that the *New York Times* ran his photo on its front page no fewer than twelve times. "Why?" Mrs. Tuchman asked. "We all know what he looks like. By packing our craving for father-worship into the same person who makes and executes policy—a system no other country uses—we have given too much greatness to the presidency."

A brief glance at the post-Roosevelt presidents shows that in trying to deal with the gap between politics and government, presidents have sometimes achieved short-term success and personal popularity, though usually at the long-run cost of increasing the burdens on themselves and their successors, not to mention their fellow citizens.

Sometimes outside factors have intervened. Thus, after winning his brilliant victory in the 1948 election, Harry Truman found himself stymied in his second term largely because of the outbreak of the Korean War, which drained resources from his domestic programs and ruined his popularity.

In other cases, presidents have made bad situations even worse. Dwight Eisenhower's muddled and passive response to the civil rights revolution, which erupted during his tenure, exacerbated the nation's already grave divisions over race.

Although his career was foreshortened, John F. Kennedy transformed the style of presidential politics in enduring ways. He irrevocably personalized presidential campaigning and the presidency itself, creating a mystique around himself while subordinating party and issues.

Trying to live up to the Kennedy legacy, and to his own grandiose pledge of a Great Society, Lyndon Johnson sought to create a consensus built around his own goals and ambitions, not a party coalition of groups committed to common interests. By sheer force of will, he tried to override disagreement and avoid debate on his policies. His prestige and his consensus became casualties of the war in Vietnam and the protest against it at home.

Richard Nixon gained the White House by catering to the resentments Johnson created and relied on this negativism to govern. But in trying to deal with his critics, Nixon abused his authority and destroyed his presidency.

Confronting a Congress made militant by the excesses of Nixon and Johnson, Gerald Ford sought to win support by distinguishing himself from Nixon. But he undercut his own efforts and added to general public cynicism by arbitrarily pardoning Nixon.

Running for the presidency in the wake of great public disillusionment with Nixon and Johnson, Jimmy Carter had early on stressed his faith in the American system of politics and government as one of the major themes of his campaign. Despite upheaval and scandal, Carter maintained that the system remained sound and vital. He made this point incessantly and so emphatically that he sometimes invited mockery, as he did one day late in his 1976 campaign against Gerald Ford, addressing a rally in Tampa. "Richard Nixon didn't hurt our system of government," I heard Carter tell that crowd, as he had told scores of other assemblages around the country. "Watergate didn't hurt our system of government," he said, and I noticed that some of his listeners looked puzzled and skeptical. "The CIA revelations didn't hurt our system of government," Carter continued with his customary litany.

At this point a young man standing near me lost patience. "It didn't help," he shouted. Those around him laughed, but Carter plunged a-head with his peroration. "Our system of government is still the basis that doesn't change, that gives us a way to correct our mistakes, to answer difficult questions, to bind ourselves together in a spirit of equity, and look at the future with confidence."

Carter had good reason to speak favorably of the system, for he had learned to use it to his advantage as a candidate. Moreover, the faith that he espoused in the system complemented his oft-repeated campaign promise to restore trust and efficiency to government through his own integrity and efficiency. Rather than attaching any fault to the system, he believed that the flaws of his predecessors were solely responsible for the failures of the presidency. But Carter underestimated the inherent difficulties of the political and governing system and overestimated his ability to overcome these obstacles. His adversary relationship with the Washington establishment, and with his own party, contributed to his inability to develop coherent policies.

Carter's failure elected Ronald Reagan. Reagan's effectiveness in promoting his personal popularity and the weakness of his opposition allowed him to make drastic changes in economic policy in his first months in the White House. But the hasty and haphazard machinations to which he resorted produced policies at war with each other, and the contradiction between his rosy promises and the gloomy economic realities soon became apparent.

Many gave Reagan credit for forcing an end to the Cold War. But whatever advantage Reagan gave his country in international affairs had to be balanced against the long-term economic problems he left behind, notably the federal budget deficit, which reached record highs in his administration. "For decades we have piled deficit upon deficit, mortgaging our future and our children's future for the temporary convenience of the present. To continue this long trend is to guarantee tremendous social, cultural, political, and economic upheaval." These somber words are Ronald Reagan's, from his first inaugural address. Intended as a battle cry for the Reagan revolution, in light of the ensuing eight years they serve better as an epitaph for his own presidency, which would haunt his unfortunate successor, George Bush.

2

The Coincumbents: The Price of Pragmatism

Even in a town where making history was the major local industry, Andrews Air Force Base, ten minutes by presidential helicopter from the White House, had always commanded special attention. For most of the past half century, presidents had departed from there on momentous missions all over the globe. Countless foreign heads of state had landed on its tarmac, amid appropriate pomp and ceremony. And no one who watched television news in November 1963 on the day that John Kennedy's presidency ended could forget the heart-wrenching return to Andrews of Air Force One bearing the grieving widow and the body of the slain president.

Yet in all the years when it had served as a backdrop to dramatic and transforming events, Andrews had never witnessed anything to rival the scene on Friday afternoon, September 7, 1990, when the legislative leaders of both parties, along with the president, gathered there for what they had chosen to call a budget summit.

Arriving by bus, the participants hauled their luggage to identical side-by-side bungalows. They marched in pairs by order of rank, behind their leaders—Senate Majority Leader George J. Mitchell of Maine and House Speaker Thomas S. Foley of Washington for the Democrats, and Senate Minority Leader Bob Dole of Kansas and House Leader Bob Michel of Illinois for the Republicans. As a homey touch, Dole brought along his pet schnauzer—and in a labored attempt at levity, presented to President George Bush a giant baseball bat dubbed the "big budget stick."

The mise-en-scène roughly resembled the opening of a summer camp, complete with name tags of a sort—orange laminated credentials emblazoned with "1990 Budget Summit." Indeed, Republican representative Silvio O. Conte of Massachusetts referred to the conclave as "Camp Run-Amok."

"It's a giant color war," joked a congressional aide. "We're the Raccoons and they're the Badgers."

These politicians badly needed a laugh. They were struggling to devise a new federal budget, with a gun at their heads. Unless they could reach an agreement on deficit reduction before October 1, the start of the new fiscal year, $85 billion in budget cuts would take effect, automatically, under the Gramm-Rudman law, the fiscal straitjacket that Congress had imposed on itself back in 1985 as an admission of its inability to deal with the deficit problem. In fact, they were under two guns, the other one representing the midterm elections due in November, when they would have to confront an increasingly impatient electorate and explain what they had done—or what they had not been able to accomplish—with the budget.

Tedium, heavily laden with anxiety, had for some time dominated their lives. Having already spent the better part of three months in a somber hearing room in the Capitol, trying to stem what seemed like an irresistible tide of red ink, they had decided to shift their deliberations to a converted cocktail lounge at the air force base. They hoped that a change of scenery, combined with the isolation from the Capitol clangor, would make their work easier.

And this notion was endorsed by no one less than the chief executive himself. "There's a new spirit of optimism that we can get an agreement," George Bush told reporters on his way into the session. But he added a note of caution. "It's going to take compromise," he warned. "Big differences remain."

And it did not take long before the underlying tension made itself evident. Dole accused the Democrats of spreading "garbage" through news leaks. He declared: "I am not certain we ought to continue to negotiate on this basis. Frankly, I am sick of it." Democratic Senate leader George Mitchell retorted that the Republicans were guilty of playing the same old Washington game.

In truth, no one expected the talks to be easy, because more was involved here than the budget. At stake in these negotiations was the future identity of both parties, an issue that, much against their will, the budget crisis had forced the party leaders to confront. The showdown brought to a head questions that they preferred to let slide by with high-sounding but empty rhetoric. The unsparing calculus of the budget document required the parties to spell out in hard numbers their goals and priorities, along with the price they were prepared to ask the electorate to pay for these objectives.

This raised questions that both parties clearly had a hard time answering. The Republicans, even though they had won control of the White House in three consecutive elections, had been unable to extend their reach to Capitol Hill and indeed had lost ground in both houses of Congress, giving rise to a new political maxim: "The Democrats can't elect a president—the Republicans can't elect anything else."

But the Republicans had an even more fundamental problem. Since the departure of Ronald Reagan after the 1988 election, they had been unable to find a way to make the conservative creed that inspired the party's activist core palatable to the electorate.

They could draw some consolation from the fact that in some respects the Democrats appeared to be in even worse condition. The inability of the Democrats to win the presidency during the previous three elections had robbed the party of the life force it needed to grow and govern. Unlike the Republicans, who at least knew what they stood for, the Democrats had lost faith in the liberalism that had once carried the party to its rendezvous with destiny.

Underlying the conundrums the leaders of the two parties faced, at their Andrews bivouac, were not only the miscalculations of the nation's current leaders but the impediments built into the system of government by the framers of the Constitution two centuries earlier. Although all presidents had endured the frustration that was James Madison's legacy to the nation he helped found, few presidents had greater cause for complaints on this score than the forty-first chief executive, George Herbert Walker Bush.

When he took office in January 1989, Bush faced a government more sharply divided along partisan lines than had any other newly elected president in the modern era. Bush and Richard Nixon were the only elected presidents in this century to enter office with both houses of Congress under opposition control. Moreover, the eighty-five-seat Democratic majority in the House represented the biggest such disadvantage for a new president in the 200-year history of the Constitution. Bush's predicament was probably the most conspicuous manifestation of the failure of either party to develop an enduring national majority during the postwar era.

His election followed eight years of mostly divided government under Reagan, a period that, interrupted only by Jimmy Carter's brief and fretful tenure, had been preceded by the eight years of division under Nixon and Ford. Republican congressman Newt Gingrich of Georgia, already a forceful voice for his House colleagues, told me at the time that Bush's stewardship would see a period of "schizophrenic muddling through," shaped by ad hoc alliances that would spring up to deal with one issue and then fade away when another controversy gave birth to another coalition. In fact, the circumstances that had overtaken the government of the United States in the closing decades of the twentieth century made such a pattern seem inevitable. The split-up of power between the presidency and the Congress—which had become the rule rather than the exception—had produced the politics of coincumbency, a condition of governance marked by stalemate and unaccountability that left both parties facing what the political scientist Walter Dean Burnham called "a choice between collision and collusion."

Faced with such a choice, most Republicans and most Democrats alike did not hesitate. Leery of rocking the ship of state and of imperiling their own positions, they plunged down the path of least resistance, haggling and bargaining along the way, as they produced a series of compromises that they touted as a demonstration of statesmanship. Genuine solutions to the nation's problems were put off for some other day, and voters were left to puzzle about the distinctions between the two parties and wonder whom to hold responsible for the national condition. It was a system with one over-riding purpose—the avoidance of risks—created by politicians who were paralyzed by the fear of the consequences of their actions.

Bush and his advisers had come to office well aware of the pitfalls of the system and of their own strategic weaknesses. "This is really a test of the system," the incoming White House chief of staff John Sununu said as he contemplated the Democratic majorities on Capitol Hill. "You look at the Constitution and I guess this is the kind of constructive tension that people planned on when they put that document together." But the framers of the Constitution, whose handiwork reflects their view of the limited scope of governmental responsibilities, would hardly have foreseen the range and scale of the burdens that confronted Bush and the congressional Democrats at the start of his presidential term.

For openers, they had to reckon with the federal budget deficit of some $150 billion, which, far from yielding to the policies Bush had so confidently prescribed during his candidacy, had instead steadily swollen to unmanageable proportions. Ranking right next to the budget on the list of difficulties was the trade deficit, which approached the budget imbalance in magnitude. And all of that was made worse by the insolvencies of the scandal-ridden savings-and-loan industry and structural flaws in nuclear weapons plants, each of which was likely to cost tens of billions to alleviate.

And this was not to mention problems of economic productivity and in-ternational competitiveness so profound that no one could claim to under-stand them fully. Also to be faced at home was the devastation wrought on society by inner-city drug use, along with other afflictions of the underclass; and overseas, the specters of terrorism and Third World debt. But of all these assorted crises and dilemmas that cried out for attention, it was the federal deficit that George Bush deemed the most urgent, the most in need of his attention. This was not just because it threatened to cause an im-mense infarction in the nation's economic structure but also because the problem had become particularly and undeniably identified with George Bush's stewardship of the country.

In simplest terms, Bush had become a victim of his own lack of convic-tions. This had been demonstrated years before, after his first significant victory in presidential politics, when he upset Ronald Reagan and won the Iowa precinct caucuses, the opening contest in the campaign for the 1980 Republican nomination. On the morning after that success, Bush swirled around the main dining room at the musty old Fort Des Moines hotel, sweeping from table to table, shaking hands and slapping backs, turning everyone's breakfast into a celebration of his triumph.

"I've got the momentum," he told everyone within earshot. "I'm on my way." When I asked him what message he would offer the citizenry now that he had emerged from his previous obscurity, he seemed puzzled. "I'm just going to keep going," he said. "I've got Big Mo."

As it turned out, momentum was most of what Bush had to offer, and that soon ran out. In a few weeks, Reagan recovered from his Iowa setback and defeated Bush decisively in the New Hampshire primary. By May, Bush was forced to drop out of the race. His fundamental problem was that he had never given voters a good reason to support him. His staff had seen disaster coming and had tried to warn him. "You're trying to substitute energy for ideas," his political director, David Keene, told Bush after his Iowa victory. "It would help if you could try to think of two or three things that you want to do when you're president."

Bush thought for a moment. "When I'm elected I'll bring in the best people and put them in charge of the government," he said.

"But what will you tell them to do?" Keene asked.

Bush just shrugged.

And eight years later, after surviving his genteel servitude as Ronald Reagan's vice president, Bush entered the Oval Office, and that question still begged an answer.

For a long time, Bush avoided ideological labels like the plague. Pressed in his 1980 presidential campaign to define himself as either a conservative or a moderate, he replied: "I don't want to be perceived as either."

"Well, you can't be both," a reporter contended.

"How do you know I can't?" Bush retorted.

After Reagan's triumph, Bush seemed more willing to place himself under the conservative rubric that by now dominated his party. "I am a conservative," Bush told the Ripon Society, one of the last strongholds of moderate Republicanism, in July 1985. "I voted along conservative lines when I was in Congress. I took conservative positions before assuming this job. I take conservative positions now."

But that meant little. By that time there was no one of consequence in the Republican party who was *not* a conservative. What sort of conservative was Bush? The traditional establishmentarian, the more contemporary neopopulist, or any of the other shadings in between that sharply divided his party? No one could ever tell which.

Bush instead allowed himself to be more or less identified, depending on the circumstances, with either of the two main branches of modern Republicanism—the Eastern Establishment traditionalism of his New England birthplace and heritage or the fast-emerging Sun Belt neopopulism of his adopted political base in Texas. That these competing forces pulled him in different directions, thus often serving to cancel each other out, did not bother him in the least. To the contrary, the result provided him with a defensive blur.

From start to finish of his career, Bush showed little interest in political ideas as such, regarding them as abstractions. He found it more comfortable to make political decisions based on opportunity for advancement and on his value structure, which was mainly defined by his sense of loyalty to organizations and the people associated with them.

That a man who harbored such a vacuum in his mind and heart could rise to the summit of his chosen profession of politics testified to his energy and his gift for establishing personal relationships that could aid and abet his ambitions. But more than that, it was a reflection of the political and governing system—for George Bush's career represented the apotheosis of the American political system. Indeed, immediately after his election, following a campaign notable even by contemporary standards for its vapidity of discourse and barrenness of content, he seemed to fit in at the Oval Office as comfortably as if he had been destined to serve there. "My constituents think he is the first normal president since Dwight Eisenhower," said former Minnesota representative and longtime Bush ally William Frenzel, midway through Bush's first year in office. "He is the guy who is like other people they know."

If, when it came to the podium, he was hardly a match for his predecessor, the Great Communicator, Bush nevertheless made his mark as the Great Ingratiator, a man who seemed to have no peer when it came to not rendering offense. Pollsters noted that not only were his favorable ratings higher than Ronald Reagan's but his negative scores were significantly lower.

Bush underlined his willingness to cooperate with the Democrats in dramatic fashion for all the nation to see during his inaugural address. "I am putting out my hand to you, Mr. Speaker," he said, turning to Speaker Jim Wright, seated nearby on the platform. "I am putting out my hand to you, Mr. Majority Leader," he said to Senator George Mitchell of Maine.

And for the most part, Democrats found him more comfortable to deal with than not only the ideologically committed Reagan but also their own party's last chief executive, Jimmy Carter. "Basically the difference between Bush and Carter and Reagan is that they said the system is bad and we're going to change the system," said the Democratic whip Tony Coelho of California when Bush took office. "I think Bush will say, 'Here's the problem. How does the system solve the problem?'"

And certainly the last thing that Coelho and his ilk among the Democrats wanted to hear was an attack on the system. They themselves had at least as much reason to feel satisfied with the system as did Bush, considering their own incumbency and considering that when Bush made his gesture of harmony to Wright and Mitchell, the Democrats had controlled the House of Representatives thirty-four straight years and the Senate for only six years less than that. But this state of euphoria was destined soon to evaporate. And by the time the president and the congressional leaders arrived at Andrews in that late Indian summer, it was hard even to remember the rosy outlook that had attended Bush's inaugural.

For this, both sides had much to answer for in the way of sins of omission and commission. But it was Bush who, as president, bore most of the blame and the burden.

The roots of the problem were in Bush's all too convenient shift on economic policy made in the Reagan years. Bush's views on such matters, like his views on most issues of the day, tended to be muddled and elastic. But one thing was clear about a man who otherwise avoided clarity like the plague: He had little use for the fancy theories of supply-side economics, which placed its faith in tax cuts as the master nostrum for the nation's welfare. When the supply-side cult first took hold in the Republican party in the 1978 congressional campaign—and nearly every Republican who counted boarded a plane chartered by the national committee to promote that idea—Bush was conspicuous by his absence. Later on, in his campaign for the presidential nomination in 1980, he directly challenged the supply-side catechism being preached around the land by Ronald Reagan. In words crafted by his press secretary, Peter Teeley, Bush dubbed the whole doctrine "economic madness" and, even more memorably, "voodoo economics."

It says all that needs to be known about George Bush that these phrases, along with his notorious "read my lips" vow not to levy new taxes, constituted the only memorable remarks the forty-first president uttered in public life, that the statements represented directly contradictory views, and that he ultimately disavowed both of them.

Once he became vice president—though his efforts to deny that he had ever used the "voodoo economics" phrase were undermined by the existence of network television tape capturing his words—Bush loyally sought to give the impression that whatever he might have said to question the supply-side doctrine, he had really and truly changed his mind. Since little of what a vice president says is held against him, Bush had the option of shifting his position on taxes once he ran for president himself. Indeed, in some ways circumstances provided good reason to do that. The deficit had burgeoned steadily in the Reagan years, fulfilling the worst fears of the critics of voodoo economics. And congressional attempts to deal with the problem had proven futile. But powerful practical reasons argued differently for a candidate for the Republican nomination.

Going back to the beginning of the Reagan era, the proponents of sup-ply-side theory had instilled into the blood and bone of the party's conserv-ative cadre the view that any tax increase was anathema. These tax-cut zealots had never accepted Bush as one of their own, nor had they sus-pended their suspicion of his lack of ardor and zeal for conservative causes. Bush had spent much of his vice presidency currying favor with conserva-tives in such an unrestrained fashion that columnist George Will likened him to "a lapdog." Was Bush willing to write off all that effort in the inter-est of leaving open the possibility of a tax increase during his presidency?

No, he was not, particularly since his political advisers, chief among them Lee Atwater, who would manage his presidential campaign, were urg-ing him to the contrary. The fact is that Bush in a way needed a firm posi-tion on something to arouse some measure of support. As vice president, he remained what he had always been—woefully inarticulate in limning some large view of national purpose, which would serve to guide the presidency he hoped to establish.

Senior leaders believed that what Republicans needed was something more than warmed-over Reaganism. "Whoever follows Ronald Reagan can't be just someone who exists within the shadow of Ronald Reagan," Frank Fahrenkopf, who had chaired the party during Reagan's first term, told me then. "He must have his own philosophy and tell the country where he wants to take it."

But Bush had trouble filling that bill. Asked about what he later came to refer to as "the vision thing" in a debate in Iowa, he declared lamely, "You have to have a vision. Mine is that education should be the number one thing." But Bush had other assets—financial support, better name recogni-tion, and the support of the party hierarchy—that would ultimately carry him through to victory. Even if he could not portray himself as a prophet of a new conservative faith, he could still succeed as long as he did not seem to be betraying the old faith.

Pressured by Atwater and fearful of the competition from New York congressman Jack Kemp, who had all but invented supply-side economics, when Bush officially announced his candidacy on October 12, 1987, he flatly declared: "I am not going to raise your taxes—period." Within forty-eight hours, that period had turned into a comma, as Bush sought to hedge his pledge under pressure from advisers who wondered how he could gov-ern if he imposed such a limit on himself. But political pressure was hard to resist. Although Kemp's candidacy faded, Bob Dole posed a serious chal-lenge in the New Hampshire primary. With his presidential hopes seem-ingly slipping away, Bush counterattacked, casting himself as a foe of taxes while depicting Dole, in a particularly stinging commercial, as a congenital tax hiker. That commercial and that issue killed Dole's candidacy and won Bush the nomination, or so most Republicans came to believe.

After that famous victory, it would have been difficult for Bush to retreat from his staunch opposition to taxes. And he ended all doubt forever, or for as long as forever lasts in a political time frame, with his acceptance speech at the Republican convention in New Orleans.

"Jack Kemp told me, 'Hit hard on taxes,'" recalled Peggy Noonan, Reagan's speechwriter who had been pressed into service as Bush's ghostwriter. But with the polls showing him trailing Democratic standard-bearer Michael Dukakis by seventeen points, it is doubtful whether Bush needed any urging from Kemp or from anyone else.

This was his darkest hour since New Hampshire, and he would use the same formula to save his hide. Noonan's draft read this way: "Congress will push me to raise taxes and I will say no. And they'll push and I'll say no and they'll push again. And all I can say to them is 'Read my lips: No new taxes.'"

More than four years later, Richard G. Darman, who became Bush's budget director, would recall for the benefit of journalist Bob Woodward that he had demanded that this pledge be deleted, denouncing it as "stupid and irresponsible." But the only objections Noonan recalled were from some unnamed aides who were more troubled by Bush's figure of speech than the substance of his words. There was no record of any previous standard-bearer making "personal organ references" in an acceptance speech, they advised her. But Bush decided that political necessity overrode such questions of delicacy. The line stayed in, the delegates roared their approval, and Bush had made himself a prisoner of his own rhetoric.

At first he escaped without penalty. With the economy roaring along in high gear, the Republican nominee quickly caught and passed Dukakis in the polls and swept to an easy victory in November. Bush's second campaign for the presidency in 1988 was as vacuous as his first in 1980. His advisers concluded that aside from stressing the favorable national condition, their best chance for success was to attack the Democratic nominee, whose own wooden personality and self-absorption made him highly vulnerable. As Eddie Mahe, a senior party consultant, told me: "We can't elect George Bush, but we can defeat Michael Dukakis."

Bush focused on half a dozen or so aspects of Dukakis's gubernatorial record—such as his veto of the law requiring the pledge of allegiance, his opposition to capital punishment, and, in particular, the weekend furlough he had granted to convicted killer Willie Horton, who had brutally assaulted a Maryland woman and her fiancé. "Clint Eastwood's answer to violent crime is: 'Go ahead, make my day,'" Bush told a campaign rally in Fort Worth. "My opponent's answer is slightly different. His motto is: 'Go ahead, have a nice weekend.'"

In a thoughtful essay summarizing the meaning of the 1988 election, Wilson Carey McWilliams pointed out that both Bush and Dukakis seemed to have more in common with each other than with any of the great presidents. Dukakis made it possible for Bush to succeed by avoiding ideas, because he avoided ideas himself.

It was, after all, Dukakis who declared that the election was not about ideology but rather about competence and then demonstrated during his candidacy that he came up short in both categories. Both candidates, McWilliams wrote, "reflected the fears and hesitancies of the contemporary public mind, but not the ability to lead or elevate it." Still, it was Bush who won the competition and therefore bore the responsibility for governing.

His inaugural address set the temporizing tone that infused his presidency. At some points in the speech, Bush sounded as if he meant to be vigorous and commanding. "A new breeze is blowing—and a nation refreshed by freedom stands ready to push on," he declared. "There is new ground to be broken and new action to be taken."

"My friends, we have work to do," Bush asserted. He went on to speak of the plight of the homeless, "lost and roaming," of the rot afflicting the cities, of the menace of drugs and crime, and the needs of children "who have nothing, no love and no normalcy."

But he had scarcely sounded this clarion call when he retracted it. "Our funds are low," Bush warned. "We have a deficit to bring down," he observed, without offering any ideas for doing so. Then he added, "We have more will than wallet"—a puzzling claim, since with sufficient will, the money could presumably be found to fatten the wallet.

Although Bush made only modest promises in the campaign and at the onset of his presidency, they were more than a match for his actions. While he styled himself as "the education president," the funds he sought to back up his words did not keep pace with inflation. The one promise he seemed most determined to keep was his "read my lips" pledge not to raise taxes. But many economists protested that a tax increase was badly needed to restore the federal government to fiscal health and allow it to deal with the problems Bush had referred to in his inaugural address.

However, Bush ignored that unsolicited advice. Not that the president and his advisers lacked data on the state of the nation's finances. As the second year of his presidency began, Budget Director Darman warned that the federal government was amassing a mountain of long-term budget commitments—ranging from federal loan guarantees and mandatory medical benefits to commitments for cleaning up nuclear weapons plants and bailing out ailing financial institutions—that was mortgaging the future of generations of taxpayers. These obligations, like the Pac-men in the popular electronic game, Darman warned, would gobble up the nation's resources.

Budget Director Darman proposed a series of marginal remedies: cutting back modestly on mandatory spending programs and depositing part of the current surplus in the Social Security Trust Fund. One solution he left unmentioned was raising taxes. But time was running out, as Darman's own figures showed: Interest on the national debt had risen to $176 billion that year, as the government continued to borrow heavily to finance its spending, and interest rates remained high. The amount of federal debt held by the public now stood at $2.2 trillion—triple that of 1980. By fiscal 1990, when the 1985 Gramm-Rudman law, designed by Congress to force itself to cut the deficit, required a budget deficit of $110 billion, the deficit turned out to be $6.1 billion over even that lofty mark.

And critics complained that the real deficit was actually twice as much as that, but had been camouflaged by bookkeeping devices such as a $65 billion loan from the Social Security Trust Fund to the Treasury Department. "No amount of tinkering with the legislative process can substitute for a commitment to get spending under control," Democratic House Speaker Tom Foley of Washington told *Time* magazine. "Some people look to procedural changes to get us out of our current mess. Will is what's required."

But will was manifestly lacking, both from the Democrats and from Bush. During his first year in the White House, Bush's unwillingness to come to grips with the deficit, and his equally notable lack of substantive accomplishment, had generated a blurry impression of his presidency. To counter that, the president and his advisers and supporters sought to foster what might be called the myth of the bifurcated presidency. Bush's strength in foreign policy, their argument ran, transcended his weakness as a domestic leader and his lack of a coherent ideology.

The myth barely concealed two obvious fallacies. The first and the most evident is that the president's burdensome domestic responsibilities can somehow be neatly severed from his more gratifying role as diplomat-in-chief. Strength abroad, of course, depends on strength at home, and the fundamental threat to U.S. security in the closing years of this century was not military but rather economic, a consequence of the dislocations in the domestic economy and the debilitating lag in education and technology.

The other fallacy was that Bush's diplomatic endeavors were born of an imagination and purpose that were made conspicuous by their absence from his domestic policies. In actuality, Bush's major foreign policy actions were mainly reactions, just like his domestic policy. Thus, his order to U.S. troops to invade Panama just before his first Christmas in the White House was spurred by the heavy criticism he had received for his failure to take advantage of the abortive military coup launched against Panamanian ruler Manuel Noriega in October 1989. The invasion succeeded in toppling Noriega but left unanswered a host of questions about the future of Panama and its relations with the United States, which years after Bush left the White House still begged an answer. The Iraqi thrust into Kuwait, which had galvanized Bush into action in the midst of the budget crisis only a few weeks before the encampment at Andrews, furnished another occasion for Bush to demonstrate his reactive style.

Bush sought to use that episode to transform the perception of himself as a temporizing caretaker, a weak and indecisive figure who was in danger of losing his grip on his own party, into that of a dynamic and forceful world leader. In this he had the considerable cooperation of the media, caught up in the drama of the military crisis and eager as always to personalize the presidency. Summing up a view widely expressed in the press at the time, the *Wall Street Journal* described the confrontation in the desert as presenting Bush with a "crucial opportunity to define his presidency."

But this view blotted out what Bush had demonstrated about himself during the first eighteen months of his stewardship. In fact, Bush's handling of the crisis in the Gulf, before and after the Iraqi attack, can best be understood not as a new definition of his presidency but as an extension and outgrowth of his past behavior. The threat to the country's economic and political security that did not become apparent until the Iraqi seizure of Kuwait was not an overnight development. Rather, it had its roots in Bush's overall failure to come to terms with the new global realities spawned by the collapse of communism and, more particularly, his shortsighted insistence on coddling the reckless ruler of Iraq, Saddam Hussein.

For all of this, Bush's ratings in the polls during the first eighteen months of his presidency were relatively high—and at one point, after the Panama invasion, reached a level above that of any other post–World War II president at a comparable point in his term. But a *Washington Post* survey taken at the same time showed that although approval for Bush was widespread, it was also shallow. "I think it's past the point where the president is the guy who can do a whole lot of good," said Wayne Doede, a landscaper from New Lenox, Illinois; "I feel he's not forceful enough." Ed Kraus, a Dayton, Ohio, firefighter, said of Bush, "The man, I think, could be a good president, but he's not the kind of man who can go out with a speech like John Kennedy did, and sway the crowd."

Perhaps the most striking measure of how little impact the public felt Bush was having on the government he headed was that when asked who has the most power in Washington, 53 percent of those interviewed said Congress; only 15 percent said the president.

What all this added up to was that in his first year in the White House, Bush succeeded in lowering expectations to the level where he could easily meet them. But that honeymoon was about to end.

The first signs of trouble came in January 1990, Bush's second year in the White House, when Budget Director Darman presented the administration's $1.23 trillion budget to Congress. The document not only proposed no tax increases but in fact embodied one major tax reduction, a cut in the capital-gains rate long favored by the president. To meet the federal deficit limits established by the Gramm-Rudman law, Bush's budget relied on spending-cut proposals that Congress had rejected in the past and on assumptions about the economy that many economists disputed.

Democratic lawmakers hammered away at the document, calling it unrealistic, too heavy on military spending, and dependent on overly optimistic economic projections. Darman shrugged off his critics. "I have yet to see a detailed plan from them," he jibed.

But it was one thing for Darman to dismiss the complaints of the Democrats on Capitol Hill, and it was quite another to actually come to grips with the ominous economic realities that confronted him and his boss, the president. The truth, as seen by Darman and his colleagues, Bush's other principal economic savants—Michael Boskin, the chairman of the Council of Economic Advisers; Roger Porter, his domestic policy chief; and Nicholas F. Brady, his treasury secretary and longtime friend—was a dark cloud hanging over the country's economic future and over the Bush presidency. The long Reagan recovery was over. The economy was headed into a recession. And unless Bush did something soon to soften its impact, his chances of regaining the White House in 1992 would go a-glimmering.

"It was probably the first and last thing they ever agreed on, or at least believed with any degree of certainty," Marlin Fitzwater, the White House press secretary, told me later. The abstruse and murky arguments over economic theory that came to dominate the inner councils of the Bush presidency had geometrically exacerbated the normal frustrations that Fitzwater faced as the administration's voice.

Something had to be done, Bush's advisers agreed. But what? Their initial reflexive response, for a capital-gains cut, won House approval in 1989 but was destined to die in the Senate. "We thought we had the votes in the House," recalled Fitzwater. "But Mitchell told us: 'Only over my dead body.'" Blocked from a tax cut, another regime in another era might have tried to stimulate the economy by increasing spending.

But if Bush's advisers believed anything at all, they believed down to the soles of their shoes that the government was already spending too much—and that increasing spending would only boost the deficit. The only remaining weapon to head off the recession, in their judgment, was, as Fitzwater put it, "for the government to quit borrowing so much money so there would be more money for the private sector to spend." And the only way to accomplish that was to cut the deficit.

Now the only road that Bush and his advisers traveled toward deficit reduction was spending cuts. But they knew from the start that this road would require Democratic approval, which would only come if the cuts were tied to tax increases. For this Darman was prepared. "This tax pledge is bad business and sooner or later we're going to have to break it," he told Fitzwater right after the election. "The trick," Darman explained, "is to mask it as much as possible, to make it politically palatable." Basically, Bush and Darman were calculating that the negotiations with the Democrats would give them cover for raising taxes, allowing them to claim that whatever they gave up in tax increases was offset by spending cuts.

But to supply-side hawks like Kemp and Gingrich, this was a mug's game. To their minds, dealing with the oncoming recession was fundamentally a political problem, not an economic problem. First they reasoned that the recession was inevitable, and no cut in the budget, whether by spending reduction, tax hike, or both, would end it. "We'll get through the recession, we'll grow our way out of it," they told Bush. As for the deficit, "The hell with it," they said. "We've lived with it for ten years and it hasn't hurt us yet."

Gingrich, Kemp, and their allies had their own alternative to deficit reduction negotiations with the Democrats. They urged Bush to design a package for economic growth, building around tax incentives to encourage investment. "Send it up the Hill," they urged Bush. "Don't expect the Democrats to pass it. But forget that. Use that package to run on in 1992. That's your reelection campaign."

But they never stood a chance. Not because of flaws in their argument, but because Bush did not consider them competent to make such an argument. "One of his failings was that he compartmentalized people," Fitzwater explained. "He only talked about the economy with economists. And he saw Kemp and Gingrich as politicians, not economists."

Bush departed from the position that had been the centerpiece of his presidential candidacy and his economic policy in an agonizingly slow series of steps. He gave a first hint in March 1990 when House Ways and Means Committee chairman Daniel J. Rostenkowski outlined a deficit reduction proposal that quite plainly included tax increases. Instead of the flat-out rejection that might have been expected, presidential spokesman Fitzwater called Rostenkowski's approach "serious and thoughtful."

Meanwhile, circumstances created mounting pressure on the president. In April, the General Accounting Office told Congress that the cost of the bailout of the debt-ridden savings-and-loan industry could run as high as $500 billion over the next decade, about triple what the administration had foreseen only the previous year. Later that same month, the Commerce Department provided more bleak news: The gross national product had grown only 2.1 percent in the first quarter of the year, while inflation had soared to 6.5 percent, the highest quarterly rate since 1981. And in May, the House of Representatives adopted a budget plan put forward by the Democratic majority that called for $13.9 billion in tax increases and rejected many of Bush's proposals for cuts in domestic spending. Republican House leaders did not even put Bush's own budget plan to a vote.

Soon after, Bush let the cat farther out of the bag when congressional leaders announced that the White House had agreed to meet with them to discuss the deficit "without preconditions," which presumably meant that the possibility of a tax increase would not be ruled out in advance. At first the talks moved slowly, and Democrats complained that Bush had so far failed to explain to the public the seriousness of the deficit crisis and the need for tax increases. But with economic prospects steadily worsening, thus swelling the anticipated size of the deficit, while the burgeoning savings-and-loan crisis added tens of billions to federal expenses, Bush came to realize that he had no choice but to change his antitax stand.

The truth arrived on a day late in June, with Congress scheduled to leave town on Friday for more than a week. Darman and Treasury Secretary Nicholas Brady were convinced that some sort of breakthrough was necessary before they left, to prevent the stalled budget talks from collapsing. Brady enjoyed special status as a longtime personal friend of Bush and his family. But Darman possessed a different sort of cachet, earned with his natural cunning and aggressiveness, augmented by the experience he had gained dating back to his role as a White House aide at the inception of the Reagan revolution. No one else could match his influence over Bush.

"Darman just walked out," Bush once remarked to a group of reporters during the budget deliberations. "And when you see him walking out, I go through a period of about sixty minutes of gloom." Out of respect for Darman's grasp of the inner power play in Washington and his command of political economics, Bush had given him more voice than anyone else in shaping his domestic agenda. And Bush found Darman's self-assured manner and cutting wit charming. While playing the part of Democratic standard-bearer Michael Dukakis during the rehearsal for the 1988 presidential campaign debate, Darman got a relaxing laugh out of Bush by donning a tank helmet, a reminder of the incident in which Dukakis made a laughingstock of himself while campaigning on a military base.

Darman was certainly not nearly that popular with others in the White House. His colleagues envied the high regard in which Bush held him—and resented the even higher regard with which he held himself. Then, too, they were put off by his ruthlessness in using his gifts to drive ahead and gain even more power and influence. Over the last decade, as Darman had steadily gained prestige and authority, he had left in his wake a trail of aggravated colleagues and embittered political rivals. Now the forty-six-year-old Darman faced the most rigorous challenge of his career as he sought to cope with the deficit, the Democrats, and the intransigent foes of taxes in his own party. Some of his fellow Republicans made no secret of their irritation at his high-handedness. "We meet every day before the next meeting just to see what Mr. Darman has in mind, so we're not surprised—as much surprised," Senator Dole quipped during the budget negotiations.

But such sniping did not deter Darman when he saw an opening to advance his strategies for dealing with the budget tangle, as he did late in June when he persuaded Bush to invite Speaker Foley, Mitchell, and Democratic House leader Richard Gephardt to the White House for breakfast on Tuesday, June 26. To ensure that those invitations were accepted, Darman first held a series of private meetings at which he hinted that Bush would take some initiative on a tax increase, without promising anything specific.

So the Democrats who arrived at the White House were hopeful but skeptical. Their host, the president, made the opening move. He produced a statement, prepared by Darman, which said only that "it is clear" that the federal deficit needs to be brought under control through, among other steps, "tax revenue increases."

But for the three Democrats this was not enough. Their party had written off its defeat in 1980 as due to the ineptitude of Jimmy Carter and blamed its 1984 debacle on Walter F. Mondale's brash promise to raise taxes. But Dukakis had steered clear of such a statement, and yet Bush had used the issue against him like a club. This was one snake the Democratic leaders did not want to bite their party again. Wary of Bush putting the burden of the tax hike on them, his breakfast guests insisted that he change the statement by adding two words that would leave no doubt about his responsibility for the tax increase.

In the rewritten statement released to the press, Bush acknowledged that "it is clear *to me*" (emphasis added) that "tax revenue increases" along with other measures were now necessary to solve the deficit problem. The die was cast. Bush and the Democrats were on the road that would take them to their September encampment at Andrews Air Force Base.

The Republicans viewed the budget negotiations as a trap set by the Democrats to ensnare Bush into backing a tax increase. They were right, of course. But Democrats faced the danger of being caught in their own trap. They could get much of the blame for any tax increase that the budget proposed and thereby lose politically. And by agreeing to the spending cuts that Bush would demand, they might antagonize their party's core constituencies. Nevertheless, they pressed on with the negotiations.

Like Bush, the Democrats were prisoners of their own emptiness. Bush, because he stood for little else, feared to break his pledge not to raise taxes, but he also feared the consequences if he failed to act. The Democrats had allowed themselves to be defined by their Republican adversaries as taxers and spenders. Now they sought to escape from that stigma, but they feared the price they would have to pay.

Although all the Democratic leaders at Andrews were troubled by this dilemma, the man who bore most of the burden of finding a successful resolution was Richard Gephardt of Missouri, the majority leader of the House of Representatives. Nominally, Gephardt had to defer to two more senior Democrats, Senate Leader George Mitchell of Maine and House Speaker Tom Foley of Washington, but he played out his own role more forcefully than they did theirs.

Although Mitchell's intense partisanship in promoting his party's interests was unquestioned, his style was restrained and moderate, reflecting the understatement characteristic of his native state. Once I encountered Mitchell waiting patiently in a long airport line for a flight back to Maine, which he seemed certain to miss, and suggested that he make himself known to the airline clerks to get to the head of line, Mitchell demurred, "Oh, I couldn't ask for special treatment." Fortunately for Mitchell, an airline clerk recognized him and hurried him on to the plane in time to keep an important speaking engagement.

Rather than a domineering personality, it was patience and tenacity, combined with shrewd judgment, that helped the Maine senator move to the forefront of the Senate, where he took over in 1989 as Democratic majority leader. In 1986, he became chairman of the Democratic Senate campaign committee and led the charge that won back the Senate for the Democrats after six years of Republican domination. In an era when Democrats felt themselves on the defensive, they found comfort in Mitchell. Named to the Senate committee probing the Iran-Contra hearings, his cool, dispassionate style served as an effective counterpoint to the often melodramatic testimony of marine colonel Oliver North. At one point, when North invoked the name of the Lord in justifying his actions, Mitchell retorted: "God does not take sides in American politics."

But aside from the limits of Mitchell's own personality, the fact was that the august body in which he served was more a reflection of its own traditions and privileges and of the prerogatives of its members, including the six-year terms they each served, than it was of the Democratic party. It was rather the House of Representatives that was the true base of the Democratic party's power and the true mirror of its infrastructure. With the collapse of the New Deal coalition and of the whole political system founded by Franklin Roosevelt and with the consequent limitation of its hopes for the presidency, the Democratic party was no longer a national party. Instead, the Democrats had made themselves into a loose affiliation of social, economic, and regional interests, which took different form and size depending on whichever particular issue was on the political agenda.

This characteristic provided the Democratic party with its greatest strength in Congress but turned into the party's greatest weakness in contesting the presidency. Unable to muster a coalition behind their positions on controversial national issues, the Democrats lost election after election for the White House. But in the struggle for control of the House of Representatives, they could fight separate skirmishes around the country, with their incumbents benefiting from the prestige and money that went with their majority status.

The Democratic Speaker of the House, Tom Foley, had not so much thrust his way to the top as much as he had sidled along with the help of circumstances, seniority, and well-placed allies. First elected in 1964, Foley served for a decade before he gained the chairmanship of the Agriculture

Committee. The previous chairman was ousted by the reform-minded post-Watergate class of Democratic House members because of his autocratic ways. In 1982, then Speaker Thomas P. O'Neill, who had become Foley's patron, made him Democratic whip, after the incumbent was defeated for reelection. That paved the way for Foley to be elected majority leader in 1986, when Jim Wright succeeded O'Neill to the speakership, upon the latter's retirement. The forced departure of Wright in 1989 under a cloud of scandal opened the door to the top post in the House to Foley.

The son of a judge and a lawyer, with early ambitions of his own to be a jurist, Foley was often said to possess a judicial temperament. Presumably, this was because he was a large man whose phlegmatic demeanor evoked an impression of solidity, which Foley's fellow Democrats believed was the right quality to help them escape the quagmire of partisan wrangling and muckraking that dragged down his predecessor.

They thought it reassuring that it was not hard to find a Republican willing to say positive things about Foley. "He is a thoughtful, bright guy who does not seek out confrontation for the sake of it," California representative Jerry Lewis, chairman of the House Republican Caucus, said after Foley's elevation to the speakership. "That is yeast from which comes compromise."

But whatever his inner strengths, Foley was plainly not eager for attention. One reason he was so obscure during his fifteen years in the House before becoming Speaker, and remained relatively so after, was his deeply ingrained caution—although he talked freely with journalists on a broad range of subjects, he almost always insisted on not being quoted by name.

As for Gephardt, he owed his rise to the leadership to persistence, skill at dealing with his peers, and adroitness at gaining favor with his seniors in rank and experience. With regard to these qualities, he differed only in degree from the other members of the Democratic leadership. But what set Gephardt apart was that his ambition reached well beyond the precincts of Capitol Hill to the nation's highest office. By the time the budget talks at Andrews got under way, Gephardt had already made one forceful thrust for the presidency. And though that had fallen short, few doubted that at some point down the political road he would again launch himself on the track for the White House.

Starting in politics at the entry level, the streets of his native St. Louis, he became the protégé of the local boss, who named him ward committeeman in 1969. This satrap maintained control of the handful of patronage jobs that went with the position. But for Gephardt the title was more important because it gave him the recognition he needed for his next step only two years later. In a campaign that established the personalized pattern that shaped his future races, he challenged the Republican alderman in the neighborhood where he had been born and raised, whose residents had known him years before as a freckle-faced youngster selling greeting cards. His voice was deeper now but no less earnest, and he still had the freckles and the quick smile that helped him gain the votes he needed to overturn his Republican foe.

In office, Gephardt gained prominence among the "Young Turks" on the city council who rallied behind the banter of civic reform. He helped blue-collar constituents fight for better police protection and garbage collection, once even responding to complaints by hiring a truck and making the pickups himself. In all of this, he was assisted by his friendship with Alderman Albert (Red) Villa, gruff ruler of St. Louis's South Side and a veteran of forty years of city politics, whom Gephardt allowed to become his mentor and who helped him make the leap to the U.S. House of Representatives in 1976.

On Capitol Hill, Gephardt followed the same pattern that had given his career its early impetus. "He succeeds best by endearing himself to his elders to the point where they delegate to him a great deal of authority," said John B. Crosby, who had worked for Gephardt on Capitol Hill. In the House, the first of Gephardt's several powerful allies among the higher-ups was veteran Kansas City congressman Richard Bolling, a revered figure among his Democratic colleagues, upon whom Gephardt had managed to make a favorable impression during his initial campaign for the seat he ultimately won. "My intuition told me that he would be stable and honest and all of the fundamental things that I wanted, and that he would also be a middle-range Democrat," Bolling would later recall.

Bolling pushed to get Gephardt placed on the powerful House Ways and Means Committee, an exceptional assignment for a freshman lawmaker. Not only that, Bolling introduced him to two of his powerful friends, House Speaker O'Neill and Representative Gillis W. Long, chairman of the Democratic Caucus, who would join Bolling in smoothing Gephardt's path to the top.

Not that Gephardt sat back and waited for help. As he had in St. Louis, he joined up with another group of Young Turks, the large assemblage of post-Watergate-era House members. "He was the fair-haired guy of leadership, and, at the same time, a leader of the bomb throwers," one long-term colleague later recalled. "He would stir the young guys up and then he'd go to Tip and say, 'The troops are restless.' And then he'd get credit from both sides."

But of all Gephardt's political talents, probably the greatest gift was the ability to adjust his beliefs, or at least his public positions, to suit the political environment he found himself in. In his early years in Congress, his votes reflected the conservative views of his blue-collar constituents—and the outlook of the businesses that contributed to his campaigns. As a freshman member of the House, with Democrat Jimmy Carter in the White House, he used his position on Ways and Means to lead the charge against hospital cost-control legislation, which he condemned as bureaucratic, though the Carter administration viewed it as the underpinning of its efforts at health reform. Instead, Gephardt backed a plan supported by the hospitals that relied on market forces to hold down skyrocketing hospital costs. By helping to defeat compulsory cost controls, Gephardt doomed the chances of health-care reform in the Carter administration, delivering a blow to the cause from which it would never fully recover.

And in Ronald Reagan's first term, Gephardt joined with the so-called Boll Weevil Democrats from the South in backing the sweeping cuts in income-tax rates, which was the heart of the so-called Reagan revolution and which many Democrats denounced as the cutting edge of "trickle-down economics." He was also a forthright foe of abortion, to a point where he backed a constitutional amendment that would override *Roe v. Wade*.

But all this was prologue to the next stage in Gephardt's career, which arrived in the mid-1980s as he moved up in the party hierarchy. He became chairman of the House Democratic Caucus, the party's policymaking arm in the House—and the horizon of his ambition expanded to include the presidency.

Then he shifted positions. From pro-life, a stance that would have made it all but impossible for him to gain his party's presidential nomination, Gephardt moved to pro-choice, explaining that although he was still troubled about abortion, advocacy of a constitutional amendment was making no headway, only polarizing society. Or, as he put it, he changed for "the sake of civil peace."

The congressman who had voted for the Reagan tax cut now vociferously criticized Reaganomics. On health care, he joined that tribune of the liberals, Senator Edward M. Kennedy, in backing a bill to impose controls on health-care costs, the sort of proposal he had successfully smothered in 1978. His own plan to encourage competition, he conceded, "was not completely doing the job."

And most important, at a time when cheap foreign competition was producing a huge U.S. trade deficit and mobilizing organized labor, the most powerful single force in the Democratic party on behalf of protectionist measures, Gephardt discovered the trade issue. Although he had no previous involvement in this field, he made a proposal, which would be the focal point of his legislative agenda, that required the United States to try to end unfair trade practices abroad through negotiations and threats of wholesale penalties. Ultimately, of course, it became the driving force behind the presidential candidacy that he launched in 1987.

Gephardt completed his ideological transformation when he hired William Carrick as his campaign manager. Carrick had formerly been a top political aide to Senator Kennedy, who had ruled himself out of the 1988 campaign, and was one of the Democratic party's canniest liberal strategists. He immediately proclaimed Gephardt's candidacy to be "an insurgency" against the Democratic establishment. But the vision of Gephardt as some sort of Midwestern Ho Chi Minh was hard to swallow. Not only did it not square with Gephardt's blue-eyed, clean-cut appearance, but more important, it was hard to reconcile with his status in the Capitol Hill hierarchy and his ties to the party's House leaders, made evident when they rushed to his side after he declared his candidacy.

And this dissonance undermined Gephardt's efforts to overtake his principal rival for the Democratic nomination in 1988, Michael Dukakis. The Massachusetts governor had won the first presidential primary in neighboring New Hampshire after Gephardt had come in first in the Iowa caucuses, and the two confronted each other in the Super Tuesday Southern primaries in mid-March.

In simplest terms, Dukakis, with his core support in the suburbs and among upscale city dwellers, reflected the beliefs and values of the party's liberal Eastern Establishment and the interests of the nation's thriving bicoastal economy. Dukakis castigated Gephardt as "the prince of darkness" for appealing to the angry side of America by exploiting the trade issue. Gephardt, hailing from America's economically hard-hit hinterland with his Missouri legacy of Truman-style populism, professed to speak for working-class voters, the foundation of classic Democratic majorities of the sort the party had been unable to assemble for a quarter of a century. He derided Dukakis as the candidate with the most money and "the least message."

Gephardt was at least half right on that point. Whatever the strengths or weaknesses of Dukakis's message, thanks to the connections that went with his job as governor of Massachusetts, he was far and away the best financed of all the Democratic candidates. As a result, the struggle for the nomination was not settled by the merits of the two arguments but rather by Dukakis's ability, in what turned out to be the decisive Super Tuesday contests across the South, to outspend his rival and drown out his message with negative television commercials.

Gephardt pulled out of the campaign in time to seek and gain reelection to his old House seat in St. Louis, returning to Washington when the new Congress opened at the start of the Bush presidency. But his mind was clearly on another office—the White House—and he seemed to be pawing the earth waiting for the 1992 campaign to arrive. "If you're in politics, that's where the real world is," he told me at the time, speaking of the presidency.

But then came the forced resignations of Speaker Wright and House Whip Tony Coelho, who had been right-hand man to Majority Leader Tom Foley. It was clear that Foley would move up to Speaker. And with Coelho out of the way, that left the road to majority leader open for Gephardt.

But taking that post, with the responsibility it entailed for the other House Democrats, would make it awkward to seek the presidency, which Gephardt badly wanted to do in 1992. Another man might have been torn by this choice. Not Gephardt. He had spent his entire career reaching for the main chance, and he did not turn away when this opportunity presented itself. Within a few days, he made assurances to Democrats in the House that he would not run for the White House in 1992, and the majority leadership was his. So far as the presidency was concerned, after all, a promise made could also be unmade.

Mindful of Gephardt's closeness to Bolling, who had a reputation as a champion of House procedures reform, and Foley's similar attachment to the late California congressman Phil Burton, another critic of the way the House carried on its business, some members speculated that the ascension of these two to the top leadership posts in the chamber presaged a new wave of change. "The reform movement will be in charge of the House," Wisconsin's David R. Obey told the *Wall Street Journal*, predicting "major institutional change" ahead.

But while some high-minded members talked about tightening rules on campaign spending and political action committee (PAC) contributions, all the close-mouthed Foley ever said was that "questions must be discussed and answered." And even that elliptical observation was more than Gephardt offered. Obey's expectations to the contrary, neither man lifted a finger for reform.

The major influence on them both came from neither of the two legendary wave makers, Burton or Bolling, but rather from the brash Coelho, who took to heart the axiom that money was the mother's milk of politics. Representative Charles B. Rangel of New York, who had been Coelho's chief rival for the whip's job, marveled at the Californian's willingness to take on and master the money-raising role that most others in the party thought unseemly. "Everyone wants the money, but no one wants to get their hands dirty," Rangel said.

Coelho did not seem to mind. And whatever his other faults, Coelho made no bones about where he stood. "I think I represent what our party used to be, as opposed to where a lot of people took it," he said of critics of his tactics during his ten years in leadership, first as campaign chairman, then as whip. "The party was eroding. We were becoming a minority party. For those people that are purists in philosophy, that's fine, because from their perspective purity is all that counts. I feel strongly about things, too, but I don't just feel strongly. I want to get things done."

Coelho did not explain explicitly what he wanted to get done, but whatever those things were, they clearly involved money, and he was just as happy to take it from big business as from anyone else. "Business has to deal with us whether they like it or not," he said. His message to the corporate PACs was blunt: "We're going to be the majority party for a long time, so it doesn't make good business sense to give to Republicans." But Fred Wertheimer of Common Cause contended that whichever party had the most votes did not matter all that much. "It is the PACs that are going to control the Senate and House, not Republicans or Democrats," he complained.

Even after Coelho left, his lesson lingered on with his apt student, Gephardt. In 1990, as Gephardt bargained with Bush's men at Andrews, he also had his mind on the elections that fall—and the presidential election in 1992. Whatever he had not learned about the value of money in politics from Tony Coelho, he learned from Michael Dukakis in 1988. Thus, as Gephardt warmed up for what many believed was another presidential candidacy, despite assurances to his House colleagues to the contrary, he raised $760,000 in money from political action committees, more than any other member of Congress.

But if taking money from huge corporations was a potential conflict of interest for Gephardt and the Democrats, it was not the only such dilemma. Overhanging the entire negotiations with Bush and the Republicans was a broader and more fundamental contradiction. In theory, the Democrats were the opposition party, arguing the case for those not satisfied with Bush and the Republicans and sharpening those distinctions in preparation for an electoral challenge to the president and the party. But in reality, the Democratic leaders at Andrews were collaborating with Bush on an effort to solve the budget problem, which, if successful, would help him gain re-election. Not incidentally, the Democratic leaders were well aware that such a solution, if it satisfied the electorate, would help their own chances of reelection, along with Bush's.

But not everyone in Bush's party believed in the political efficacy of balancing the budget, which was why the differences within each party were often at least as great as the disagreements between the two. Some of these differences were ideological, as in the case of the GOP whip, Gingrich, and his cohorts in the House, notably Dick Armey of Texas. Back in July, Armey, who was only in his third term but had become a force in the House, pushed through the House Republican Conference a resolution that, in the face of Bush's stated intention to break his pledge on taxes, flatly rejected any new taxes along with any cuts in Medicare. Right after that, Gingrich made clear that although he would keep his seat at the bargaining table during negotiations, he would have no part of any agreement that called for new taxes.

Democrats had their rifts, too, in part because of institutional prerogatives. In the first week of the Andrews meeting, when Gephardt met one-on-one with Bush's man Darman, the budget director made clear to Gephardt that he would cut a separate deal with Senator Robert Byrd of West Virginia on discretionary spending, which makes up about one-third of the budget, all the areas not covered by entitlement programs. Without Byrd onboard, Darman told Gephardt, he knew he had no chance to get approval in the Senate. Byrd knew exactly what he wanted, Gephardt was sure of that. And now Gephardt was equally sure that whatever it was, Darman would see that he got it.

He did, but in the process, Darman gained something *he* wanted, which was to have fateful consequences. Instead of compelling Congress to target the deficit, as the Gramm-Rudman law did, Darman wanted Congress to target spending. Congress could not really control the deficit, since it depended on revenues, which in turn depended on the state of the economy. But levels of spending on discretionary programs, as contrasted with entitlement programs, could be controlled. This was what Darman wanted Byrd to approve.

The deal he offered Byrd was part of a five-year budget agreement. Byrd would get extra billions to spend on domestic programs, including pork-barrel projects in West Virginia, in the early years of the agreement, in return for which Byrd would sign off on limits, or "caps" as they were called, on discretionary spending, which would get tighter over the five-year period. Byrd, as Matthew Miller, who would later become a senior adviser in Clinton's budget office, pointed out, figured he would take the cash and worry about the caps later. In the years to come, Byrd assumed Democrats would find a way to raise those limits. But Darman calculated that once in place, bolstered by the force of inertia, the caps would prove too risky a target for the Democrats to challenge. And he would prove to be right.

But other problems, having to do with issues and temperament, confronted the negotiators. After the first few days, Phil Gramm, progenitor of Gramm-Rudman, laid down the law. His support, considered in its way just as vital to Republican Senate votes as Byrd's was to Democratic support, was dependent on a cut in entitlement costs totaling $120 billion over the five-year span of the agreement.

When Gramm made his announcement, Gephardt and the Democrats were in despair, trying to figure out a way to reach Gramm's bottom line. Gephardt brought the problem home with him to brood about in the Virginia suburbs and barely slept that night. Driving back to Andrews the next morning, with one of his aides at the wheel, Gephardt pulled out some sheets on entitlements from the last budget and went to work on a yellow legal pad.

At Andrews, Gephardt showed his numbers to his colleagues and they decided to go all-out, making cuts that they had always considered off-limits. They worked on it all that day and on through the weekend, and at the first session Monday morning, they proudly laid their handiwork before John Sununu, Bush's chief of staff.

In his two years in Washington, Sununu had built a reputation for unsurpassed arrogance and unpleasantness, and on this occasion, he lived up to his billing. After glancing at the paper briefly, he contemptuously tossed it away. "This is only $100 billion," he snapped. "Where's the other $20 billion?"

This was nit-picking on a scale beyond anything the Democrats had ever witnessed. For the moment, they were struck dumb with outrage. Then they protested bitterly. As the argument raged, Dole, taking in the scene and realizing that the talks were about to collapse, scribbled a note and passed it on to Darman, who glanced at it quickly, cleared his throat, and said: "I think we had better caucus." And the Republicans left the room.

When they returned, the Democrats were still furious.

Byrd administered an old-fashioned West Virginia tongue-lashing to Sununu and Darman, calling them "arrogant" and "rude." An angry Leon Panetta of California, chairman of the House Budget Committee, weary not only of Sununu but of Darman and his high-handed style, demanded to know if Darman was trying to browbeat the Democrats, much as he bullied his own staff at the budget agency.

But Darman refused to stay on the defensive. "Look," he shouted back at Panetta, "I'm your only friend here." Despite the harsh exchanges, by allowing the lawmakers to vent their frustration, the episode probably helped keep the negotiations alive.

All told, the talks at Andrews dragged on for eleven days. During one break, some Republican bargainers played nine holes on the base golf course—though other Republicans were annoyed when House Whip William H. Gray showed up for talks in tennis clothes. Food became a high point—especially the vanilla ice cream and hot-fudge sauce served at the snack bar and the Officers' Club regular Monday night prime-rib special.

"Maybe it would have ended sooner if the food wasn't so good," said one of the Republican negotiators. "It wasn't going to end before prime-rib night rolled around again. On Monday night, we had our prime rib and left."

"We had hit the wall," a member of the Democratic bargaining team conceded later. On Monday, September 17, they pulled up stakes at Andrews, their isolation having outlived its usefulness.

Back in Washington talks resumed on the following Wednesday in Speaker Foley's office, limited this time to the so-called Big Eight—Foley, Gephardt, and Mitchell for the Democrats; and for the Republicans, Senate Leader Dole, House Leader Bob Michel, and the White House contingent of Sununu, Darman, and Brady.

The ten days at Andrews had already produced consensus on a number of specifics that laid a foundation for an ultimate agreement—notably billions in tax increases on luxury goods, cigarettes, liquor, beer, wine, insurance companies, and airline passenger travel over the next five years. But one major sticking point remained: Bush's repeated demand for a sharp cut in the tax on capital gains—profits from the sale of stocks, bonds, and other assets. This, the Democrats said, they would only concede in exchange for a boost in taxes on the very rich, an idea that the Republicans resisted.

On Sunday afternoon, September 23, the fifth day of wrangling in the Speaker's office, Gephardt lost patience with Sununu's refusal to consider the surtax on the rich. "Why," he asked, not petulantly, but in a conversational tone, as one politician to another, "do you want to protect people making over $1 million a year?"

Sununu did not blink an eye. "It's the American dream," he replied.

George Mitchell snorted. "It's the American experience," he snapped, "that the more money you make, the less tax you pay."

That finished the idea of trading a capital-gains cut for a boost in taxes on the rich.

Talks went on into yet another week, the third since the excursion to Andrews. The Democrats took heart from the Republican willingness to drop the demand for a reduction in capital-gains tax, which they decided showed the GOP's willingness to make a deal. The Republicans comforted themselves with the fact that even if they had been forced to agree to increasing taxes, they had blocked Democratic efforts to raise income tax *rates*; that would have amounted to a repudiation of supply-side theory. Perhaps most important, both sides knew that time was running out on the October 1 deadline under Gramm-Rudman, which would impose $85 billion worth of automatic, across-the-board spending cuts.

On Friday, September 28, the Big Eight talked through the night and seemed close to agreement. But when they returned the next night, both sides wanted changes. They argued even later than the night before, until finally each side gave up and simply surrendered to the pressures for accord. Their plan embodied sweeping tax increases and spending cuts designed to slash the federal budget deficit by $40 billion during the next fiscal year and by a total of $500 billion over the next five years. In addition to the increased levies on gasoline, cigarettes, beer, and luxury goods amounting to $134 billion over the next five years, the harsh steps included a boost in Medicare premiums and a scaling back of itemized deductions for all taxpayers with incomes above $100,000—not to mention Darman's spending caps that would cut federal outlays by more than $180 billion by 1995.

Even so, the agreement fell a full $10 billion short of the $50-billion reduction that negotiators originally wanted to achieve. And despite this fiscal blueprint, which was the largest deficit reduction plan ever proposed, the deficit for the new fiscal year was still expected to top $250 billion—in good measure because of the slowdown in the nation's economy, which was just beginning to be felt and would have fateful consequences.

The negotiators set Sunday, the final day in September, for a public unveiling of their handiwork. But each side had a bad case of negotiator's remorse. Early that morning, Darman called on Byrd in his Senate office, trying to get the Appropriations Committee chairman to agree to lower the caps on discretionary spending. But the crusty old lawmaker stood his ground. Then it was the Democrats' turn to try to rework the deal to their advantage. Gephardt met with Darman to persuade him to agree to cut more out of defense and put the difference into social programs.

Darman would have none of it. He reminded Gephardt that Bush had gone to the United Nations that morning to bolster support for the vast Desert Shield military buildup then unfolding in the Persian Gulf. "He's on his way back now," Darman snapped at Gephardt. "You have fifteen minutes to make up your minds."

Gephardt consulted with Foley and Mitchell. The mood was somber. They had achieved an agreement. But now that they had reached their goal, the satisfaction they might have expected to feel was ruined by their awareness of the price they had paid—the tax hikes that would hit their own constituents and the spending limits that would drain the energy and imagination that had been the party's life force for half a century. "We were sick with what we had done," one of them later confessed to his aides. But they had agreed they had no choice but to accept the hard bargain they had made. "We're going ahead," Gephardt told Darman.

They gathered for the announcement in the Rose Garden, where Bush did the honors. "It is balanced, it is fair, and in my view it is what the United States of America needs at this point in its history," the president said.

"The alternative to this agreement is fiscal chaos," Gephardt said. He conceded disagreement. "What delayed us for months is what has divided us for a decade," he explained. "The parties to these talks continue to have deep disagreements over values, the role of government, and the fairness of our taxes. But we all made compromises in the national interest."

Given the lack of enthusiasm for the plan among its own progenitors, the reaction from the rest of Congress and the public was only to be expected. The trouble started even before the Rose Garden announcement. At a meeting with his party's leadership beforehand, Bush pleaded with them for support, with particular emphasis on Gingrich.

"I haven't read it yet," the whip said. "I'm going to read it and I'll see what I think." But it was an ill omen that he chose to absent himself from the Rose Garden ceremonies.

The verdict was already in from the House Republican Caucus. Its members voiced their anger at a closed-door session that was so raucous the dissonance echoed in the hall outside. Congressman Christopher Cox of California, a former aide in the Reagan White House, called the budget agreement "an economic Yalta and a complete sellout." Cox added: "The American people won't buy it and certainly the Republican Conference won't buy it."

Democratic reaction was only a trifle less negative. "I have great reservations about supporting the agreement until I look realistically at the alternatives," said Congressman Julian C. Dixon of Los Angeles. "The impact of the gas tax is going to hit very hard in Southern California. It's not a done deal."

New York's Democratic governor Mario M. Cuomo, regarded as the last remaining champion of the party's liberal creed, was more emphatic. He called the deal a "surrender to the failed policies of the past." Complaining bitterly about the "regressive" tax increases, the governor said, "It makes things worse for the middle class, the elderly, the states, and local governments. The winners are the handful of people who are the richest in the country."

On Sunday, the day of the announcement, Congress quickly pushed through a stopgap resolution to continue funding for current programs and delay the automatic spending cuts that would have been mandated under Gramm-Rudman. The next step, or so the plan's sponsors hoped, would come on Friday, when both houses would adopt a formal budget resolution for fiscal year 1991, with detailed spending instructions that followed the outlines of the plan, then adopt another stopgap resolution to keep the government running a while longer.

But it was clear from the initial reaction that this schedule faced rough sledding. In desperation, Bush went on national television on the Tuesday after the announcement to plead for public support for the deal. But he was whistling in the wind. His own party had turned against him. Republican members were outraged at the $134 billion in tax increases in the measure, and Democrats complained that the tax increases on gasoline, liquor, and Medicare were regressive.

Gephardt was not deaf to their reaction. On Wednesday, his hometown newspaper, the *St. Louis Post Dispatch*, carried an interview with the Democratic majority leader in which he said, "I despise the package," though he claimed he would try and ram it through the House.

It never had a chance. A bizarre coalition of conservative Republicans and liberal Democrats voted it down on October 5 by a 254 to 179 vote, with 105 out of 176 House Republicans defying the president by rejecting the plan on which he had staked the future of his presidency. That night, Bush refused to sign emergency legislation to maintain federal spending, and the government thereupon pulled the plug on all but its most critical operations at midnight. Bush made plain who he felt ought to bear the blame—the Democratic-controlled Congress. "It is deeply discouraging that the governing bodies of this country would wrangle with the nation's fiscal affairs for nearly a year and fail," the president said.

Meanwhile, Darman invited the Democrats back to the White House. "It would be a shame for all this work and progress we made to go to waste," he said. Democrats were willing to talk, and, on Monday, Bush agreed to sign another stopgap funding measure, which ended the three-day government shutdown.

Back at the bargaining table, the haggling once again came down to a trade of capital gains for a tax increase. Then Bush got into the act. At his press conference on October 9, he said the idea of a tax-rate trade-off was "on the table." But when Senate Republicans protested, Bush changed his mind the next day. Now the trade was off the table, he said.

Bush was jogging when puzzled reporters asked him about his reversal of field. "Read my hips," he told them. Without meaning to, the president had signaled his own irrelevance in words more devastating than any of his critics might have delivered.

The rest was anticlimactic. Over the next three weeks, the Democrats cobbled together most of the pieces of the "despised" package, minus some of its more odious features, such as the increase in Medicare premiums. And with Bush no longer a factor to be reckoned with—following his "read my hips" quip, he avoided any public discussion of the budget—they wrote in a 3-percent increase on the rate for taxpayers in the highest brackets, ignoring the cut in capital-gains rates that Bush had fervently sought for so long. Having spurned the bargain proffered to him by the Democrats, Bush got the short end of the stick—in his eyes.

The chief lesson that emerged both for politics and public policy is that pragmatism is sometimes less practical than principle. Dick Darman had devised the summit approach and the Democrats had gone along with it, based on the pragmatic premise that no budget agreement could ever be reached in public because, by definition, cutting the deficit requires politically unpopular tax increases and spending cuts. But the way the deal was carried out gave the political process another black eye, contributing to the already intense public cynicism plaguing both parties.

The *New York Times* complained: "Whatever anyone thinks of the new deficit-reduction package, the process that produced the 1991 budget was a frightening display of government-in-secret. Members who battled and bargained into the wee hours are only now discovering the full content of what they approved. There is a better way, called telling it like it is."

Darman and the Democrats each intended to use the other to shield themselves from blame. In the process, the Republicans repudiated the one idea that most clearly identified them, while the Democrats showed themselves willing to compromise any idea for the sake of being able to declare a victory, no matter how empty. In fact, by agreeing to Darman's spending caps and enacting a so-called pay-as-you-go formula, which would require any new spending to be covered by new taxes or cuts in other spending, the Democrats effectively forfeited the central reason for their existence—the use of government to solve problems. And along with it, they abandoned hope of the much-talked-about post–Cold War peace dividend, which many had counted on to reinvigorate the party.

"The congressional Democrats sold their birthright when they made that budget deal," Rochelle Horowitz, political director of the American Federation of Teachers and an influential member of the Democratic National Committee (DNC), told me. "They destroyed their potential as an opposition party."

Over the long run, Bush too would turn out to be a big loser. He lost the support of his party, whose officeholders, to survive the midterm election in relatively respectable shape, distanced themselves from the president. Edward J. Rollins, director of the National Republican Campaign Committee, sent a memo to his party's candidates advising them that they should "not hesitate to oppose either the president" or his policies.

An Associated Press survey two weeks before the midterm election showed that of 100 Republican candidates who had filmed endorsement advertisements with Bush, only a handful had decided to put the commercials on the air. More important for his reelection prospects in 1992, Bush lost the confidence of the electorate.

But he was shielded from the consequences of this for some time to come by his decision to go to war against Saddam Hussein in the Persian Gulf ten weeks after the midterm election and the budget deal. The public, which had been sharply divided, rallied around Bush once the shooting started, sending his poll ratings soaring.

The Democrats, weakened by the budget deal, were thrown into disarray. In the immediate aftermath of the budget agreement, some of their leaders talked about resurrecting economic fairness as a political issue. But the case was unconvincing, particularly in view of all the machinations that had preceded the final agreement. In the midterm elections, few Democrats wanted to campaign on the belated budget agreement, which even in revised form was not regarded as pleasing to voters. And the party's modest gains in the off-year voting—eight seats in the House, one in the Senate—hardly suggested that they had found the new battle cry they needed, considering that they were competing against a party led by a president who had just revoked the pledge that was central to his election. All the Democrats had been able to achieve was to get Bush to share the blame for raising taxes.

And this was soon overshadowed as the nation moved toward a showdown in the Gulf. From the beginning, Democrats had been uncertain about how to respond to Bush's venture in the Gulf. Mindful of their reputation for being "soft" on defense, they had held back from challenging Bush at the start of the military buildup, which they conceivably might have done by invoking the War Powers Resolution. Instead, they waited until the massive deployment of U.S. forces had been completed, then plunged into a Capitol Hill debate over whether Bush should be authorized to use force, an argument from which most of the meaning had been drained by Bush's announcement that he would send U.S. troops into battle regardless of what Congress did.

In the aftermath of the military victory in February, the Democrats seemed like punch-drunk fighters, uncertain even about which corner to choose for their retreat. Their torpor was consistent with the actions of their party's congressional leadership in the budget deal, which had blurred the Democrats' traditional identity as a party committed to use government for the benefit of the disadvantaged.

Even as Bush's poll ratings soared, the economic indices showed the nation to be in the midst of a serious recession, a condition that in the past had never failed to rally Democratic voters to the party's candidates. Indeed, within two weeks of the midterm elections, Bush received a prophetic memorandum from Fred Malek, the former Nixon aide who would become his 1992 presidential campaign manager, who warned that the current recession "has the clear potential of becoming deeper, larger, and more destructive than the 1981–82 recession." Moreover, despite Malek's urgings that Bush should rectify the public's sense of government insensitivity to the growing economic threat, Bush gave no evidence that he was prepared to deal with the recession. Yet so dispirited were the Democrats that their leaders, for the most part, seemed unable to absorb this reality and plan a course of action based upon it.

In the wake of the U.S. triumph in the Persian Gulf and the new surge in President Bush's popularity, Democrats were so disheartened about their party's chances of winning the White House in 1992 that some talked of drafting an uncharismatic but respected legislative leader to serve as a sort of caretaker nominee. Such a candidate—House Speaker Foley's name was frequently mentioned—might be a sacrificial lamb, but, said Ted Van Dyk, a veteran of Democratic presidential campaigns going back to 1964, "At least he'd run a dignified race, and we'd get our share of wins in Congress."

On paper, at least, the Democrats had no shortage of potential contenders for the 1992 nomination. On Capitol Hill, the leading prospects were Gephardt and Tennessee senator Albert Gore Jr., both veterans of the 1988 nomination contest; Texas senator Lloyd Bentsen, the 1988 vice presidential candidate; and Georgia senator Sam Nunn, who had led the congressional opposition to the use of force in the Gulf. Among governors, the most prominent possibility was New York's Cuomo.

But less than a year before the nominating process would officially get under way, not one of these prospects had offered himself as a candidate or given any meaningful signal that he intended to do so. And some Democrats fretted that the current gloomy outlook for their presidential hopes would become a self-fulfilling prophecy by discouraging their strongest prospects from entering the race. "You could wind up with a potentially vulnerable incumbent and no one strong enough to exploit that vulnerability," Democratic pollster Mark Mellman said.

How did the party of Franklin Roosevelt and Harry Truman, of Jack Kennedy and Lyndon Johnson, of the New Deal and the Fair Deal, of the New Frontier and the Great Society, get into such a fix? The budget deal of 1990 offered a clue to the answer. But this bargain was really a symptom of causes that went further back in the party's recent fretful history, to the last time the Democrats had governed the country from the White House.

3

The Prince of Ambivalence

IN JULY 1979, with his presidency slipping away, Jimmy Carter sought a boost from the nation's Democratic governors, then gathered in Louisville, Kentucky, for a conference of all governors from both parties. He got what he wanted, an endorsement for his as yet unannounced candidacy for reelection in the face of an anticipated challenge from the champion of party liberals—Senator Edward M. Kennedy of Massachusetts.

But he also got something he certainly did not want—a lecture on political leadership from the most junior of all the Democratic governors in terms of age and length of service. This was William Jefferson Clinton of Arkansas, a fellow Southerner who had honed his talent at the best schools the North had to offer, a Rhodes scholar and a country hustler, a man of considerable gifts but of even greater ambitions and appetites, a new face who had already made a great noise in his party and yet would not turn thirty-three for another month.

Besides all this, Clinton was a Carter friend and ally of some years' standing. Carter had helped Clinton when the young man had run unsuccessfully for Congress in 1974, his first try for public office, and Carter served in the newly created position of national Democratic campaign chairman, a position created by the party hierarchy in a vain attempt to bury the Georgian and his all-too-evident lust for the White House. In 1976, Clinton had returned the favor to his benefactor, having led Carter's successful presidential campaign in Arkansas after he himself had been assured of election as the state's attorney general.

And in his current predicament, the president needed all the help he could get from his friends. That the president had brought much of his trouble on himself made things no easier. He had rushed home from a Far

Eastern trip to confront a citizenry seething with discontent because of energy shortages, a problem he had been grappling with fruitlessly ever since he had entered the White House.

Now conditions had plainly worsened. Gasoline was scarce and prices were soaring. The shortage seemed to have taken over national life. Millions of Americans were sweating it out in gasoline lines and junking vacation plans. Domestic policy adviser Stuart Eizenstat sounded the alarm: "Nothing which has occurred in the administration to date has added so much water to our ship," Eizenstat wrote. "Nothing else has so frustrated, confused, angered the American people—or so targeted their distress at you personally."

But Carter, having returned home, did not really confront the problem. Instead, having scheduled a speech on the issue, he postponed it. Withdrawing to the presidential retreat at Camp David, he brooded over what to do next while seeking the counsel of prominent citizens from both parties and nearly every walk of life. In the midst of these deliberations, which sowed bewilderment far and wide, Carter dispatched his vice president, Walter Mondale, to secure the blessing of the Democratic governors for his candidacy.

For any incumbent president, such an endorsement should be something to be taken for granted. That Carter felt he had to ask for it spoke volumes about his political weakness the year before his lease on the White House ran out. It also irritated a few of the governors who viewed the request as unsuitable. Most went along, including Clinton, who nevertheless used the occasion to offer Mondale a few words of advice to be passed on to the president.

Carter was in trouble, Clinton observed, because people "feel no sense of movement or involvement with the president," and then he laid down an indictment of Carter's governance that included the limpness of his oratory, the negativeness of his energy proposals, and his administration's lack of coordination in dealing with energy. As if that was not enough, Clinton expanded on his views in remarks to reporters. "The president is not a great orator," Clinton said, stating the obvious. Indeed, Carter's delivery of speeches in the White House had caused Milton Gwirtzman, a Democratic speechwriter, to remark that if Carter had given FDR's "nothing to fear but fear itself" address, the Great Depression would still be raging.

Recalling the speech Carter had given early in his presidency, in which he had likened the effort to deal with the energy crisis to the "moral equivalent of war," Clinton said Carter had sounded "almost like a seventeenth-century Puritan bringing bad news to the country. What people are looking for is someone who will say that this is the moral equivalent of a war of independence—and that everybody has some role and some mission to play."

Powerful bonds of history and politics link Carter and Clinton together. They are the only two Democrats to sit in the White House in the final three decades of the twentieth century. And it is no coincidence that both were governors, and particularly Southern governors. Both ran against Republican incumbents—Carter against Ford in the wake of the Watergate scandal, Clinton against Bush in the midst of a painful recession—who arguably could have been defeated by any reasonably qualified Democrat from any region of the country. But both were selected in large measure because of their Southern origins, out of the conviction of the Democratic leaders that only with a Southern candidate could they reclaim the unquestioned loyalty of the Old Confederacy.

In both cases, this rationale would prove to have only limited and short-term validity. In both cases, their tenure in office turned their home country against them with the special bitterness bred by a sense of betrayal. Yet this lesson, borne out by the fact that Carter lost every Southern state but his own in his failed effort to win reelection, would be forgotten or ignored by the Democratic leaders who rallied to Clinton's side only twelve years later.

But for all the similarities, sharp differences distinguished these two Southern politicians. As to Clinton, his behavior at Louisville in that troublesome summer was what the political world would ultimately come to recognize as a vintage performance. He managed to have things both ways—loyally voting to pledge support for Carter and at the same time bolstering his personal identity as a new figure on the national stage with strong ideas of his own.

This characteristic underlined perhaps the major distinction between Clinton and Carter. The younger man was far more supple in the practice of their mutual profession; if his rhetoric was unremarkable, at least it went down easy. And whereas Carter, as Clinton suggested, tended to talk at people or, even worse, down to them, his words shaped only by the particular conceit in his own mind, Clinton's public utterances were defined by what he conceived to be the concerns of his audience, to which he sought to match whatever point he wanted to make, giving each listener, as he had said, "some role and some mission to play."

The truth was, as most of his colleagues recognized, Clinton had offered Carter sound advice. The approach he recommended to Carter was just what Clinton would have done—indeed, had undoubtedly already done numerous times on his path to the governorship. But the larger truth, as Clinton himself would have recognized had he been a bit older and wiser, was that no one had the slightest chance of getting Carter to do anything of the sort.

Carter had heard advice like that in the past. Had he been able to follow it, he might have done better in struggling against the tides of political misfortune that seemed to be overwhelming his presidency and his party.

The disastrous impact of Carter's tenure in the White House would leave the Democratic party with the same sense of futility as the baseball manager who watched in growing anguish as his right fielder dropped one easy fly ball after another. After a few innings of this, the manager could take no more and dispatched another player to take over the position. But then the substitute muffed the first balls hit to him, too, as if in mimicry of the player he had replaced. When the inning was over, the manager demanded an explanation. "I'm sorry, Skipper," the replacement said, "but that guy screwed up right field so bad no one else can play it." So it was that Jimmy Carter made such a mess of his presidency that for years it seemed no Democrat would be able to hold the job again.

Not that Carter did not face a challenge of immense proportions. "The time is ripe for a political realignment in America, for construction of a new political coalition," Patrick Caddell, who was Carter's pollster in his 1976 campaign against Gerald Ford and the most farsighted of his political advisers, had written to the president-elect a few weeks before inauguration day. But this was more than just an opportunity; it was an imperative. For the same turbulence that gave Carter and the Democrats the opening to create a new majority assured that the president and his party would be doomed to defeat if they failed to seize the day.

The most fundamental problem Carter faced was the slowdown of the economic growth that had made it possible for past Democratic presidents to hold the support of the party's various constituencies by distributing to them the largesse of government. As Caddell had warned Carter in an early memorandum on political strategy: "The Democrats are by definition over-promisers; they are expensive." Now it seemed that this was an expense the country could no longer afford. "Our budget people must be made sensitive to spending what we have well," Caddell admonished, "rather than thinking up new ways to spend."

An outsider not tied to the left or the right or to any element of the existing power structure, Carter had wide freedom of action. Even so, he faced the formidable task of creating a political base to support his policies. "We must devise a context that is neither traditionally liberal nor traditionally conservative, one that cuts across traditional ideology," Caddell wrote. "What we require is not stew, composed of bits and pieces of old policies, but a fundamentally new ideology."

Franklin Roosevelt had created the old formula. But his once-invincible alliance lost part of its reason for being in the early post–World War II years with the spread of affluence. In the 1960s, under the pressure of the Vietnam War and the civil rights revolution, it crumbled, allowing Richard Nixon to thrust himself and his "silent majority" of white middle-class supporters to the forefront of American politics.

Because of Watergate, the Democrats had been given a chance to reverse the tides of history. And they had chosen Jimmy Carter to meet that challenge. But this was not a chance they had genuinely earned. That would have required coming to grips with both the limitations of the New Deal and the distortions of the political system, by developing a set of goals and beliefs based on this understanding. This would have taken time and demanded imagination and a willingness to assume risks.

Instead, when the Democrats found that—no thanks to anything they had accomplished—a discredited Richard Nixon had been driven from the White House less than two years after his triumphant election, they sought the shortest, and what seemed to be the easiest, road back to the top of the political heat. And what could be a safer bet than nominating a Southern white man who could get blacks to vote for him?

The fever of the times inclined them toward that choice. The burden of the polling evidence was that the "silent majority" of middle-class Americans, which Nixon had rallied to his side and which had given him his 1972 landslide victory, had been undermined by scandal, inflation, and recession. Only one in ten Americans was optimistic about the nation's future, compared with three out of four a decade earlier, when the Great Society was still rich in promise and Lyndon Johnson had yet to make the irrevocable decision to escalate the war in Vietnam. Cynicism was rampant. Nearly seven out of ten believed their government "consistently lies to the people," a view extending to political promises both left and right.

The public attitude would probably cause most immediate damage to the Republicans because they controlled the White House. But the long-range implications were more serious for liberal Democrats, simply because government activism is the basic tenet of liberalism. When people lose faith in government, liberals have a hard time staying in business.

The immediate cause of the widespread mistrust of government was obviously Watergate, for which liberals could blame Republicans. But liberals could not escape responsibility for other contributors to citizen alienation—the Great Society, which had fallen dramatically short of the high expectations Lyndon Johnson created for it, and, of course, the Vietnam War, in which two liberal Democratic presidents, Kennedy and Johnson, had expanded the U.S. role. The war had divided liberals, and in its aftermath, many liberals now argued that the war, by its waste of resources and its inherent savagery, had betrayed basic liberal beliefs. Others contended that it was the critics of the war who were the betrayers, through their undermining of the nation's will to fight. And these divisions had paved the way for the downfall of the Democrats in the 1968 and 1972 presidential elections.

Carter and his advisers were quick to see the implications of the defeat and divisiveness that gripped the Democratic party in the wake of the 1968 and 1972 defeats. Under these circumstances, they realized the party would be less concerned with ideology than with finding a way to return to the White House.

Another factor that favored Carter was the threat of a successful and disruptive George Wallace candidacy. Wallace had demonstrated his powerful appeal not just to white Southerners but to working-class voters in the North when he ran as an independent candidate in 1968. In 1972, competing for the Democratic party nomination, he had already made a formidable showing by early spring, when he was cut down by a would-be assassin's bullet.

The sector of the party—the liberals—that would ordinarily have been most concerned with issue positions was the same group most worried about Wallace. Near panic, they sought a Southerner who could defeat Wallace on his home ground. Carter, who had established his bona fides on civil rights by renouncing segregation as governor of Georgia, eagerly offered himself up for the job. No one was sure where Carter stood exactly on most issues, but Andrew Young, the black civil-rights leader who had dealt with Carter in Georgia, reassured the many liberal politicians who asked him if "Carter was all right on race."

Young usually added: "There are a lot of other questions I may have." But the worried liberals heard only the reassuring "all right on race" and shut their ears and minds to the "other questions." Meanwhile, with strong liberal backing, Carter routed Wallace in the Florida primary, a success that assured him the nomination. And then he stumbled to victory by a hair's breadth in November, after a campaign that called more attention to his personal idiosyncrasies than to his policy beliefs and goals.

Certainly, the hurdles he faced as president were not of the kind that could readily be surmounted by anyone. But what was blameworthy about Carter's response was not that he did not quickly develop a new ideology but that he never really tried, and never really acknowledged the need for it.

Carter saw himself as a problem solver, guided by his twin verities of trust and competence, and not as a politician, certainly not as the founder of a new political coalition. So he forged ahead on all fronts, heedless of political consequences, promoting the comprehensive solutions so close to his heart. If his policies seemed to other politicians to be disjointed and inconsistent, Carter was not disturbed, so confident was he of the rightness of his beliefs, so certain that he would prevail because the merit of his ideas would inevitably be rewarded.

It was this attitude that ultimately led to Carter's self-destructive conduct in the summer of 1979, when, following his sojourn at Camp David, he proclaimed the nation to be suffering "a crisis of confidence." Given the ballyhoo preceding that belated address, Carter needed a strong message that outlined a clear answer to the problems confronting the country, something along the lines of what Clinton had suggested in the governors' session at Louisville. Instead, the so-called malaise speech that Carter did deliver was an exercise in self-indulgence, in which the president invited his fellow citizens to wallow in guilt and share his frustration. Rather than an expression of leadership, it was a tacit admission by the president that after three years of trying to govern he had lost his way.

At the time, Ronald Reagan was gearing up for his 1980 presidential candidacy, and pollster Richard Wirthlin, who was the Reagan counterpart of Caddell, was "absolutely ecstatic" about Carter's talk. "He completely misread the perception of what people wanted a leader to be," Wirthlin told me later. "He set us up with a perfect foil. It made him sound impotent. It was the most important political speech in the last four years."

Carter's abortive attempt to use the shortage of gasoline to revive his presidency left him a political cripple, ill-equipped to deal with the November 1979 seizure of the U.S. embassy in Teheran by Muslim extremists. As with the gasoline shortage that summer, Carter sought to use the hostage episode to dramatize his presidency. "At the height of the Civil War, Abraham Lincoln said, 'I have but one task and that is to save the Union,'" Carter declared. "Now I must devote my considered efforts to resolving the Iranian crisis."

The seizure of the hostages was an outrage and an affront to the government and people of the United States. But it was scarcely to be compared to the Civil War. It was in reality an event whose impact was mostly symbolic, and Carter, by his response, enlarged that impact and made the damage enduring, a cross that Democrats would have to bear years into the future.

Nearly fifteen years after Carter left the White House, Newt Gingrich would still be able to gloat over the president's failure to free the hostages. "There's a competent party in this country called Republicans and an incompetent party called Democrats," he told a Young Republican conference shortly after the Republican triumph in the 1994 midterm elections. "One system won a war. The other system—the last time it was in power—couldn't get eight helicopters across the desert," an allusion to the failed military mission Carter launched in a vain effort to get the hostages out of captivity.

In retrospect, it is apparent that the death throes of Jimmy Carter's presidency began with his malaise speech in the summer of 1979. That address, and the events immediately following, reflected and reinforced Carter's failures as a leader, chiefly because of his inability to develop a coherent political vision and to build a coalition to support his programs. Carter was accepted by the leaders of his party as their nominee in the post-Watergate election of 1976 because he promised something different than the traditional liberal creed, which they had come to believe had lost its appeal. As president, he lived up to much that he had promised. He was a man of exceptional rectitude, possessed of great energy, and marked by intense commitment to the causes he believed to be right. His tenure was untarnished by any serious scandal, and he preserved the peace. Yet he failed dramatically and decisively. And the lesson from that failure should have been that finding a successful formula for politics and governance is a far more complex matter than finding a fresh face and moving a few degrees in the direction of the political center.

"Our people have turned to the federal government and found it isolated from the mainstream of our nation's life," Carter declared in his malaise speech. In essence, Ronald Reagan won the 1980 presidential campaign by reminding people that it was Carter whom they had chosen to head that government. And Carter's party would spend the next twelve years trying to dig out from under his legacy.

Bill Clinton was one of the early victims of the Carter presidency. In 1980, as the Democratic incumbent president lost every state in the South except Georgia, Arkansas voters also rejected Clinton after one term in office. Clinton suffered particularly because as chairman of Carter's campaign in Arkansas in the 1976 election, he was closely linked to the president in the minds of voters. Then, too, the Carter administration's use of Fort Chaffee in Arkansas to house Cuban refugees, who subsequently rioted, set off a wave of anxiety and resentment throughout Clinton's state in the midst of his efforts to gain a second term.

But Clinton also took some of the blame himself, concluding he had tried to do too much too fast, without first building enough public support. When Clinton came to power in Little Rock, he seemed to be a typical product of his liberal educational background at Georgetown University and Yale Law School and of the liberal activism that had energized the Democratic party in the 1960s. Clinton had been active in the protest movement against the Vietnam War and had broken into presidential politics in 1972 as Texas coordinator for George McGovern's presidential candidacy, which, in addition to stopping the war, was committed to infusing the nation's domestic policies with McGovern's brand of Prairie populism.

Sure enough, in his first term in the statehouse, Clinton championed such liberal causes as environmental reform, energy conservation, and scrutiny of utility company rates. And he pushed through the legislature an increase in auto license fees to pay for highway improvements, which proved to be wildly unpopular, particularly in rural parts.

After his rejection, Clinton was prepared to mend his ways. "I have made mistakes," he told the state's voters when he campaigned for reelection in 1982. And "if you'll give me a chance to serve again, you'll have a governor who has learned from defeat that you can't lead without listening." Clinton won back the statehouse. But the trauma of defeat left its mark, encouraging his inherent proclivities to calculate every move and hedge every bet, a behavior pattern that would come to stamp his presidency.

"He came back as someone who wouldn't make any move without a poll," said Thomas McCrae, the former president of the Winthrop Rockefeller Foundation and a political rival of Clinton's in Arkansas. "Here was someone who had been brash and kind of exciting, was kind of cowed by the experience, and came back very cautious."

His admirers justified his tactics as an expression of pragmatism. The 1980 loss, claimed Scott Trotter, who had been an official of the Arkansas Department of Energy in Clinton's first term, "made him stronger as an individual, as someone who can take the heat and take the pressure. I think it also made him really think about what types of issues he was going to get involved in; what's the downside, what's the upside, who will be opposed to me, how sweeping an issue it will be, and how will it affect my political career?"

In collaboration with his once-and-future political adviser, a New York–born and bred political consultant named Richard Morris, Clinton decided to make education reform the focus of his efforts. Certainly, the schools were in need of improvement. In 1978, just as Clinton was assuming office for the first time, an outside study of Arkansas's schools had concluded they were the worst in the nation. But it did not occur to Clinton to change this situation until he was in his second term and was looking for an issue that would have broad appeal but would incur few political risks.

Clinton's first step in school reform was to set a pattern he would follow long afterward. He established a commission to look into the problem headed by his wife, Hillary Rodham Clinton, who had begun using her husband's last name after discovering that by styling herself as simply "Hillary Rodham," she had cost him political points in the conservative state he governed.

Then Clinton devised ways to get conservative support. One was to finance the program by increasing the sales tax, the most regressive of levies but the easiest to get through the legislature. The other was to couple the substantive reforms, which included such things as curriculum upgrading and reduced class size, with so-called competence tests for teachers.

This last infuriated the teachers' union, which was exactly what Clinton and Morris had been counting on. By attacking Clinton, the union won him the sympathy and support of Arkansans who resented the influence of this liberal special-interest group. And it also helped to separate him from the Democratic left in general, a tactic that was designed to assist his national political ambitions, just as was the enactment of the reforms.

The substantive results were modest. As a result of reforms, the state of Arkansas spent more money on its schools than it had in the past; but a decade after they were enacted, the state still ranked near the bottom in such things as overall student test scores, per-pupil expenditures on education, and average teachers' salaries. However, in political terms, the reform had a huge payoff. It gave Clinton national attention and identified him with an issue—education—a public responsibility that even people who were critical of government thought demanded attention.

If Clinton needed further justification for the conservatism and caution that now guided his political course, after his initial liberal orientation, it seemed to be provided by the experience of his own party on the presidential battlefield. When it came to winning back the White House, the Democrats were getting nowhere fast.

Carter's 1980 defeat had given the Republicans another chance at the presidency, despite the ignominy of Watergate, and Ronald Reagan had taken full advantage of it. Riding a wave of prosperity, which fueled his own personal popularity, Reagan won a landslide reelection in 1984, crushing Walter Mondale, who had been Carter's vice president and for that reason was probably the weakest candidate the Democrats could have chosen except Carter himself.

But Mondale was not the only problem. It was the whole liberal ethos that had once dominated the party that Clinton now faulted. At the convention in San Francisco that nominated Mondale, Democratic governor Richard Lamm remarked that he had been moved by Mario Cuomo's keynote speech, which electrified the delegates. Clinton responded: "Come on, what did it really say about the issues we're trying to raise?"

In overwhelming Mondale that year, Reagan drained blue-collar voters, Catholics, and Southern whites away from their traditional home in the Democratic party, creating a new coalition of his own. And by the time Michael Dukakis rose to accept the 1988 nomination at the Atlanta convention, after a seemingly interminable speech by Clinton, which some thought would leave him a laughingstock for life, the departure of these groups had left the Democrats only a shadow of their former selves. Not only that, rising tensions among blacks and Jews, the most important remaining constituency groups, had strained the bonds of the remnants of Roosevelt's alliance. As Berkeley political scientist and old-line Democratic activist Austin Ranney put it: "The old fault lines of American politics—when you tapped hard that's where the cleavages would fall—those fault lines are gone."

Clinton himself had no clearer idea of how to replace that time-honored configuration than Jimmy Carter had. But for the time being, he concentrated instead on carving out a niche for himself, in part through his efforts as a founding member of the Democratic Leadership Council (DLC), created to put some space between Democratic officeholders and the regular party organization. He also took pains to establish himself as a mover and shaker with the National Governors Association, becoming its chairman in 1988, which enhanced his national reputation as an advocate of reform in such high-profile areas as welfare and health care, in addition to education. Clinton's prominent roles in the leadership council and the governors' association, like his schooling at Georgetown and Oxford Universities and Yale Law School and his involvement in the antiwar movement and the 1972

McGovern campaign, not to mention the contacts of Hillary Rodham Clinton, helped him to cultivate and maintain a far-flung network of personal allies. These supporters were people he could—and did—call on for political help, opening doors to influential political leaders and organizations around the land and, perhaps most important of all, giving him access to the financial resources needed to mount a presidential campaign.

Members of this informal and widespread group, as well as others who had known Clinton since his adolescence, had always reckoned that it was only a question of time before he ran for the presidency. In the spring of 1987, a few months after his reelection to a four-year term as governor, that moment appeared to have come for Clinton, and he began readying himself for a candidacy in 1988.

He was in the midst of preparations when the political world was shaken by the forced withdrawal from the Democratic presidential field of Gary Hart, following the disclosure of his weekend assignation with a Miami model, which seemed to lend credence to persistent rumors of his extensive extramarital sexual involvements. The departure of Hart, who had come close to upsetting Walter Mondale in 1984 and had been the early front-runner in 1988, left the Democratic competition wide open. That was the good news.

The bad news was that Hart's blunder made certain that any candidate would have to face intense scrutiny of his private life. And if there was any politician for whom such inspection posed a problem, it was Clinton. Nearly everyone in politics or journalism in or out of Arkansas whose business it was to know and care about prominent politicians had heard rumors of Clinton's womanizing. Reporters did not have to ask politicians about the issue—politicians asked *them.*

While Clinton brooded about what to do, his longtime aide Betsey Wright confronted him with a list of women whose names had been linked to his own. After a lengthy session, she advised him, by her own later account, not to run—out of consideration for his wife and their daughter, Chelsea. That was enough for Clinton. He let it be known that he would sit out 1988.

But that period was not a dead loss for Clinton so far as his presidential ambitions were concerned. By watching the performance of the ultimate nominee and his fellow governor, Michael Dukakis, Clinton was able to gain valuable insight into the importance of money in winning a presidential nomination. Helped immeasurably by his position as governor of a major industrial state and by his ability to tap into the ethnic pride of the Greek-American community, Dukakis had raised nearly $15 million by early spring, more than twice as much as his nearest rivals, Gephardt and Al Gore. Fund-raising was such a high priority for Dukakis that one aide jokingly called him "the vampire candidate—by day he works at the statehouse, then at night, he swoops down on some unsuspecting city and sucks up their money." But the advantage was nothing for his rivals to laugh at. William Carrick, campaign manager for Gephardt, grumbled, "Whatever mistakes the Dukakis campaign made, they had the funds to recover from." This was a lesson Clinton would absorb and profit from in times to come.

Unfortunately, Dukakis did not fully realize how much difference his fat bank account made to the outcome of the competition for the Democratic nomination. It allowed him to win that contest without ever identifying himself or explaining to voters why he should be their president. Not since the Democrats nominated Jimmy Carter, another former governor, in 1976 has either party picked as its standard-bearer anyone whose beliefs and persona were so little known.

The haze over Dukakis's candidacy stirred anxiety among fellow Democrats, who assumed Dukakis would use his acceptance speech at the convention to better define himself. Dukakis and his advisers, made complacent by their relatively easy stroll to the nomination, saw no need for that. "We see this as an opportunity to go back to our strengths and communicate them to the voters," Campaign Communications Director Leslie Dach told me. What Dach did not realize was that Dukakis's strength was in his bankroll, and he would not have that advantage in the general election campaign against George Bush.

Indeed, Dukakis set himself up for the negative onslaught Bush launched against him. "Dukakis was a blank slate," said Eddie Mahe, GOP consultant and informal adviser to the Bush campaign. That allowed Republicans to define him the way they wanted to—as heartless, mindless, and a certified liberal. By the time they were finished, Dukakis was fortunate to carry the ten states he did win.

In the wake of Dukakis's defeat, Clinton remained a potent presence on the national stage. In the spring of 1989, he seemed the logical person to interview for a story I was doing for the *Los Angeles Times* about economic nationalism—the movement then gaining support among Democrats to regain the economic ground the United States had lost to Japan and other trading nations in the previous two decades. This was an idea Richard Gephardt had been promoting vigorously. But the story needed other voices, and I knew Clinton had spoken out on this subject often at the National Governors Association and in other forums. And I assumed he would welcome the chance to give his views on a matter of substance, as distinguished from the superficial and tactical aspects of politics on which politicians often complain that journalists concentrate.

To my surprise, Clinton resisted the idea. He claimed, through his press secretary, that he was either too busy or had little to say on the issue. And when he finally did agree to an interview, after I offered to come to Little Rock at any time that was convenient, his continued reluctance was evident.

Instead of turning on the famous Clinton charm I had heard about and witnessed, he was distant and indeed seemed suspicious of the whole enterprise.

What I came to realize from this and later experience was that as eager as he was for national attention, he was uncomfortable dealing with the press in situations that he had not created for his own purposes.

He certainly did not lack for information on the subject. We talked for nearly an hour, seated in the coffee shop of the Excelsior Hotel on a Sunday morning, until his wife and their daughter came to fetch him away to some family occasion. And during that time, he said just about everything that could be said on the subject, without actually making clear his own position. On the one hand, Clinton said, with public anger and anxiety over foreign economic clout approaching xenophobic levels, the idea of reasserting American strength in the world could be "a major political issue" in the midterm elections in 1990 and in the presidential campaign of 1992— "even more" of an issue than it had been in 1988 when Gephardt had built his victory in the Iowa caucuses around a commercial denouncing the Hyundai and other cheap imported cars.

Yet, on the other hand, he came down foursquare against jingoism. "You can't blame the Germans or the Japanese for the fact that we are undereducated," he argued. "You can't blame them for the money we waste in the draining effect of the federal deficit—or the fact that we'd rather spend money bailing out the savings-and-loan industry or promoting mergers and acquisitions than investing in emerging technologies." That made it sound as though this country needed an industrial policy, just the sort of government activism Democrats have always liked to peddle.

But once again, Clinton flashed an amber light against seeking to rally the populace behind that banner. "If you try to be a simplistic demagogue, unless everything goes to hell in a handbasket, that's not going to work."

Throughout his remarks, Clinton sprinkled his favorite buzzword for the day—"ambivalent." Americans feel "a deep ambivalence" about foreign competition and free trade and about most other public issues as well, he said. "You had two candidates in the last election—Dukakis and Bush— who were deeply ambivalent," he asserted, "and that reflects the ambivalence of the American public."

Looking back on that election, Clinton offered the unremarkable guess that "if there had been a Roosevelt or a Lincoln running, they would have won in a walk." But then he thought of still another caveat. "Keep in mind that Roosevelt ran on a balanced budget and Lincoln said slavery didn't matter."

Coming back to the present, Clinton said, "There is a struggle going on in both parties now—an attempt to break out of traditional molds."

Could a strong leader carry this out, or would it take some crisis such as a deep recession? "I can't answer that," Clinton said. "It's waiting for at least a clearer direction. And it may take hard times to get that."

It was clear from that conversation, and became even clearer during his candidacy for the presidency that followed two years later, that Clinton not only preached ambivalence, he practiced it. He had a talent for avoiding controversy and political risk either by avoiding taking a position or by taking two or three positions, each stated with equal fervor or conviction. A classic example was his reaction to the congressional vote authorizing President Bush to use military force against Iraq. "I guess I would have voted with the majority, if it was a close vote," Clinton said, "but I agree with the arguments the minority made."

As Clinton reached national prominence during the 1992 campaign, it became the fashion to attribute this behavior pattern to his turbulent childhood, a notion that Clinton himself encouraged by recounting some of the traumas he had encountered early in life. He was born three months after the death of his father in an auto accident and left in the care of his grandparents by a mother determined to finish her education in a distant city. His stepfather was a drunk, often a mean one, and Clinton himself, after he reached adolescence, intervened to prevent Roger Clinton from physically abusing his mother.

On one occasion, his mother recalled watching her son, who at fourteen was a head taller than his stepfather, walk over to the older man's chair. "Daddy, stand up," he said. "What I have to say to you, I want you to be standing up." The boy helped the older man get to his feet. "I don't know what I will do if you ever strike my mother again," he said. "I would advise you never to strike her again." Years later, recounting the incident to an interviewer, Clinton said: "I couldn't wait to get big enough to know there would be peace in my home."

By his own account, as well as the recollections of friends and close associates, the bringing of peace to his mother's home was a shaping event for Bill Clinton, one that set a course for his life and his life's work. Yet a year after this transformation had taken place, Clinton himself, in a deposition given during his mother's divorce proceedings, said that the physical abuse had continued until just the month before, when the police had to be summoned to his home because of his stepfather's battering his mother. Although this contradiction does not alter Clinton's claim that he endured a troubled childhood and adolescence, it does show that he and his admirers had learned to shape this experience to his political advantage.

As a result of the searing experiences of his childhood, or so Clinton and his supporters sought to suggest, the young man became imbued with an impulse that, fortunately for him and the citizenry, helped to make him exceptionally well suited for the stewardship of a fractious and fragmented nation: a dogged determination to forge consensus and to defuse polarizing conflict.

There was and is no way to confirm or disprove the connection between Clinton's stressful upbringing and continuing effort to disguise, blur, and deny differences that became the hallmark of his professional style. There is abundant anecdotal evidence that offspring of alcoholic parents go to great lengths to avoid disagreements as adults. But in Clinton's case, his devotion to compromise and conciliation might also be due simply to the presence of a boundless ambition, coupled with an absence of firm conviction.

In either case, what difference does it make? Only that the calculated efforts to depict these youthful experiences as definitive of the grown man demonstrate the extent to which Clinton and his inner circle were willing, even eager, to exploit his personal life to advance the public man. And this tactic takes on significance in view of Clinton's and his partisans' indignant reaction to the exposure of certain less sympathetic aspects of his personal life.

The last question I asked Clinton in our Little Rock interview was whether he would run for the presidency in 1992. "I haven't made up my mind," he said, and added that he had not even decided whether to seek another term as governor. A year later, he had answered the second question in the affirmative and had won another four-year term handily. The campaign was otherwise noteworthy for his answer to a question about whether he would forswear any idea of running for president in 1992 and serve out his full four-year term as governor.

At the time, Clinton was ahead of his Republican challenger in the polls. But his opponent, Sheffield Nelson, a former Democrat who was head of the state's largest gas utility, was well financed, knowledgeable about state government, and not to be taken lightly. The campaign had become nastier the longer it went on, and Clinton knew that the idea that he might be using the governor's office as a springboard for the White House could be used against him. He decided to kill that notion once and for all. A man often devoted to the uses of ambiguity, he could not have been more forthright in his answer: "You bet," Clinton had replied. "I'm going to serve four years. I made that decision when I decided to run. I'm being considered as a candidate for governor. That's the job I want. That's the job I'll do for the next four years."

For Stanley B. Greenberg, the pollster for Clinton's gubernatorial campaign, who saw him as a presidential potential, the news was a disappointment. And it added to his surprise when only four months after election day, in the early spring of 1991, Greenberg was summoned by Gloria Cabe, Clinton's deputy chief of staff, to a meeting at the governor's mansion in Little Rock to discuss a Clinton presidential bid.

"I thought he wasn't going to run," Greenberg good-naturedly chided Cabe. Greenberg chose not to believe that his client had meant to mislead the voters of Arkansas. "I think he thought he wasn't going to run," he said later.

What, then, changed his mind? Certainly nothing that happened in Arkansas. The 1991 winter legislative session had been a triumph, particularly in contrast to the frustration of past sessions. Clinton had won an in-crease in pay for teachers, approval of several new programs he had long sought, and, most important, a hike in the state's corporate income tax—the first such increase in more than two decades—to finance improvements in the state's colleges and vocational schools. It appeared that he could look forward to four fruitful years, allowing him to cap his career in that state and still give him ample time to prepare for a presidential run in 1996, when he would be only forty-six.

But on the national scene, there had been a dramatic change—the culmi-nation of the Gulf War in a great military triumph for the United States and a great political triumph for George Bush. But if for most Democrats it was the worst of times, for Clinton it was the best opportunity for the White House he was ever likely to get.

As Greenberg and others in the group of inner-circle advisers met with Clinton in the comfortably furnished stone mansion, with its windows looking out on the spacious lawn, their first agenda item was to consider who might get in the race. Any review of the Democratic order of battle pointed to three candidates, all of whom had more experience and larger reputations on the national scene than Clinton.

First in seniority was Texas senator Lloyd Bentsen, who had won admi-ration as Dukakis's running mate in 1988 and would command the loyalty of many party leaders around the country. Then there was Senator Al Gore from the next-door state of Tennessee, who had been "the last white man standing" in the battle against Dukakis in 1988 and who might seriously eat into Clinton's potential Southern base. Finally, but certainly not least, Richard Gephardt, the House majority leader, from another next-door state, Missouri, and the conqueror of the Iowa precinct caucuses, could threaten to make inroads among most of Clinton's potential fund-raising sources.

Yet all three men had ready-made excuses not to run and had indicated they intended to let the cup pass for this quadrennial. Bentsen could claim age—he was, after all, seventy. Gore could plead family obligations, be-cause his young son was still recovering from the serious injuries he had suffered in an auto accident. And Gephardt could point to the promise he had made to his colleagues in the House when they elected him Speaker, that he would stay on the job and not run for the presidency in 1992.

And although all these reasons had some foundation in truth, few peo-ple in the Democratic party or sitting in that room with Clinton believed they would hold much water if George Bush's poll standings were closer to 50 percent than to 100 percent. Even if any or all three of these politicians should run, in the somewhat subjective view of the men at the meeting that March day and in the opinion of Clinton's other confidants, none had overwhelming strength. "We sensed an absence of leadership at the top of the party," Clinton's longtime friend Derek Shearer said. "There's nobody we'd look at and say, 'that's the leader of the Democratic party, that's the heir apparent.'"

Of course this view could not be accepted without a grain of salt. To some extent, Shearer and the others saw what they wanted to see. But their opinion could not be entirely discounted, either. And what this meant for Clinton, conscious of the personal baggage he carried that had kept him out of the race in 1988, was that even if his womanizing became an issue, the rivals he faced might not be strong enough to take advantage of it.

The next question was whether the game was worth the candle. What would be the point in Clinton's running, even if he could gain the nomination against a weak field, if he could not win election?

Pollster Greenberg had the answer to this. The Persian Gulf boom was only temporary, he argued. Americans had nurtured doubts about George Bush all along, he contended. And once the glow from the Gulf War lifted, those misgivings would reassert themselves and drag the president down.

Apart from Greenberg's analysis, Shearer could point to hard evidence to support his belief that the time was right if Clinton wanted to be president. And Clinton's team of advisers ticked off these points to him, one after another: The economy continued to drag along in the recession that had begun the previous fall. And the previous summer, before the Persian Gulf crisis heated up, Bush had been on the defensive because of his failure to mount domestic initiatives. Besides all this, Clinton's friends counseled him, 1992 promised to be a defining moment for Democrats. Bush might or might not be beatable, but the 1992 primaries almost certainly would serve as the introduction and shakedown period for the new, post-Vietnam generation of Democratic presidential contenders. If Clinton wanted to be part of that group—an ambition that had long burned inside him—he could not afford not to run, his friends told him. "If he ever wanted to be president of the United States, this was the time," Shearer said.

Clinton himself seemed to accept the notion in theory. But in practice, he had doubts. One was about breaking his promise to the voters of Arkansas not to run again. "If I'm going to run for change," Clinton asked friends, "would it look like I was betraying my ideals?" It was a pregnant question, one he brooded on for months and even asked the citizens of Arkansas about. On the July Fourth weekend, the freshly reelected governor toured the state, asking citizens whether they would object to his breaking his promise. He even asked his daughter, Chelsea, whether she would be troubled by her father's breaking his word.

When politicians ask such questions, they invariably get the answer they want, which is how it turned out with Clinton. No, neither Chelsea nor the voters of Arkansas whom Clinton confronted had any objection. Still another more fundamental problem remained: What would be the basis of his candidacy, and how would that go over with Democratic primary voters? Clinton was convinced that the Democrats needed to make some departure from their past in order to stand a chance of regaining the presidency in November, and he was not alone in that belief.

"Everyone at the end of 1988 recognized the desperate need for a new Democratic message that would take some of the traditional legacy of the Democratic party and cast it in language that would resonate in the 1990s," said Michael McCurry, who had been an adviser to two presidential candidates—John Glenn in 1984 and Bruce Babbitt in 1988—and had tried and failed to perform this sort of political alchemy. McCurry would work for another failed candidacy, Bob Kerrey's in 1992, before becoming Clinton's White House press secretary.

But finding the proper mix was not going to be easy, for Clinton or anyone else, because any such solution would have to contend with a complex and long-standing Democratic deficiency. To put it bluntly, the Democrats were losing because they were not getting enough white votes, a problem that went back nearly half a century to the party's break with racial segregation and its support for civil rights.

There was a measure of poetic justice in this. For the better part of a century after the Civil War, the Democratic party was able to survive and compete against the Republicans because for all intents and purposes, it owned the South. And the reason for this was that the Democratic party had served all this time as a bulwark for the racism that was the foundation of Southern economic and social life. The Democrats kept faith with that record from the end of Reconstruction through the presidency of Franklin Roosevelt; willing though he was to wage a world war against the darkest stain of bigotry and racism, Roosevelt was reluctant to lift a finger against white supremacy in the American South. Not until the Truman presidency did the Democrats move against discrimination even in a limited way, and it remained for the first Southern president, Lyndon Johnson of Texas, to once and for all smash the racial barriers.

But the linkage of racism to politics, which had endured for all those decades to the great benefit of the Democrats, could not be easily sundered without creating havoc throughout the South—and without the Democrats paying an enormous price, which at least matched the benefits they had enjoyed and continued to enjoy into the 1990s.

In the ten presidential elections since Franklin D. Roosevelt's fourth and last term in 1944, Democrats received more than 50 percent of the white vote only once—in 1964, when Democratic president Lyndon B. Johnson trounced Republican senator Barry Goldwater before the full impact of his drive for civil rights had been felt in Dixie. And in the six elections since 1964, only one Democrat, Jimmy Carter in 1976, carried more than 40 percent of the white vote and was the only Democrat to win any of those five elections. The culmination of this disastrous trend for Democrats came in 1984, when Walter F. Mondale carried only 35 percent of the white vote and one state—his own Minnesota. His showing was even worse among white men, only about 30 percent of whom voted for Mondale.

Understandably shaken by these results, the Democratic party leadership went through a long postelection period of soul-searching and brainstorming, with often frustrating results. One outgrowth of this reappraisal, the Democratic Leadership Council—formed to provide political coverage for Democrats leery of linkage with the liberal interest groups involved in the national Democratic party—turned instead to many of the same corporations and wealthy individual contributors who backed the Republican party. Indeed, when the organization held an annual convention in Cleveland in 1991, presided over by Clinton, it was so overrun by lobbyists and corporate figures that it refused to provide the press with a list of these self-selected delegates. As the *Washington Post* writer David Broder reported at the time:

> The Cleveland convention did not look or feel like a Democratic gathering. You looked around the floor and saw few teachers or union members, few blacks and even fewer Hispanics. In their place, you had dozens of corporate lobbyists who pay the DLC's bills in return for access to its influential congressional members and governors. Many of the lobbyist-delegates acknowledge being Republicans; one was a top staffer for Spiro Agnew. But they were in there voting on resolutions, just as if they really cared about the Democrats' winning.

Still another attempt at shifting the party's ideological direction was the creation of the Super Tuesday primary, covering Democrats in fourteen Southern and border states. The theory underlying this arrangement was that the concentration of all these supposedly conservative electorates at one crucial point in the political calendar would create a huge stumbling block for liberal candidates and a big advantage for conservatives. But this strategy, like countless other plans offered as panaceas for the illness of the system, ignored reality: the exodus of white conservatives from the Democratic party throughout the South for the past decade, leaving blacks and white liberals in a dominant role. The result was that the big winners on Super Tuesday in 1988 were two candidates liberal enough to fulfill the worst nightmares of the architects of Super Tuesday—Michael Dukakis, who did particularly well in South Florida and among Latinos in Texas; and Jesse Jackson, who captured black voters across the South.

Dukakis's ultimate failure was a severe blow to Democrats who had imagined that with Reagan gone from the scene they would be able to regain the White House. As a matter of fact, a close look at the 1988 returns gave reason for hope, at least by comparison with the disaster of 1984.

Dukakis carried ten states, compared to one for Mondale. And he won majorities among blue-collar workers, non-college-educated voters, and those below the median family-income line, all groups Reagan had won four years earlier. Since Dukakis had waged a notably dispirited and bloodless campaign, except for a last-minute burst of "I'm-on-your-side" populism, these figures suggested that expanding and strengthening that appeal might pay large dividends.

But this was not the path most party leaders chose to take, certainly not the leadership of the DLC. Serving the interests of the disadvantaged over nearly half a century was what had brought on their present predicament, or so they had come to believe.

"Our economic legislation reached out to help people of all kinds, particularly the nonrich," said Harry McPherson, looking back on the Democratic legacy to which he had contributed as a White House and Senate aide to Lyndon Johnson. "Our social legislation—civil rights and education— was meant to empower new groups, the women's movement, the gay rights group, and so on."

The trouble was, McPherson contended, that giving to these new groups seemed to mean taking away from another group: white middle-class Americans, especially males. "These men were the original stockholders in this country," McPherson said. "And to them, the Democratic party was in effect watering the stock."

The self-styled centrist forces, based in the DLC, now set out to wrest power away from these so-called new groups, whom DLC president Al From dubbed "liberal fundamentalists." Thus, the tactics and policy devised by the DLC for winning back the middle class had the twofold purpose of both appealing to the middle class and alienating the activist left, or what remained of it, in Democratic ranks. This strategy was carried forward none too subtly by a "declaration of principles" promulgated in the spring of 1990, which committed the organization to the cause of "equal opportunity," not "equal outcomes," and urged Democrats to "expand opportunity, not government."

In case anyone did not get the point of this rhetoric, Al From, a man not given to finesse, followed it up by not inviting Jesse Jackson, the Democratic party's most prominent black leader, to address the DLC's Cleveland convention—this, although Jackson had twice run for the Democratic nomination and collected more votes and delegates than any of the party leaders who were asked to speak in Cleveland. Moreover, Jackson had given speeches at past DLC meetings and had been well received. Indeed, addressing a DLC gathering in Atlanta early in the 1988 campaign, the liberal Jackson seemed to make a point of his willingness to coexist with the conservative DLC members within the Democratic party. "A party needs two wings to fly," he quipped. But by now the DLC wanted to shear off the left wing. Explaining the reason for snubbing Jackson, From said that Jackson represented "the old politics."

To replace the "old politics," the DLC planned to rally behind a New Democrat. And the obvious choice, of course, was Bill Clinton, the DLC chairman who was there to test out the themes for his still-unannounced presidential candidacy. "Why have the Democrats been shut out of the White House for all these years?" Clinton asked rhetorically. "I'll tell you why," he said. "Because too many of the people who used to vote for us, the very burdened middle class we're talking about, have not trusted us in national elections to defend our national interests abroad, to put their values in our social policy at home or to take their tax money and spend it with discipline." To get back into the good graces of the electorate, Clinton said the party needed to embrace the idea of economic opportunity rather than dependence on government. It must also be ready to insist on greater responsibility from citizens, for example, welfare mothers. "We must demand that everybody who can go to work does it," Clinton said. "For work is the best social program this country has ever devised."

This collection of homilies was more of a lecture than a political speech. It was an exercise drawn from From's inoculation program, part of an effort to rehabilitate the Democrats' reputation and intended to demonstrate to the middle class—that is, white voters—that Democrats had broken with their high-taxing, free-spending past and should be considered reasonably qualified to run the government. For one reason or another, the electorate was fed up with the way the Republicans were running the government.

In making these points to the audience of lobbyists and self-styled centrist officeholders, Clinton was preaching to the choir, telling them what they already believed. But in the view of Clinton's advisers, the speech accomplished its purpose—which was not to get across a presold argument but rather to persuade those in attendance that Clinton would be the best messenger for that argument in competing for the party's nomination the next year.

Clinton's next big opportunity to break with the "old politics" came later that year at the National Governors Association in Seattle, which made health-care reform the centerpiece of its agenda. It was also the centerpiece of the Democratic party's legislative agenda on Capitol Hill, and, in the mind of many Democrats, their best issue against George Bush in next year's presidential election.

Health care was certainly a problem, as everyone conceded. But dependence on the federal government as the nation's chief problem solver was strictly old politics, and that was not Clinton's style. As cochairman of the governors' task force on health care, Clinton made clear that he believed the best thing the federal government could do was to stay out of the way while experimentation with innovative reforms went forward at the state level. At the meeting's opening press conference, Clinton said it was un-likely that any "national solution" to the health-care problem could be reached in the next year or so. The most constructive action that Washing-ton could take, Clinton contended, was to relax its various mandates on the way states run and fund their Medicaid programs, giving them broad free-dom to design "radically different" solutions to health-care problems, espe-cially the need to control costs.

Before undertaking a "tax-and-spend approach" by the federal govern-ment, Clinton said, "we think there should be some structural reform, and we think the states should lead the way."

Asked about legislation pending on the Hill, backed by the top Demo-cratic congressional leaders, that would extend health insurance to the 34 million Americans now lacking coverage by requiring all employers either to offer insurance to their workers or to pay a tax into a fund that would cover workers otherwise unprotected, Clinton made clear he was unim-pressed.

"My opinion is that if you pass a law [to extend insurance coverage] . . . which does nothing to deal with the underlying growth and inefficiency of the American health-care system . . . we will solve one problem without solving another problem. We still might have runaway costs," he said.

It would be "presumptuous" of him to tell the senators that "they should wait ten years to pass that bill," Clinton said. But he offered this general advice to sponsors of such legislation in general: "Don't do it unless you're willing to get some cost controls into it." And he added: "Nothing I have seen in the Congress makes me think they are prepared to do that."

Paul Tully, the Democratic party's national political director, who would later work closely with Clinton on his reelection campaign, was furious, and so were Democratic congressional staffers at the conference. Monica Healy, an aide to the Democratic Senate leader George J. Mitchell of Maine, took issue with Clinton's contention that the Senate proposal to ex-tend health-care coverage neglected cost-control issues.

She pointed to five pages of provisions calling for reducing unnecessary care and eliminating unnecessary administrative costs. But Clinton had made his point and advanced his candidacy.

It would not be long before he would have to dispute the same argu-ments again—only this time, as president, he would find himself on the other side of the health-care debate.

All preparations had been made for his official candidacy except for one step: another form of inoculation, this time against revelations of the wom-anizing that had marked his personal life and kept him from running for president four years earlier. In the past when this issue had been raised, Clinton had brushed off the questions, contending that candidates should be allowed "a privacy zone."

But that defense had not really settled anything, and now that he was about to formally declare himself, his advisers convinced him that something more ought to be done. As with everything Clinton had done that spring and summer, this was carefully calculated. In midsummer, he arranged to be the guest at a press breakfast in Washington, surprising his hosts by bringing his wife, Hillary. He was clearly braced for questions about his personal life, and when the first one was asked, he jumped on it like a baseball slugger going after a fat pitch.

First, he dismissed the question as unworthy of discussion in a presidential campaign. "This is the sort of thing they were interested in Rome when they were in decline, too," he said.

Then, with Hillary Rodham Clinton at his side, he laid down his position:

> What you need to know is that we have been together for almost twenty years and have been married almost sixteen, and we are committed to our marriage and its obligations, to our child and to each other. We love each other very much. Like nearly anybody that's been together twenty years, our relationship has not been perfect or free of difficulties. But we feel good about where we are. We believe in our obligations. And we intend to be together thirty or forty years from now, regardless [of] whether I run for president or not. And I think that ought to be enough.

But that turned out to be a judgment that before long he would be obliged to drastically amend.

4

The Contender: Who Else *Is* There?

THIS IS NOT YOUR NORMAL RUN of Democratic candidates," former Massachusetts senator Paul E. Tsongas said of himself and the five other seekers after the 1992 Democratic presidential nomination early in the competition. "There are a lot of free thinkers, a lot of people who are unpredictable." He also might have added that in the view of most politicians and journalists, there were a lot of unknowns, like Tsongas himself, and a lot of unelectables.

After agonizing over his decision all summer and fall, Mario Cuomo, the one Democrat who had the prestige and resources to become the instant front-runner if he announced his intention to run, finally decided in mid-December that he could not break away from his duties as governor to run for the presidency. The vagaries and consequences of Mario Cuomo's thinking are perhaps worth a separate book. But in regard to the 1992 campaign, all that needs to be said is that although some of Clinton's advisers claimed they hoped the New Yorker would enter the race, providing a contrast with their own "New Democrat" candidate, "there was," in the words of pollster Stan Greenberg, "a universal sigh of relief even from those people with bravado who said they wanted him in."

With Cuomo out, the only two candidates who were considered to have the stature to compete vigorously against Clinton were the two senators in the race, both from the Midwest—Tom Harkin of Iowa and Bob Kerrey of Nebraska. And by the time Clinton himself officially entered the field in October 1991, each appeared to have a special advantage. This was because, just as Clinton's pollster Stanley Greenberg had predicted, the political environment had markedly changed since spring, when Clinton had first begun to seriously contemplate his candidacy. The national sense of euphoria over the Gulf War that had benefited Bush had faded, and the president's poll ratings had begun what would be a steady decline from their stratospheric heights.

The reason for this was not hard to find. The recession that Bush had hoped to prevent by his agreement to raise taxes and then had hoped would soon lift was instead tightening its hold on the country. The hard times had made voters, particularly Democrats, more receptive to the idea of government solving their problems. Potentially, this mood seemed to favor Harkin, the strongest believer in an activist government in the field, and Kerrey, who built his candidacy around the idea of health-care reform as a solution to what many viewed as the nation's most serious economic problem, the health insurance crisis.

The most dramatic evidence of the change came in November 1991 in Pennsylvania, when an obscure former aide to John Kennedy named Harris Wofford trounced Richard Thornburgh, Bush's former attorney general and former governor of the state, in an election that Wofford made into a referendum on Bush's presidency. Guided by a transplanted Cajun consultant named James Carville, Wofford made health care his key issue. His most compelling commercial claimed that a citizen had as much right to a doctor as to a lawyer.

Both Carville and health care would help to shape Clinton's future. But at that moment, Clinton was mainly concerned with preventing Harkin and Kerrey from gaining an advantage on him by exploiting the opportunities the recession had presented to them. And for this, Clinton needed something besides the reformist rhetoric of the DLC. He began to broaden and redefine the New Democrat message in his announcement speech in Little Rock on October 3. To begin with, he sought to dismiss Harkin as lacking in substance. The Iowan had been scoring points among Democratic audiences by indicting Bush and the Republicans for preaching "a message of greed that pits race against race, creed against creed, sex against sex, old against young, class against class." But he had been short on constructive answers. And when Clinton said: "We're not going to get positive change just by Bush bashing," it was clear to whom he referred.

Clinton also continued to try to separate himself from the "old politics" that had shaped Democratic rhetoric and programs in the past. "The change we must make isn't liberal or conservative," he said. "It's both, and it's different."

But having laid down that hazy disclaimer, Clinton moved to neutralize Kerrey by abruptly endorsing the idea of national health reform—a notion he had vigorously dismissed only two months before at the governors conference in Seattle. "Opportunity for all means reforming the health-care system," the newly minted candidate declared. "I pledge to the American people that in the first year of a Clinton administration, we will present a plan to Congress . . . to provide affordable quality health care for all Americans."

Returning to his theme of responsibility, Clinton repeated his pledge to put welfare mothers to work. But now, mindful of the economic pressures on the citizenry, he injected a strong dose of populism by extending his demand for responsibility to include people at the top, whom he charged as being "the most irresponsible people of all" during the 1980s.

"How can you ask people who work or who are poor to behave responsibly," he demanded, "when they know that the heads of our biggest companies raised their own pay in the last decade by four times the percentage their workers' pay went up."

Continuing to mix messages in his next major speech at his alma mater, Georgetown University, Clinton talked of a "New Covenant" for economic change "that isn't liberal or conservative . . . that empowers people, rewards work, and organizes Americans to compete and win again." But then he unveiled a program to get the nation out of the recession in a hurry, which could have come right out of the liberal playbook of Harry Truman or Lyndon Johnson—or Tom Harkin. The top item on his agenda, which would become the centerpiece of his program for economic revival before it was discarded, was a middle-class tax cut that would mean $350 a year for the average family. And he would also accelerate federal spending on highway construction to create 45,000 new jobs, increase the ceiling on Federal Housing Administration (FHA) mortgage guarantees to expedite new home buying, and pressure banks to ease credit-card rates and not to foreclose on business loans.

Competing with his rivals for the backing of the Democratic state chairs at their meeting in Chicago, Clinton once again blended DLC revisionism with old-fashioned populism. "We have to reinvent the way the government operates," he told the party leaders. But well aware of the appeal of health care identified with Kerrey's candidacy, Clinton refused to yield any ground on this issue newly dear to his heart. "We are the only country in the world where the government does not help control health-care costs and provide decent health care for every one of its citizens," he lamented. And he repeated his pledge to devote his first year in the White House to pushing through "a national health-care plan the American people can be proud of."

The speech was a rip-roaring success, but the capper came when he responded to a question, planted by his aides, about the frequently heard criticism that as a New Democrat he was not a true Democrat at heart but really only a slicked-up Republican.

The old-fashioned Democratic faith was bred into him, blood and bone, Clinton claimed. "I am a Democrat by heritage, instinct, and conviction," he said. "Why, my grandfather used to say that when he died he would go to Roosevelt," he declared.

The audience, supposedly hardened political pros, lapped it up. Next day, the *Washington Post*, in a page-one story, reported that Clinton "had jumped out of the pack of Democratic contenders" and "outdistanced his announced rivals" for the nomination. While this was an overly portentous judgment to impose upon the rendering of one speech, the story, which was widely circulated by the Clinton staff, became a self-fulfilling prophecy. It helped him create an aura of success that none of the other candidates possessed.

He also had a problem no one else had—and one that would not go away. At a reception at the Chicago meeting on the night before Clinton spoke, one of the party leaders, a woman from a Southern state, confided in me that not too long before, she had attended a party function that Clinton also addressed. "There were about ten women there, and I knew that at least two of them had slept with him. That's a ratio of one in five," she pointed out. She wondered whether that ratio prevailed elsewhere, and if so, what that would mean if Clinton were the nominee.

She was not the only one concerned about Clinton's womanizing. "A lot of us are worried that this could turn out to be a problem," Jeff Neubauer, the Wisconsin state chairman and a Clinton admirer, told me at the meeting. "If this stuff is going to come out, we would rather it come out now than when he is so far in front that it would be too late to do anything about it."

But this problem remained nothing more than a cloud hovering over Clinton's head as the year drew to an end. The favorable publicity he had been getting from his stump appearances in Chicago and elsewhere around the country was augmented by his victory in a straw poll at a Florida Democratic convention, which testified to his strength in the South. This attention also helped boost him into the fund-raising lead nationally and allowed him to expand his organization in New Hampshire while reinforcing his natural base in the South. "The tide is rising around the country for him, and New Hampshire is part of it," said Jim Monahan, director of the Kerrey campaign in the home state of the nation's first presidential primary.

Clinton's network of friends also paid dividends to his candidacy. Campaign manager David Wilhelm, a Chicago operative with labor union ties, helped gain Clinton substantial support inside the American Federation of State, County, and Municipal Employees and the American Federation of Teachers, spoiling the liberal Harkin's chances of aligning the labor movement solidly behind his own candidacy. Georgetown schoolmate Roger Altman, an investment banker, had opened doors on Wall Street to Clinton's campaign treasury. Anti–Vietnam War comrade Harold Ickes of New York, an adviser to the 1980 Kennedy campaign and the 1988 Jackson campaign, had signed on to Clinton's bandwagon, providing entrée to the Democratic left for this New Democrat.

But nothing helped Clinton more than the weakness of his competition, a circumstance his advisers had shrewdly anticipated. As 1991 ended, over a drink at a Washington New Year's Eve party, AFL-CIO president Lane Kirkland asked influential lawyer-lobbyist Harry McPherson, a loyal Clinton booster: "Why has the Washington establishment anointed Clinton for the nomination?"

"Who else is there?" McPherson retorted. "We aren't talking about a field of Lyndon Johnson and Adlai Stevenson and Hubert Humphrey."

Indeed, the two candidates—expected to be his leading rivals and, together with Clinton, considered the "top tier" of the Democratic field—were having difficulty making headway. By year's end, Harkin had been unable to develop a theme that went beyond his contempt for Bush and the Reagan era. Neither had Kerrey—a Medal of Honor winner who had lost a leg in Vietnam, still young and handsome, a son of the heartland, as well as a dedicated advocate of health reform, whom his admirers viewed as a plumed knight who would ride to their party's rescue. But as his press secretary Mike McCurry conceded: "Kerrey has yet to put his message together in a way that is digestible and consistent."

The other three candidates who were regarded as making up the second tier each faced enormous handicaps. Virginia governor L. Douglas Wilder, the first black to be elected a governor in the nation's history, had inexplicably chosen to base his candidacy on the theme of fiscal discipline, an unlikely message to appeal to black voters—and his limited experience on the national scene hurt his cause across the board. Wilder would drop out of the race in January, unable to raise funds to keep going.

Tsongas, a former Massachusetts senator, was an unprepossessing figure trying to win Democratic votes with a campaign that, like Wilder's, was based on contrarian economic philosophies for a Democrat—belt tightening and budget balancing. He had waged a winning fight against cancer, which had forced him to leave the Senate, but that episode left a question mark about his health. California governor Edmund G. (Jerry) Brown had more experience running for president than anyone else in the field, having twice tried for the Democratic nomination, in 1976 and 1980, as well as having served two terms as California's governor. But he had been out of public office for five years, and during his career in and out of office, he had earned a reputation for erratic behavior bordering on downright flakiness. Nevertheless, it was these latter two candidates from the second tier, Tsongas and Brown, who would prove to be Clinton's toughest and most enduring competitors.

Tsongas was tough from the beginning. Aided by his early start—he had announced his candidacy in April 1991—and by the familiarity gained from having held office in a neighboring state, he was running neck and neck with Clinton in New Hampshire early in 1992. The reason that both were ahead was that they were the best prepared to talk about the recession, which had already devastated the nation's first primary state.

Even New Hampshire's Republican governor, Judd Greg, acknowledged the hard times. "We're no longer in a recession," he said, as he grimly cut government services across the board to deal with a $200-million deficit over the next two years. "We're somewhere between a recession and a depression, so I call it a repression."

The jobless rate, a mere 2.4 percent in 1988, the year Bush was elected, had soared to 7 percent, higher than even during the somber days of the 1982 recession. The number of families on food stamps had increased by 50 percent over the previous year, the highest rate of increase in the nation, and bankruptcies had jumped by nearly 100 percent.

To deal with the crisis, Tsongas, who called himself a probusiness liberal, offered a book full of ideas—*A Call to Economic Arms*—which became the hallmark of his candidacy. Among other breaks with liberal Democratic orthodoxy, he proposed stepped-up research into nuclear energy development, cuts in capital-gains taxes, and easing antitrust laws to allow U.S. companies to become more competitive abroad. What is good for business is often good for labor and the rest of the nation, too, Tsongas claimed.

Clinton had a book of his own—a red, white, and blue pamphlet labeled "A Plan for America's Future." Along with copies of Clinton's major speeches, it contained seventeen pages of proposals that delineated Clinton's centrist vision of America, headed by a middle-class income-tax cut and including such ideas as creating an investment tax credit for small- and medium-sized companies, limiting the increases in spending on government programs to the rate of increase in personal incomes, and requiring welfare recipients to eventually take a job. Subjected to close scrutiny, all these schemes left many questions unanswered. But politically, they were priceless. Regardless of their merit, or lack of it, these proposals demonstrated that the candidates who offered them were at least mindful of the economic plague that had descended upon the country, and the state, and this was more than could be said of George Bush.

In this distressed environment, Clinton started off the new year with a shrewdly timed move that caught Tsongas and his other rivals off guard: his first television commercial, which promoted his program for economic recovery. "I'm Bill Clinton, and I believe you deserve more than thirty-second ads or vague promises," the candidate said. "That's why I've offered a comprehensive plan to get our economy moving again." Within a week, Clinton had made a huge gain in the polls, moving up 13 points from 20 percent and a close race with Tsongas, to 33 percent and a clear lead. Greenberg was stunned.

Everyone else was impressed. If Clinton could hold his lead in New Hampshire, he could clean up on the 1992 version of Super Tuesday on

March 10, when eleven states voted, eight in his native South. Suddenly, his nomination seemed inevitable. *Time* and *Newsweek* put him on their covers. Still, amidst the ballyhoo, a measure of skepticism remained. "Is Bill Clinton for Real?" *Time* headlined. "Anointed—prematurely—as the front runner, he remains an enigma," the story declared. And in the Clinton campaign itself, fingers were firmly crossed. Everyone realized that it was still very early in the campaign. And the specter of womanizing still hung over his head.

In mid-January, even as he was climbing in the polls, the supermarket tabloid *Star* published an article based on an old lawsuit by a former Arkansas state employee, Larry Nichols, who claimed he had been fired because he knew too much about Clinton's extramarital affairs. It was an old story, Clinton's staff pointed out, and most of the women named by Nichols had denied any involvement with Clinton.

Still, it raised the issue in public for the first time in the campaign. Concerned Clinton aides found a way to answer back: through the candidate's wife. A couple of nights after the *Star* story broke, as Clinton was stumping with his spouse in Bedford, New Hampshire, a woman in the crowd asked Hillary if she thought the charges about her husband's infidelity were a relevant issue in the campaign. In New Hampshire, most people shy away from raising such embarrassing subjects, so the question bore every evidence of being arranged by the Clinton staff. At any rate, Hillary Clinton knocked it out of the park.

"From my perspective, our marriage is a strong marriage. We love each other," she said, her voice breaking slightly. "We support each other, and we have had a lot of strong and important experiences together that have meant a lot to us. In any marriage, there are issues that come up between two people who are married that I think are their business," she said.

Then she made two points that were central to the Clinton campaign defense against allegations into his personal life, arguments that would persist, along with the charges, into his presidency. One was privacy: "It is very important to me that what I care about most in this world—which is my family, what we mean to each other and what we've done together— have some realm of protection from public life," she said; the other, that the allegations were essentially a distraction from the main purpose of the presidential campaign, which in the case of this state was to find ways to relieve the economic distress of its citizens. "Is anything about our marriage important enough to the people of New Hampshire as whether or not they will have a chance to keep their own families together?" At the back of the room, James Carville, the Harris Wofford consultant who had become Clinton's chief strategist, let out a whoop of joy and relief.

Carville cheered too soon. The very next night, during a televised debate in New Hampshire, Clinton was asked by Cokie Roberts, the moderator, whether the rumors that he had had affairs with several women would hurt his candidacy. Clinton laid the blame for the rumors at the feet of Republicans from his home state. "This last episode was a pack of lies," he said. "I think the American people are sick and tired of that kind of negative politics. They want somebody who can lead." This was another part of the defense against the charges—blaming them on Clinton's political enemies. But the hard fact remained that the womanizing issue, the issue that Clinton feared the most, was becoming more prominent and more respectable for opponents to raise.

Thus, there was reason for Clinton to be uneasy late in January when I wheedled some time with him for an interview in New Hampshire. I had flown up with him from Washington in his small chartered jet, hoping to talk to him on the plane. But the exertions of the stump had so strained his voice that his doctor had warned him to avoid talking over the roar of a plane's engines, so we chatted instead in his car, on the way from Manchester airport to the Holiday Inn where he was staying.

I was struck by Clinton's effort to cast himself apart from and above other politicians. He owed his success, he contended, to what he called "the nonpolitical nature" of his campaign.

"I've developed a clear message, a specific plan, and I have reached out to people and asked them to discuss it with me, to discuss their lives," he said. "At these town meetings we've been doing, I never mention my opponents unless I'm complimenting them about something. And sometimes I even forget to bash Bush a little."

In fact, of course, it was a rare day when Clinton forgot to blast the president, more than a little. As for his Democratic opponents, whatever he did or did not say in his town meetings, he had aired the first negative commercial of the campaign. The ad denounced "politicians in Washington" for taking a pay raise, an unmistakable reference to Kerrey and Harkin, both of whom had supported a recent boost in pay for senators. By contrast, Clinton said in the ad, "In eleven years as governor, I've never had a pay raise. And as president, I'll veto pay raises in Washington until middle-class incomes are going up again."

Nevertheless, Clinton told me, "I've just not engaged at all in the sort of political calculation and handicapping in my public discussions that other politicians do. My life's work in public life has been trying to effect progress and positive change through education and economic development. Those are the issues that have taken center stage in this election. And I think people are beginning to feel a pretty good comfort level with me and what I'm trying to do."

Still and all, Clinton volunteered, he had no intention of sitting on his lead. "I tell you this. I'm not going to become more cautious and more passive. I'm going to try to keep the hard edge on my message. I'm going to keep trying to raise the stakes in debate. And I'm going to continue to break new ground."

I asked Clinton how he would reconcile his groundbreaking role in the DLC with the Democratic party's liberal tradition and the liberal goals of its constituencies. "I think of the DLC as an engine of ideas which go beyond the labels of left and right and unifies people around values and ideas in a way that allows liberals and conservatives to come together," Clinton said. "That is always the best thing in a Democratic society, if when you have to change you can redefine a new majority where you can be for change in terms of traditional values." In other words, Clinton claimed he and his party could have things both ways—with change and traditional values. But that was a tall order.

Just before we arrived at the Holiday Inn and the interview ended, I asked him, without referring directly to the allegations against him, to what degree he thought a candidate's personal behavior was relevant to the sort of president he would be.

"That is a question that every American has to answer for himself," he said. "The question I would ask back is: To what extent is that the real reason the press pursues these matters with such relentlessness?"

It was a deft response, shifting the burden of the issue of personal behavior from the candidate onto the press. It was an argument that Clinton would soon have a chance to test, in a way that would prove to be a crucible for his candidacy and that would come close to shattering it.

I did not know how timely that question would turn out to be. The night before my interview with Clinton, his staff in Little Rock had learned that the *Star*, in its relentless way, was about to emit another of what would come to be called "bimbo eruptions"—only this would be by far the most serious yet. The source of the accusation that Clinton would confront soon after he set forth from the Holiday Inn was a Little Rock nightclub singer named Gennifer Flowers, whom Clinton had helped get on his state's payroll. The gist of Flowers's story, for which the *Star* had paid an undisclosed sum, was that she had had a sexual relationship with Clinton over a period of a dozen years, concluding in 1989. And what was more, she had tapes to back up the story.

Indeed, the *Star* story includes quotations from tapes that Flowers made of her telephone conversations with Clinton, who at one point, according to this record, told her that "as long as everyone hangs tough" there will be no problems. "If they ever hit you with it, just say 'No' and go on," he added. Clinton claimed the quotes were "distorted" and taken out of context and denied that he had had a sexual relationship with Flowers. But when he was asked if he thought he could persuade people that he was telling the truth, he said: "I don't know if I can."

In that judgment, he was right on the money. Because that day would change Clinton's candidacy and his career forever. It was only the first in a

long and seemingly endless series of allegations that would redefine his political persona and reshape the Democratic race. But it was particularly important because it made him vulnerable to the other charges. The initial impact was subtle but significant. Asked by polling interviewers whether they
thought the allegations about Clinton's womanizing would change their
minds on whom to support, the vast majority of voters invariably said no.

But when pressed, it became clear that the charges had influenced their
overall reaction to Clinton, and not for the better. "I'm not sure he's willing
to level" with voters about the costs of his economic program, said Dan
Harkinson, a thirty-nine-year-old lawyer in Rochester, New Hampshire,
one of a group of voters interviewed by the *Los Angeles Times* after a televised candidate debate three weeks before the primary vote. "I felt he was
holding something back," twenty-nine-year-old Jackie Lawson, an accountant, said when asked about Clinton's position on health care. "I don't
quite trust him," said Bob Ciderberry, a fifty-two-year-old construction
contractor.

"The polls on the adultery charges in a curious way give Clinton the benefit of the doubt," said Harrison Hickman, a pollster for Bob Kerrey.
"Should it matter? For most people? The answer is no." But what his polls
also demonstrated, Hickman said, is that the adultery issue "opens the
door" to questions about Clinton's basic credibility.

That sort of skepticism would be a large cross for any candidate to bear.
But it was a particular problem for Clinton, who had set himself the task of
doing what Jimmy Carter was unable to do—forging a new coalition, or as
he had put it on the day the Gennifer Flowers charges exploded, "defining a
new majority." The saving grace for Clinton was that the voters in New
Hampshire seemed to be asking themselves the same question Harry
McPherson had put to Lane Kirkland on New Year's Eve: "Who else is
there?"

None of Clinton's rivals showed signs of catching on as an alternative.
Although the poll ratings made out Paul Tsongas to be Clinton's chief rival
in the state, New Hampshire had trouble picturing him as president. The
group of voters interviewed by the *Los Angeles Times* after they watched
the debate argued among themselves over whether Tsongas reminded them
more of television's Mr. Rogers or the *Saturday Night Live* character Father
Guido Sarducci. "Whichever," said Dan Harkinson, "he just doesn't come
across as what I consider presidential."

Clinton's burden, and his advantage as well, was that he had overshadowed all the other candidates. "This race right now is a referendum on
Clinton," said pollster Greenberg.

Two weeks after the airing of the Gennifer Flowers charges, that referendum became harder to win when a new, and in some ways even more serious, controversy shook Clinton's candidacy. This time it was the disclosure

that Clinton had schemed to get himself admitted to the ROTC program at
the University of Arkansas in 1968 while he was a Rhodes scholar, so he
could avoid being drafted into the Vietnam War. But then Clinton passed
up the chance to join ROTC and reentered the draft pool, or so he contended in a letter he wrote at the time.

Out of concern that he had compromised his principles in order to "protect myself from physical harm," he wrote, and due to his desire to "maintain my political viability within the system," he decided not to become a
draft resister but to "accept the draft in spite of my beliefs." As it turned
out, Clinton was never drafted, and circumstances suggested he probably
could have assumed that he would not be.

Clinton said he hoped voters would see the letter as the testament of a
"conflicted and thoughtful young man" who "loved his country but hated
the war," who "wanted to go home and do what I could to work for
progress." But many saw its convoluted and self-serving logic as portraying
a young man so consumed by expediency and ambition that he lacked the
courage either to serve his country or to openly resist the draft for a war he
did not believe in.

"Meltdown" was the way Greenberg described the impact of these twin
hammer blows on Clinton's support in New Hampshire.

As Clinton's poll ratings sank and Tsongas surged ahead in New Hampshire, something close to panic seized the Democratic establishment. Frantic efforts were made on Capitol Hill to persuade some new champion to
enter the race. But those who had rejected the opportunity the previous
summer had not become more courageous at this later date, and no one
else materialized.

For his part, spurred by adversity and desperation, Clinton fought back,
campaigning nonstop, by bus and by plane, in walking tours and on television call-in shows, thrusting himself at voters to regain their support and
trust.

The funds that had filled his campaign coffers during the bright days of
December helped pay for television time, to fly around the state, and for a
massive canvassing effort to deliver videotapes of Clinton's life story to tens
of thousands of targeted voters across the state.

This effort was abetted in no small measure by Tsongas, who, with victory in sight, seemed to freeze, cutting back his schedule to one appearance
a day. That stirred renewed speculation that Tsongas's health might be
troubling him. The best he could do in response was to urge journalists to
watch him do his swimming workouts, the regimen that had helped him recover from cancer. But this was a task that few reporters were willing to impose upon themselves.

Meanwhile, the storm over Clinton drowned out the efforts of the two
men who had been anticipated to be his chief rivals—Kerrey and Harkin—

to at last make something of their candidacies. It was all between Clinton and Tsongas, and in the end, Clinton benefited both from his own energy and Tsongas's lethargy. He finished in second place, seven points behind Tsongas.

By any objective measurement, it was a stunning victory for Tsongas, who had been given no chance at all, and a huge setback for Clinton, who had been ahead by double digits. The margin Tsongas won by was bigger than Jimmy Carter's advantage over Morris Udall, which had boosted Carter into the nomination and the presidency. But that night, Clinton transformed reality. While Tsongas waited for the final returns to come in, Clinton rushed to the television cameras and, using a phrase crafted by his staff, announced, "New Hampshire has made me the Comeback Kid." With that masterstroke of spin control, Clinton robbed Tsongas of the psychological boost that he should have expected to gain from his victory in New Hampshire. Instead, it was Clinton who had somehow contrived to gain the momentum as the campaign moved on.

He also had a clear strategy, which was to exploit his natural base in the South. There he was aided by the friendly Democratic governors he had cultivated over the years. Regardless of the flaws in his character and candidacy that had been exposed in New Hampshire, they were bound to Bill Clinton by the strongest force in American politics: self-interest. Clinton was one of their own and, these barons of the Southern Democracy believed, far more likely to respond to their needs and respect their prerogatives than any of his rivals. And Clinton could rely on a network of personal alliances to reinforce this commonality.

In Georgia, for example, where Clinton had made his major commitment in the March 3 delegate contests, while conceding Maine and Maryland to Tsongas, he was greatly aided by Governor Zell Miller, who was a client of Clinton's own chief strategist, James Carville. In fact, long before, Miller had decided to move his state's primary to the week prior to the other Southern contests, thus assuring extra attention for his state—creating a potential jump-start for Clinton's efforts in the South.

The Clinton team under Carville lost no time in seizing this opportunity. "On the afternoon of New Hampshire, the exit polls said we were going to finish second, and I said, 'Yeah, that's it, I'm going down to Atlanta now,'" Carville recalled later. "We were playing tough. Zell came out the next day, and we were lining people up, and we were shooting every tenth one that didn't fall in line. This was our turf and we knew we were going to be there." With friends like Miller, Clinton could overcome foes like Tsongas without much trouble.

As for the other former members of the "top tier": Tom Harkin's candidacy collapsed in the week after New Hampshire, and only Kerrey remained to fight on. Sustained for a while by defeating Harkin in the South

Dakota primary on February 25, Kerrey came to Georgia mainly to denounce Clinton over his avoidance of the draft and for flaws in his character. In particular, Clinton's efforts to portray himself as being victimized by his political enemies got Kerrey's dander up. "Let me tell you where I go over the edge on this thing," Kerrey explained at a press conference. "It should not surprise you to discover that it was the men and women who went to Vietnam who suffered. All of a sudden in this campaign the sympathy is going to someone who didn't go." In the most damning indictment that any Democrat of prominence had yet leveled at Clinton, Kerrey accused the favorite of party leaders of "an evasion of responsibility."

"We've got to be able to nominate somebody who is capable of asking for a sacrifice to rebuild this nation, and I'm conscious of what a sacrifice is all about," said Kerrey, referring to his amputated leg. "Bill Clinton is a friend of mine. But if he is the nominee, he will be the issue and he will not be able to win." If Clinton became the standard-bearer, Kerrey warned, in a phrase that lingered in memory after his own candidacy had evaporated, "He is going to be opened up like a soft peanut."

This harsh rhetoric may have caused Georgians to reflect on Clinton's missteps. But it did little for Kerrey, who did not have enough of a campaign organization in Georgia to take advantage of Clinton's weaknesses.

Similarly, Clinton was able to overcome his own ill temper and lack of discipline and gain the lion's share of the critical black vote. When Clinton was told, erroneously, early in the delegate struggles in the South that Jackson had decided to back Harkin for the nomination, he exploded in a barely coherent tirade in front of an open microphone and television cameras. "For him to do this to me is an act of absolute dishonor," he declared. "Everything he has bragged about—he has gushed to me about trust and trust and trust—and it's a back-stabbing thing to do."

Tsongas had sought to exploit the incident in a radio commercial. But it had no impact. Jackson himself was of course not on the ballot to benefit from Clinton's blunder. And Tsongas was in no position to gain black support, since he was even less well known to Southern blacks than to whites. Clinton, however, had worked this lode from the first, relying as usual on a network of personal contacts, such as black congressman John Lewis of Atlanta.

"That is the first thing I said in this campaign when I went to work," Carville recalled. "I said you can cut this thing any way you want, but unless you have Southern blacks in there, you can't figure this thing." Even with Douglas Wilder in the race, Clinton was convinced he would win blacks; and Wilder's withdrawal, of course, in effect clinched the deal.

If anyone in Clinton's campaign saw the irony of the candidate who championed efforts to bring white voters back into the party depending for his success on black votes, it did not impede such efforts, which turned out to spell the doom of Clinton's competitors. As Paul Goldman, who had been Wilder's campaign manager, remarked, "When they let the DLC get the Jackson vote, you don't have to be a Harvard scholar to figure there ain't a lot left" for Clinton's rivals. Clinton won Georgia with nearly 60 percent of the vote, to Tsongas's less than 25 percent, and carried the black vote by huge margins—not only by six to one in Georgia but also by more than two to one in Maryland, even though Tsongas won that state.

More than that, the exit polls defined the limit of Tsongas's candidacy and his neoconservative economic message. His strength was among voters earning $60,000 a year or more—slim pickings in Democratic primaries. And even as the votes were being counted, Clinton sought to exploit that limitation in the Super Tuesday contests that fell the week after the Georgia primary. Doing so involved another dramatic redefinition of what it meant to be a New Democrat. Clinton, who set out to challenge his party's prevailing liberal doctrine, now challenged Tsongas from the left.

Campaigning in Florida for the Super Tuesday vote, he spoke of next Tuesday's balloting as offering a "clear choice" between two Democrats. His own economic recovery program "puts people first," Clinton claimed, whereas Tsongas's offered "a refined version of Eighties-style trickle-down economics." Clinton really rubbed it in when he charged that Tsongas's advocacy of a capital-gains tax cut would primarily benefit wealthy individuals and amounted to an attempt to generate "growth without fairness"—even though Clinton's program for economic revival, his "Plan for America's Future," included his own version of a capital-gains tax cut.

"We had growth and no fairness in the 1980s," Clinton said. "What happened? No more fairness and lower growth. It doesn't work. It's bad economics." That argument, which Clinton sharpened by accusing Tsongas of planning to tamper with cost-of-living increases for Social Security, paid off big on Super Tuesday, when Clinton, back in his position as front-runner, swept all seven of the Southern and border states contested.

Once again, as in the Georgia primary, blacks made a big contribution to Clinton's victory, giving him about 80 percent of their vote across the South, contrasted with the 60 percent of the white vote he won. Outspent and outmaneuvered in the competition, Tsongas had been reduced to toting around a toy panda bear to symbolize Clinton's eagerness to cater to Democratic interest groups. "I'm going to tell you something, Bill Clinton, you're not going to pander your way into the White House as long as I'm around," he declared on election night, amid the ashes of defeat.

But Tsongas lacked the resources and will to back up his bluster in the primaries—in Illinois and elsewhere in the Midwest—that followed the Southern contest. He seemed unable to separate himself from the economic abstractions he cherished, which he used to justify his case for economic austerity. Back in his Boston headquarters, his staff knew their candidate was making no progress when, on his first day of hustling for votes in the Illinois primary, they saw him on the network news lecturing black high-school students, desperate to find work in Chicago's tight job market, on the need for a capital-gains tax cut.

On the campaign trail, Tsongas presented the reverse image of Clinton, who promised to lift the nation out of its economic doldrums with an assortment of nostrums guaranteed to benefit all and pain none. For his part, "Tsongas tells people they have to sacrifice, in order to balance the budget, but he doesn't ever explain what the rewards will be," his pollster, Irwin (Tubby) Harrison complained.

But if Clinton had little to fear from his rivals, new disclosures about his past made it seem once again that he himself was the most serious threat to his own candidacy. The latest revelations had to do with financial dealings, his own and his wife's, back in Arkansas, relating in particular to their joint investment in a real estate development in an Ozark resort called Whitewater.

But the charges were complicated and hard for the public to grasp. And Clinton, now made confident by his successes in the South, fought back even more vehemently than he had in New Hampshire, seeking to turn the issue against his foes. When, during a campaign debate two days before the Illinois vote, Jerry Brown attacked the Clintons for their alleged conflicts of interest in Arkansas, Clinton ignored the specifics of the charges, instead calling Brown a liar who was "not worthy of being on the same platform" with Hillary Rodham Clinton. "Let me tell you something, Jerry," said Clinton, shaking his finger in anger at Brown. "I don't care what you say about me. But you ought to be ashamed of yourself for jumping on my wife." Clinton then called Brown an unprincipled politician who "reinvents himself every year or two," willing to "say anything" to get elected—thus, in effect, taking words out of the mouths of his own critics, who felt that this was an apt description of Clinton himself.

Once again, as in New Hampshire, Clinton turned to the theme of the attacks on his past behavior, representing a digression that was against the public's interest. "The American people can spot somebody who's on their side, and they desperately want this election to be about them," he said in Chicago. "They're tired of the politics of personal destruction. They would like to have one election where the focus would be on them and their future instead of all these things that divert our attention."

It was this argument that had now gained acceptance among the party leaders who had nursed misgivings about Clinton's candidacy, even as they had cheered his performance in Chicago in November. And they suppressed whatever doubts might have still plagued them, because the party was too far committed to Clinton now. I called the Southern party leader, who in Chicago had expressed concern about Clinton's extramarital involvements. Was she still troubled? "I thought about it some more," she said, "and I decided that if we had used that standard in the past, John Kennedy would never have been president. I think Clinton is our best candidate." And what made him seem so strong, she and her colleagues believed, was that he was from the South and could reclaim for the Democrats the irredenta that had now fallen under Republican hegemony.

For all the doubts and misgivings that the campaign had raised about his beliefs and character, Clinton remained what he had been on New Year's Eve in 1991, the anointed candidate of the establishment. This unspoken attitude was formalized just before the Chicago primary, when Ron Brown, the national chairman of the Democratic party, in an extraordinary departure from the neutrality demanded of him by custom and law, denounced Jerry Brown and Paul Tsongas for their criticism of Clinton, particularly for calling him "unelectable." Declaring that Clinton had undergone more scrutiny than any political leader in the past twenty years, Ron Brown praised him for "taking all the shots and standing up there." Ron wanted Jerry Brown, in particular, to stop his attacks on the Clintons, but, the party chairman said, "You can't control Jerry Brown."

He was certainly right about that, as the next few weeks would show. After Clinton vanquished Tsongas in the Illinois and Michigan primaries in mid-March, Tsongas took himself out of the race, apparently leaving Clinton a clear road to the nomination. His only remaining rival was Jerry Brown, considered too zany to be nominated, let alone elected. But the public uncertainty with Clinton was such that nothing could be taken for granted.

Brown stunned Clinton and most other Democrats by winning the primary in Connecticut on March 24. Suddenly, Clinton seemed vulnerable again. He had hoped to be regarded as the certain nominee, to use the New York battleground as a rehearsal stage for the general election. Instead, he was forced to wage a bitter contest against Brown, which the country's most raucous electorate and intrusive press corps transformed into an audience-participation show.

At the start, nearly everything Clinton tried to do seemed to go wrong. An evening rally turned into a confrontation between Clinton and a young AIDS activist who shouted at the candidate, "I'm dying from AIDS; you're dying from ambition."

With that taunt still ringing in his ears, Clinton awoke the next morning to face allegations in a *New York Times* article that while governor, he had maneuvered the Arkansas legislature to weaken a state government ethics bill that allowed him to shield himself from scrutiny. Visiting a Harlem hospital, Clinton found himself drowned out by the noisy protests of Alliance party candidate Lenora Fulani and her supporters.

With the tabloids and the talk shows hounding him, Clinton fed their blood lust by belatedly admitting, after repeated denials, that he had once

smoked marijuana, claiming that he had not inhaled, a response that provoked a nationwide wave of derision and a memorable headline in the *New
York Daily News:* "Weed Asked Him That!" Later that month at the Oscar
ceremonies in Hollywood, comedian Billy Crystal, serving as master of ceremonies, brought down the house by simply uttering the words: "He didn't
inhale," and then shaking his head.

Clinton and his staff soon realized they could do little to help themselves
in this setting—except to hurt Brown. After his upset victory in Connecticut on March 26, Brown charged into New York "riding a wave of disaf-
fection" with the political system, as Clinton's New York campaign manager, Harold Ickes, put it, and threatening to eclipse Clinton as an agent of
change and win the April 12 primary. But Clinton finally stopped Brown's
momentum by using the same tactic he had employed against Tsongas—
turning Brown's own message against him.

The main target was Brown's characteristically ill-considered proposal to
transform the tax system by instituting a flat tax, an idea that Clinton contended would hit hardest at the low-income voters whom Brown claimed to
be championing. What is more, Clinton claimed, Brown would benefit
from his own flat-tax proposal and pointedly noted that the former California governor had declined to release his tax returns.

For his part, Brown made Clinton's task easier by dramatizing his pledge
to make the Reverend Jesse Jackson his running mate, an idea that sent a
chill of apprehension through Jewish voters, who still recalled Jackson's
characterization of their city as "Hymietown." "The Jesse Jackson thing
was the stake in the heart," Brown adviser Michael Ford later told me.
Brown's campaign collapsed. He finished third behind not only Clinton but
also Tsongas, whose own candidacy had been revived more or less in ab-
sentia by his local supporters.

The results removed any remaining doubts that Clinton would gain the
nomination. But it left a lot of other questions about his candidacy. Exit
poll results showed that only 35 percent of the primary voters agreed with
the statement that Clinton had the honesty and integrity to be president,
whereas 35 percent disagreed and 30 percent were not sure. And only
about half of those who voted for Brown and Tsongas were prepared to say
that they would probably vote for Clinton against Bush in the fall.

"In terms of the fall, he is a dead, stone loser," Tsongas's pollster, Tubby
Harrison, told me. And now, as Clinton limped on through the California
primary, beating the discredited Brown by a margin of only seven points
and heading on to the July convention in New York, a new threat loomed,
born out of the same discontent with the status quo that Clinton had been
struggling to tap into with his own candidacy.

It had all begun, as with so many other phenomena of modern American
politics, on a television talk show back on February 20. The timing was

auspicious. Two days before, Tsongas's victory in New Hampshire had left the Democratic party in confusion and anxiety. Three weeks before that, the monthly economic indicators showed a sharp drop in the growth rate from the month before, going down nearly to zero, while unemployment climbed. President Bush's approval rating was in the low forties. Appearing with Larry King, the interviewer notorious for massaging the egos of his guests, was billionaire Ross Perot. Making it seem that the words had to be dragged out of him, Perot mingled a string of butchered metaphors about putting on the gloves, climbing a cliff, and putting the shoe on the other foot, suggesting he might indeed run for president "if all these nice people who have written to me" would get his name on the ballot in all fifty states. "I can certainly pay for my own campaign," Perot reminded his potential supporters. "But I want you to have skin in the game."

All this was not quite as spontaneous as it appeared. Earlier that month, Perot had met with a group of civic leaders in Nashville, Tennessee, and his stated willingness to run had been reported in the *Nashville Tennessean*. That story had caused barely a ripple, except to prompt King's invitation to Perot. But with King's huge audience, the impact was seismic. On the morning after the show, the switchboard at Perot's firm, Electronic Data Process, crashed under an overload of calls. An 800 number was installed along with a phone bank, and calls flooded in at the rate of 90,000 an hour.

They kept coming. In the first three weeks of March, the total reached 1 million. For his part, Perot said he would be willing to spend $50 million to $100 million to advance his own candidacy. But it was more than money that was pushing Perot; rather it was a matching of the man and the mood of the country.

There was nothing new about the idea of Perot running for president. Back in 1987, after he gave a speech to the National Governors Association, its chairman suggested that Perot ought to set his cap for the White House. The chairman at the time was Bill Clinton of Arkansas. But Perot had never run for anything. Politics seemed an unlikely field of endeavor for a man whose ability to make billions was matched only by his refusal to suffer fools—a category that often seemed to encompass in Perot's mind everybody who disagreed with him.

A champion salesman for IBM, he left his job, complaining that his bosses did not pay enough attention to his suggestions, and founded a computer firm that brought him vast wealth. But after he sold his data-systems firm to General Motors, his attempt to streamline the automaker's bureaucratic operations led to a collision of ideas and egos. The effort was scrapped, and Perot severed his ties with GM but gained a $700-million settlement that assuaged his wounded feelings.

Perot soon thrust his ideas and freewheeling approach into the world outside business. In the mid-1980s, he helped push through a sweeping reform of the Texas school system, notable mostly for the "no pass–no play rule" it imposed on high-school athletes. Less successfully, he launched a prolonged and bitter campaign to prod the Defense Department into making more of an effort to gain information about American prisoners of war still held captive in Vietnam.

He brought this same abrasive, egomaniacal style to his presidential campaign. In April, for the first time subjected, by a panel of editors, to the sharp scrutiny routinely applied to full-fledged presidential candidates, Perot bridled. "Do we have to be rude and adversarial?" he asked. And at one point, "Can't we just talk?" Then, in a remark that foreshadowed later events during his in-again, out-again pursuit of the White House, he said, "I'm not driven to do this. Matter of fact, the more I'm in it, the less interesting it becomes."

Despite his crankiness, and despite, or perhaps because of, the fact that the public knew relatively little about him or his views, he had the enormous appeal of an outsider challenger, independent because of his wealth of any interest group, and this all transformed the presidential politics of 1992. From February 20 to the California primary, a period of little more than three months, Perot went from zero to leadership in the polls, with the incumbent president, George Bush, trailing him—and Bill Clinton, the presumptive Democratic nominee, in third place.

Within another month, by the time he withdrew, Perot had qualified for the ballot in twenty-four states, and his volunteers had collected enough signatures for him to qualify for sixteen others. During that time, by the testimony of Tom Luce, the Texas Republican who had served as chairman of the Bush petition committee, Perot had not spent a single cent either for television ads or petition drives. He had shelled out $6 million—small change by the standards of presidential campaigns—to create an organization and a staff, which subsequently became absorbed with complying with the Federal Election Commission (FEC) rules and with the requirements of each state for ballot placement.

Stunned and frightened, the political establishment struck back. Gerald Ford warned that Perot's candidacy could force the election into the House of Representatives, setting off a "constitutional crisis." White House press secretary Marlin Fitzwater called Perot a "monster." Vice President Quayle's wife, Marilyn, said that it is "worrisome . . . that you can in essence buy an election without standing for anything."

The press dug into Perot's past and unearthed a treasure trove of idiosyncrasy. Apart from once referring to the navy, in a letter to a congressman as "a fairly Godless organization," he had also regularly dealt with his antagonists in public and private life with tactics so high-handed that they often barely fell short of illegality, such as conducting investigations of his own children and of then vice president Bush.

Perot's response to this wave of disclosures did not help his by now tarnished reputation. He claimed that the "Opposition Research" group of the Republican party had launched an effort to redefine his personality. He said he had evidence to support this charge but declined to disclose it. Suddenly, on July 16, on the very night Clinton would be nominated by the Democratic party in New York, Perot pulled out of the race. He feared that his candidacy might force the election into the House, he said, the same concern Ford had expressed, and be "disruptive" to the country. He would not endorse either Bush or Clinton, but he did have a good word to say about the Democrats, who "had done a brilliant job in coming back," as he said. Although not many paid much attention at the time, he also left the door yawning to allow his return, urging his supporters to keep up their efforts to get his name on the ballot.

Both Perot's brief domination of the national political scene and his temporary departure from it could not have been better timed from the standpoint of Clinton's candidacy. When the former started, Clinton was "damaged goods," as Greenberg later admitted, and the time before the convention had to be used to rehabilitate his candidacy. But no serious effort was made to define and clarify his policy positions beyond the constantly amended hodgepodge that got him through the campaign.

Now his advisers set out to change the public's view of Clinton himself. "We had decided that biography was critical," Greenberg said. And this turned into a contorted campaign, built around television and radio talk shows—such as Arsenio Hall's show and MTV—in which Clinton could ramble on about himself without fear of the pointed questions the more structured news talk shows would fire at him.

The relevance of what he said was often far from clear. Asked whether his appearance on the Arsenio Hall show, wearing wraparound sunglasses and playing the saxophone, might make him seem unpresidential, Clinton replied, "I've been playing the sax since I was nine. It's a part of who I am." His strategist Carville added: "This was the real Bill Clinton. That's not to say he wears sunglasses indoors. But it is to say that he likes to have fun."

Pretty flimsy, perhaps. But it was one way to get voters to forget the testimony of Gennifer Flowers and that in his own letter to Colonel Holmes of the ROTC.

More seriously, Clinton set out in dramatic fashion to underline what had been one of his early and important themes, the perception of himself as a champion of the middle class, that is, of white values. It was in this context that during a talk with Jackson's Rainbow Coalition in June of the election year, he attacked the rap singer Sister Souljah. Sister had appeared before the group the preceding day; Clinton's criticism was, by implication, of Jackson himself, who had praised her contributions to his coalition.

Sister had made herself a target of convenience a month earlier in an interview with the *Washington Post*. As a way of expressing her empathy with the blacks in Los Angeles who had rioted following the Rodney King police-beating acquittals, she asked: "I mean, if black people kill black people every day, why not have a week and kill white people?"

This heavy-handed irony was just what Clinton was looking for. Sister Souljah's remarks, he told the Rainbow Coalition meeting, "are filled with the kind of hatred that you do not honor." He was making a point of criticizing her, he said, because "she has a big influence on a lot of people."

Jackson had not been warned about what Clinton was up to, an oversight that, calculated or not, was bound to assure his indignation. Wondering aloud why Clinton had made those remarks to the audience, Jackson said, "Perhaps he was aiming for an audience that was not here," and that seemed to explain matters as well as anything.

In more substantive areas, Clinton proposed yet another new economic plan—the most striking feature of which was his scaling back of the middle-class tax-cut proposal that had once been the core idea in his agenda for revival. Indeed, his aides made certain that the tax cut was not even mentioned in the Democratic platform, which had been drafted not long before in New Mexico. In a classic touch of his trademark eclecticism, Clinton made a point of citing an idea that he had incorporated from each of his rivals into his own proposal. "I listened to them all and listened to the debate, and I learned something," he claimed. "So all of them can say that part of them is in this plan."

But Clinton's main concern continued to be with imagery and symbolism. His most important symbolic act was his choice of Al Gore as a vice president. Vice presidential choices are always said to be the first important decision a new nominee must make. They are also by definition, because of the nature of the vice presidency, one of the least substantive. But the symbolism matters because it reflects the nominee's sense of priorities.

The usual purpose of vice presidential candidates is to balance the ticket, to compensate for some weakness on the part of the standard-bearer. Thus, John Kennedy chose Lyndon Johnson to aid him in the South. And Jimmy Carter selected Walter Mondale to bolster his relations with Northern liberals. Yet Clinton flew in the face of such conventional logic by picking another Southerner, a man just as conservative as he was, thus reaffirming his commitment to the white South. The striking aspect of this choice, so far as the Democratic party was concerned, was not just that Clinton made it but that no one else disputed it or complained about it, so drained of vitality and confidence were the liberals who had once dominated the party.

Yet there was an element of balance in the Gore selection, more subtle than the usual geographical or ideological considerations and not without significance. Unlike Clinton, whose whole career had been in state government, Gore was a man of Congress, with fifteen years in the House and Senate. And his strengths, in national defense and the environment, were both areas in which Clinton needed reinforcement. But perhaps most important of all, wooden, dull Al Gore was unassailably wholesome. A Vietnam War veteran, no one had ever reason to doubt his loyalty to his country or his fidelity to his wife, Mary Elizabeth, also called Tipper. In her own right, Gore's spouse presented a helpful contrast to the Democratic candidate for First Lady—Hillary Rodham Clinton, who, during the course of the campaign, had once sneered at the idea that instead of pursuing her professional career she might have "stayed home and baked cookies." For her part, Tipper Gore was widely known for her battle against pornography in popular music and her devotion to her own children; and she seemed like just the sort of person who would enjoy whipping up a batch of goodies for them and their friends. Together, the Gores provided a solid counterweight to the misgivings stirred by the past behavior of the nominee and the outspoken feminism of his wife.

The final symbolic stroke came at the convention, with the presentation of an hour-long film biography turned out with the slickness to be expected from its producers, Harry and Linda Bloodworth-Thomason, the creators of the TV sitcoms *Designing Women* and *Evening Shade.* The Clinton film focused on every obstacle the candidate had overcome, every hardship he had confronted along the long climb from his difficult origins in the little town of Hope, Arkansas. "I still believe in America," Clinton declared at the conclusion. "And I still believe in a place called Hope."

Both the Clintons were said to have wept when the film was previewed for them. "It's *good,*" the nominee-to-be proclaimed. But then he insisted that the section on Vietnam should be edited out lest it revive the controversy over his draft. "I hate all this stuff," Clinton said afterward by one account. "This is not what American politics should be about."

This was mindful of his constant complaint during the campaign whenever his relationship with Gennifer Flowers or his avoidance of the draft or his conflicts of interest as governor were brought up: "This campaign is not about me—it's about the issues." But of course he *was* the issue, as Bob Kerrey had foreseen earlier that year. To a degree, this was true of all candidates for the presidency. But it was especially true of Clinton because he repeatedly offered the story of his own life as an earnest portrayal of his intentions in the presidency and because his background provided so much reason to doubt him.

"My life is a testament to the fact that the American dream works," he was fond of saying. "I got to live by the rules that work in America, and I wound up here today, running for president of the United States of America." And so it was that he announced at the convention that he was accepting the nomination "in the name of all those who do the work, pay the taxes, raise the kids, and play by the rules; in the name of the hardworking Americans who make up our forgotten middle class. I am a product of that middle class. And when I am president you will be forgotten no more."

Clinton promised change in America, as he had throughout the campaign. But he did not make clear how he was going to achieve this change, because he seemed intent on changing everything at once.

"Government is in the way," he declared in his best DLC style. But then he went on to promise to use government to help create millions of new jobs, dozens of new industries, college educations for all who wanted them, and cheap health care for all who needed it.

But what he said that night mattered little. The big news of the day had come earlier with Ross Perot's announcement that he was withdrawing from the race. Some in Clinton's camp fretted that the timing of this announcement would detract from Clinton's big moment in New York. But setting aside whether that mattered much, the fact was that Perot's candidacy had already done Clinton a great service. The constant controversy Perot had provoked during those late-spring and early-summer weeks had helped the public forget, or at least overlook, for the time being, all the reasons it had for doubting Clinton. And his withdrawal, just as Clinton and Gore staged their political coming-out party, was a catalyst that led to a reshuffling of the political order of battle.

Three days after Clinton's nomination and Perot's withdrawal, just as Clinton and Gore were setting out with their families on a bus safari around the land, which would dominate television coverage for a week, a new Gallup poll showed Clinton, who only a few weeks before had been dead last in a three-man race, now holding a commanding twenty-point lead over Bush in a two-man race. With Perot out of contention, voters had taken a second look at Clinton and had once again asked themselves: "Who else is there?" The only answer was Bush, and he was no answer at all.

In effect, the general election campaign was over before it officially began. The voters had not yet spoken, but most had made up their minds. And although Clinton's margin narrowed as some voters returned to the Republican fold and others declared for Perot when he reentered the race at the start of October, the outcome was never in doubt.

Sometime in the months following Desert Storm, during the long economic collapse, Bush forfeited his claim to leadership on the one aspect of the national condition that mattered most to Americans—their ability to provide for themselves and their families. Bush stumbled through the convention in Houston in mid-August, allowing himself to be overshadowed by Patrick J. Buchanan and other prophets of cultural conservatism. "We lacked a message and we were in such a floundering state at the White House, we grabbed family values," recalled William Kristol, then chief of staff to Vice President Quayle and one of the more thoughtful members of Bush's board of strategy.

But there was probably not any issue that could substitute for the economic message that Bush had given to Clinton. Bush himself could find nothing to say to convince Americans that they had misjudged him. In mid-September, by finally unveiling his plan for economic recovery, grandly titled "Agenda for American Renewal," Bush briefly fostered the impression that he wanted to turn the presidential campaign into a high-level debate over economic policy. But it was very late in the game for that. And neither the president nor his advisers believed they could turn the economy to their advantage.

The real thrust of the White House strategy became apparent less than a week after the economic plan emerged, when the president addressed the National Guard Association's Salt Lake City convention and sought to renew the controversy over Clinton's Vietnam War draft record. His voice choked with emotion, Bush, by unmistakable implication, questioned whether Clinton met the "highest standard" for sending young Americans into battle as commander in chief. This was just part of the overall strategy to exploit the public's mistrust of Clinton—and to echo the question Bush had raised in his Houston acceptance speech: He had asked Americans, "Who do you trust to make change work for you?"

"The biggest thing that's going to happen in the next seven weeks is that people are going to know a lot more about Clinton than they do now," Bush campaign pollster Fred Steeper told me in September after both conventions were over. But actually, the Republicans were unable to tell voters much more about Clinton than they already knew. Some would never vote for him for these reasons. But others had made their peace with Clinton because of what they already knew about Bush. In the abstract, the argument about trust seemed potent. But coming from the man who had instructed the country to "read my lips" the last time he ran for president, it had become painfully hollow.

With a comfortable lead, Clinton had a chance to lay down a clear course of action for his presidency. He did not take it. "One of the worst things we ever did for George Bush was let him get elected without a plan for what he would do as president," Clinton used to claim early in his presidential campaign. "We let George Bush get elected on the cheap . . . on 'read my lips' and 'the other guy's a bum.'" But as election day neared, Clinton rarely used that line. It would have raised questions about his own performance on the hustings, where he waged a campaign designed to bring an electoral majority but not a clear mandate for governing.

Many other politicians have played that same expedient game—but Clinton's situation was different. He had been the clear front-runner in the race since the midsummer Democratic convention and thus had the opportunity to be explicit. Moreover, by promising that his presidency would portend dramatic change in the government, he generated high expectations for himself. Weeks before the ballots were counted, it was already clear that Clinton would not be able to keep his promises to reduce the deficit, renovate the infrastructure, and reform health care and education without asking for belt-tightening, of one sort or another, that would impinge upon the lives of all but the least advantaged voters. And yet he had done nothing to prepare the citizenry for that sort of imposition on their lives.

As he stumped across the land, Clinton often called on voters to "have the courage" to change the country. But he never mentioned the word "sacrifice." To the contrary, when he stumped through the Farm Belt he promised his audiences, long dependent on federal support for agriculture, that, unlike Bush, he would as president "put government on your side." And though he prided himself, as "a different kind of Democrat," on his willingness to challenge the party's traditional constituencies, he seemed as eager as any hack member of Congress to please all sides. Addressing a rally in Portland, Oregon, he described himself as "progrowth and proenvironment, probusiness and pro working families."

Asked at a meeting with editors and reporters of the *Los Angeles Times* about his reluctance to call for sacrifice, Clinton referred to the "assumption abroad in the land" that the only way to reduce the budget deficit "is to punish the middle class and lower middle class." But, he added, "I don't believe that. I have told everybody who will listen that it takes courage to change; I'm not talking about sacrifice." Clinton did say that no president could do much to change the national condition, "unless people are willing to change their private conduct, too. Unless there is a real commitment to higher productivity in the private sector, unless every middle-class American is willing to change their behavior in the workplace, commit themselves to a lifetime of education and training." But this was a huge cop-out. Private conduct could not implement change on the scale Clinton liked to promise unless it was backed by fundamental shifts in federal policy that would, for example, make education and training readily available. At any rate, Clinton himself, based on his own behavior, seemed like a poor person to make that argument.

On election day, Clinton captured 43 percent of the popular vote and 370 electoral votes; 38 percent of the popular vote and 168 electoral votes went to Bush. Perot won no electoral votes, but his 19 percent of the popular vote was the big surprise of the election, the largest share for any independent candidate since former president Theodore Roosevelt, running on the Bull Moose ticket in 1912, had won 27 percent.

Clinton and Gore's Southern roots had only limited impact. Bush carried Texas and Florida, the two biggest Southern states, along with most of the rest, leaving Clinton only Georgia and Louisiana to go along with his own Arkansas and Gore's Tennessee. Bush still won more white votes than Clinton did—and won far more in the South, where Clinton took only 34 percent of the Southern white vote. What it all boiled down to was that the Reagan-Bush era in American politics ended just as it had begun twelve years before—with the massive repudiation of a president undone by economic distress. As it was summed up most succinctly and most famously by the four-word motto emblazoned on a sign in the Clinton campaign headquarters: "It's the economy, stupid."

More than one-third of the voters felt they were financially worse off than they were four years before, and the majority of them voted for Clinton. And throughout his long march to the White House, he never passed up a chance to cite the rising figures on layoffs, bankruptcies, foreclosures, and other gloomy indicators of decline that fueled dissatisfaction with the Bush administration, a presidency that recorded the slowest economic growth of any such period during the post–World War II era.

Clinton's decisive victory also contravened claims that had been advanced by Republicans—and generally conceded by Democrats—as explanations for GOP domination of presidential politics for more than a decade. The GOP strategists had contended that their party assured itself of a permanent lease on the White House by fashioning a message that appealed to the electorate's aversion to government—particularly the threat of higher taxes and increased spending—and its reverence for traditional values. Bush and his team expended everything they had in time, energy, and money to pound those themes home in their campaign against Clinton in 1992, as the GOP had done so effectively against Democratic standard-bearers Walter Mondale in 1984 and Michael Dukakis in 1988. But these time-tested battle cries failed to arouse voters, who were preoccupied with the nation's prolonged economic slump. Indeed, Clinton's support withstood this buffeting even though his proposals for raising taxes by $150 billion and spending by $220 billion, as well as the fact that he was beset by allegations of philandering and shirking the draft, made him in some ways an easier mark for such attacks than either Mondale or Dukakis. When all the votes had been counted, Republican professionals privately confessed their belief that the environment was such that Michael Dukakis, the hapless loser of 1988, probably could have defeated Bush in 1992. They also argued convincingly that Clinton would certainly have come a cropper in the good times of 1988.

But if the election demonstrated that the Republican claims were fallacious, it left a huge question looming for the new president: What did he have to offer an electorate that now, instead of asking "Who else is there?" would be more likely to wonder, "What have you done for me lately?" Moreover, in trying to find an answer, Clinton would be up against a new adversary—a politician in the other party and in the legislative branch of the government, a fellow Southerner who seemed fully as resourceful, and as ambitious, as Clinton himself.

5

The Prophet: Back to the Future

IT SCARCELY DESERVES THE NAME OF PARTY." Such was the judgment of political scientist V. O. Key Jr., writing in his magisterial 1950s study, *Southern Politics*, of the Republican party in the South. "It wavers somewhat between an esoteric cult on the order of a lodge and a conspiracy for plunder in accord with the accepted customs of our politics. Its exact position on the cult conspiracy scale wavers from place to place and from time to time."

The last half of the twentieth century, which followed the publication of Key's opus, has been a period of seismic turmoil and change in American politics, no more so anywhere than in the Southern states. Well before the conclusion of this era, by the time Bill Clinton of Arkansas began planning his drive for the White House, the Republican party in the South had matured into a powerful entity that, in many places, dominated its Democratic opposition. But even after all these years of accomplishment for Republicans, even as Newt Gingrich of Georgia was rising to claim a place among the party's national leadership, V. O. Key's scornful indictment came close to accurately describing the Republican party in the House of Representatives.

Like the Republican party in the South of 1950, the Republican party in the House had been in the minority for so long—forty unbroken years, and forty-six out of the last fifty by the time Bill Clinton was inaugurated president and members of the 103rd Congress took their oath of office—that most of the Republican members of the House had given up any realistic hope of changing their situation.

The partisan imbalance in the House of Representatives had become an additional distortion of the political system, growing out of the structural distortions engineered by its eighteenth-century creators. The constitutional separation of powers allowed the Democrats to construct a majority in the House, regardless of which party controlled the White House or, for that matter, the Senate. And in the modern era, this advantage had become self-reinforcing. The power of incumbency to establish political identity, to shape debate, and, last but certainly not least, to gain financial support seemed to outweigh all the other forces in the political system. During the entire period of Democratic dominance, the reelection rate for incumbency averaged well above 90 percent; and in 1990, it reached 96 percent, leaving Republicans to flounder in despair and frustration. Ultimately, their situation changed for the better, in large measure because of the enhanced status of the Republican party in the South, reflecting the changes that had taken place in that region since V. O. Key's time.

But in 1993, this favorable prospect was not at all clear to the members of the Republican contingent in the House, where, even after gaining nine seats in the 1992 election, they counted only 176 members out of 435. Seeing no realistic chance of improving their situation, many of them continued to make their main objective holding on to their own positions in public life as best they could, which often meant accommodating themselves to Democratic demands.

As might be expected, the Democrats took full advantage of this situation. "If we have a united Democratic position, Republicans are irrelevant," boasted Democratic congressman Henry Waxman of California in 1986. And far from understanding the Republican complaints and attacks on the one-sided relationship that prevailed, Democrats resented it. "When you have owned the plantation, the idea that one of your slaves wants to drink out of the same glass is clearly an assault," said Newt Gingrich of the tension between the two parties in the House. "Seen by the slave, it's simply the fact that it's a hot day."

Since he entered the House in 1979, Gingrich had made the principal objective of his career to rouse his GOP colleagues, to help overturn the Democratic behemoth. And it was his continued dedication to this purpose, as the 103rd Congress opened and the new president prepared to take the office, that made him Clinton's most dangerous adversary in Washington.

Not everyone realized that yet. After all, Bob Dole was the ranking Republican official left in the federal government. Dole was, and had been for some time, the leader of the Senate Republicans. Gingrich was the House whip, a position he had gained only three years before, and still technically junior to the veteran House Republican leader Bob Michel. Moreover, Dole was certainly nobody to be dismissed. He had already run for the presidency twice, and he loomed as the early favorite of the party establishment for 1996.

For the time being, though, Dole was more concerned with staking out the turf in his own party than in frustrating Clinton. He would stand in the president's way only to the extent that he saw that as necessary to keep ahead of the Republican competition for the only prize left in political life that he wanted—the presidency. Moreover, Dole was a man who liked to work within the system, and always had, since coming to Washington more than thirty years before. Gingrich was the man who was at war with the system; he had been since he came to Washington fourteen years before, and always would be.

Jim Wright, the Texan whom Gingrich dethroned as Speaker of the House, afterward denounced Gingrich as a "nihilist, intent on destroying and demoralizing the existing order." But Wright, whose judgment on Gingrich was understandably colored, missed part of the point. Certainly, Gingrich did want to bring down the existing order—at least so far as it ruled the House of Representatives. But the Gingrich that the Democrats confronted at the start of the Clinton presidency was no nihilist. To the contrary, Gingrich was a demagogue of sorts, with strongly held beliefs and values. To be sure, he did not hesitate to emphasize some convictions above others—depending on circumstances and on the weakness of his enemies—in order to reach the goals he set for himself in politics. But these beliefs, harnessed to his ambition, defined Gingrich's presence on Capitol Hill and separated him from Dole—who rarely argued over beliefs and issues and who was solely a negotiator and a bargainer, not a demagogue—and made him more dangerous to Clinton, a president elected with a shaky plurality and a blurry set of beliefs.

Clinton and Gingrich differed not only in the intensity of their convictions but in their view of the personal experiences that had shaped them. Both men's lives reflected the fragmentation and tensions that had destabilized American society—and American politics—in the years after World War II.

An army brat, Gingrich, like Clinton, bounced around during his childhood and adolescence, even more than Clinton had. Young Newt's mother, like Clinton's, went through a divorce, and her remarriage created a tense relationship between her son and his stepfather, who had once, in a burst of temper at young Newt, picked him up and held him against the wall by his shoulders while bawling him out.

Clinton later contended that his life epitomized the American dream. Gingrich, with a better developed sense of irony, and considerably more candor, referred to his upbringing as "a classic psychodrama."

Yet despite these differences in style and tone, these two men shared some fundamentals. Both set out on self-proclaimed missions to alter their parties. And both came from the South, that forcing ground for political change. Just as the postwar social and economic upheavals that transformed the South of V. O. Key's day opened the doors in the national Democratic party to Clinton, so they paved the way for Gingrich to pursue his ambitions in the Republican party. Amidst upheaval in Dixie—its dramatic transformation from a Democratic fiefdom into a bulwark of Republicanism—most of the restraints and barriers on how individuals progressed up the political career ladder crumbled, and the door was opened wide for young men like Gingrich and Clinton to tailor their own credos to suit their own ambitions.

In later years, Gingrich liked to recall the defining experience of his early years: a visit as a fifteen-year-old, while his father was stationed in France on the battlefield at Verdun, one of the worst slaughterhouses in the Great War. "I can still feel the sense of horror and reality which overcame me then," he wrote in his 1984 book, *Window of Opportunity*. "It is the driving force which pushed me into history and politics and molded my life."

However much his soul was seared by that episode, there were more pragmatic and contemporary influences that shaped his entry into politics. In 1960, his family had moved from his father's billet in Germany to Georgia, still a foundation stone of the Southern Democratic politics then, therefore offering more opportunity to a newcomer in the Republican party. Even before he arrived, he spelled out his career plan to a high-school teacher in Stuttgart, Germany. "I would go to Georgia, help create a Republican party, and win a national office."

On his way to his political career, he got married—to his high-school math teacher, who was seven years his senior, which caused a bitter breach in his family. Then he trained as a historian, first at Emory University and then at Tulane University. During the course of his schooling, he got caught up to some degree with the liberal enthusiasms of the time—defense of the environment and opposition to the war in Vietnam and to racial segregation, which was nearly as prevalent in the South of the 1960s as it was in V. O. Key's time. Civil rights in particular captured Gingrich's attention because he saw black votes as opening the path for the Republican party in the South.

One of Gingrich's principal heroes at the time was Fifth Circuit Court judge John Minor Wisdom, whose rulings in that circuit, which included much of the South, greatly advanced the cause of civil rights, all the more so because of Wisdom's Southern origins. He also enrolled one of his daughters in a mostly black Head Start program and arranged for Ernest "Dutch" Morial, a black who would become the first of his race to be elected mayor of New Orleans, to be put on the speaker's list at a campus discussion group.

While at Tulane, Gingrich signed on for his first presidential campaign— as a Louisiana organizer for the 1968 candidacy of Nelson Rockefeller. He told some people that he was mainly interested in the experience he would gain. But he also said that Rockefeller had a better chance to win black votes than the front-runner for the nomination and the party's ultimate standard-bearer, Richard Nixon, for whom Gingrich had little use, anyway. Whatever his motivation, Gingrich worked hard to recruit black supporters for Rockefeller, telling blacks that they could hardly count on the Democrats, with their deep ties to the racial barriers that ruled the South, to aid in the battle against segregation.

Outside of Gingrich's group in New Orleans, Rockefeller's candidacy went nowhere in Louisiana or elsewhere in the South. At the convention, Louisiana cast most of its votes for Nixon, none for Rockefeller, and a handful for a newcomer on the presidential scene from the West—Ronald Reagan, the governor of California and already viewed by conservatives as the heir to their leader, Barry Goldwater. Yet Gingrich himself did not come away empty-handed. In addition to the experience of working in an actual presidential campaign, he acquired the credentials of a moderate Republican, which was convenient for him in his next venue, teaching at West Georgia State College, while he prepared himself for the congressional seat that was his goal.

In those days, to gain acceptance on a college campus, even at a backwater such as West Georgia State, any Republican was better off being a moderate. The conservative cause had yet to achieve the intellectual prominence it would attain in the Reagan era. And although moderate Republicans hardly marched in the vanguard of progressivism, they were more willing to adjust to the changes overtaking the South than were the Old Guard Democrats.

Gingrich himself embodied the anomalies that marked the moderate Republicans. He was ultraconservative in taste and manner—he wore a suit and tie to class—leading one friend to label him "a relic of the Fifties." Yet intellectually, he made himself an earnest adept of every trendy cause and train of thought from the 1960s. So immersed was he in futurism that he taught a noncredit course on this subject at Tulane, with a reading list that featured management guru Peter Drucker and writer Alvin Toffler, who would become beacons on his path.

"Anything that was new, he was interested in," recalled Don Wagner, who taught with Gingrich at West Georgia State College. When Gingrich applied to chair the history department after he had been there only one year and was turned down, he cofounded an environmental studies program, then a path-breaking event. Bright, imaginative, audacious at times, Gingrich "always had a big picture in his head," one of his colleagues said.

Still, his friends on the faculty thought he was never fully comfortable in academic life. It was merely a staging ground for his political career, and by 1974, he was ready for his first major political venture—challenging John J. Flynt, the veteran Democratic incumbent in the Sixth Congressional District of Georgia.

The nature of his opponent, the changing times, and the makeup of the Sixth District all shaped Gingrich's early political identity. Flynt was a retrograde figure who had first entered Congress in 1955, when the state was not much different from the South that V. O. Key described. The South changed, but not Flynt. As dean of the Georgia delegation, he had convened periodic meetings of its members. But when Andrew Young, Georgia's first black member of Congress, joined the delegation in 1972, Flynt stopped holding meetings.

The Voting Rights Act of 1970, which opened the doors of the House to Young, started to make black political power a reality throughout the South. And in 1970, Jimmy Carter, who won the governorship of Georgia and ordered that Martin Luther King's portrait be hung in the state capitol building, made the cover of *Time* magazine and launched himself on the pathway to the White House. Running to succeed Carter in 1974, archsegregationist Lester Maddox, promising to remove King's portrait from its new platform, lost the election.

As race relations changed in the South, so did population patterns, the suburbs swelling at the expense of rural and urban areas. When Flynt entered Congress, twenty years before Gingrich took him on, the Sixth District was a slice of the Deep South—farm country, small towns, and one middle-sized city, Macon. But as the suburbs around metropolitan Atlanta boomed, the farm folk followed the call of opportunity. The district had to be moved north, to the edge of suburban Atlanta, attracting a group of citizens who wanted to be part of the middle class but were uncertain whether they really belonged. Some from the small towns fretted about whether they could adjust to big-city tensions and demands. Others had fled Atlanta itself and brought with them their uneasiness about the blacks and poor who remained behind in their old and decaying neighborhoods.

The newly formed Sixth District was no liberal stronghold. But its citizens of both races wanted something different from hard-line racial antagonism, which was what John J. Flynt continued to offer.

Gingrich ran as the agent of change, pounding Flynt with some of the same ammunition he would later fire against members of the Democratic majority in the House of Representatives. He planned to transform the GOP, he told his supporters, into a reform party that would attract blacks and women and moderate conservatives. Avoid the conservative label, Gingrich admonished his staff, except when the qualifier "moderate" was added.

Indeed, at times Gingrich did not sound like any kind of a conservative, moderate or otherwise. Talking to the Junior Chamber of Commerce in his district, Gingrich evoked memories of Tom Watson, Georgia's greatest populist. The "special interests" dominated Congress and fleeced ordinary Americans, he charged. To give the average citizen a fair shake in the marketplace, Gingrich promised to launch congressional probes into high corporate profits and vowed to hold the big corporations accountable for the way they deployed their vast earnings.

Gingrich's stance, and particularly the contrast with his opponent, gained him some unlikely political bedfellows. The League of Conservation Voters and the Sierra Club backed him for his environmental stands. The liberal National Committee for an Effective Congress, eager to help anyone who would challenge the dragon Flynt, sent money. And the steadfastly Democratic *Atlanta Constitution*, after conceding that 1974, in the wake of Watergate and President Ford's pardon of Nixon, was a bad year for Republicans, nevertheless contended that "in this particular race, party labels are of no moment." Chiding Flynt for failing to keep up with the changes in the district, the paper applauded the thirty-one-year-old Gingrich, whom it called "a relatively young man with the proper amount of maturity for his concern with the environment, the economy, and national defense." Gingrich, said the *Constitution*, stood for "the new approach, the search for innovative solutions to nagging and growing problems."

In a bad year for Republicans, innovation lost out to incumbency, but by only two points. And Gingrich was back after Flynt's seat again in 1976, hitting out harder than ever. He called the incumbent the tool of special interests and contended he had used his post as chairman of the House Ethics Committee to shield his sleazy House cronies from answering for their misconduct.

For his part, Flynt set the tone for the defense of his seat when he refused to debate Gingrich on the grounds that "if you lie down with dogs, you get up with fleas." Unfortunately for Gingrich, with Jimmy Carter heading the Democratic ticket, it was another bad year for Republicans in Georgia. Despite a second *Constitution* endorsement, Flynt again edged him out.

Defeat left Gingrich broke. But a group of supporters chipped in $13,000—about half his salary as a professor—to provide Gingrich with a subsidy to write a futuristic novel about World War III. Gingrich's wealthy backers gained a tax shelter, so that, in effect, the subsidy came from the U.S. Treasury. Gingrich took his family to Europe to research the book and actually completed the manuscript, but it never saw the light of day. What mattered most to him was that the book scheme helped him make it through the next two years—to the 1978 elections, when he tried again.

This time the seat was open. Flynt had announced his retirement, having capped his career with an episode that lent credence to Gingrich's complaints about his stewardship of the House Ethics Committee. When the committee began the probe into the so-called Koreagate scandal, objections from a bipartisan group of House members about Flynt's coziness with some of the suspected culprits among his colleagues forced Speaker O'Neill to remove him from effective control of the investigation.

With Flynt out of the way, Gingrich competed against Democratic state senator Virginia Shapard, who made the mistake, once she had won the Democratic primary, of taking victory for granted and Gingrich too lightly, an error other politicians would continue to make in the years to come. Shapard rarely mentioned her opponent by name except to refer to him as "Professor Gingrich," as though, gibed the *Constitution*, "he was a near-sighted Mr. Magoo, whose vision stopped at the ivied walls."

On the other side, Republican party strategists in Washington realized that following his two near misses, in an off-year election, with the White House occupied by a Democratic president whose popularity was steadily diminishing, Gingrich was a good bet to win. Now was the time for the party to come to the aid of the candidate. The national GOP sent the two-time loser money and dispatched a couple of hired guns to run his campaign. Gingrich's third try for the House took on the aspect that would become common in the campaigns that first Republicans, and ultimately many Democrats, ran in the 1980s—heavy advertising, most of it negative. On most issues of any consequence, Shapard was just about as conservative as Gingrich and therefore was just as suited to the tastes of the district. But Gingrich's advertising, particularly in newspapers and leaflets, "went after every rural Southern prejudice we could think of," one campaign official later acknowledged.

One flier contrasted family-man Gingrich with his opponent, claiming that she would leave her husband and children behind if the district voters sent her to Congress. Frederick Allen, a columnist for the *Constitution*, which abandoned its previous support of Gingrich and this time backed his opponent, accused Gingrich of verging on racism, specifically by depicting Senator Shapard as an ally of black state legislator Julian Bond in opposing welfare reform proposals, when she herself had offered her own proposal for welfare reform. "This year Gingrich has taken the low road," Allen lamented. But it was the path that got him 54 percent of the vote and a ticket to Washington.

Gingrich's brief political career had so far mirrored the metamorphosis of Southern politics in that period. He had started out in 1968 working for Nelson Rockefeller, when the Democratic party was still viewed as a bastion of segregation and the way was open to the Republicans to find common ground with black voters, working-class whites, and well-educated, affluent whites concerned about issues such as abortion and schools. And his populist rhetoric in his first campaign against Flynt, along with his focus on the environment, suggested that Gingrich himself might be headed in that direction. Indeed, during the 1978 campaign, even while his handlers were race baiting for votes against Shapard, Gingrich hustled for support in black areas of the district "like a certified Democrat," the *Constitution* reported. "He goes to churches, talks at black gatherings, walks the streets." He even promised if elected to set up a mobile office to serve blacks.

But over the past few years' events, racial polarization on the national level made moderate Republicanism, with its benign view of race relations and its acceptance of government's role in society, a less attractive option for Gingrich in the South. Like most politicians in both parties, he took the path of least resistance. The Democrats, driven by their leadership in the urban North, made black voters their base in the South but stopped short of also reaching out to low-income whites and forging a majority coalition. The Republicans reacted by appealing to the white voters who felt themselves threatened by the black gains and abandoned by Democrats. Most of the competition between the two parties was aimed at reaching middle-class white voters and business interests.

Still, having gained office, Gingrich at first resisted foreclosing the chance to march toward broader horizons that had beckoned to him a decade earlier. He did not want to be pigeonholed. He promised Atlantans that he would "lean very heavily" on liberal Democratic congressmen Wyche Fowler and Elliott Levitas for guidance on issues that concerned the city, and he pledged to work closely with the Democratic-dominated Georgia delegation on the Hill. "Between elections," he said, "we've got to work for the country and work on issues and not on party."

Gingrich made a point of dismissing talk about his conservatism. "Maybe faced with the problems of the late twentieth century, what we need to do is invent new ideological boxes," he said. "We have not yet defined the word that would explain the politics that would make sense to this country."

It was a historian's answer. And in the years to come, Gingrich would continue to lean heavily on the lessons of the past, sometimes for guidance, often merely to help him make a point. But after 1978, Gingrich was no longer a professor and an amateur politician; he had become an amateur historian, but a professional politician. And so it was the tide of events in the present and what they portended for the future that would shape his answers to the problems of the late twentieth century, not the past he liked so much to talk about.

"He had an uncanny knack of seeing where things are going," recalled Ben Kennedy, a Gingrich colleague at West Georgia State, who voted for Gingrich in his first two House campaigns—but never again. Gingrich reminded Kennedy of the nineteenth-century politician Alexandre Auguste Ledru-Rollin, who, during one of the numerous political upheavals that shook France during his era, raced outside to join a mob of his supporters that was surging through the street, off to storm some likely barricade. "Ah, well," he confessed later. "I am their leader, I really had to follow them."

And despite his reassuring words about working for the country, not for the party, Gingrich's priorities shifted dramatically once he got to Washington. Guy Vander Jagt, the House Republican campaign committee chairman, commissioned him to draft a plan to make the Republican the majority party.

It was a tall order. To ready himself for the task, Gingrich set about putting his own life in order in a way that left a glaring mark on his career. "America needs a return to moral values," an early Gingrich campaign flier declared—a theme that served as a Gingrich hallmark during the years he sought to become the Sixth District's member of Congress. To all outward appearances, his own life seemed to embody that idea. Gingrich and his wife, Jackie, the high-school geometry teacher whom Newt had married when he was nineteen, were regularly in attendance at the local Baptist church where Gingrich taught Sunday school. And it seemed to townspeople that wherever they went together, Newt and Jackie always held hands.

But beneath the surface, rifts developed in this May-December alliance. A marriage counselor did not seem to help. Gingrich's dalliances with other women, several of them volunteers in his campaign, became common gossip among members of his staff. The move to Washington heightened the tensions between the couple. Gingrich told friends that because his wife, Jackie, was considerably overweight and he was near the end of his first term, he filed for divorce.

"I'm either going to get a divorce or I'm going to have a nervous breakdown," he explained to his mother. The divorce was made messier by the fact that Jackie was afflicted with uterine cancer, and while she was recovering from surgery, Gingrich paid a visit to her hospital room to hash over the terms of the divorce, until she threw him out. Despite the unfavorable publicity in his hometown paper two weeks before election day, Gingrich won easily. "There must have been some quiet, angry white males out there . . . who felt trashed by women," one of his staffers later reflected. In the first year of his second term, Gingrich married Marianne Ginther, whom he had met at a Republican fund-raiser in Ohio in 1980, a union that, as Gingrich later conceded, had its share of stresses and strains, which he once gave little better than a fifty-fifty chance of surviving.

Looking back on that period a few years after divorcing Jackie, Gingrich later claimed that his private behavior so contradicted the homilies he preached to his constituents that "I began to stop saying them in public." And that decision impelled him to get a divorce. "If I was disintegrating enough as a person that I could not say those things," he explained, "then I needed to get my life straight, not quit saying them." Soon after the divorce, he began saying "those things" again. And traditional values became one of the cornerstones of his view of the world and of his political catechism.

Years later, after he had become Speaker of the House, Gingrich brought up his past and present personal difficulties in a talk to a gathering of the Christian Coalition, the most potent political organization of the Religious Right. He complained that liberal journalists accused him and other Republicans, who championed family values but who had been divorced, of hypocrisy. The liberal view, Gingrich contended, is that "the only people you should listen to are social therapists, who do not believe in God and who will tell you that you should simply relax and accept your decay and your depravity because it's the most you've got." As for himself and other conservatives, Gingrich claimed: "We emphasize family precisely because it's hard."

Whatever the merits of Gingrich's rationalizations for the conflict between what he preached and what he practiced might seem, his divorce had removed a substantial obstacle to his carrying out the assignment Vander Jagt had given. Now he could concentrate all his energy and time on the formidable task.

For Gingrich, satisfaction with the Republican success in the 1980 election in winning back the White House and capturing the Senate, was mixed with frustration because of the results in the House: a net gain of thirty-four over their preelection holdings, which still left them with only 192 seats, twenty-six short of the 218 needed for a majority. What was especially troubling was that this 192 figure had come to represent a sort of high-water mark that Republicans had reached twice previously in the period since the Eisenhower era, when they had last, briefly, controlled the House.

But on those previous occasions, each of which followed Richard Nixon's two presidential victories, they had gone no further but had instead fallen back. Sure enough, history repeated itself. In the first two years of Reagan's presidency, the economy soured, unemployment soared to the highest levels since the Great Depression, and in the 1982 elections, the GOP House members paid the price. The loss of twenty-six seats set them back on their heels and made the dream of a majority farther off.

Disconsolate, Gingrich paid a visit to Richard Nixon in New York, seeking his counsel. On the face of things, this was hard to explain. In his early days in politics, Gingrich had been no great fan of Nixon. And whatever his other accomplishments, Nixon had been singularly unsuccessful at helping to create a Republican congressional majority. When he was inaugurated for the first time in 1969, he was the first president in this century to take office with both houses of the Congress controlled by the opposition. In the midterm election of 1970, despite a massive effort on his part, which included intensive campaigning by his vice president, Spiro Agnew, the best that Nixon could do for his party was to gain two Senate seats—not nearly enough to threaten Democratic control of that body. Meanwhile, in the House, the Republicans lost nine seats. In his 1972 campaign, Nixon lost interest in the GOP's congressional prospects, and his campaign was conspicuous for its lack of attention to House and Senate races.

This indifference particularly exasperated Bob Dole, then chairman of the Republican National Committee, who sought to turn the huge lead Nixon enjoyed over Democratic standard-bearer George McGovern to the advantage of other Republican candidates. Nixon and his personal advisers wanted no part of any strategy that might jeopardize Nixon's own status.

Such was their disdain for their own party that when Dole sought to arrange the presentation of a sweater bearing the GOP's elephant emblem to Mrs. Nixon, he was turned down. "We have to appeal to donkeys," a Nixon aide told him. "I'll give her a donkey next week," Dole replied, but to no avail.

Why then did Gingrich call on Nixon with this particular problem? Because to Gingrich, and other politicians, not all of them Republicans, Nixon less than ten years after his fall from grace had become a figure of almost mythic proportions, an antihero whose career embodied unspoken and unsavory truths about the uses of power in American politics. Nixon had been punished, Nixon admirers privately believed, not because what he had done in perpetrating Watergate was really much out of the ordinary but because he had been caught doing it by his enemies. In their eyes, the ostracism Nixon had suffered only testified to his grasp of realpolitik.

For his part, Nixon, then in the midst of his sustained endeavor to rehabilitate himself, was happy to oblige. His thinking, it turned out, was no more profound than it had ever been. No one member of the House, even one so energetic and dedicated as Gingrich himself, Nixon said, could make the Republicans into a majority alone. "Get help," the oracle advised. And also get ideas. Recalling his own service in the House, during one term in which the Republicans *had* been in the majority, Nixon remembered an insufficiency of substantive thinking needed to drive legislation and generate public enthusiasm.

It is hard to believe that Gingrich, given his imagination and his sense of history, could not have worked out this rudimentary formula for success by himself. But since this wisdom had come to him from Nixon's lips, it probably carried more force than if it had been generated by Gingrich's own mind.

Gingrich quickly recruited a dozen or so of his colleagues—young men like himself, junior in rank, ideologically attuned—and got them to band together under the rubric of the Conservative Opportunity Society (COS). Their objective was nothing less than the crushing of the opposition, referred to as "the liberal welfare state," and creating "a governing majority." Before long, Gingrich and his cohorts had an agenda of sorts, stressing such fundamental Gingrich concepts as individual empowerment and traditional values at home along with aggressive pursuit of U.S. interests abroad, all with a heavy overlay of that Gingrich cornerstone, futurism.

Literally defined, futurism seeks life's meaning in the future, rather than in the present. But in Gingrich's mind, this concept had a somewhat altered twist. He called himself a "conservative futurist"; when he looked to the future, Gingrich explained, he sought to find ways to recapture what he regarded as the best in the past to redirect the present. The goal that always remained uppermost in Gingrich's thinking was the revival of the role played by the GOP as the nation's dominant and activist party in the closing years of the nineteenth century. As he put it, "I'm a modernizer who is suggesting we leap back an entire span and claim our own heritage again."

All this produced from Gingrich's newly conceived Conservative Opportunity Society was a back-to-the-future agenda that promoted such revisions in the political structure as the line-item veto, the balanced budget, and a welfare system that would somehow be more in tune with the work ethic. None of this was original—some leaders in both parties had advocated the same sort of reforms. Nor was it clear that these ideas would genuinely appeal to voters. Gingrich claimed to have tested and refined his agenda by analyzing polling and focus-group results. And he proudly labeled its components "65-percent" issues—meaning they enjoyed the support of about two-thirds of the populace. But as Gingrich himself knew, such results meant little unless voters, when asked if they favored a balanced budget, were first told what benefits they would have to give up to get one.

Nevertheless, the Conservative Opportunity Society agenda did play an important role in Gingrich's own rise. It helped to give his new organization some identity, contesting in an arena where, as Nixon had pointed out, ideas were few and far between. And it provided Gingrich's followers with something positive to hold them together against their adversaries, of whom there were plenty, not only among the Democrats but also among fellow Republicans.

Within the Republican party, Gingrich and his allies expended much of their energy in battles not only against pragmatic Republicans who believed in the need to compromise with the Democrats in order to survive politically, but also against other conservatives whose political and economic priorities differed from his own particularly over-fiscal policy—issues of taxes and the deficit. The disagreements in this area first emerged late in the summer of Reagan's first year in the White House, when most Republicans were still celebrating the enactment by the Democratic Congress of the package of sweeping tax cuts and huge increases in defense spending Reagan had proposed. David Stockman, whose responsibility as budget director was to measure the impact of this one-two punch, soon realized that the almost certain outcome would be to send interest rates soaring, plunge the economy into recession, and probably wreck the Reagan presidency. In desperation, Stockman sought support from the White House for a massive antidote to this danger, which included among its options delaying the next two installments of the much-heralded Reagan tax cut in return for congressional action to postpone Social Security cost-of-living increases for a year and to slash domestic spending. But opposition to these responses mounted even before Stockman could get final assent from the president. And Gingrich and his society were right in the middle of the fight, as Stockman discovered when he flew to Atlanta that September to speak at a fundraiser for Gingrich.

Gingrich, whom Stockman regarded as "an interesting combination of intellectual ideologue and political street fighter," lived up to his reputation. "You guys are making a fatal mistake," Gingrich warned Stockman, a note of defiance in his voice. He wanted no part of delaying the tax cut, or of tampering with Social Security, or of any other move that would hurt politically. And he claimed that neither did many others in the House. "You've taken us for granted. Just because the White House makes a decision, it doesn't mean that everyone else just falls in line." Give the Republicans on the Hill a chance to take a crack at the deficit, Gingrich demanded. "We'll find a better answer."

"Gingrich was whistling through his hat," Stockman thought. "There weren't any better answers." For Stockman, a true believer in conservatism, this was a frustrating turn of events. If the fundamental conservative objective of trimming back government was ever to be achieved, now was the time for it. And his remedy, in return for a postponement of the planned tax cut, would, he believed, move the government toward that ultimate conservative goal. But like other Republicans, Gingrich did not want to pay the price of putting off the tax cut, which was, after all, the spoonful of sugar that made the harsh medicine of Reaganomics go down.

"Push had come to shove," Stockman observed later of Gingrich. "And now, for all his conservative talk, he too was flinching." It turned out, though, that Reagan also flinched, refusing to delay the tax cuts. Interest rates soared, as Stockman had foreseen, and the economy headed south.

The next year, the tax and deficit issue reared its troublesome head again, this time spearheaded by Bob Dole, the chairman of the Senate Finance Committee, who, driven by his abiding obsession with fiscal red ink, pushed a $98-billion tax hike through the Senate, backed by nearly every GOP senator. But in the House, the supply-siders, Gingrich prominent among them, erupted in open rebellion. Persuaded that the tax hike was needed to lower the astronomically high interest rates and keep the recession from deepening, the White House went all out for the bill, warning House Republicans that if they opposed the measure, the president would not raise funds for their reelection campaigns. Contrariwise, the president's agents assured House Democrats, who worried that their GOP challengers might use a tax increase vote against them, that Reagan would send them thank-you letters that they could use in *their* reelection campaigns.

Gingrich was just as furious about this deficit-reduction legislation as he had been over Stockman's nascent plan for curbing the deficit the year before. Taking the floor of the House, he declared: "On this particular bill the president is trying to score a touchdown for liberalism, for the liberal welfare state, for big government, for the Internal Revenue Service, for multinational corporations, and for the various forces that consistently voted against the president." But Gingrich was outgunned. The tax hike passed the House, too, though more Democrats voted for it than Republicans, and became the law of the land.

But Gingrich carried on to fight another day. The next battleground was the 1984 Republican Convention in Dallas. Disturbed because Reagan had just signed another hefty tax increase, Gingrich and New York congressman Jack Kemp, who had helped to make tax cuts the hallmark of Reagan-era Republicanism, set out to forestall such violations of supply-side doctrine in the future by writing a no-tax pledge into the party platform. They had to contend against White House aides who resisted anything that would limit Reagan's flexibility. But Gingrich and his allies responded by saying in effect, "Unless you guys can get Ronald Reagan to come out personally and say to the public that he is for tax increases, we're gonna win this fight." That settled matters and the antitax forces had their way with the platform. "We decided that 'no tax increase' was going to be the dividing line in the party and the dividing line in the country," Gingrich recalled later.

But the victory at Dallas, and the other skirmishes on Capitol Hill that followed, left Gingrich and his allies facing a lingering problem that would haunt them for the next decade and more. As good conservatives, they were pledged to balance the budget. But as Stockman had perceived earlier, they were also just as firmly against taking the politically risky steps necessary to accomplish this—curbing entitlements or domestic programs with massive voter support or raising taxes. Indeed, despite Gingrich's constant lamenting about the "liberal welfare state," by the time he had served three terms in the House, he did seem prepared to pay a political price to change it.

As the *Atlantic* pointed out in May 1985, Gingrich appeared unwilling to attack such pillars of this entity he so despised as Social Security, Medicare, farm subsidies, affirmative action, and a domestic content bill to restrict automobile imports—all of which, as he recognized, had the backing of potent constituencies among the electorate. For example, a Ford plant that provided thousands of jobs in his district explained his support for domestic content measures. For Gingrich, as for most members of the House, Republican and Democrat, conservative and liberal, the needs of his district came first, indeed had to come first or he would not be in Congress. Thus, although the rhetoric of the right, which Gingrich proclaimed at every chance, demanded overthrow of the system, until that upheaval took place, when it came down to the nitty-gritty, Gingrich worked within the system to serve the interests of his district and himself.

The intraparty battles they fought gave focus and cohesion to Gingrich and his band of insurgents, but it was their attacks on the Democrats that gained them momentum and ultimately victory. In fact, the Democrats paved the road to power for Gingrich, a development explained by the culture of the majority in the House of Representatives, which had characteristics just as striking as the culture of the minority.

Several common aspects shaped each group. A sense of permanence defined the contingents of each party. Just as the Republicans abandoned hope that they could ever gain control of the House in the face of continued Democratic domination, so the Democrats took for granted that they could not be displaced. Frustration was another powerful force. If the Republicans were limited by their role as permanent congressional minority, the Democrats were limited in what they could accomplish by the fact that the White House was almost always in charge of the other party. This was the situation that prevailed for twenty of the twenty-four years between 1968 and 1992. And the one four-year break in that stretch, during which Jimmy Carter was the president, was because of Carter's insulation from his own party, in its way as frustrating as the years when the Republicans ruled.

As a consequence of this combination of permanence and frustration, Democrats who came to the House with large ambitions to change the social or economic system before long went elsewhere—or ultimately their ambitions dwindled away. Those who remained considered themselves part of the status quo, with an interest in protecting it. Like animals burrowing into a cleft on the side of a mountain, they made themselves as comfortable as possible. Their horizons were limited, and their existence was governed by relationships with their constituents, to whose day-in, day-out needs they catered; with organized interest groups, whether representing an ideology, an industry, or a labor union, whom they sought to placate in return for their support; and with the federal bureaucracy that they funded and relied on to satisfy their constituents and their favored interest groups.

Even though they seemed to have a great deal of power in a limited sphere, most members functioning in this environment became smug, complacent, insensitive, and somewhat arrogant. A few lost perspective and common sense and gave in to greed, lust, and other of the baser human instincts. Their collective behavior suggested that if, as Lord Acton posited, absolute power corrupts absolutely, limited power creates at least a limited degree of corruption.

"Corrupt" was the word Gingrich favored above all others to describe the Democratic hegemony in the House. And he set out to dramatize any evidence he could find to support his indictment, exhibiting little or no restraint. In his freshman year in the House, Gingrich launched an attack on Representative Charles Diggs, a Detroit Democrat, demanding that Diggs be expelled after he was accused of diverting money from his payroll for his personal use. Ultimately, Diggs was convicted and resigned. But Gingrich's attacks, prior to any formal legal proceedings in the case, outraged the Democratic leadership, and some suspected him of catering to bigotry, because Diggs was black. "The precious presumption of innocence was openly flouted by the brash young Georgian," Jim Wright later complained.

Next, Gingrich prodded the House into censuring rather than simply reprimanding Massachusetts senator Gerry Studds for having sex with a male congressional page. Demonstrating a sense of fairness, he sought and got the same penalty for Republican representative Daniel Crane of Illinois for having had sex with a female page.

But Gingrich's not-so-civil war against the Democrats became broader, more substantive, and more effective with the emergence of C-Span as the widely used medium for monitoring the doings of Congress. The cable TV channel had begun its coverage of Congress in 1979, but it was little watched for the first few years of its coverage. Gingrich and his allies in the Conservative Opportunity Society soon turned it into what one Washington journalist termed a political "Field of Dreams." Spearheaded by Gingrich ally Robert Walker of Pennsylvania, they seized upon two little-known parts of the congressional rules—"special orders," for which the end of the day is reserved, and "one minutes," intervals at the start of legislative sessions during which members of Congress may talk about anything they choose—and exploited them to harass the Democrats and heckle their leaders and also to promote their own ideas.

Although most of the time the Republican assault team was speaking to an empty chamber, no one outside the House knew that because the television camera focused only on the Speaker. At any rate, the COS members were reaching millions of voters in their living rooms. Just as important, the Democrats, who in the days before the C-Span era preferred to ignore Gingrich and his cohorts, now felt obliged to strike back, with mixed results.

In the spring of 1984, Gingrich and Walker went before the C-Span cameras to condemn and deride a "Dear Commandante" letter that Democrats had written to Nicaragua's Sandinista leader Daniel Ortega asking for assurances that forthcoming national elections would be conducted fairly and openly. Gingrich called the Democrats appeasers and charged them with having a "pessimistic, defeatist, and skeptical view toward the American role in the world."

This was too much for Speaker O'Neill, whose good friend Representative Edward Boland of Massachusetts was among those being held up to public scorn. With Walker at the microphone, O'Neill ordered that the C-Span camera pan the entire chamber, showing the empty seats. "Walker looked like a fool," O'Neill later recalled. Had O'Neill let the matter rest, he would have done himself and his party a service. But the Democrats were genuinely indignant, not only because they felt their patriotism had been attacked but also because of the Republican failure to warn their targets of the televised barrage. Going to the well of the House to join the debate, O'Neill called the Republican tactics "the lowest thing I have ever seen in my thirty-two years in Congress."

That was just the sort of opening Republican whip Trent Lott had been awaiting. He immediately and successfully moved that O'Neill's remarks be "taken down," that is, stripped from the record. Thus, O'Neill brought down upon himself the first such rebuke for a House Speaker in the history of the body, and Gingrich and his cohorts won an important victory, which gained them new respect from Republican moderates who had shied away from their aggressive tactics.

The Democrats further polarized partisan relations in the House early the next year, when they refused to seat Republican Richard D. McIntyre, who had apparently defeated the incumbent Democrat Frank McCloskey in a close election in Indiana. The Indiana secretary of state had certified that McIntyre had won by thirty-four votes, and the Republicans were furious. A long dispute ensued until the House voted to seat Democrat McCloskey, with ten Democrats joining the solid Republican contingent in opposition.

That settled, the entire Republican membership walked out of the House in protest. Afterward, Richard Cheney of Wyoming, a sober and respected figure, asked, "What choice does a self-respecting Republican have except confrontation? There's absolutely nothing to be gained by cooperating with Democrats at this point." With Democratic help, Gingrich had set the stage for his boldest attack yet.

The elevation of Jim Wright to the speakership in 1987 provided the opportunity. Gingrich had long been seeking a prominent target to dramatize his crusade against Democratic corruption in the House. And he had talked darkly of driving Tip O'Neill from the House and had labeled him as corrupt. It was true that O'Neill had some dirty laundry having to do with his personal finances that the *New York Times* had washed out in public. But for all his bluff and hearty manner, O'Neill was a shrewd operator, too shrewd to allow Gingrich an opening. Moreover, O'Neill's congeniality softened his partisan edges and won him a good many friends on both sides of the aisle to shield him from the likes of Gingrich.

Wright was a different sort of man. Although the speakership of the U.S. House of Representatives had long been associated with power, most Speakers have preferred to use their power behind the legislative scenes. That was not the case with Speaker Wright, who, on assuming the leadership of the House from O'Neill, shook up Capitol Hill and the White House, thrusting himself into public debate on sensitive issues.

Wright's personal outlook and political philosophy had been shaped over the years both by his ties to freewheeling Texas entrepreneurs and by his populist background as a young man coming of age in the depths of the Great Depression. Born in Fort Worth in the early 1920s, he spent much of his youth shifting with his family from one Dust Bowl Texas community to another.

As with many of his generation, his service in World War II boosted his career in politics. His medals and combat record as a bomber pilot helped him win election to the Texas legislature and then as mayor of Weatherford, Texas. He took his seat in Congress from Fort Worth in November 1954, in the election that would begin forty years of Democratic majorities.

His skill as an orator and his success in getting defense contracts for his district solidified his standing with his constituents, but it was seniority and his natural aggressiveness that boosted him in the House, until in 1977 his Democratic colleagues made him majority leader. In the early years of the Reagan presidency, he used this post to battle the new chief executive's efforts to cut back the role of the federal government. He scored enough points to rouse the anger of David Stockman, who regarded the Texan as "a snake-oil vendor par excellence, a demagogue of frightening proportions."

But Stockman's scorn did not slow Wright down one bit. No sooner had O'Neill announced early in 1984 that he planned to retire after the 1986 elections than Wright began planning to run for the speakership. By February 1985, Wright announced that he had the backing of more than 75 percent of Democratic House members, thus effectively assuring himself of the prize that he officially claimed nearly two years later.

At the House podium he soon made it clear that he planned to make the most of his office, in some ways more than any other Speaker in recent memory, by plunging into the nation's tangled relations with Nicaragua. Wright's involvement began in August 1987, when the new Speaker agreed to join with President Reagan in supporting a new proposal to end the fighting in that tormented land. That maneuver spurred Central American leaders to offer a peace plan of their own, which Wright promptly embraced. Moreover, in November, when Nicaraguan president Ortega came to Washington, he met with Wright to discuss his own peace proposal before unveiling it publicly.

Incensed at being upstaged in this heavy-handed fashion, the Reagan administration accused Wright of undercutting U.S. policy in Central America. But Wright stood his ground, pointing out that it was President Reagan himself who had drawn him into Central American diplomacy in the first place.

On domestic issues, Wright also made waves—and enemies—on both sides of the aisle, by proposing a delay in the tax-rate reduction for upper-income taxpayers called for in the 1986 tax-reform bill. This antagonized Republicans and made Democrats uneasy.

By now, Wright's behavior had made clear how he differed from O'Neill and had also demonstrated the limits to what a Speaker could do, unless he was willing to risk causing problems for himself. A highly partisan figure, so unquestioned in his loyalty to the liberal creed, Tip O'Neill was nevertheless a man who enjoyed good fellowship, a man who liked the cut and thrust of politics for its own sake. But Wright took little joy from such matters. And although his populist roots gave tone to his rhetoric and a direction to his career, what mattered most with him was not ideology but sheer ambition. Gingrich, watching Wright's rise to power in the House, saw and understood this, studied Wright's strengths and weaknesses, and calculated how to deal with them, as if measuring the new Speaker for his political coffin. "If Wright ever consolidates his power, he will be a very formidable man," Gingrich told Wright's biographer. "We have to take him on early to prevent that."

The chance Gingrich was looking for came, innocuously enough, with the indiscretions of another Democrat, Fernand St. Germain of Rhode Island, chairman of the House Banking Committee. It was St. Germain, as would become clearer later, who, in his role as chairman, had presided over one of the massive abuses of the public by private interests in modern times—the savings-and-loan scandal. Moreover, his interventions with federal regulators on behalf of banks did not go unrewarded. Among the favors offered and obtained, besides the chance to buy stock in one of the befriended institutions, was 100-percent financing for stock purchases. Such advantages had presumably helped St. Germain accumulate $2 million during a quarter century on the public payroll. But when the House Ethics Committee looked into this, it concluded that whatever sins St. Germain had committed did not rise to the level that required disciplinary action.

For his part, Gingrich was both enraged at this insensitivity to wrongdoing and delighted at the opportunity it presented him. If ever evidence arose to support his claim of Democratic corruption, this was it. And he set out to dramatize both St. Germain's misconduct and the Ethics Committee's tolerance of this behavior and to link Wright to the entire mess. Gingrich began his campaign by forcing a vote on a motion to reopen the ethics committee probe. The motion lost, as he knew it would. But now he had the Democrats—Jim Wright's Democrats—on record as unwilling to deal with blatant evidence of corruption.

Gingrich swung into action. He wrote letters to Common Cause, citing the misconduct of the Democrats. He used C-Span and television talk shows to trumpet his cause. And as he traveled around the country making speeches, he made it a point to seek out local reporters and editorial writers, offering his evidence against Wright. "Look, I don't think Jim Wright's a Mafia don," he conceded to an interviewer. But he explained: "Wright is a useful keystone to a much bigger structure. I'll just keep pounding away on his ethics."

Gingrich counted on the media, liberal as it was, to help him. "The media values its liberal bias less than it values honesty in government," he said. And what the media valued most of all, Gingrich realized, was a good fight. "When you give them confrontations, you get attention," he pointed out.

He was right about that. The media not only published his charges, but as time went on, journalists dug up new charges of their own. Wright's hubris gave them plenty of ammunition.

Gingrich had seen his crusade against Wright as serving, among other purposes, to counterattack Democratic charges of misconduct against Reagan's attorney general, Ed Meese. This longtime Reagan adviser was under investigation because of his connection to Wedtech Corporation, a New York defense contractor that, in its efforts to gain business for itself, had bribed at least one member of Congress.

But in fact, both Meese and Wright were caught up in a zeitgeist, the implications of which went far beyond such partisan maneuvering. Indeed, Gingrich's assault on Wright came amid growing distress among Americans that their society was undergoing a period of moral upheaval and change. Among teenagers, the suicide rate was increasing and so was the rate of births out of wedlock. Adults faced a growing threat from AIDS. And the general sense of uneasiness was aggravated by disclosures of misbehavior against prominent officials and private individuals customarily looked upon to exemplify and uphold standards of conduct.

The most serious of these assorted examples of misconduct was the Iran-Contra affair, which demonstrated willful disregard of the law at the highest levels of the Reagan administration and stirred whispered talk of impeachment. In summing up its investigation into this tangled series of events, a congressional select committee quoted Supreme Court Justice Louis Brandeis: "If the government becomes a law breaker, it breeds contempt for law; it invites every man to become a law unto himself; it invites anarchy."

Amid these revelations, which increased cynicism about politics and government, other disclosures tarnished the perception of the corporate world. Ivan Boesky, a major figure in the 1986 insider-trading scandals on Wall Street, went to jail for three years. Three other investment bankers were charged with plotting to trade information between two leading financial firms so that they could profit from investments in corporate takeovers. In Detroit, the Chrysler Corporation, which had not long before become the beneficiary of a multibillion-dollar bailout from the federal government, was indicted by that same government for tinkering with the odometers of 60,000 autos already driven by company executives so that consumers could be duped into buying the cars as new.

The taint of scandal extended even to the pulpit. The television evangelist Reverend Jim Bakker resigned his ministry after admitting to engaging in extramarital sex seven years earlier, claiming that he had been betrayed into the encounter "by treacherous former friends" who then conspired to blackmail him in an effort to gain control of his business interests, which included an amusement park, a hotel, and a satellite television system. The revelation that Bakker's wife, Tammy, his cohost on a daily television talk program, was undergoing treatment for drug dependency compounded the damage.

This tide of miscreancy undermined Wright's chances of surviving Gingrich's assault. With all this going on, an aroused press and public were in no mood to tolerate anything that smacked of hanky-panky from an official as powerful and prominent as the Speaker of the House.

Now not only Gingrich but also the media were poking into Wright's affairs. Particularly troublesome was the disclosure by the *Washington Post* that Wright had received an enormous royalty on a book contract for a collection of his reflections, many copies of which were bought by his political supporters, thus circumventing the legal limits on campaign contributions.

Democrats reacted to this barrage of charges by filing their own complaint against Gingrich with the House Ethics Committee, alleging that Gingrich violated House rules with a partnership he created in 1984 to promote his book *Window of Opportunity*. This arrangement was similar to, but on a larger scale than, the tax shelter scheme he had contrived to subsidize the novel he had written after his 1976 defeat by John Flynt. But that allegation was too late to save Wright. Soon, Common Cause was on his case, echoing Gingrich's demand for an investigation.

In the face of this hubbub, in June 1988, the House Ethics Committee launched an inquiry not only into Gingrich's book deal but also Wright's intervention with federal regulators on behalf of bankers in his state and sundry other matters.

Bush's election brought no surcease for Wright, as the new president, seeking to separate himself from the atmosphere of sleaze surrounding his predecessor, named a special commission to "take a fresh look" at existing ethical standards for all three branches of government and then to propose a brand new ethical code. "It's not really very complicated," Bush said of the high standards he purported to seek for public servants. "It's a question of knowing right from wrong, avoiding conflicts of interest, bending over backwards to see that there's not even a perception of conflict of interest."

But it was nowhere near that simple, as Bush found out when he sent the name of former Texas senator John Tower to the Senate to be confirmed as defense secretary. Because he was an ex-senator, Tower expected that his former colleagues would give him an easy ride to confirmation. But in the prevailing environment, charged with moral and ethical sensitivity, his experience turned into an ordeal. Tower appeared to be a walking embodiment of the darkest suspicions festering in the public mind about behavior in the corridors of power. His former colleagues grilled him not only about potential conflicts of interest stemming from the fat consulting fees that he had received from defense contractors but also about allegations of womanizing and drunkenness. After a prolonged and bitter fight, the Senate rejected his nomination in a vote that closely tracked party lines.

His fellow Texan's demise was bad news for Wright. Unable to prevent Tower's defeat, Republicans were not going to let Wright escape, and the

Ethics Committee knew it. On April 17, the committee issued a "statement of violations" against Wright, in which he was charged with sixty-nine specific instances of violating House rules dealing with acceptance of gifts and outside income. At first the Speaker fought back, denying any wrongdoing. But it soon became clear he was waging a losing battle, as his colleagues fretted that the controversy surrounding him would spread to threaten other members of his party. Giving substance to these apprehensions, majority whip Coelho decided that he would quit the House rather than stand up to an investigation into charges that he had illegally used campaign contributions to purchase $100,000 in junk bonds.

Finally, Wright threw in the towel. In his emotional farewell address, he called for an end to "self-appointed vigilantes carrying out personal vendettas against members of the other party" and offered his own resignation as "a propitiation for all of this season of bad will that has grown up among us."

But it would take more than Wright's departure to calm the roiling waters on Capitol Hill. Democrats seethed. "No way" can Democrats forgive or forget the trauma of Wright's resignation, declared Bill Richardson of New Mexico. "I feel like I'm in a battle zone."

And even some Republicans were taken aback at the stunning success of Gingrich's assault on Wright. House Republican leader Bob Michel said that Gingrich would have to be "much more responsible." This was particularly true because as it turned out, the defeat of Tower's nomination had provided a double windfall for Gingrich. Not only had it given the Republicans a partisan motive for attacking Wright, but it had led to a vacancy in the House leadership, since Bush selected Dick Cheney, the GOP whip, to fill the job at the Pentagon initially earmarked for Tower. No sooner was Cheney easily confirmed than Gingrich took over his old post as whip.

Gingrich, who had sat impassively next to Michel during Wright's hour-long speech of resignation, his hands folded in his lap, afterward ducked out of the House chamber without a word to reporters. His name was on everyone's lips, but for once he had nothing to say. He was too busy plotting his next move.

His objective, a Republican majority in the House, remained an improbable goal. But Gingrich was now in a better position than ever to reach it because of Wright's departure and his own elevation to the whip position, making him second only to Leader Michel in the GOP pecking order. Forcing Wright out had gained him, along with new enemies, increasing respect, particularly from Republicans who saw that however abrasive his aggressive methods were, they worked. Gingrich "had the vision to build the majority party and the strength and charisma to do it," Nancy Johnson of Connecticut told her shocked fellow moderates in the House when they asked how she could have backed Gingrich for the whip's job. On his election, Gingrich himself promised his new constituents on Capitol Hill "a new era based on greater activism, new ideas and energy and an aggressive effort to build a GOP majority in the House."

To reach that goal, he set out to exploit another asset that had fallen into his lap three years earlier, just as fortuitously as the whip's job had opened up. This was GOPAC, a party-building political action committee that had been created by Pierre S. du Pont IV, Delaware's former governor and congressman, to aid state and local office seekers. Over the long run, Pete du Pont hoped to create a "farm team" from which Republicans could recruit candidates for the House. In 1986, when he decided to run for president, du Pont turned his brainchild over to Gingrich, who quickly made two key changes in keeping with his own priorities, and those included, along with electing more Republicans to the House, establishing an ideological framework for governing.

Instead of limiting GOPAC aid to state and local candidates, who someday might run for the House, under the Gingrich regime help would also go directly to likely House candidates, thus speeding up the timetable for takeover. Just as important, GOPAC's considerable resources, much of which had come from a dozen or so wealthy businessmen, would be used not to bankroll candidates but to indoctrinate them with the ideas that Gingrich conceived to be necessary for the Republicans to achieve a majority in the House. The Republicans had always had plenty of money, Gingrich pointed out to du Pont. If money could win control of the House, the Republicans would already have taken over. No, Gingrich said, what the Republicans really needed was not money but ideas.

Gingrich of course already had plenty of ideas. He came to Congress with them in 1978, developed them further with the Conservative Opportunity Society, and spelled them out in his book *Window of Opportunity*. But now GOPAC could help him translate those ideas into the Republican majority of his dreams.

At a GOPAC meeting with officials and contributors and other Republican strategists in August 1989, Gingrich outlined his plan for a GOP takeover. They gathered at the North Pole Basin, a lodge in the Colorado Rockies owned by Howard Bo Callaway, the wealthy Republican political operative whom Gingrich had taken on to supervise the day-in, day-out operations of GOPAC.

The site was well chosen to provide privacy and opportunity for contemplation. After driving fifteen miles from Crested Butte in a four-wheel-drive vehicle, the visitors came to Callaway's spread, about 11,000 feet above sea level, just below the timberline. They slept in cabins, with indoor plumbing but no heat except for fireplaces, and conferred in a larger cabin with a dining room that seated twelve. The invitation promised "libations of high quality and adequate quantity and anything else you might desire except telephones, television, and the distractions of the city."

During the course of the deliberations that continued intermittently for the next year at the Colorado retreat, and in more comfortably appointed hotel rooms in Washington, the GOPAC planners paid much tribute to the importance of specific issues in bringing about this political transformation. But the fact was that after ticking off the nation's major problems—crime, drugs, education, urban decay, economic decline, and the instability of the family—they passed over them in short order, promising themselves they would formulate more detailed solutions after the 1990 elections.

For the present, they devoted most of their time and effort to tactics and strategy, and the approach reflected the influence of marketing techniques common to political consultants, shaped by the Republican faith in free enterprise and Gingrich's own fascination with technology. "We are on the way to becoming the Bell Labs of politics," Gingrich declared. "That's the closest model you can find to what we do, and nobody else is in that business. The first thing you need at Bell Labs is a Thomas Edison, and the second thing you need is a real understanding of how you go from scientific theory to a marketable product."

No one ever doubted who would fill Edison's role. The outline of the path GOPAC would blaze to political success was less evident, except that it seemingly relied on a smattering of New Age thinking, combined with Dale Carnegie. For example, the six-step model for making decisions about important issues went like this: "What is my objective? What is presently happening? What do I want to have happening given the constraints of the current reality? What are others doing to stop me from getting what I want? What am/are I/we doing to stop me/us from getting what I/we want? What is my program? Who is in charge of what, and by when?"

Whatever the idiom, the agenda laid out two months before the first meeting had the outward appearance of a major and serious undertaking. The goal: to create a three-year plan to pave the way for the election in 1992 of huge Republican majorities in the Congress—56 seats in the Senate, 240 seats in the House, along with retention of the White House, which was almost taken for granted. A more particular objective, which might have been assumed to not need saying, was stated anyway: "Newt must be reelected."

That point did not go overlooked. Although GOPAC itself was legally barred from contributing directly to federal candidates, its big financial supporters as individuals gave more than $120,000 to Gingrich's 1990 reelection campaign, in which he faced a formidable Democratic challenger. GOPAC's blueprint aimed for GOP control of both houses of Congress, as well as the White House, but it was seizure of the House of Representatives that mattered most to the planners. In part, this was because it had been for so long under Democratic rule. But there was another reason: Because the members of the House must go back to their constituents every two years for reelection, Gingrich and others saw it as the branch of the government most susceptible to the fundamental changes they intended to create throughout the political system.

"That's why I got involved in this business in 1966 to get Republican control of the House of Representatives," Eddie Mahe, the veteran consultant who was deeply involved in the GOPAC efforts, told me later. "Because that's where all the power rests. If the government is operating properly, the House is what defines the agenda for the country. It's the only place that voters have any real opportunity to have any significant influence."

Indeed, in Gingrich's eyes, the chance to take over the House outweighed even whatever personal ambition he might have for the highest office in the land. "I made a very conscious decision a decade ago to avoid running for president, because if you run for president everything becomes very transactional," he told GOPAC leaders. "You have to be in Iowa on this date to approve this person to run this precinct—you can't do that and think. Furthermore, once you start moving in that direction, people can look at you and say, 'Oh yeah, I see what you want.' They don't listen to the message anymore. They now listen to a sales pitch. That's a totally different dynamic."

Although from the beginning everyone involved recognized Gingrich's preeminence in this enterprise, he saw no harm in occasionally reminding his colleagues of this point. "I start with the premise that all this assumes that my health holds up, that I can get reelected, that I can get reelected as whip, and that the ethics charges somehow get handled," he remarked at one point. "If you want to bet against those four, then all this is somehow irrelevant."

Nevertheless, his role was not always easy to define. The planners all agreed that Gingrich should play the role of "wagon-train leader, and that is not a function that can be delegated extensively with any strong expectation of success." Still, the preference of his fellow leaders was that Gingrich should also function as a "senior partner," who would lead with the collaboration of other partners, rather than as a "general." But it was in another role, as historian, that Gingrich made his most important contribution to the takeover plan.

GOPAC strategists had picked 1992 as the target year because they assumed this would be a year of great opportunity for the Republicans, a year in which their candidates would face fewer Democratic incumbents than usual. Given the big population shifts in the 1980s, from cities to suburbs, from the Frost Belt to the Sun Belt, they anticipated that the 1990 census would produce substantial redrawing of the lines marking congressional districts. This would leave many Democratic incumbents with a choice between running on unfamiliar ground, sometimes against another redistricted incumbent, and retiring. Indeed, by one GOPAC reckoning, there would be more than 170 such districts in 1992—40 percent of the House. In addition, it was expected that retirements would increase because 1992 would be the last year in which lawmakers who had been in office for at least twelve years could convert their accumulated campaign funds to personal use if they left office. About eighty members fell into that category, and the GOPAC planners guessed a sizable number of them would take the money and run.

"Nineteen hundred and ninety-two looked like it would be the year," the consultant Eddie Mahe, involved in the planning, recalled. And time and again, Bo Callaway told his cohorts: "The moon, the stars, and the planets will all be lined up in our favor."

But for the Republicans to exploit these opportunities, President Bush would not only have to win reelection handily—the planners were not worried about that in 1989, with Bush riding high in the polls—but he would also have to carry a good many Republicans along with him. The trouble was, nothing of the sort had happened in the recent past. Nixon and Reagan had both won landslide reelection victories, but Republicans had gained only twelve seats in 1972 and seventeen in 1984, leaving the Democrats firmly in control. And in 1956, when Dwight Eisenhower was reelected by a 10-million-vote margin, the Republicans actually lost three seats in the House. In fact, no president's coattails had been long enough to provide gains for his party on the scale the GOP would need to recapture the House since Harry Truman had run in 1948.

And as Gingrich saw it, that was just the point, for the basis of his strategy, which reflected his back-to-the-future outlook on the world, was built around the idea of George Bush following the examples of Truman and another Democratic president, Franklin Roosevelt. It was Truman who had recaptured control of the House for the Democrats after they had lost it in the postwar transition election of 1946. Immediately after that election, Truman had promoted a package of liberal domestic proposals modeled after the New Deal. And when his agenda was rejected by the GOP majorities on Capitol Hill, Truman ran against the "do-nothing Republican Congress," and not only got himself reelected but helped his party gain seventy-six seats in the House and nine in the Senate. Roosevelt, of course, had defined his presidency and the New Deal during his first 100 days in office, when he pushed through a sweeping series of economic reforms. In the process, he established a benchmark that no president had been able to approach since, though nearly all had been measured against it.

It was Gingrich's plan to combine these two episodes—Truman's defiance of an opposition-controlled Congress and FDR's historic legislative accomplishments—as a paradigm for George Bush and the Republicans. As laid out in the preliminary agenda, Gingrich was to present to Bush "the framework for a 'governing 100 days in 1993' campaign" and urge the president to make this plan his own and implement it in cooperation with the Republican party and "the conservative movement."

The "governing 100 days" concept would be best carried out, the planning group suggested, if "Bush would review his agenda and ask himself, 'What programs would I be enacting if Republicans held a Congressional majority.'" Once he had answered that question, the planners hoped Bush would submit his ideas to Capitol Hill, demanding they be written into law; and when the majority Democrats rejected them, as they surely would, he could then take his case to the people, win his own reelection, and carry the Republicans into the majority on Capitol Hill, as Truman had done for the Democrats in 1948.

Of course, the circumstances surrounding those two dramatic chapters in political history differed sharply from the present reality that faced the incumbent Republican president and the GOP minority in the House. In Truman's time, Americans were still basically Democratic, had been since the Great Depression, and were still fearful that the Republicans might undo the New Deal reforms if they had the chance. The Republicans had no such hold on the populace. Roosevelt's "first 100 Days" came as Americans, reeling from the impact of the worst economic collapse anyone could remember, were eager for almost any action that offered the hope of relief from this disaster. And finally, and perhaps most important, no one who knew George Bush was reminded of the boldness, strength, and imagination that distinguished Roosevelt and Truman. The proposed strategy was so far removed from anything that Bush had ever done in the past that the planning group itself acknowledged this. "He has been a largely managerial president thus far, and the proposed 'governing 100 days' model implies a certain level of conflict and confrontation that the president may be unwilling to demonstrate."

Such hope as there was that Bush might go along rested on the premise, as Eddie Mahe later put it, that "since he believed nothing, there was an expectation that this would be on his agenda because he didn't have anything else." Gingrich himself put the matter more delicately. "If you wait for George Bush to figure out on his own what his strategy is going to be, to launch an aggressive strategy, we might as well just write off the next election," he told his cohorts. Rather, the way to go about it, he counseled, was to say to the president, "Look, if you ever want to deliver a Republican majority in this country in Congress, this is the only strategy that will get you there."

But care had to be taken in fashioning the strategy; and bearing in mind Bush's own nature, Gingrich cautioned his colleagues: "Now that means it has to be designed so he can do it, that he can be comfortable with it. Because you can't design a drop-back, long-passing offense with this guy," he said, turning to an analogy from the gridiron and then mixing in another metaphor: "But if we design a meat grinder and it makes sense to him, he will live out a meat grinder for three years."

Whatever Bush's limitations, Gingrich found the Republican president more imaginative than the two top Republicans on Capitol Hill, Senate Leader Dole and his own superior, House Leader Michel. "You go to the Republican party leadership, which is George Bush, Bob Michel, and Bob Dole, and you suggest any strategy and only one of those three are going to understand it, and that's the president," he said. Michel and Dole he considered to be among "the significant number of fairly senior Republicans who are committed to a minority values system in which being pleasant and being invited to the right dinner is more important than winning." Dole "frankly doesn't give a damn" about fighting for conservative causes, Gingrich said, describing the senator as overseeing a "passive, backward-oriented" faction of the party.

This cleavage among Republicans obviously made Gingrich's challenge to the Democrats that much more difficult. It was only reasonable to assume that his mistrust of Dole and Michel was mutual. Indeed, Gingrich appeared on television and lashed out at Democrats while Michel was in the midst of trying to bargain with them; Michel's staff burst into groans or laughter, while Michel himself shook his head in frustration. Moreover, personal feelings aside, if Michel and Dole were half as pedestrian in their thinking as Gingrich accused them of being, why should they support such a scheme as Gingrich proposed?

Still, GOPAC pushed ahead on plans to draw up an agenda comprising "a series of sweeping legislative initiatives put forth as a gentleman's agreement between the Republican party and the American people." This would be Exhibit A in showing how the Republicans planned to govern once they had full control of the government, proving that there was "more than a dime's worth of difference between Republicans and Democrats."

By November 1990, GOPAC had developed a "prototype agenda" that Republicans would pledge to enact into law during the first 100 days of the 103rd Congress if they were in command on Capitol Hill. The prototype was completed just in time for the collapse of the plan. Bush's revocation of his no-new-taxes promise would have made any pledge on his part hollow indeed. Moreover, Gingrich's refusal to go along with the budget agreement left a legacy of bitterness that would have made agreement on an agenda impossible. As the battle over the tax hike raged in October 1990, Gingrich found himself at a fund-raising dinner for House Republicans, posing for a photograph with Bush. "I'm really sorry this is happening," he told the president. Bush turned to him, and declared in heartfelt tones: "You are killing us, you are just killing us."

Against this background, it was inevitable the 1990 election, in which GOPAC planners had sought "a measure of success" to get them started on their 1992 takeover plan, threw cold water on those hopes. The net result was that Democrats strengthened their already powerful grip on both houses of Congress, and on the state level, scored successes in key governors' races, which bolstered their ability to influence the reapportionment process that would follow the 1990 census.

Matters could have been even worse for Republicans and GOPAC. Gingrich, by 1,000 votes, barely won reelection, edging out a candidate to whom the national Democratic party had given only minimal assistance—a significant contrast to the huge helping hand GOPAC contributors had given Gingrich. But the news was bad enough, seeming to provide proof of the invincibility of the system that Gingrich proposed to challenge. Although polling data had suggested that a rebellion against incumbents might be taking shape, more than 96 percent of 406 House incumbents seeking reelection were returned to office.

The most evident explanation was money. Only twenty-three challengers were able to raise even half as much money as the incumbent. One reason for this was that political action committees gave nineteen times as much to sitting lawmakers as to their foes. Said Common Cause president Fred Wertheimer: "House members are shielded by a wall of political money that makes them nearly invincible."

In the end, the most damning verdict delivered by the citizenry was not against either party or any one candidate but against the political system. Only 36.4 percent of the voting-age population, little better than one out of three, went to the polls, tying the last off-year election in 1986 as the second lowest since 1942, when the nation was in the midst of World War II.

But for Bush it was easy to shrug off the election and ride to glory on the sense of crisis engendered by the Gulf War. In January 1991, as the air war against Iraq got under way, with the idea of the White House endorsing the GOPAC strategy more remote than ever, Gingrich told members of the team that their takeover might need to be postponed for two more years beyond the initial 1992 target date. "The most we can ask of the White House is that they not be a liability," Gingrich said. "I want to say just for the record that we may or may not succeed for 1992, but 1992 must be our goal for the sense of urgency that it places on us."

Still, Gingrich did not entirely give up hope. The war seemed to provide Bush with a new lease on political life, and Gingrich, when I interviewed him at the time, urged the president to take advantage by following in Truman's footsteps. "We ought to put Democrats in the position where they either pass the president's agenda or they prove publicly that they are against the future," he said. Other Republicans egged Bush on, too. "Popularity is an opportunity," argued GOPAC's founder, Pete du Pont, who had lost out to Bush in the 1988 presidential campaign but remained one of the president's sharpest critics on the right. "If you don't use it, it evaporates."

But neither Gingrich nor du Pont had the ear of the White House. Bush chose to deliver his first postelection address on domestic policy just a few hours before he announced the end of the Mideast war. It consisted mainly of familiar proposals, repackaged under the rubric of "opportunity and choice," favorite buzzwords for conservatives, but it was drowned out on this occasion by the jubilation over the triumph in the Mideast. By giving the speech on a day when nobody cared about domestic policy, Bush made clear that he felt the same way himself.

And so Bush forfeited the opening Gingrich had envisaged for him. The whip made one final effort in September 1992, when he proposed to the White House that the president and Republican congressional candidates gather on the Capitol steps to mutually endorse a common agenda. But it was too late in the game for anything of the sort to work. The White House had no interest and as Robert Teeter, Bush's campaign chairman, put it, the idea "died its own death."

From Gingrich's standpoint, the 1992 campaign thus turned into one of the great wasted opportunities of modern politics. If ever there was a president who could have benefited from a policy agenda, it was George Bush. Moreover, if ever there was a Congress where the majority was ripe for overthrow, it was the Democratic-controlled 102d Congress.

The trouble started in July 1991, when the Senate voted to give itself a pay raise, bringing its members' annual salary up to the House level of $125,100. The action stirred widespread public criticism, in part because the Senate gave no advance notice of its action and also because of the hard times afflicting the country.

Later that same year, the Senate Ethics Committee "strongly and severely" reprimanded Democratic senator Alan Cranston of California for "improper and repugnant" conduct in seeking to help thrift operator Charles H. Keating Jr., a major fund-raiser, in his dealings with federal regulators. Cranston apologized but showed little remorse, contending that many other senators had been similarly helpful to contributors. Indeed, earlier in the session, four other senators—Republican John McCain of Arizona and Democrats John Glenn of Ohio, Donald W. Riegle Jr. of Michigan, and Dennis DeConcini of Arizona—were given lighter rebukes for their efforts on behalf of Keating, who also contributed to their campaigns.

In October, another furor was stirred when it was disclosed that some members of the House of Representatives routinely wrote checks on the private bank maintained for them when there were no funds to cover them. Reacting to the wave of public indignation, the House shut down the bank and launched an inquiry into the bouncing of more than 8,300 checks by at least 134 lawmakers.

The next year, the banking scandal burgeoned, helping to create what Speaker Tom Foley called "the Congress from hell." Further investigation of the House Bank disclosed that more than 300 current and former members had written nearly 20,000 bad checks, some running into the tens of thousands of dollars. After a bitter and embarrassing controversy, the House reluctantly agreed to release all the names of the offenders, which included a number of prominent Republicans, among them three former House members who had moved up to the Bush cabinet—Defense Secretary Dick Cheney, Labor Secretary Lynn Martin, and Agriculture Secretary Edward Madigan.

On top of the furor over the House Bank came allegations of irregularities involving the House Post Office. Members of the House, it was alleged, were converting official expense vouchers or checks for campaign contributions into cash through transactions disguised as stamp purchases. Speaker Foley, already under fire for his lax handling of the bank scandal, came in for more unwelcome attention when it was disclosed that his wife, Heather, who also served as his chief of staff, was summoned to testify before the grand jury probing into possible obstruction of justice in the House Post Office investigation. A five-month inquiry by a bipartisan House task force produced a split verdict. Democrats on the task force blamed the post office's managers, clearing members of any serious wrongdoing, while the Republicans put the onus on the Democrats, contending that individual members had taken advantage of special privileges. But three House Democrats—most prominent among them Ways and Means chairman Dan Rostenkowski of Illinois—who were subpoenaed by a federal grand jury looking into the mess, did not help their party's image when they refused to testify, citing the Fifth Amendment protection against self-incrimination.

The charges hurt both parties, and Congress as an institution. A Gallup poll conducted in March found that disapproval of Congress's performance had jumped to nearly 80 percent from about 50 percent the previous July. Asked whether members of Congress understood the problems of people like themselves, three out of four of those interviewed said no. And despite attempts to minimize the significance of the House Bank revelations, nearly nine out of ten said that it was indeed "a big deal" that members wrote bad checks on their accounts. Still, most of the blame fell on the Democrats, simply because, as the public fully realized, they were in charge.

Concern about the darkening public mood, combined with the burden of coping with redistricting, contributed to a post–World War II record number of retirements. No fewer than fifty-three members quit politics, in addition to the thirteen members who gave up their seats to seek higher office. And a record number of those who did not quit voluntarily were sent packing by their discontented constituents in party primaries. All told, twenty House incumbents were beaten in primaries, breaking the previous post–World War II high of eighteen, set in 1946.

The vulnerability of the House to change was thus roughly as great as the GOPAC planners had foreseen three years earlier. But the results were not as dramatic. The voters sent 110 new House members to Washington, and of the 348 incumbents who had survived primary challenges, twenty-four were rejected. The reelection of 324 sitting House members worked out to a winning percentage for incumbents of 88 percent, the worst survival record in almost twenty years and sharply down from the 96-percent rate of two years earlier.

In partisan terms, the overall results in the House were a big disappointment for the Republicans, who gained only nine seats. But the fact that they had made this advance in the face of a recession and encumbered with a Republican president who gave voters little reason to support him or his party offered reason for hope.

Gingrich also found consolation in other aspects of GOPAC's performance. If GOPAC had not fulfilled Gingrich's chief ambition, it had still carried out the role Gingrich had conceived for it as a gigantic "propaganda machine," supplying party activists and potential candidates with ideas, information, and rhetoric. True, in the process of reaching that end, money had been lavished on projects of dubious value. Also, the emphasis on Gingrich's own thinking—"Newt's world," as it was referred to in GOPAC's internal memoranda—at times seemed disproportionate.

Enclosed along with an audiotape of a Gingrich speech sent to prospective recruits was a list of words and phrases frequently used by Gingrich. "The words and phrases are powerful," recipients were advised. "Memorize as many as possible. And remember that, like any tool, these words will not help if they are not used."

Still and all, GOPAC filled a vacuum created by the almost total absence of similar efforts by the regular party organization or anyone else. It generated interest and activity among potential candidates and supporters by flooding the grassroots with videos, audiotapes, and all sorts of other political mail. During 1989, GOPAC mailed a questionnaire to every Republican legislator in America. "Our goal is to control the U.S. House of Representatives by electing people like you to state legislatures and encouraging them to run for Congress," the questionnaire explained. "You comprise the Republican Farm Team for Congress. We need your help in providing information. The better we know you and your opinions, the more effective we will be. Please take the time to fill out this questionnaire."

Of the farm-team members recruited by the questionnaire, more than thirty actually ran for Congress in 1990 or 1992. In 1990, nine of them won office. And after the 1992 election, GOPAC claimed that "forty-one of the forty-eight freshmen Republican members of the House in 1993 were GOPAC alumni; they'd either participated in our live training sessions, received our direct financial support, or used our audio and video training tapes."

For futurist Gingrich, this was something to build on. And for him the goal remained the same. But changed circumstances meant that he would have to drop his Truman-Roosevelt scenario and find some other route to forging a Republican majority in the House. "It is virtually impossible for a party to strengthen its position in the House at the same time that it occupies the White House," Brookings Institution political scientist Thomas Mann had written in 1987, citing the regular patterns of American politics that had persisted for most of two centuries. "In this sense, House Republicans have been victims of their party's success in presidential elections." Following that reasoning, Mann concluded, as did many other scholars and politicians, that for the Republicans to gain a majority in the House, they must first lose the White House.

But when I mentioned this theory to Republican National chairman Lee Atwater in 1989, a few months before his death from a brain tumor, he said: "No thanks, I'll try some other way." Gingrich had tried another way, but it had not worked. But the 1992 election had dealt him a different hand—a Democratic president with only a tenuous hold on the electorate and a shaky grip on himself. And now Bill Clinton's weaknesses would determine how Gingrich played his cards.

6

The Unraveling

IN EARLY FEBRUARY 1992, Bill Clinton's presidential candidacy was on life support. The controversies about his womanizing and avoiding the draft had sent his poll standings into free fall; he was now ten points behind Paul Tsongas—"St. Paul" as the Clinton people derisively called him—over whom he had once held a commanding lead. Clinton sought to blame his troubles on some sort of Republican conspiracy. "People ask me sometimes during the course of the last three weeks how I've sustained all these obviously very well-planned and coordinated negative hits," Clinton told a crowd of supporters at a fund-raising dinner in Jonesboro, in his home state. "And I said," he added with bitter humor, "'Oh, this is just an ordinary election week in Arkansas.'"

If neither the accusation nor the joke was persuasive, Clinton still possessed one important source of comfort—money. On his way back to New Hampshire from his visit to Jonesboro, he stopped off in New York City for a major fund-raiser. The setting for the dinner was the Sheraton Center, a nondescript hostelry in midtown Manhattan. But the take was eye-popping. When Clinton departed the Big Apple that night, his campaign's bank balance was healthier by $750,000, all due to the generosity of the moguls of Wall Street.

Clinton's staff had no trouble finding a way to spend the money. It paid for two half-hour television programs on the Thursday and Friday before the New Hampshire vote, which, by rehabilitating Clinton's character, helped him regain enough of his previous support to make his "Comeback Kid" claim on primary night.

It was not just the intrinsic value of the cash raised from New York's financial community, as important as that was, that mattered. "That dinner signaled to a lot of people that some very smart money was behind Clinton," Paul Carey, who headed the candidate's fund-raising in New York, pointed out. "It was critical to Clinton's campaign."

New York's brokers and bankers had good reason to open their wallets for this sometime populist from Arkansas. They considered themselves, above all, to be pragmatists; in politics, as on the Big Board, they liked to bet on winners. And for all Clinton's recent troubles, to Wall Street, having sized up his opposition, he still looked like a winner.

Beyond that, he had come well recommended. At Goldman, Sachs, one of the nation's most powerful investment banking firms, whose employees and partners would ultimately give $100,000 to Clinton's drive for the nomination, Clinton was touted by two of the firm's senior partners—Kenneth Brody and Robert Rubin. Brody's urging struck a particular chord among his colleagues. "Ken made the case that Clinton was one of the few presidential candidates who could have become a Goldman partner," one said.

Robert Rubin's influence also carried great weight at the firm and in the intertwined worlds of politics and high finance. The cochairman of Goldman, Sachs, with an estimated net worth of $100 million, was known as a Democrat with relatively liberal ideas—which was to say he was a fixture among the "limousine liberals" of the Northeast, like Felix Rohatyn, people who bought their way into the good graces of the ruling Democratic power structure and whose investments, whatever help they provided for the Democratic party, invariably paid off handsomely for the donors.

With this in mind, the generosity of Wall Street and particularly Goldman, Sachs did not stop in February or with New Hampshire. By May 1992, a computer survey showed that securities and investment company executives had given Clinton well over half a million dollars, placing them second only to lawyers and lobbyists in their generosity to the candidate.

In addition to their own lavish contributions to Clinton's campaign, Goldman, Sachs partners and their spouses raised at least $1 million more from others for the Democratic presidential nominee. As Clinton's prospects brightened that spring and summer, Rubin, whose name was already being dropped as a potential secretary of the treasury, and other Goldman, Sachs partners helped raise $4.2 million to fund the Democratic party. And Rubin and his wife contributed $275,000 from their personal foundation to help finance the Democratic convention, which nominated Clinton in their own city of New York.

In truth, though, Clinton's presidential candidacy had made him a magnet for Wall Street contributions in 1992, but his ties to the financial community, and to Goldman, Sachs in particular, well preceded the campaign. The *Los Angeles Times* disclosed that Clinton, during his tenure as governor, had made a practice of rewarding Arkansas's financial elite with lucrative state business and low-interest loans, while soliciting them for millions of dollars in political contributions and campaign loans.

The key to this convenient relationship was the Arkansas Development Finance Authority, established by Clinton to issue mostly tax-free bonds to fund low-interest loans for projects from housing to business development. All told, the development authority helped generate more than $90 million in business loans. And the recipients of those loans, along with the bankers, bond brokers, and attorneys who benefited by handling these deals, became a pool of contributors to Clinton's political campaigns.

Such sources donated and loaned $2.7 million to his 1990 race for governor and his presidential campaign. In Clinton's gubernatorial race alone, which he needed to win to maintain his prospects for the presidency, those who benefited from the finance authority gave $400,300—nearly one-fifth of the total raised—whereas bankers, brokers, and lawyers, who got little or none of its business, gave only $51,600. And not surprisingly, among the beneficiaries of the finance authority's business was Goldman, Sachs, which helped to underwrite $400 million in bonds issued by the agency.

Now, as he prepared to move into the White House, Clinton's connections with high finance were deeper and stronger than ever, and the stakes in Washington were far greater than they had been in Little Rock. As governor, Clinton had been able to reward his favored financiers with government contracts and easy money to aid them in pursuing their ventures. Now, though, the prizes in Clinton's power to bestow would go far beyond the petty patronage at the disposal of the government of Arkansas. As president of the United States, Clinton would be positioned to make—indeed, would be responsible for making—the far-reaching policy decisions that would determine the future of the national economy.

As Clinton commenced his first year as the forty-second president of the United States, its economy was in a state of crisis, entering a fateful period where actions of the federal government would decide its course well into the next century. And it was just as clear that as a result of political circumstance and personal predilection, the new president—a man who could have made it as an investment banker—was closely aligned with one of the nation's most entrenched and influential sources of power, the world of Wall Street. And though many Americans had different points of view and varying stakes in the managing of the economy, no other segment of society was as determined to get its own way in the great debate over the course of commerce and the means of making a living.

This conflict had raged since the birth of the republic and, in the contemporary debate, echoes rang of Jackson's assault on the Bank of the United States and Bryan's denunciation of the cross of gold. This ongoing argument had its roots in the clashing visions of America conceived by two of the founders of the republic: Jefferson and Hamilton. Looking to history's horizons, Jefferson, whose views Jackson later expanded and strengthened, contemplated an agrarian nation of small freeholders. Hamilton, anticipating the rise of capitalism, then in its nascent stage, foresaw a burgeoning state, closely allied to those who controlled and manipulated wealth.

As the years passed, the battle changed somewhat in form and appearance. The agrarian freeholders whom Jefferson cherished were supplanted by a vast polyglot new class of urban laborers, clerks, and small entrepreneurs. They made up the debtor class. The great mercantile interests that Hamilton sought to promote had been transmuted first into owners of railroads and textile mills and later into operators of enterprises dealing in a technology that was complex beyond previous imaginings. Whatever shape their enterprises took, they were the creditor class. And one central disagreement that more than any other issue determined to what extent any group of Americans could share in the nation's wealth, divided these groups. This dispute was over the price of money. At no time was the difference any more significant or consequential than it was at the end of 1992 as Bill Clinton prepared to take over the stewardship of the U.S. economy.

To understand this conflict, it was necessary to understand the economy. Clinton, of course, realized that the economy was in trouble. The glib slogan of his campaign—"It's the economy, stupid"—certified that. Yet Clinton and his aides thought of the economic slump that had brought them to power as a function of Bush's failure to act, just as his predecessor as Democratic president, Jimmy Carter, had thought of the nation's political difficulties as symptomatic only of the defects of Nixon and Ford.

In fact, the difficulties of the economy far predated Bush and reached back into the 1970s, starting even before Carter's own tenure, when the postwar economic boom in wages suddenly ground to a halt. With the deindustrialization of America, marked by the shift from manufacturing to a service economy and the erosion of the trade-union movement, wages not only stopped rising but went into decline. At first, no alarm was sounded, because the slowdown was assumed to be temporary. The signs of trouble were still overlooked in the 1980s, when Ronald Reagan ruled and Americans thought themselves engulfed by affluence.

In fact, affluence was limited to a fortunate few, as a study by the Joint Economic Committee of Congress demonstrated. Based on Census Bureau data and released in January 1992, a year before Clinton took office, the study confirmed a phenomenon called "middle-class squeeze," to which Michael Dukakis had vainly tried to call voters' attention when he campaigned against George Bush in 1988. During the much-heralded decade of the 1980s, the study showed, a large majority of two-earner families with children had to work harder, not to get ahead but simply not to fall behind.

Not only did living standards decline for millions of Americans, but inequities in the economy increased. On the one hand, for families making more than $63,000—the richest 20 percent of the nation, or the wealthiest one-fifth of America—times were good. Their incomes increased by 15 percent. On the other hand, those making less than $35,000—two-fifths of all two-earner families—saw their incomes level off and often drop, despite longer hours worked. Families in the middle of the income ladder were able to increase their incomes slightly during the 1980s, but only because wives greatly increased the hours they worked. Measured in terms of the time parents had left for their children after time spent working, these families actually lost ground. For married couples, the average income growth in the 1980s was one-half the growth in the 1970s and one-fifth the growth during the 1950s and 1960s.

One central fact about this study made it particularly gloomy. Previous surveys had focused on the hard times endured by individual workers because of declining wages. The January 1992 study showed the way that trends in earnings of men and women combined to boost the income of those who were already doing well while holding down the income of families who were struggling. Hourly income did go up for one group of male workers—but only one—those already in the top fifth of incomes. As a result, the gap between low-wage and high-wage workers got wider. Men in the lowest income group earned an hourly wage that was 31 percent of that earned by men in the top income group back in 1979. By 1989, their hourly earnings were only 25 percent of those in the top group.

As bad as conditions were in the Reagan era, they got steadily worse after Bush took over. In September 1992, a new Census Bureau study showed that economic stagnation in the first three years of the Bush administration had wiped out whatever meager gains middle-class Americans had made in the late 1980s, causing the middle class to lose ground financially and ultimately swelling the ranks of the poor to a twenty-seven-year high.

Of all the sectors of American society, none had suffered more or fallen further behind than America's cities, once the proud citadels of urban Democratic politics, now merely decaying enclaves on a landscape shaped by white flight and suburban sprawl. As Bush headed into what would be the final year of his presidency, advocates for the cities demanded help, contending that only by returning the cities to their roles as the economic and social wellspring of the nation could the overall economy be salvaged. In a report for the U.S. Conference of Mayors, the Economic Policy Institute, a Washington think tank, called for massive spending for housing, public transportation, water and sewer systems, and other urban needs, which would create jobs critical to reviving the economy. The cost was enough to take the breath away from the nation's political leaders—from $60 billion to $125 billion annually, though the report claimed these outlays could be offset by reductions in military spending and increases in the personal and corporate income tax. In a separate report, "State of Black America 1992," the National Urban League reiterated a two-year-old call for a Marshall Plan for America's cities that would allocate $50 billion a year over the next decade to domestic priorities. "Cost is not the issue," Billy J. Tidwell Jr., director of research for the Urban League, claimed. "The real issue is the nation's priorities and our appreciation of what best serves the national interests."

How would this fit into Bill Clinton's priorities, into the New Democratic concept of the national interest that he would spend the year of 1992 formulating? No one, certainly including Clinton himself, knew what being a New Democrat entailed—only that it had to represent a break from old Democratic practices, like pouring billions into the cities.

The extended debate among economists about how to bring the nation back to economic health, even if it offered no ready answer, at least laid out the complexities of the problems he would have to deal with. Freed from the urgent pressures that burdened political leaders, the economists could take the long view. The real problem, as they saw it, was not the Bush slump, as painful and frustrating as its impact was. The worse news was that when this recession finally lifted, the United States would still confront a future of stagnant living standards. The way out of this hole, the economists more or less agreed, was to boost savings and investment.

The question was how? Each answer was encrusted with its own set of difficulties. Possible remedies included a middle-class tax cut, which would do wonders politically but have only transient economic impact; a capital-gains tax cut, which would please the business community but whose benefits for the rest of the economy would be doubtful; an investment tax credit, which would have the same advantage and the same drawback; increased spending on public works, which would help wherever it was done, but not necessarily anyplace else. One group of economists saw a built-in drawback to all these nostrums. Any increase in spending or cut in tax revenue, they believed, was very likely to expand the federal budget deficit, and that would result in deepening the nation's debt and risking higher interest rates, which, they argued, would make the fundamental problem worse.

Clinton was in a quandary. Not only were the problems thorny, but he was ill-prepared to deal with them. No single approach offered itself as the right answer to the prolonged problem of slow growth. Instead, he would have to choose from among a variety of answers, each of which might do some good, and also some harm. Which course one tried would depend on what one believed and whose ox one was prepared to have gored. But to pursue any such course meant that groundwork had to have been laid earlier on. Clinton would have had to spell out his course of action during the campaign, making clear who would benefit most and who might bear some pain in the short run as a price for long-range gains. Then he would have had a mandate to act. Candidate Clinton, however, had done nothing of the sort—instead, he had gone off in several directions at once.

In keeping with New Democrat doctrine, spawned by the self-described centrists of the Democratic Leadership Council, Clinton had paid constant tribute to middle-class Americans, whose well-being he promised to enhance largely by cutting their taxes, reforming welfare, and "reinventing government." But his campaign rhetoric also consisted of a blend of liberal populist pledges to narrow the fast-widening gap between rich and poor and to revitalize the economy with a plan to "rebuild America" through a public investment in the infrastructure, education, and the environment. Along with this came a smattering of resentment at the greed of multilateral corporations and the American trading partners, intended to offset the economic nationalist themes sounded by Ross Perot.

Clinton's situation, as he took office, would have been far different if he had woven these diverse ideological strands into a cohesive policy fabric of his own, drawing on the strengths of each set of beliefs. This, however, was beyond the nature of a man committed to ambiguity. As the twists and turns of his candidacy had shown—from right to left and back again—he had no guidepost beyond the relentless pursuit of expediency. Thus, his presidency, like his candidacy, would be distinguished by its disjointedness. Monday's triumph would have as its sequel Tuesday's debacle. On Wednesday, the left would attack him, Thursday the right would take its turn, and, by Friday, it might be the center taking him on. As a natural-born dodger and ducker, he adjusted to this pattern. Nowhere, though, could he find consistent support—what politicians call a base—because no one knew enough about him to trust him with the stewardship of their interests for longer than the period between morning and nightfall of the same day. He had survived over the long run and prospered as a candidate because he could offset his own failures by exploiting the weaknesses of his foes. Now, in the White House, he held center stage, and for the time being, no adversary was formidable enough to draw attention from Clinton's own contradictions.

In this predicament, confronting multiple uncertainties, Clinton inevitably turned for guidance to the financial leaders who had done so much to make him president. As they had freely given him money, now they cheerfully gave him advice, and gained power in return.

The top economic policy job in the Clinton White House went to Texas senator Lloyd Bentsen, whom the new president made treasury secretary. With this choice, Clinton gave the corporate world—which might have been upset about the prospect of facing a Democratic president for the first time in twelve years—abundant reason to relax. At the same time, he caused consternation among those in the Democratic party who had taken candidate Clinton's populist rhetoric to heart.

Business worships consistency, and no one could fault Lloyd Bentsen for lacking that trait. In any dispute among Democrats between conservatives and liberals, it was always clear that Bentsen would come down on the conservative side. In any argument between big business and its foes—whether consumers, the federal government, or organized labor—Bentsen could be found standing up for the side of business. Indeed, when then-congressman George Bush ran for the Senate in 1970, a good many liberal Democrats gave him their backing, viewing their party's candidate, Lloyd Bentsen, as too conservative. Bush welcomed the liberals aboard his bandwagon, confident he could hold the conservative support. "If Bentsen is going to try to go to my right, he's going to have to step off the ends of the earth," Bush boasted. Yet Bentsen managed to do just that, which is how Bush came to be U.S. ambassador to the United Nations, while Bentsen launched his long Senate career.

Occasionally, Bentsen misjudged his audience. In 1976, he calculated that the Democratic party would rebound from George McGovern's landslide defeat in 1972 by nominating a conservative. He was right about that. Even as an antidote to McGovernism, though, Bentsen was too hard for Democrats to swallow. They settled for the more moderate Jimmy Carter. Bentsen shrugged off that setback. And during Ronald Reagan's first year in the White House, he helped rally Democratic support to expand the new president's sweeping tax-cut proposals—pushing for bigger business tax reductions than even Reagan had contemplated. Meanwhile, as chair of the Senate Finance Committee, he earned the nickname "Loophole Lloyd" for his success in legislating tax breaks for real estate, oil and gas producers, and an array of other industries.

Life in Bentsen's world of wealth and privilege sometimes dulled his perspective. The disclosure in 1987 that he had invited special-interest lobbyists to join a club whose main function was to have regular breakfast meetings with Lloyd Bentsen—for a $10,000 fee—forced him to break up the club. Still, he kept his hand out as one of Capitol Hill's leading recipients of campaign contributions from political action committees.

In 1988, Bentsen finally made it to the Democratic national ticket—as Michael Dukakis's vice presidential running mate. With the polish and security that come with wealth and power, Bentsen humiliated his Republican counterpart, Dan Quayle, in their televised debate: "You're no Jack Kennedy," he scolded—the most memorable words Bentsen ever uttered in public life.

Of far greater consequence, though noticed by no one at all at the time, was the advice he gave running-mate Dukakis, to lay off the savings-and-loan scandal as a campaign issue against Bush and the Republicans. Handled aggressively enough, that issue, with its overtones of corruption and greed, might, some Democrats believed, turn the electorate against Bush. However, it would certainly have caused discomfiture to the savings-and-loan industry, to which Bentsen's ties were many and strong.

To understand where Bentsen's loyalties and beliefs lay, it was necessary only to look at his campaign contributions. He had collected more than $200,000 from finance, insurance, and real estate concerns, and a like amount from lawyers and lobbyists—including $9,550 from Baker and Botts, the Houston law firm of one of Bentsen's predecessors at the Treasury Department, fellow Texan James A. Baker III. Bentsen also took in $13,500 from the Wall Street finance house of Goldman, Sachs, largesse bound to make for a harmonious spirit in the Clinton cabinet, where the redoubtable Rubin would hold the job of head of the newly established Economic Security Council.

Bentsen's own role was spelled out by the man who appointed him well before he took the oath of office. "The secretary of the treasury will continue to be the principal economic spokesperson after the president for this administration," Clinton said reassuringly after creating Rubin's post. "The treasury will still be the place where the president's economic views are spoken for after the president does it."

Tradition, though, had to make room and allowances for Robert Rubin. In every new administration, men take offices with high-sounding titles but are soon revealed as hollow figures who occupy little more than sinecures. Such was not to be the case with Rubin. He made the Economic Security Council into a power center, ensuring his own prominence and influence. One measure of a presidential appointee's true significance is which meetings he passes up and which he attends. Many a gathering of economic policymakers in the early weeks of Clinton's presidency never caught a glimpse of Rubin, because he judged them unworthy of his presence. Significantly, at Clinton's first meeting with congressional leaders in the White House, called to discuss his economic agenda, Rubin was conspicuously present at his president's side. Likewise, when Clinton met privately with Federal Reserve chairman Alan Greenspan, Rubin was also front and center. And when Clinton wanted his cabinet secretaries to round out their budget proposals, the requests went out over Rubin's signature.

For his part, Bentsen took Rubin's emergence in stride. While he quietly maneuvered in the background, where he liked to operate, the fifty-four-year-old Rubin was content to let the seventy-one-year-old Bentsen fulfill the role the president wanted him to play—as chief spokesman. The two men were hardly strangers. During his tenure at Goldman, Sachs, Rubin had served as Bentsen's personal financial adviser. More important, on the great questions of economic policy, which now faced Clinton and divided some of his other advisers, Rubin and Clinton saw eye to eye.

The most fundamental question of all had to do with reducing the deficit. For Democrats, this was particularly sensitive, bearing with it a special onus that invited comparison to the issue of world communism. With the collapse of the Soviet Union and the end of the Cold War, Democrats had appeared to be freed from one of the great burdens that had faced them through nearly the whole of the postwar era—the reputation for being "soft" on communism.

This stigma had been stamped on the American consciousness in the late 1940s, first by the supposed sellout of Eastern Europe at Yalta by FDR, then by the "loss" of China to the Communists by Truman, which many believe drove Lyndon Johnson into the quagmire of Vietnam. "Liberal Democrats were suspect on the Communist issue," Harry McPherson, a Johnson aide, wrote years after the war. "If they were 'soft' on Communists at home or abroad, they would find their legislative programs stopped cold by charges of complicity." Horace Busby, one of Johnson's closest confidants, believed that Johnson was "very much afraid" that, if he pulled out of Vietnam, "the Republicans would say this man is just like Truman and Acheson; he's selling out in Asia."

Now, the budget deficit had turned into a similar nightmare for the Democrats—and with even less justification. For the first thirty years after the war, Democrats were assigned most of the responsibility for the deficit, because of their support for expanding government—though, in fact, during the postwar years, Republican presidents Eisenhower and Nixon often collaborated with Democrats in Congress, backing new efforts by the federal government, notably the interstate-highway program launched under Eisenhower and the establishment of cost-of-living allowances (now famous by their acronym, COLAs) under Nixon. In fact, the budget deficit when the last Democratic president, Jimmy Carter, turned the White House over to Republican Ronald Reagan was a mere pittance: $79 billion. It started soaring in Reagan's first term, climbing to $221 billion by 1986 and reaching over $300 billion in Bush's final years in the White House.

For most of this time, the Republicans seemed to care very little about the deficit. They could hardly afford to call attention to it during the Reagan years, because that would only remind people of Reagan's fractured promise to balance the budget and cut taxes. It was the Democrats who became obsessed with the deficit, because it kept them from using government for the purposes to which their party was dedicated. Among some Democrats, notably New York senator Daniel Patrick Moynihan, it became an article of faith that the Republicans had created the deficit to paralyze the Democrats.

It was this obsession that compelled the Democrats into a series of self-destructive acts. Notable among their follies was their 1984 nominee Walter Mondale's pledge to raise taxes for no other reason than to abolish the deficit. Whoever Americans elected in November would have to raise taxes, Mondale declared in his acceptance speech. "The difference is, he won't tell you. I just did." The forty-nine-state landslide that followed explains the determination of the Democratic congressional leadership to avoid blame for the 1990 tax increase by getting Bush actively to support this boost, which was supposed to bring the deficit down to earth. But the party's deficit phobia led to the decision of Democratic congressional leaders to accept Richard Darman's plan for limiting government spending, which, in the long run, would turn out to be just as injurious to the Democrats as bearing the blame for the deficit.

In the dawn of the Clinton presidency, the deficit obsession became even deeper, in part because Bentsen and Rubin persuaded Clinton that as a result of the recession, the federal tide of red ink could rise to the level of $500 billion before the end of the year 2000. Prior to this surge of anxiety, Clinton had cast deficit reduction as simply part of his overall effort to revive the economy and had made trimming the deficit a distinctly secondary objective to reviving the economy. In the book *Putting People First*, published over the names of Clinton and Gore as the bible of the Democratic presidential campaign, the word "deficit" does not even appear until page twenty-seven. At that point, after a lengthy summary of Clinton's ideas for economic revival, including such measures as health-care reform, worker training, and educational and welfare reform, this sentence appears before a table of spending proposals: "The plan not only pays for every penny in new investments with new savings but—even with modest growth estimates—will cut the deficit in half by 1996."

Yet within a few weeks of the election, the idea of deficit reduction would be transformed from merely a byproduct of the Clinton recovery plan into its main goal. And that change would reshape the Clinton presidency for its entire history.

This change would come about largely because of the influence of the money men—Bentsen and Rubin—who persuaded Clinton to accept their outlook, the outlook of Wall Street, as the ideological premise of his presidency. Their accomplishment was made easier by the fact that Clinton had no clear ideology of his own.

Clinton's adoption of the Wall Street credo, advocated by the conservative Democrat Bentsen and the supposedly liberal Democrat Rubin, soon elevated another economic policymaker, who could not claim to be any sort of Democrat, to a position of far-reaching influence. He was Alan Greenspan, now nearing sixty-three, who had begun playing the power game in Washington when Bill Clinton was still struggling to get started in politics in Arkansas and who now ruled the Federal Reserve Board of Governors.

With his stooped posture and habitually melancholy expression, Greenspan certainly did not look the part of one of the nation's movers and shakers. He disdained appearances. For him, the exercise of power was strictly an inside game. "He is a survivor," said Washington power broker Robert S. Strauss, the former chairman of the Democratic National Committee. Strauss, a member of the same power-broker breed, was very different from Greenspan in that he was a paradigm of ostentation, whereas Greenspan was a model of self-effacement. Strauss tooted his own horn and got far more attention—which was what he really craved—than influence. The highest pinnacle he reached in his career was appointment as U.S. trade ambassador in the failed presidency of Jimmy Carter.

Greenspan, by contrast, let others sing his praises and rose to become chairman of the Federal Reserve system, the most powerful and secretive force in the shaping of U.S. economic policy. "He is one of the best political operators in this town, and yet you never hear people talk about him in political terms," Strauss marveled. "Most people don't even think that he knows anything about politics, which shows you how good he is at it."

In a city famed for its bluster, Greenspan, like one of the computers on which he relied, operated silently, efficiently, and coldly. Unmarried* and childless at age sixty-two, his favorite mode of relaxation, apart from listening to classical music and playing tennis, was to tackle complex economics-related mathematics problems. "I think you can deal with people in one of two ways, either by force or by persuasion," he once observed. "If you can't deal with them by persuasion, you are not as effective. And I don't enjoy confrontation, to tell you the truth," he added. "I can do it if necessary, I can be as hard as anybody I know, but I don't like it."

Although Greenspan had already been a force in four Republican presidencies, going back to Richard Nixon, it would be under a Democratic president, Bill Clinton, that he achieved unprecedented levels of power. He gave Clinton and his economic advisers what they most wanted—credibility with the financial interests on whose goodwill they believed the nation's chances of prosperity, and Clinton's prospects for political success, depended. For in the green-eyeshade world of tight-money Republicanism, no one embodied the principles of fiscal austerity more faithfully than Alan Greenspan. Indeed, soon after he had first taken over the helm at the Federal Reserve in summer 1987, as Ronald Reagan's choice to succeed Paul Volcker, he raised interest rates, in part to show Wall Street he could be just as tough as Volcker, whose own ham-handed approach to monetary policy had helped demolish the Carter presidency, had propelled the country into the 1982 recession, and had set the stage for the economic binge of the 1980s.

Greenspan's present eminence could hardly have been foreseen from his first job—as a jazz musician. A graduate of Juilliard as a teenager, he played tenor sax for $55 a week in Child's Paramount, the Times Square restaurant that was a feature of the Broadway jazz scene during the wartime years. Between sets, some of Greenspan's fellow musicians would rush next door to Walgreen's drugstore, a favorite hangout for marijuana users, and light up reefers. As for Greenspan, not only did he not touch drugs, but his old boss recalled: "He never even took a drink." Instead, the bookish young man tended to the band payroll and spent his free time in the midst of Manhattan's wartime uproar reading college economics texts.

---

*He would later marry NBC News correspondent Andrea Mitchell.

His discipline paid off. He graduated from New York University summa cum laude in economics, earned a master's degree there, and went on to study for his doctorate at Columbia University under Arthur F. Burns, who would become chairman of the Federal Reserve under Nixon. Meanwhile, Greenspan married an aspiring painter named Joan Mitchell, who introduced him to someone whose overall influence on his thinking would be even greater than Burns's. This was the novelist and cult heroine Ayn Rand, a refugee from Soviet communism whose books championed a quasi-Nietzschean creed she billed as radical capitalism. Rand's characters were monuments to boundless individualism and unabashed selfishness. In her 1943 best-seller *The Fountainhead*, architect Howard Roark, the prototypical Rand hero, blew up a housing project he had planned because bureaucrats tampered with the initial design. Greenspan and his new wife fell under Rand's spell, joining the "collective" of disciples who met regularly to steep themselves in her doctrines.

Greenspan's marriage collapsed in less than a year, but his friendship with Rand endured until her death in 1982 and served as an entrée for Greenspan to the intellectual ferment then bubbling among conservatives dissatisfied with the passivity of the Eisenhower era. "Alan is my disciple philosophically," Rand said in a 1974 interview. "He is an advocate of full laissez-faire capitalism, but neither he nor I expect it overnight."

Still, Greenspan did what he could to advance the cause. His link with Rand brought him into the 1968 Nixon presidential campaign and, ultimately, into Nixon's ill-fated second administration, as chairman of the Council of Economic Advisers, an appointment he accepted only after shrewdly insisting on assurances by aides to Vice President Ford that he would be kept on if Ford succeeded to the Oval Office. That promise was kept, and Greenspan's faith in the free market soon underwent its most rigorous test. With consumer prices climbing, Greenspan persuaded the new president that what the economy needed was a stiff dose of spending cuts and tax increases, bundled together under the soon-to-be-infamous battle cry of "Whip Inflation Now," handily abbreviated as WIN.

As unemployment soared, though, WIN soon became a synonym for fiasco. Under Greenspan's tutelage, Ford had proclaimed inflation to be "domestic enemy number one." In reality, however, recession, not inflation, was the nation's real problem. That development did not faze Greenspan. In 1974, in the midst of the slump, he told a Washington audience made up mostly of groups of consumers and minorities that stockbrokers on Wall Street, not poor people, were suffering the most in the recession that was then straining the economy. His remarks were met with catcalls and boos and made front-page headlines across the country the next day.

Nevertheless, Greenspan stayed on through Ford's tenure in the White House, and after Ford's defeat in 1976, he returned to New York to pick up where he had left off as an economic consultant. In the early 1980s, his

success at his work brought him among other clients a West Coast real estate operator named Charles H. Keating Jr. and his Lincoln Savings and
Loan. If there was anything amiss in the way Keating and Lincoln were
operating, it was not apparent to Greenspan. He gave their activities,
which ultimately ripened into the worst-case example of the savings-and-
loan crisis, his seal of approval. Indeed, early in 1985, Greenspan wrote a
letter to the Federal Home Loan Bank of San Francisco arguing that Lincoln Savings deserved an exemption from regulations that limited to 10
percent a savings and loan's direct investment in real estate projects.
Greenspan claimed that Lincoln was "financially strong" and that Lincoln posed no "foreseeable risk to the Federal Savings and Loan Insurance Corp." Such advice bolstered Keating's own far-flung efforts to restrain federal regulators from moving against him when he was ultimately
convicted of fraud and racketeering.

Many involved with Keating were tarred with the brush of scandal that ruined Keating and came to symbolize the corruption of an entire industry. Because his own connection came several years before these disasters,
Greenspan escaped any stigma, and during the Bush presidency, while the
savings-and-loan scandal burgeoned, Greenspan's own influence as chairman
of the Federal Reserve grew. "Whenever there are major economic decisions
to be made, [Greenspan] is in on them," a delighted Federal Reserve official
told a journalist. "His voice is listened to."

One reason for Greenspan's power was that his own style and inclinations
suited well the Federal Reserve, the institution he headed. It was the Federal
Reserve, and its relationship to the markets and to the government, that
defined and dominated the making of national economic policy and contravened the most fundamental principles of Democratic self-government.
Many ingredients went into creating the role and the influence of the Fed, but
the single critical factor was unaccountability. In almost total secrecy, the Fed
made decisions that controlled policy and shaped the lives of Americans.
Moreover, even when information about the Fed's actions leaked out or was
belatedly divulged, the knowledge was of limited value because the decision-
makers could not be made to answer for what they had done. The dirty little
secret about this syndrome was that it served the convenience and interest of
the elected officials, who were supposedly responsible for making economic
policy. When things went wrong, all they had to do was throw up their hands
and blame the Fed, comfortable in the knowledge that everyone knew they
could do nothing about it.

Thus, the unaccountability was twofold. Not only was the Fed not responsible for its actions, but its existence made it possible for elected officials to
evade responsibility. The potential for this system to wreak havoc on the lives
of ordinary citizens had been dramatically illustrated when Clinton's most recent Democratic predecessor in the White House appointed Paul Volcker as

chairman of the Fed in October 1979. Volcker did not tell Carter exactly what he was going to do. He did not have to. With inflation on the rise and Wall Street restless, anyone who knew anything about Volcker's tight-fisted approach to economic policy realized that he was going to squeeze credit.

Just before he made the choice, Bert Lance, Carter's old banking crony from Georgia, sent word to warn the president off. Volcker's appointment would mean higher interest rates and higher unemployment, Lance said. The outcome of the 1980 election would be "mortgaged" to the Federal Reserve. Carter shrugged off that advice. He had other voices to heed, as Stuart Eizenstat, the president's chief domestic adviser, later acknowledged. "Volcker was selected because he was the candidate of Wall Street," Eizenstat said. "This was their price, in effect," for promising to maintain stability in the markets.

Whatever Wall Street actually did for Carter, the president paid a high price in return. Bert Lance's worst fears were fulfilled. Volcker attacked inflation with a new weapon. Instead of raising short-term interest rates, he set out to limit that supply of money—with devastating effects for millions of Americans. Interest rates soared to unprecedented heights, and unemployment climbed along with the price of money. Worst of all, inflation continued to skyrocket, too.

Ultimately, inflation subsided, though at the cost of another recession in 1982, the most severe since the Great Depression. Still, Wall Street was happy. But it was too late for Carter, who was crushed by Reagan in 1980. Volcker's cure took too heavy a toll. As usual, the Fed denied the implications of its own actions. When asked at the time if its draconian measures against inflation would lead to slower growth and higher unemployment, Volcker blandly replied: "I don't think it will have important effects in that connection." Given the forces that shape the economy, which were certainly well known to Volcker, that was as close to a bald-faced lie as an economic policymaker could tell. "There wasn't any question that the Fed knew that recession would follow" its tightening of the money supply, a former Fed official said later.

Late in the election campaign, Carter tried the old political trick of blaming the Fed for the country's economic troubles. Carter, however, had too many other weaknesses, and the economic conditions were such that the electorate was unwilling to tolerate his presence in the White House any longer. After serving two uneasy four-year terms under Reagan, during which his power grew, Volcker was finally eased out in 1987 and replaced by Greenspan.

With Volcker's departure, Reagan's advisers breathed a sigh of relief. Although Volcker and Greenspan practiced the same tight-fisted approach to the economy, Greenspan lacked the prestige to exercise the great clout wielded by Volcker. No sooner did he assume his new post, though, than

Greenspan began to grow in stature, approaching Volcker-like dimensions by the time Bush had replaced Reagan and faced the onset of the 1990 recession.

One reason for Greenspan's importance was that Bush, like other presidents, used him as a shield to deflect criticism of his policies. Greenspan demonstrated his power during the deadlock over budget talks on Capitol Hill in 1990. He sent word to both sides that if no agreement was reached, interest rates would likely rise and the stock market would tumble.

Now with Democrat Clinton in the White House, Republican appointee Greenspan was going to get another boost in his prestige far beyond anything that had been granted to him under Bush. Just as Carter had reached out to a conservative economist to bolster his stock with Wall Street, so did Clinton, who, in the postelection weeks of 1992, was striving to reconcile the promises of his campaign with economic reality. Like Carter, he wanted the security blanket of Wall Street, but he did not have to appoint a conservative as Fed chairman. Greenspan was *already* on the job, thus Clinton's task was easier. With the connivance and urging of Lloyd Bentsen and Bob Rubin, the new chief executive set out to make Greenspan, Republican champion of Wall Street, part of his New Democratic presidency.

His first move was to invite Greenspan to Little Rock for luncheon early in December. Their meeting would, of course, be private. Before he even arrived there, Greenspan showed Clinton and the financial markets just how strong a hand he believed he had by sending the president a message of where he stood—in public. Two days prior to the lunch in Little Rock, Greenspan took the extraordinary step of releasing a letter he had sent the previous week to Congressman Henry B. Gonzalez, chairman of the House Banking Committee, who, like other Fed critics, had been pressing for lower interest rates to speed the still-sputtering recovery. In a November 5 letter to Greenspan, Gonzalez had warned that the Fed's cautious approach could prolong the economic downturn. He accused the Fed of "choking the economy down to recession levels by its insistence on maintaining a slow annual monetary growth rate." Greenspan's reply was couched in the arcane and indirect language favored by the Fed. His aides made clear, though, that the chairman had put the kibosh on the notion of lower interest rates—and hard. The Fed was confident that the economy was already on its way to recovery, Greenspan told Gonzalez, and no more easing was needed. In fact, far from contemplating any easing of credit, Greenspan told Gonzalez, the central bank was seriously considering reducing its targets for money-supply growth next year—the tactics that Volcker had used to drain away inflation, but which first drained away the lifeblood of the economy.

The letter's release served to put Clinton on notice as to where Greenspan stood. In their luncheon, the ex-saxophone player stuck to the tune he had played in his letter—with elaborations. Short-term rates, the rates the Fed directly controlled, were just about where they should be,

Greenspan told the president-elect, as Bob Woodward reconstructed the conversation in *The Agenda*. Of course, he understood the president wanted to ease credit. In that regard, though, the president should be thinking about long-term rates, which really were more important anyhow, since they influenced the long-range planning of serious investors.

Greenspan and Clinton could agree that long-term rates were too high, and had been too high for too long a time. There was a reason for this, Greenspan explained, as if he were an economics professor lecturing a bright—but green—student. The bondholders and traders who set long-term rates were not greedy, just frightened. They still had nightmares about the inflation that had raged in the last two years of the Carter presidency. With the federal deficit soaring and seemingly out of control, they feared that nightmare would return at any moment.

Greenspan knew of a way to deal with these fears, he claimed, and Clinton himself could do it. What Wall Street wanted from the president was proof that he was worried about the deficit. Thus reassured, the bondholders and traders would reduce long-term rates, the housing market would boom, and so would consumer spending in general. Prosperity would return to the land.

Now, in many ways, this was an outrageously narrow and self-serving argument. First of all, the supposed link between the budget deficit and inflation was hard to prove. The deficit had been soaring for more than a dozen years. Yet since the 1982 recession, inflation had remained under control, averaging less than 3 percent. Second, one reason the deficit was so high was the recession and slow growth of the Bush years, during which Greenspan had been one of the chief shapers of economic policy. The course Greenspan now advocated was to reduce the deficit in order to revive the economy.

Of course, there was another and more direct approach, which was for Clinton to follow the mandate of his own candidacy. This involved reviving the economy through a broad array of government actions, some of which involved increased spending. As a by-product, the deficit would almost certainly go down.

Clinton had found it expedient to advocate this course during his candidacy, but his commitment to it was no deeper than it was to the other policies he had advocated. To stick to the promises of his campaign would bring down upon him the disapproval of the very forces to whom he was already so indebted: Robert Rubin and the investment bankers of Wall Street. For Clinton, the best course seemed to be to stay on their good side, particularly when he would have the backing of such a reasonable conservative as Alan Greenspan.

"We can do business," Clinton told his vice president–elect, Al Gore, after the lunch with Greenspan. Indeed, they could. The main condition for the alliance was now agreed to: The president would make deficit reduction the major objective of his economic program.

After that, events followed in train. In mid-January, Bentsen reported to Greenspan on the deliberations of the Clinton economic team and the agreement to pursue deficit reduction. If Bentsen thought he would get a firm promise from Greenspan in return, he was mistaken. Instead, the Fed chairman smiled his famously enigmatic smile and said that he would cooperate with Clinton "within limits," leaving the president and his advisers to fathom the exact meaning of those words.

When it came to seeing that Clinton lived up to his end of the bargain, though, Greenspan was not shy. In February, Rubin forwarded a memo from his staff to Clinton, raising concerns that deficit reduction might hurt consumer demand and slow down the recovery. "Greenspan believes that a major deficit reduction will lead to interest changes more than offsetting the demand effect," the memo stated. And so it was that deficit reduction became the Holy Grail of Clinton's economic policy.

During his first year in the White House, Clinton's ill-defined New Democrat credo produced policies that contradicted his campaign promises not only in the economic arena but also on other issues. The most politically damaging example was the controversy over gays in the military. Competing against other Democratic candidates for gay support, Clinton took an early stand in support of admitting homosexuals into the armed services. This was by no means the top item on the gay political agenda, which was headed by the gay and lesbian civil rights bill pending before Congress. On that issue, claiming he was concerned about the need to clarify technical issues, Clinton dragged his feet. Thus, his backing for gays in service served as his bona fides in the gay community. The gay movement was grateful enough for its leaders to later claim to have raised more than $3 million to support Clinton's candidacy. In the long run, Clinton was to pay a high price for this backing. This trouble should have been foreseen and avoided. Although the promise attracted little attention during the campaign, gay leader David Mixner, Clinton's chief contact with the movement, sought to warn Clinton's staff a week before the election that any attempt to press gay rights issues could create a serious backlash. "I urged them to have a detailed plan for our issues and cautioned them on the number of enemies the gay community had in the political process," he later recalled.

Disregarding the warning, Clinton announced less than two weeks after his election that he intended to stick to his campaign promise to allow gays into the military, without devising a strategy for building support or defusing the opposition. Sure enough, as Mixner had foreseen, the proposal came under fire from the Joint Chiefs of Staff, led by Colin Powell, and from Capitol Hill, where it was spearheaded by Senator Sam Nunn of Georgia, the most influential figure in Congress on national defense issues.

Facing a threat by Republicans in Congress to write the existing Department of Defense policy banning gays into law, Clinton backed off. The week after his inauguration, he agreed to postpone action for six months, when he would prepare a draft executive order dealing with the issue. That order turned out to be another compromise—the celebrated policy of "don't ask, don't tell." Recruits would no longer be questioned about their sexual orientation, but gays in the service could not talk about their preference—on pain of being discharged. This arrangement had the backing of the Joint Chiefs and was acceptable to congressional leadership, but the six-month-long flap caused inestimable damage to the president.

On the one hand, Clinton appeared to many Americans, particularly in the South, as having sacrificed the traditions of military service and impinged on the welfare of the troops in order to pay a political debt to a minority many of them despised. On the other hand, to the gay community and its liberal supporters, the president was viewed as unwilling to stand firm on an issue he himself had described as a matter of high principle.

Nevertheless, it was the economic issue that was to prove the major stumbling block as Clinton sought to resolve the conflict between his campaign promises—his pledge to revive the economy through expansion of federal investments in education, job training, and the infrastructure, along with a tax cut for the middle class—and his vow to cut the deficit in half in four years. This Herculean labor had taken on added difficulty as estimates of the size of the deficit after four years increased.

As the president's struggles to resolve the dilemma unfolded over the opening months of his presidency, each step along the way seemed to do further damage to his credibility. On February 15, in his first televised address to the nation since taking office, the president, who as a candidate had promised to deliver a middle-class tax cut, declared that he could not set the economy right without raising taxes on the middle class. He called on virtually all Americans to endure sacrifice to pay for the economic-growth and deficit-reduction program.

To distract attention from the burdens he proposed to impose, Clinton depicted himself as the embattled leader of a crusade for the public good fighting special interests and defenders of the status quo. "Within minutes of the time I conclude my address to Congress Wednesday night, the special interests will be out in force," he warned his fellow citizens. "Those that profited from the status quo will oppose the changes that we seek. They are the defenders of decline. And we must be the architects of the future."

Even Clinton's allies voiced misgivings about the public reaction to the call for sacrifice, particularly since Clinton had promised during his candidacy that no sacrifice was needed. "I think the president will have a much more difficult time selling deficit reduction and public sacrifice than he realizes," said former Michigan governor James J. Blanchard, a close friend and adviser of the president. He had himself been driven from office by dissatisfaction with his economic policies. "There is no political future in administering pain to people."

Two nights later, the president unveiled his economic program in a lengthy address to a joint session of Congress. He asked for enactment of $496 billion in tax increases and spending cuts in a sweeping four-year program to revive the economy and reduce the deficit, warning that failure to act would be "condemning our children and our children's children to a lesser life than we enjoyed." To revive the economy, in addition to a $31-billion short-term stimulus package, Clinton proposed spending $160 billion on "investment" programs that, he argued, would improve the economy over the long run. That $160 billion represented a $60 billion drop-off in the $220 billion the president had promised to spend on investment during the campaign—a result of the new emphasis on deficit reduction.

That evening in the Capitol, apart from Clinton himself, Alan Greenspan probably attracted more attention than anyone else. This was because he had been given the most prominent seat in the House—next to First Lady Hillary Rodham Clinton. By placing him there, Clinton had assured that all the world would know that his economic plan had the tacit approval of the chairman of the Fed. In a sense, that would be helpful. In another sense, Clinton was taking a huge risk. Following in the footsteps of Jimmy Carter twelve years earlier, he was making his economic plan and his presidency hostage to the goodwill of the chairman of the central bank.

Clinton's economic blueprint reversed the classic role of Democrats in modern times. For more than half a century, Democrats had raised taxes to finance the expansion of the federal government, which, in turn, expanded the Democrats' political support. This formula was capsulized best by FDR's right-hand man, Harry Hopkins, who, in the heyday of the New Deal, reputedly boasted: "We shall tax and tax, and spend and spend, and elect and elect." What Clinton had decided to do was just tax and tax, not spend and spend, and that raised doubts about whether he would be able to elect anybody, including himself.

Not only had he given the Republicans ammunition to attack what they justifiably called the largest tax increase in the nation's history, but what was worse, little of the money he intended to raise was earmarked for the sort of activism that had allowed the Democrats to dominate national politics for more than a generation. Instead, Clinton intended to use the revenues to invest in the theory held by Greenspan, Bentsen, and Rubin—that cutting the deficit would drive down interest rates enough to fulfill the promise of economic growth that had been the platform of Clinton's campaign for the White House.

The first casualty of this strategy was Clinton's short-term $31-billion stimulus package intended to create 500,000 new jobs that very year. "Our immediate priority," Clinton declared in an address to the Congress, "must be to create jobs—create jobs now." That was about all that he said. With the absence of strong leadership that would have roused the public, the plan fell victim to a determined Republican filibuster led by Bob Dole. When the legislation died in April, both Democrats and Republicans tried to make political hay out of the vote.

"The Republicans think they won today, but what a hollow victory it is for them," contended Democratic senator Barbara Boxer of California. "We are in a jobs recession and we needed this bill to give employment a lift." The triumphant Dole, however, threw the president's reasoning back in his teeth. The Republicans did not want to enact programs that would increase the federal deficit, Dole said. "It's just a bump in the road for President Clinton," Dole said. "He ought to rejoice—the taxpayers won this one."

The next bump was public investment, which had been the bulwark of Clinton's recovery program. Faced with pressure from Republicans and conservatives in his own party, the president began scrapping the billions of dollars in education, job training, research, and public-works spending he had called for in his budget—transforming his bold dreams into little more than small demonstration projects. The immediate cause of the problem was the spending ceiling imposed in the 1990 budget agreement—the quid wrung by Darman from the Democrats in exchange for the quo of Bush raising taxes. Under the agreement, which turned fiscal policy into a zero-sum game, the only way that Clinton could get funding for his investment initiatives was to persuade Congress to agree to offsetting cuts in existing spending programs.

When Clinton's staff reminded him of this obstacle to his spending plans, the president was said to have exploded in rage, pounding his fist on his chair and demanding to know why he had not been sufficiently warned about the spending ceilings. This may have impressed those present, but the tantrum mainly served to illustrate Clinton's obsession with blaming others rather than himself when things went wrong. Darman's spending caps were hardly a state secret. A president who fancied himself a policy wonk and who was innocent of their significance might just as well lose his temper, since his ignorance was inexcusable.

Despite the spending ceilings, Clinton's Democratic allies sought to depict him as indignant and determined to prevail in the struggle over his public investment proposals. "The president intends to make a fight for his investments," said House budget chairman—and Andrews summit veteran—Leon Panetta. "Having said that, I think he recognizes [that] the administration faces a tough battle."

But to rid himself of the "Old Democrat" tax-and-spend stigma, Clinton had converted himself into a tax-and-cut president. It was a position without a constituency.

Liberals in Clinton's own party were willing to raise taxes, but only in return for funding government programs. They were drowned out by Republicans and conservative Democrats, who opposed any new taxes and were interested only in more spending cuts. Among this cohort, a bipartisan group of four senators, led by Oklahoma senator David L. Boren, a key figure in the Senate Finance Committee and a man Clinton presumed to be his ally, struck the most devastating blow to Clinton's plans. Boren declared his opposition to the new energy tax proposed by the president, which would add about $10 per month to the total energy bill of an average family in order to raise $40 billion. He would make up the difference by cutting spending—not the president's proposals for new investments, but spending for *existing* programs. Clinton made a great show of defending the energy tax. "It's basically a $40-billion shift away from wealthy Americans right onto people just above the poverty line, the elderly and the working poor," he said.

In fact, the White House was now in full retreat. After winning the votes needed for approval of the controversial tax in the House by promising hard-pressed Democratic legislators not to abandon the measure, the administration caved in before the Senate voted and the energy tax disappeared, to be replaced by a minuscule increase in the gasoline tax. Clinton lost not only more than two-thirds of the revenue he had hoped to raise from the energy tax to help the disadvantaged but a substantial portion of his remaining credibility.

Still, the White House pushed for approval of what was now little more than a shell of the economic plan the president had proposed. By the time the legislation neared the vote on final passage, the amount earmarked for deficit reduction had soared from $336 billion to nearly $500 billion. Much of the difference was made up by cuts in investment. Noting that the plan closely resembled the 1990 budget deal that emerged from the Andrews Summit—which turned out to be a flop—the *New York Times* complained: "Mr. Clinton promised voters more than a rehash. He pledged to end the consumption frenzy of the 1980's by turning the Federal budget toward investments in infrastructure, children, and training. But Congress is veering in a different direction. Unless it turns around, and fast, Mr. Clinton's victory in getting a deficit-reduction package through Congress will be hollow."

The *Times* turned out to be right. By the time the budget passed Congress, all that was left of the president's investment proposal amounted to a mere $50 billion, less than one-fourth of what he had promised during the campaign.

"President Clinton's Economic Plan. Victory, August 6" was the slogan emblazoned on the T-shirts passed out by the victors in the White House. "I've seen lots of presidents and lots of victories," said Lloyd Bentsen, "but this is the sweetest."

For him and other members of the economic elite, it was. Corporate profits would soar to new levels in the next twelve months, while median household incomes sank.

As for Greenspan, he was back to business as usual. In 1992, right after the election, Greenspan had promised the president that cutting the deficit would revive the economy by bringing down interest rates. Yet it would take more than a promised $500 billion in deficit reduction to rid Alan Greenspan's mind of the fear of inflation. Every time growth bubbled up, he moved in. Before the fateful election of 1994, he was to raise short-term interest rates six times, driving up mortgage rates and consumer costs and contributing to the national mood of unease that seemed to intensify with each month of the Clinton presidency.

Although the passage of the economic program was hailed as a great victory within the White House, the months of skirmishing and retreats by Clinton had left the public confused about the new president and his purposes, as the soundings taken by Clinton's own pollster, Stanley Greenberg, showed. "One of the central problems we face is the perception that there is no coherence or principle or purpose to the president's actions," Greenberg wrote. "People see him mired in the legislative process. They see him compromising."

The most obvious way for Clinton to get on track was for him to go forward with his much-heralded health-reform plan, which, next to the broad objective of reviving the economy, had been the linchpin of his campaign. Nevertheless, another objective beckoned, the North American Free Trade Agreement covering U.S. trade with Canada and Mexico, which had been conceived and nurtured by Clinton's two Republican predecessors in the White House but which his economic advisers now urged him to adopt as his own offspring. Clinton had decided to support the trade pact during his campaign, despite the bitter opposition of the AFL-CIO and his own occasional bursts of economic nationalist rhetoric, as a way of countering Republican criticism that as a candidate whose sole experience had been limited to the governorship of Arkansas, he had no interest in international affairs.

For a president who needed to assemble a new coalition to succeed in office, NAFTA was a political nightmare. It pitted labor against business, farmers against industry, region against region. Its backers claimed that the agreement, by eliminating tariffs on virtually all goods traded between the United States, Mexico, and Canada, would create hundreds of thousands of jobs for Americans. But its foes warned that it would cost at least as many jobs when manufacturers relocated plants south of the border, where cheap labor could make goods for duty-free export to the United States.

The big winners would be manufacturers that rely on higher-skilled labor that is hard to match in Mexico. By bringing down tariffs on U.S.-made goods, NAFTA would open new markets for their goods. The losers would be concentrated among low-skilled industries, where jobs had already been disappearing due to a combination of automation and cheap foreign labor. The Amalgamated Clothing and Textile Workers Union, for example, predicted that 500,000 U.S. jobs would disappear over the next five years if the trade pact was enacted. California and other states along the U.S.-Mexican border expected to profit handsomely from the expanding Mexican market. By contrast, the smokestack industries of the Northeast and Midwest and their workers would take it on the chin.

In view of these cross-pressures, Clinton hesitated. Some among his advisers urged him to avoid making a major effort for NAFTA, arguing that his time would be better spent promoting health reform, which had already been overly delayed. Besides, others argued, why get into a fight with organized labor—still the most powerful single force within the Democratic party.

That was just the point, insisted Treasury Secretary Bentsen, who led the fight for NAFTA within the cabinet. Using the same perverse logic that had led Clinton to attack Sister Souljah during the campaign to separate himself from Jesse Jackson, Bentsen contended that it was important for Clinton to show his political courage by battling the AFL-CIO. Besides, he claimed that America's role as a world leader was at stake, an argument that, even though it had lost much of its force since the end of the Cold War, Bentsen shrewdly calculated would nevertheless appeal to a president uncertain of his ground on foreign affairs.

Advice to push ahead on NAFTA also came from David Gergen, the veteran of three previous Republican presidencies, whom Clinton, in a startling admission of his administration's early unsteadiness, had recruited from the world of journalism and given an influential role in his White House that May. As communications director for Republican Ronald Reagan, Gergen had helped to promote the very same economic policies that Democrat Clinton had vowed to reverse when he campaigned for the White House. Yet this did not seem to matter to Clinton as much as Gergen's supposed ability to help steady his presidency after its first wobbly months in power, a problem that Gergen, among others, had pointed out. "He's not only gone off track, he's going around in circles," he had said of his boss-to-be in an interview only two weeks before his appointment.

Gergen was one of the new breed of political technicians prized more for their manipulative skills than for their substantive beliefs, people who made their living and their reputations on the premise that perception mattered more than substance—at least in the short term. Thus, Gergen was remembered and praised most not for any policy initiative he had fostered but rather for the cunning suggestion that Reagan take maximum advantage of the goodwill toward him that followed the abortive attempt on his life by making his first post-assassination-attempt appearance a speech to a joint session of Congress.

Both Gergen and Clinton understood that the first requirement for successful manipulation of public opinion for political advantage is to claim total disinterest in politics. "The message here is we are rising above politics," Clinton declared in announcing that Gergen would take the position of counselor to the president. Gergen himself struck the same note. "The country really wants people in this city to get together and stop all this savage partisanship," he said.

Gergen immediately demonstrated that his commitment to tactics and superficiality was as strong as ever. His first action in his new job was to reverse the ill-conceived order to close the door linking the press briefing room with the rest of the White House. The change did little to help the basic problems of Clinton's presidency, but it predictably got Gergen himself a flood of favorable publicity from grateful journalists.

Pitching in to help Bentsen in his fight for NAFTA, Gergen took Thomas F. (Mack) McLarty (the former Clinton boyhood chum, who before long would be replaced as White House chief of staff by Leon Panetta) to see Gergen's old boss, Richard Nixon, another NAFTA enthusiast. Nixon contended that Clinton should fight for the treaty, even at the risk of defeat. "He must take an issue and lose," Nixon advised. "Losing sometimes means a win," he added, a maxim he had evidently not absorbed until after his departure from the presidency.

Once committed to the NAFTA cause, Clinton went all out. To offset the opposition, Clinton arranged for former presidents Ford, Bush, and Carter to join him at the White House in a bipartisan show of support for the agreement and dispatched Gore to tackle NAFTA foe Ross Perot in a televised debate. Gore was shrewd enough to allow Perot to self-destruct. Meanwhile, the White House mounted a massive lobbying effort that contrasted sharply—as Jesse Jackson later acidly pointed out—with the futile efforts made on behalf of the economic stimulus. And so by late November, Clinton had another victory to celebrate, but one for which he had paid a price in time and energy that could have been used for his health-care reform. If losing, as Nixon had suggested, could produce a victory, Clinton now had to face the danger that his victory in NAFTA could lead to defeat on health care.

Given the political and economic setting, the adoption of major health-care reform should have been a certainty. The need was evident. More than twenty years earlier in 1970, *Business Week* called health care a $60-billion-a-year crisis. By the time Clinton arrived in the White House, the cost was over $800 billion a year, and the share of the nation's gross domestic product given over to health care had nearly doubled to over 13 percent. Moreover, more than 38 million Americans, about 17 percent of the population under age sixty-five, had no coverage—and another 40 million were underinsured. Furthermore, conditions continued to worsen. Midway through Clinton's first year in the White House, a poll showed that for nearly one-half of working Americans, health-care coverage had been cut back or costs had been raised in the past two years, and in the past year alone, more than 1 million American families, many of them members of the much-cherished middle class, had lost their insurance.

Public support for reform was on the rise. In George Bush's early years in the White House, polls showed that two-thirds of Americans supported national health insurance. Bush ignored the issue, as he did nearly every other domestic concern. And this was to cost him politically in the special Senate election in Pennsylvania in 1991 when Democrat Harris Wofford won a stunning upset largely by pledging to support national health insurance. To dramatize the need, Wofford, who had been appointed to fill the vacancy left by the death of Republican John Heinz, proposed legislation to deny himself and his fellow lawmakers the free medical care they were receiving from the government until they enacted some form of national health insurance.

In the wake of Wofford's triumph, Democratic candidates for the presidency, Clinton among them, fell all over themselves trying to come up with the most appealing plan. Even Bush offered something. Yet a poll taken as the 1992 general election campaign was getting under way in earnest showed that by a margin of better than two to one, voters thought Clinton would do a better job than Bush of providing affordable coverage.

Right after Clinton's election, Republicans jumped on the reform bandwagon. GOP senator John Chafee of Rhode Island introduced legislation to provide universal coverage through a system of mandates on individuals to buy insurance. Even such traditionally unyielding foes of anything that smacked of "socialized medicine," such as the American Medical Association and the Health Insurance Association of America, backed plans that aimed at universal coverage through requiring employers to insure their workers. Backing for employer mandates also came from the U.S. Chamber of Commerce, along with many of its most important corporate members.

No wonder the architects of the White House scheme were euphoric when the president at long last unveiled his plan on September 23, 1993, in a speech to both houses of Congress. "This health-care system of ours is badly broken and it is time to fix it," Clinton said. A reformed system, he contended, should be more secure, simpler for patients and doctors, less expensive, but structured to preserve freedom of choice and quality of care. Displaying a small, credit-card-sized "health-care security card" emblazoned with the presidential seal, Clinton told his audience that under his plan all Americans would be guaranteed comprehensive health benefits. "Let us agree on this," Clinton said. "Before this Congress finishes its work next year, you will pass, and I will sign, legislation to guarantee this security to every citizen of this country."

To accomplish his two major goals—health coverage for all Americans, while at the same time restraining the rapid escalation of health-care costs—Clinton proposed mandating employers to provide coverage to all their workers. This would establish a network of regional health-care alliances, essentially huge purchasing cooperatives, that would negotiate with doctors, hospitals, and other health-care providers to set fees and restrain spending.

The speech was a smash hit. The next day, pollster Greenberg let the White House know that about two-thirds of the public approved of what the president said he wanted to do. By December, polls showed Clinton's plan with a seventeen-point edge over alternative proposals. And press commentary was widely favorable.

Yet even at this moment of apparent triumph, the seeds of defeat had already been sown. The main reason for failure was the president. National health insurance was for him an issue of convenience, not a matter of conviction. He did not *really* believe the federal government should be involved in health reform—as he had made plain at the governors' conference in Seattle only a few weeks before he announced his presidential candidacy. Forced by the political dynamics of the campaign for the nomination to endorse the idea, he was the last of the major candidates to propound a plan, and his was notably lacking in specifics.

Once in office, health-care reform became a pawn in his tangled relationship with Hillary Rodham Clinton. Having helped to salvage her husband's presidential candidacy by her loyal defense of him in the midst of scandal, she now claimed as her reward the leadership of the health-reform drive. It was an unprecedented grant of power to a First Lady, who, having been neither elected by the voters nor confirmed by the Congress, was accountable to no one, not necessarily even her husband. Moreover, her decision to conduct the crucial initial deliberations by her task force in absolute secrecy antagonized friend and foe alike, forfeited a badly needed opportunity to build public support, and instead fostered suspicions about her motives and purposes.

During the campaign, Clinton had promised a plan by the first 100 days of his presidency. This was postponed first until after the economic proposal, then until after the vote on NAFTA. The plan's potential allies, cut off from the White House by a shield of secrecy, began to squabble among themselves and lose interest. The foes of reform, however, gathered strength, bolstered by other signs of Clinton's political weakness and lack of resolve, including the burgeoning scandal over Whitewater.

And in the fall of 1993, when the time came for Clinton finally to unveil his plan to the public, he chose the most conservative of the three major approaches. Passed up were the single-payer system, which would have been financed by payroll taxes, and the "play or pay" approach, which would have required all employers to either provide health insurance for their workers or help subsidize government coverage of the uninsured. Instead, in another effort to establish his identity as a New Democrat, the president settled on a version of managed competition, essentially a market-oriented reform stressing the preservation of the existing system.

Designed to placate the foes of national health insurance, Clinton's proposal offered little to generate enthusiasm from supporters of the idea. An internal White House memo written late in December 1993 noted that "the complexity of our bill and the huge levels of misinformation and misunderstanding about it" were retarding efforts by unions and other potential backers to get their members behind the legislation. The intricate workings of the reformed system—epitomized by the arrangement for providing insurance through a network of regional health-care alliances—resulted from Clinton's determination to conceal as much as possible the fact that this was indeed a government program. The emphasis on regulation, as a substitute for direct government action, added to the complexities of the plan.

Moreover, these attempts at camouflage only succeeded in irritating potential allies without fooling the sworn enemies of health reform. Texas senator Phil Gramm, who sought to make his opposition to Clinton's proposal the foundation of his campaign for the Republican presidential nomination, never tired of repeating the charge that Clinton wanted to "remake the world's greatest health-care system into the image of the post office." And in a memorable and telling nationally televised critique of the president's plan, Senator Dole displayed a series of charts resembling Rube Goldberg cartoons, to demonstrate its cumbersomeness.

The First Lady later claimed that the health-reform drive crashed against a wall of public cynicism. "There is so much skepticism, even cynicism, about the political process," she said, that "huge amounts of money spent to convey an intense, negative message has a very powerful impact."

Polling data demonstrate the fallacy of that rationalization. Americans do not really spend a lot of time thinking about government in the abstract. To be sure, if asked whether they trust government or not, many will say no. Still, their attitude toward concrete programs is very different. The wave of cynicism about government has done little to erode public support for such institutions as Medicare, Social Security, or the armed forces—all of which the vast majority of citizens regard as necessary to their lives and to the country's welfare. Clinton had the opportunity, the resources, and the responsibility not to persuade voters to think better about government but rather to make them understand that effective health reform depended on a major role for government and that the net result would change their lives for the better. By shirking that obligation, he helped his enemies destroy the program.

Clinton himself delivered the fatal blow in an episode that underlined the ambiguity that had undermined the chances for reform all along. Ever since he had introduced his plan, Clinton had made clear that two aspects were central to his vision of reform: universal coverage, in which he had pledged before a national television audience to veto any health reform that did not provide it, and employer mandates. But speaking at the annual conference of the nation's governors in Boston in late July 1994, Clinton abruptly retreated from both demands, agreeing to accept legislation that got "somewhere in the ballpark" of universal coverage and did not call for employer mandates, "if we knew that we were moving toward full coverage."

Clinton's words stunned his allies in Congress, where House and Senate leaders were poised at an extraordinarily delicate moment in their efforts to put together legislation that retained the controversial employer mandate along with universal coverage.

In a panic, the White House sought to contend that the president had not really changed his position. That reassurance did not comfort Clinton's supporters on the Hill, who remembered other Clinton retreats in the face of political difficulty—notably on the economic program the year before— and they privately conceded the doom of their efforts.

The impact of Clinton's latest waffle was evident not only from the reaction of his supporters but also from his foes, as I found out when I went to Los Angeles to cover a meeting of the Republican National Committee the weekend after Clinton's speech. For most of the health-care debate, the Republicans had been persuaded that they could not afford the political price of blocking reform. Many of their leaders felt obliged either to offer their own plans or to work toward a compromise with Clinton. Now the president's mishandling of the issue, capped by his speech to the governors, had changed their view. The committee members cheered when former defense secretary Dick Cheney, a 1996 presidential hopeful, declared: "There is absolutely no reason why we have to have a [health] package passed by November." At the same time, members from thirteen states in the GOP's Southern region, stretching from Florida to Texas, unanimously adopted a resolution calling for a delay in health-care legislation then pending in Congress until after the November elections.

Bob Dole captured the new Republican mood, touting his own reform proposal, which offered fewer benefits at lower cost than Democratic-backed alternatives. Significantly, though, he also sounded willing to consider waiting until next year. "We don't have to do it all this year," he said in his talk to committee members. "We don't have to do any of it this year. You know, Congress meets every year," he added.

When, in September, Senate Democratic leader Mitchell announced the death of health reform, the impact extended beyond that issue itself. It was another measure of Clinton's failure to keep faith with the middle-class constituency he had sought to make his own. One of the first acts of his presidency had been to renege on his pledge of a tax cut for the middle class. His economic program was mainly designed to aid the owners and investors of business rather than middle-class wage-earning families, which wound up paying a tax increase on gasoline, along with a tax hike on Social Security benefits for the better-off among them, while their wages continued to stagnate.

National health reform had been another big boon Clinton promised to the middle class. It would assure families of protection even if they lost their jobs. And it would keep premiums from getting out of sight. None of this happened. Clinton failed to provide even the most minimal improvements, such as portability of insurance from one job to another and a guarantee of coverage for previously existing conditions. All this represented a failure on both policy and substantive levels.

Clinton had broken faith with the middle class in another area, too—and that was character. The most troublesome questions about his character stemmed from the Whitewater controversy. The Clintons had managed to fend off queries about their 1978 investment in a planned resort development in the Ozarks during the campaign. By the fall of 1993, though, Whitewater was back in the news. The Resolution Trust Corporation (RTC), which for years had been sorting out the causes and consequences of the failure of Little Rock's Madison Guaranty Savings and Loan, asked the Justice Department for a criminal investigation into whether Madison funds were illegally diverted to pay the personal and political debts of politicians, among them Arkansas's former governor Bill Clinton. Clinton insisted both he and the First Lady "did nothing improper," but the charges soon spread to include allegations that the White House and administration officials had interfered with the RTC investigation, and the First Lady became an important focus of the controversy because of her role as counsel to Madison Guaranty and because of investments she had made. Republicans in Congress pressed for hearings, and the Justice Department appointed an independent counsel to investigate. Although all this was enormously complicated, two concerns emerged from the finagling and confusion—whether Whitewater had been a means for Clinton to use his position as governor to advance the private financial interests of himself and his wife and whether he had sought to cover up whatever he had done since he became president.

The president's difficulties over Whitewater were compounded in December 1993 by new allegations of womanizing, which revived recollections of the Gennifer Flowers case that had besmirched his candidacy in New Hampshire. According to the fresh charges, published in the magazine *Spectator* and the *Los Angeles Times*, during his tenure as governor of Arkansas, Clinton had used state troopers to act as intermediaries to arrange and conceal extramarital sexual liaisons. The White House denied the stories. Two months later, though, a former state employee named Paula Corbin Jones, claiming that she wanted to restore her "good reputation," charged that then governor Clinton made sexual advances toward her in his hotel room during a 1991 conference in Little Rock, and she filed suit against the president for sexual harassment. Clinton's lawyers claimed that as a sitting president, he could not be sued—an issue that went to the Supreme Court for resolution.

Clinton's allies denounced reckless journalists and sore-loser Republicans for stirring the scandal pot. "Republicans have lost some of their old reliable issues," such as welfare and crime, Democratic National chairman David Wilhelm told me. "So, in order to slow the president down and stop the progress, they've latched on to Whitewater." Yet underlying these allegations was a more fundamental political struggle over character, values, and the allegiance of the middle class. It was a struggle Clinton himself had initiated in the campaign and continued in his presidency. At nearly every opportunity, the president presented himself as the champion of middle-class people "who play by the rules," a phrase right out of his pollster's lexicon. As a self-proclaimed "different kind of Democrat," he frequently used religious assemblages as forums, stressed religious themes, and deplored how far national life had strayed from the influence of the Almighty. "I think God wants us to sit down and talk to one another and see what values we share and see how we can put them inside the millions and millions of Americans who are living in chaos," Clinton said in a speech to fellow Yale Law School alumni in the first autumn of his presidency.

On occasion, Clinton seemed blatantly to contradict himself with his own words. Addressing inner-city junior high school students in Washington, he made a moving plea for sexual restraint and family values, stressing that sex is not "sport" but a "solemn responsibility." Nevertheless, five days later, addressing auto workers in Shreveport, Louisiana, Clinton recalled owning a pickup truck that he carpeted with Astroturf in the bed. Amid laughter from the audience, Clinton added: "You don't want to know why, but I did." Ten days after that, he tried to explain away the prurient implication of that remark. "I carried my luggage back there. It wasn't for what everybody thought it was for when I made the comment, I can tell you that."

Clinton's stress on morality was part of a well-calculated strategy. "What we tried to do and what Clinton tried to do with us was articulate values which were the underpinning of a public agenda," Al From, head of the Democratic Leadership Council, told me. "I think he's changed the agenda dramatically in the way he's conducted his office. I'm not going to talk about his personal conduct."

Whether From wanted to talk about it or not, it was clear that Clinton's rhetorical allegiance to values and character had been buried under the allegations of improper financial gains from the Whitewater real estate investment and the accusations of sexual misconduct. Equally troublesome to the Clintons' image was Hillary Clinton's $90,000-plus earnings on her $1,000 investment in the commodities markets, a profit that hardly squared with the president's regular denunciation during the campaign of "cheating and cutting corners the way Republicans and their friends do."

Looking ahead to the 1994 elections, Republican strategist William Kristol told me: "If Clinton can convince people he is doing the right thing in health care and other areas, I think that would outweigh a fair amount of character flaws. But to do that, a president needs trust, because you can never prove your programs will work right away, and Clinton does not have anything like that trust."

7

The Crybaby

Starting early in Clinton's second year in the White House, one day every week a dozen or so of his political advisers, briefing books and notes in hand, trooped to a meeting room hidden away in the White House basement. There they spent the better part of two hours planning Clinton's role in the November midterm elections. Their leader was Clinton's deputy chief of staff and chief troubleshooter, Harold Ickes, whose new role as campaign overseer drained time away from his efforts to muster support for Clinton's health-care reform and to contain damage from the Whitewater affair. His assignment testified to the recognition by President Clinton, shared by the Republican high command, that the midterm balloting would go a long way toward defining the political future.

Ickes and his crew faced a sobering task. From the beginning, the 1994 midterm election loomed as an uphill march for Democrats and a golden opportunity for Republicans. History was the most evident factor working against the Democrats and in favor of the GOP. Not since 1934, when a grateful electorate rewarded Franklin D. Roosevelt and his Democrats for checking the ravages of the Great Depression, has the party controlling the White House failed to lose ground in a midterm election. Given Bill Clinton's fitful start in the White House, no one supposed that his administration would be an exception to that rule.

Indeed, to the contrary, the Democrats now feared that their victory in the presidential election would be their undoing in the midterm. Their well-founded anxiety reflected the ultimate triumph of Madison's scheme of restraint through countervailing ambitions. His design had produced the gridlock that marked the government for the twelve years when Republican presidents Reagan and Bush had been pitted against the Democratic majorities in the House, and half the time in the Senate, too. This stalemate had not only frustrated the electorate but further debilitated and fractured the parties, undermining their ability to govern even when one or the other controlled both the legislative and executive branches.

The Democratic capture of the White House in 1992 meant that the 1994 campaign was the first midterm election since 1978 in which either party had full responsibility for both the presidency and the Congress. And this shift of power in the presidency, instead of providing the party with the opportunity it had long sought to revitalize itself, was turning into a terrible burden. For the first time since 1980, Democrats had nobody but themselves to blame for the country's problems, a reality the Republicans sought to exploit to the fullest. "With all the talk by the president about the end of gridlock, he's made it clear to the American people that the Democrats are in charge of the White House and the Congress," said New York representative Bill Paxon, chairman of the House Republican Campaign Committee, who had been given the seemingly hopeless task of transforming the long-term Republican minority in the House into a majority: "And when the public is not happy with the job they are doing." Despite the much-heralded pairing of a Democratic president with a Democratic-controlled Congress, three out of five respondents interviewed by pollster Lou Harris at the end of Clinton's first year believed that legislative gridlock still existed in the capital. While acknowledging the problem, Clinton's advisers struggled to put the best face on the Democratic predicament. "Like it or not, we have responsibility for government," Stanley B. Greenberg, Clinton's chief pollster, told party leaders gathered in Albuquerque in June of Clinton's first year in office. "It would be easier to be outside, easier not to take responsibility, easier not to be held accountable. I think what we will find, hopefully, is that taking responsibility is a good message."

In reality, that was wishful thinking in the face of the Democratic failure to define a position on the economy that would gain the support of a clear-cut majority of the middle class. Ohio party chairman Harry Meshel blamed both Clinton and the party that had elected him for the failure to build public backing for Clinton's program. "We are not showing the strength of the issues that we are trying to promote," he told me. When I asked who was to blame, he said: "I'd like to see everyone share in that responsibility. That means the White House and the national committee and us at the state level. It's everybody's job." Meshel conceded that for all the talk of a unified effort, Clinton's problems had been aggravated by opposition from within his own party on Capitol Hill. "We have to understand that members of the House and Senate are still going to fight to protect their own interests in their own districts," Meshel said. "Everyone is worried about preserving what they've got."

In the final roll-call votes on the president's economic program in the House and Senate, Democrats had presented a united front. By that time, though, various factions of rebellious lawmakers in Clinton's own party had nibbled away at the program, blunting its effectiveness, confusing the public, and demonstrating that the maxim for Capitol Hill propounded by Joe Jacobs (and recalled by Lloyd Cutler during the Carter presidency) still prevailed: "It's every man for theirself."

Moreover, these retreats in the face of congressional opposition came on top of the decision made by the president himself, on the advice of his economic advisers, to make the main thrust of his economic program deficit reduction rather than the direct measures to invigorate the economy that he had promised in the campaign.

Mindful of poll results that showed public support for the president on the decline, Democrats were fearful of the future. "Wait until the fourth quarter of this year," Tom O'Donnell, chief of staff to House Democratic leader Gephardt, told me that summer. "If Clinton's numbers stay where they are now, the members up here will be nervous."

As the year wore on, the Democratic Congress made it possible for Clinton to claim some accomplishments. In addition to enacting his economic plan and approving NAFTA, Congress adopted the Brady Bill, the first major gun-control law since 1981; breathed new life into the tradition of volunteerism by establishing a modest national service program; and reenacted the family-leave bill that the Democrats had passed under Bush only to have him veto it. Climaxing a five-year struggle, legislators also approved the so-called motor-voter bill, which required states to provide eligible citizens the chance to register to vote when they renewed their driver's license.

Still, none of these measures addressed the fundamental discontent that had gripped the public and had set the tone for the 1994 campaign. The president's main problem was his failure to deal effectively with the economic grievances that had paved his way to the White House.

Despite indicators that suggested a relatively strong recovery from the recession that had contributed to President Bush's defeat, wages, benefits, and living standards for the average worker continued to decline. During Clinton's first full year in the White House, median family income fell to an inflation-adjusted 1 percent. That left median household income stuck at its lowest level in a decade, more than 7 percent below its 1989 peak. The Democrats liked to boast that the economic revival had created new jobs, but a good portion of them were only temporary, part-time, or low-paying. Moreover, the lion's share of the rewards the economy provided were going to a relatively narrow segment of the electorate—highly educated, affluent households—thereby widening the already broad economic gulfs between different groups of Americans, which Clinton had pledged to bridge during his campaign against Bush. In addition, the corporate cutbacks and layoffs that had been the hallmark of the early 1990s left deep scars on the psyche of average workers, making them far more fearful of the future and far less willing to pressure their employers for higher salaries and benefits.

"There is a squeeze on American workers today," Alan Sinai, chief economist at Lehman Brothers Global Economics in New York, said. "Productivity gains and low inflation are coming on the backs of American workers. We've got what looks like the healthiest economy in decades, but that doesn't sound good if you are working two or three jobs without any benefits, and your wife is working, and you're just keeping even with where you used to be, and you don't have much leisure time or time for your family."

Voters frustrated by economic stagnation blamed not only Clinton but also the way the government in general ran the country. "Clinton has done some good things, but things are just not as good as they should be," complained Charles Daniel, a fifty-year-old mechanical supervisor for a construction company in Liberty, Texas, interviewed after he responded to a *Los Angeles Times* poll. "We're still at the same pace of life that we've been at for the last three years. People are still out of work, and companies are still moving overseas."

"Clinton? I don't care for him at all. I don't think he's doing anything," said Beryl Stevenson, a retiree in Madison, New Jersey. "I really don't think things are getting any better. Prices keep going up, and incomes certainly are not."

Foreign policy was causing trouble for Clinton, too. The basic criticism resembled the complaints about his domestic policy: Abroad, as at home, the president lacked a sense of conviction about how he should lead the country. In domestic policy, this haziness caused him to compromise and temporize. But in foreign policy, it led him to reverse Teddy Roosevelt's famous dictum by speaking loudly but carrying a small stick, a pattern he followed from Bosnia to North Korea, from Haiti to the People's Republic of China. His supporters blamed his difficulties on the turbulent state of post–Cold War diplomacy, which had forced him to sail on uncharted seas. Whereas some Americans urged him to steer clear of foreign crises, others demanded stronger action. "You're damned if you do and damned if you don't," Democratic National Committee chairman David Wilhelm argued. "These are tough and difficult situations."

This, of course, is precisely the challenge of presidential leadership. Clinton's critics, some of them in his own party, argued that he was making the job more difficult with his inconsistencies. "You can't go Chinese menu week by week on foreign policy and expect the American people to support you," said Hodding Carter III, who was spokesman for the State Department during the Carter administration.

Republicans leaped to the attack. Gingrich scoffed at Clinton's initiative for dealing with the potential flood of refugees from Haiti by establishing seaborne processing centers. "There is a level of sloppiness about this administration that is kind of scary," he said. When Clinton held a ninety-minute televised press conference to demonstrate his grasp of foreign affairs, Bob Dole responded with mockery: "You shouldn't have to have a television show with someone scripting the answers to demonstrate what you know about leadership," Dole declared.

Democrats were disturbed, too, not only by the implications of Clinton's zigging and zagging on the U.S. position in the world but also by what that inconsistency suggested about Clinton's overall capacity for leadership. "My concern is that there are some people who would say he can't stand up to people on the world scene and be strong because he's not a strong person," Michael McCurry, then State Department spokesman, soon to go over to the White House to become Clinton's press secretary, told me in early 1994. "All this other stuff ain't going to be a political liability. But the cumulative impression that he lacks the discipline to be a world leader goes to the threshold question about his presidency."

Weighed down by his uneven performance at home and abroad, Clinton's approval rating in public opinion polls slumped, rarely rising over 50 percent. In November, on the anniversary of his election, his rating in a Washington Post–ABC News poll was at only 49 percent, lower than any of his post–World War II predecessors in the White House at that point in their tenure, except for Ronald Reagan, who had been caught in the onset of the 1982 recession. Clinton's average approval scores during his first year in office were lower for that period than for any chief executive—except for the unelected Gerald Ford—since regular presidential polling began in the days of Franklin Roosevelt.

The discontent extended beyond Clinton. A *Los Angeles Times* poll in December 1993 showed that only one in ten Americans had much confidence in Congress—less than one-half the number who had felt that way in April 1991. A Gallup poll released on February 23, 1994, showed that only one in five believed they could trust the federal government all or some of the time—little more than one-half the percentage of citizens who told pollsters they felt they could trust the government in the midst of the Watergate scandal in 1974. Most periods of low confidence have been triggered by war or a steep rise in inflation or unemployment. What puzzled Clinton's advisers about the country's indigo mood was that the nation was at peace, with most economic indicators pointing upward. They overlooked the fact that for more than a decade, average families had been trapped on an economic treadmill, unable to improve their lot or assure the future for their children. The cumulative impact of this condition was to sour the public's view of the entire political system.

Underlying this negativism, a crazy quilt of conflicting attitudes made it impossible to assemble a majority coalition in support of any cause except to throw the rascals out—the rascals being whoever happened to hold power. Increasing demands for government to solve problems from crime to health care clashed with sharp disagreement over which problems should take priority and with widespread skepticism about government's ability to solve anything. "The poor are dissatisfied because government is helping the rich, and the rich are unhappy because government is raising their taxes but doing nothing about crime," UCLA political scientist John Petrocik pointed out. "For different reasons you can find a constituency of dissatisfaction almost everywhere."

This mood created fertile ground for such reforms as constitutional amendments requiring the balanced budget and term limits, both backed by the middle-class supporters of Ross Perot's presidential candidacy. Because of their comfortable economic circumstances, they viewed the government not as a provider of benefits but as a threat to their well-being. Supporters of the balanced-budget amendment such as Dan Palmer, California director of United We Stand America, the political organization founded by Perot, claimed that the key to public discontent was a growing awareness of chronic overspending by government. "People are concerned that the government lacks integrity," Palmer said, "that it lives by rules different from the rules others of us live by. We all manage to live within our means and manage not to spend our children's future."

Backers of term-limits proposals argued that the way to restore public confidence was to break the power of long-entrenched incumbents and curb the influence of special interests by forcing more frequent turnovers in office. "The way things work now," said Russ Verney, a national strategist for United We Stand, "you get a congressman sitting on a powerful committee with special interest money who runs against a well-meaning challenger and crushes him. The people who go to Washington aren't bad to begin with, but they get stuck in a process that makes them insiders instead of reformers."

Another measure of public discontent—and the president's weakness—was a series of Republican victories that began even before Clinton officially took office. GOP challenger Paul Coverdell defeated incumbent Democrat senator Wyche Fowler in a special runoff election in Georgia two weeks after the vote that swept Clinton into power. That June, Texas Republican Kay Bailey Hutchison overwhelmed Democratic senator Bob Krueger—who had been appointed to fill the vacancy left by Lloyd Bentsen—by running against Clinton's economic program.

Meanwhile, the nation's two biggest urban centers, long the symbol of Democratic power, fell under GOP control with the election of wealthy businessman Richard Riordan in Los Angeles and the victory of former U.S. attorney Rudolph W. Giuliani in New York. The New York outcome was a particularly ill omen for Democrats dependent for their success on interracial support, because whites, who made up 55 percent of the city's population, provided 85 percent of Giuliani's vote. The tide also turned against the Democrats in competition for the only two governorships at stake that year. In

New Jersey, Republican Christine Todd Whitman ousted James Florio, who had brought on his doom by pushing through a big tax increase, thus reinforcing the impression of Democrats as taxers and spenders, which Clinton and many congressional Democrats has been struggling to live down. And in Virginia, voters demonstrated their weariness with Democratic rule by electing former Republican Congressman George F. Allen instead of Democratic attorney general Mary Sue Terry, who would have been the state's fourth consecutive Democratic governor since 1981.

The trend continued in 1994 when, in a May special election, Democrats lost a Kentucky House seat they had held for 129 years, an outcome that underlined the powerful political considerations that reinforced the constitutional strictures separating the legislature and the executive, even when both were under the control of the same party. During the twelve years of the Ronald Reagan–George Bush presidencies, Democratic candidates could tailor their campaigns to suit local tastes with minimal concern about the national party. Now they had to answer for Clinton's policies, too, and this could be a heavy burden, especially in the South and other conservative areas where neither the president nor his policies were popular.

The victorious Republican Ron Lewis, a minister and owner of a fundamentalist bookstore, who received 55 percent of the vote to 45 percent for Democrat Joe Prather, centered his campaign on linking Prather to Clinton, even running a commercial that depicted Clinton's face blending into Prather's. In a district Bush carried in 1992, Prather concluded that he should keep his distance from Clinton and from the national party, refusing financial support or any other type of help. After the election, Democratic National Committee chairman David Wilhelm denounced Prather for failing to stick with Clinton. "The lesson here is that Democrats should run as Democrats," Wilhelm said.

But looking ahead to the November elections, other Democrats drew a different conclusion, pointing out that far from being an asset in the South, the former Arkansas governor had made himself into a liability. Southerners now felt betrayed by what they viewed as Clinton's liberal policies, such as his tax increase and his support for gays in the military. Character played a part, too. "A lot of Southern whites look at Clinton and they think he isn't being straight with them," said Merle Black of Emory University, an authority on the politics of the South. "They don't think he has the kind of moral stature they expect in a president." "There's no doubt about it that in parts of the South it's just very hard right now to run stride for stride with Clinton," said Saul Shorr, a Democratic consultant for half a dozen Democratic House candidates in the South. "It's going to be a tough year for Democrats."

The bleak public mood had a palpable effect on the midterm campaign from the very start. One of the incongruities of the separated American political system is the significant impact on the election of a host of idiosyncratic factors that have more to do with the peculiar mechanics of electing the Congress than with broad questions of public policy. The principal peculiarity is, of course, that House and Senate candidates run every two and six years, respectively, in contests that only occasionally coincide with presidential reelections.

As recently as two years earlier, Republicans had no chance of winning a large batch of House seats, simply because they did not field candidates for them. This was most often true in the South, where in many districts the Democrats seemed to hold an unassailable advantage. In contrast, Democrats contested nearly every race. Thus, Republicans left sixty-one Democratic seats unchallenged in 1988, forty-six in 1990, and seventeen in 1992. But that picture changed dramatically in 1994 as the onetime Democratic advantage in the South disappeared—despite or, more accurately, because of their Southern president. Republicans left only a handful of seats unchallenged and actually filed more candidates for the House than the Democrats did.

As for the Democrats, they worried not only about a shortage of strong challengers but about a disturbing tendency by their incumbents to call it a day, thereby adding to Democratic vulnerabilities. In the Senate, which the Democrats controlled with fifty-six seats to forty-four for the Republicans, six Democratic members of the class of 1994 decided to retire, against only three Republicans. This compounded the numerical disadvantage the Democrats faced in having to defend twenty-two seats against only thirteen for the Republicans.

Democrats were similarly handicapped in the contest for the House of Representatives, in which they had held nearly eighty more seats than the Republicans until the retirement of twenty Democratic incumbents, compared with only seven Republican retirements. The net result of the retirements and departures for other reasons by House members was to leave the Democrats with thirty-one open seats to defend, against only twenty-one for the Republicans.

Reapportionment exacerbated the Democratic problems in the House, contributing to the decisions by some of their members to retire. Moreover, unlike past reapportionments, which Democratic legislators and governors had usually shaped to their partisan advantage, the new district lines created after the 1990 census were more often drawn impartially by courts, creating genuinely competitive districts, thus making it harder than in the past for incumbents to retain their seats.

These mechanical factors would play a large part in determining the success or failure of the broad strategic blueprints of the two parties. Determined to make the most of Clinton's low standing in the polls and the sour public mood, Republicans sought to cast the election as a referendum on the party in power. For their part, the Democrats, relying on the axiom that all politics is local, tried to wage each campaign separately, focusing on the strengths and accomplishments of their individual candidates.

When Representative Louise Slaughter's Republican challenger assailed her as a tax-and-spend liberal, she changed the subject. Instead of discussing national issues, she pointed to the rewards that she had helped her constituents in Rochester, New York, win from Washington: an airport expansion, a new high-tech research facility, and harbor improvements to protect against the ravages of Lake Ontario. "Nationally, there's an anti-incumbent mood, and a mood against President Clinton," Slaughter's media consultant Joe Trippi explained. "If you get enmeshed in that, you lose. But if you can get voters to focus on what you as a member of Congress have done for local people, you have a good chance of winning."

These were the tactics the Democrats had followed during twelve years of Republican presidencies in maintaining their hold on Congress, but Clinton's presence in the White House, and his unpopularity, made the Democratic task far more difficult. As their candidates tried to distance themselves from the president and his sagging poll ratings, Republican candidates sought ways to link them to the president. "Republicans are telling voters these Democrats are not independent," said pollster Bill McInturff, whose firm counsels some sixty GOP House and Senate candidates. "Every time their votes were needed, they voted for the president."

Even Democratic challengers found it hard to totally separate themselves from the president. "I think you are going to run into problems if you pretend you don't know the man," David Nagle, a Democratic congressional challenger in Waterloo, Iowa, told me. "I think the proper thing to say is: 'I'm going to work with the president when I agree with him.' But you're better off talking about your solutions to problems than his solutions."

Because of the nature of their office, which obliges them to deal more with national than with local issues, Democratic Senate candidates had a harder time putting distance between themselves and the president than did House candidates. But most tried, anyway. In their commercials, Democratic Senate candidates, even incumbents, commonly depicted the federal government as a menacing force that needed to be wrestled to the ground, while stressing their local roots and loyalties. "You'll see me fighting for Utah," Pat Shea, Democratic challenger in Utah, promised. "Working hard for Virginia" is the way incumbent Chuck Robb described himself to Old Dominion voters, while incumbent Jeff Bingaman depicted himself as "standing up for New Mexico." In Montana, challenger Jack Mudd claimed as a prime credential the fact that "he is not a politician" and "he has never held office." I had to view fifty commercials before I could find even one mention of Clinton's name.

Republican Senate challengers showed no such reluctance about using the president's name. In New Mexico, an ad for Colin McMillan, the GOP chal-

lenger running against Senator Jeff Bingaman, depicted Clinton making his
since-broken promise not to raise taxes on the middle class. Tennessee Republican Bill Frist, running against Jim Sasser, leaned heavily on an ad that
showed the visages of Clinton, Massachusetts senator Edward M. Kennedy,
indicted Illinois Democratic representative Daniel J. Rostenkowski, along
with Sasser's, carved on Mount Rushmore. In Virginia, Republican Ollie
North's commercial claimed that Senator Chuck Robb voted with Clinton 95
percent of the time and "voted to help Bill Clinton raise your taxes."

By far the most ambitious step the Republicans took toward nationaliz-
ing the campaign was the promulgation of their Contract with America,
which represented a fulfillment of Gingrich's GOPAC dream, conceived
when Republicans controlled the White House. Just as having their own
party's president in the White House turned into a heavy burden for Democratic congressional leaders to bear, so the absence of a Republican president was a great boon to Gingrich, who was free to push ahead on his own.

At a boisterous, flag-waving rally on the west front of the Capitol held
less than ten weeks before election day, Gingrich mustered about 300 Republican incumbents and challengers. Most signed on to a ten-point manifesto whose provisions Republicans promised to bring to a vote within the
first 100 days of the new Congress, provided they had won control of the
House, an eventuality that almost no one but Gingrich foresaw. The Contract with America combined social issues—an anticrime package and a
two-year limit for welfare payments—with right-wing populism, including
a term-limits amendment and such standard Republican economic nostrums as a capital-gains tax cut and a balanced-budget amendment. "This
is a first step toward renewing American civilization," said Gingrich, never
one to understate the momentousness of an occasion. "If America fails, our
children will live on a dark and bloody planet."

To avoid divisiveness, the Contract skirted such moral issues as school
prayer and abortion, so dear to the heart of Christian conservatives among
the Republican rank and file. Thus, Gingrich set out to claim the moral
high ground for his party, his ham-handed manner reminiscent of his effort
while stumping for Bush during the 1992 campaign to exploit the then
much-publicized custody battle between Woody Allen and his former in-
amorata, Mia Farrow. Alluding to Allen's profession of love for one of Farrow's adopted daughters as reflecting the "weird values" represented by the
Democratic opposition, Gingrich declared: "Woody Allen having nonincest
with a nondaughter to whom he was a nonfather because they were a non-
family fits the Democratic platform perfectly."

In the face of a storm of protest, the Bush campaign had disavowed his
remark. That, however, did not faze Gingrich. In the closing days of the
1994 campaign, he cited the case of Susan Smith, the South Carolina
mother who had drowned her two children and then claimed they had been

abducted, as a reminder of the moral decay afflicting American society. "How a mother can kill her two children, fourteen months and three years, in hopes that her boyfriend would like her, is just a sign of how sick the system is, and I think people want change," Gingrich declared. "The only way you get change is to vote Republican."

Vice President Gore denounced Gingrich's remarks as "outrageous." Aside from objecting to Republican claims and rhetoric, though, Democrats did not have much to say for themselves. In a sense, the Republican Contract became their major issue on a national level. They modified their localized strategy enough to counterattack with a $2-million multistate advertising campaign. Seizing upon the Contract's most obvious weakness— the contradiction between its commitment to a constitutional amendment balancing the budget and its endorsement of a wide range of budget-busting tax breaks—they charged that if Republicans had their way, the deficit would grow by $800 billion, the rich would get tax cuts, and Medicare and Social Security recipients would pay the price.

A measure of the Democrats' ideological and moral bankruptcy was the White House selection of former California representative Tony Coelho as a senior adviser to the Democratic National Committee to take charge of the campaign. To Democratic problems growing out of the Whitewater controversy and the Paula Corbin Jones sexual harassment case, the fifty-two-year-old Coelho, who had become an investment banker in New York, brought his own personal baggage—allegations of financial impropriety in his personal investments, which led him to resign his House seat in 1989 in the wake of the Jim Wright controversy.

With Coelho at the helm of the party that had once assured Americans that they had nothing to fear but fear itself, Democrats threw themselves into a massive effort to frighten voters into backing their candidates in hopes of staving off disaster. A Republican victory, the Democrats claimed, would threaten women with a loss of the right to abortion, senior citizens with cuts in Medicare and Social Security, and all citizens with a chilling of their First Amendment rights, as Republicans pandered to their Christian conservative allies.

Using scare tactics, Democrats tried to offset the threat of the low turnout that darkened their election prospects. Their party regularly faced this problem because of its dependence on low-income voters, usually less likely to go to the polls than the more affluent and better educated citizens who generally back the GOP. But Clinton had heightened the turnout problem with his New Democrat agenda, emphasizing fiscal discipline and free trade, doctrines that held little appeal for the working-class voters who made up the Democratic base.

In fact, neither party aroused enthusiasm among any segment of the electorate. Disappointment with the president and with the Democratic congress dominated the political climate as election day approached. A *Los Angeles Times* poll in October showed Clinton's approval rating lingering well below 50 percent, with voters giving him remarkably little credit for any accomplishments, even in areas where he had, in fact, won victories. And on a number of issues across the board, such as crime, welfare reform, and the budget deficit, voters had come to conclude by a narrow margin that Republicans could do a better job than Democrats. Even on health care, where the Democrats once enjoyed a big advantage, the Republicans had drawn even. Yet the support for Republicans reflected a rejection of the Democrats rather than backing for key Republican initiatives. A plurality of those interviewed said they would prefer to "stick with President Clinton's programs" for the economy rather than "return to the types of programs put forth by Ronald Reagan when he was president." By a margin of nearly two to one, those polled thought the government should spend more on domestic programs. Asked about the Republican promise in the Contract with America to cut taxes, increase defense spending, and still balance the budget—the same pledge made and broken by Ronald Reagan—55 percent called that idea "unrealistic," whereas only 30 percent viewed it as realistic. In point of fact, for all the attention the Contract had gained within the Washington Beltway and even though Gingrich had taken out a full-page ad in *TV Guide* to promote it, more than four out of five of those polled said they had never even heard of it.

Rather than fervor for the Contract, it was disgust with the Democrats that generated the electoral whirlwind that swept across the country on November 8, bearing out every ill omen for the Democrats and bringing in a GOP victory on a scale far beyond the wildest dreams of all but a few of its strategists. Before the vote, Democrats had contended that the resentful mood of the electorate was really directed against incumbents in general, not just Democrats. But the GOP tide ran so strong that not a single Republican incumbent for major office—House, Senate, or governorship—was defeated, whereas Democratic incumbents were swept out of office on a wholesale basis. The most dramatic success for Republicans was in the House of Representatives, where they gained fifty-two seats and took command of the House for the first time since 1954 with a majority of 230 to 204 Democrats and one independent.

The Republican gain was the biggest in an off-year election since the first postwar election of 1946, when voter resentment at the shortages and disruptions created by postwar conversion gained fifty-five House seats for the GOP. No fewer than thirty-four Democratic incumbents were defeated, including Speaker Tom Foley, seeking his sixteenth term, the first time a House Speaker had been rejected by the voters since 1862. Republicans added seats in every region of the country, but the biggest gain was in Dixie, where their capture of nineteen House seats from the Democrats gave Republicans for the first time since Reconstruction a majority of the congressional seats in the thirteen states of the Old Confederacy.

On the Senate side, Republicans established control for the first time since 1986 by winning the six seats made vacant by Democratic retirements and defeating two incumbent Democrats—Jim Sasser of Tennessee, who had hoped to succeed retiring Democratic Senate leader George Mitchell of Maine, and Harris Wofford of Pennsylvania, whose upset victory in the fall of 1991 had foretold the Democratic success in 1992—and thrust health care to the top of the national issue agenda.

Republicans won big among the governorships, too. The election left them in charge of eight of the nine largest states, including New York, where voters sent liberal champion and perennial Democratic presidential prospect Mario Cuomo into unplanned retirement.

The White House seemed in a state of shock. In private, Clinton berated his aides and strategists for not serving him well, but in public he tried to accept at least part of the blame—for not fulfilling the fervent but vague promises of change he had made to the electorate. Voters "were saying, 'Look, we just don't like what we see when we watch Washington, and you haven't done much about that . . . Democrats are in charge; we're holding you accountable,'" Clinton said at a press conference the day after the election. Recalling his 1992 election campaign, Clinton promised to try to deliver on his central promises of greater economic security for the middle class and broader opportunity for all. "I'm not going to compromise on my convictions," Clinton insisted.

But those convictions still remained unclear, even to Clinton himself, as was evidenced by his early attempts to articulate a new message that responded to the voters' evident displeasure with what he and Congress had delivered during the previous two years. He told the audience at his undergraduate alma mater, Georgetown, that the public was angry and upset because these are not "normal times," asserting that he thought his administration had made a good start at addressing the nation's problems and that he was stunned to find that the public violently disagreed. Looking weary, Clinton said that the way the administration and Congress had recently done their business was "messy" and "almost revolting." The speech was supposed to be an overview of Clinton's foreign policy and a kickoff to Clinton's trip to the Asian economic summit. His rambling remarks were unplanned—and unwelcome to his staff.

Clinton seemed to be seeking advice from everywhere except from within himself, and his own uncertainty was intensified by the conflicting counsel he received about his course for the next two years. Some advisers argued that Clinton should emphasize his efforts to define himself as a New Democrat; others contended that he should revive the populist themes that had also been a major part of his 1992 campaign message. Paul Begala, who had worked closely with James Carville on the 1992 campaign and continued to advise the president, suggested that it was most likely Clinton would pursue both courses at once—and that would certainly be consistent with what he had done in the past.

The Republicans were plagued by no such ambiguity. Some votes in close House races were still being counted when the presumptive Speaker of the newly elected 104th Congress bulled ahead on the course he had set for himself. For Gingrich, the election results offered the best opportunity yet presented to him to overcome the frustrations and inhibitions imposed by the Constitution. His earlier efforts to create a Republican majority had failed miserably in 1992 because of the total disinterest of his own party's president in Gingrich's plan for promoting a Republican agenda that would unite the chief executive with the congressional Republicans. Bush's failure to go along or to develop any significant agenda of his own cost him the presidency and ruined Gingrich's dream.

Now, thanks in large measure to Bush's Democratic successor, whose fretful stewardship of the nation did far more to help Gingrich's cause than George Bush ever did, Gingrich had achieved the majority and the power he sought. But control of the House and the speakership was only one part of Gingrich's dream. The other part was establishment of the conservative agenda he had been constructing all his life. And it was to this task that he immediately committed his time and energy.

Mindful of the impediments of the constitutional system, Gingrich was driven by a combination of ambition and zeal into acting as if that system did not exist. Instead, he behaved as if he, not Clinton, were chief executive, or, more precisely, as if the Founding Fathers had created a parliamentary system of government and Gingrich was prime minister, a figure combining Benjamin Disraeli's guile and Margaret Thatcher's resolve. It was a momentous bluff, yet for a time, he seemed to be carrying it off, because no one else on the scene was prepared to challenge him.

Gingrich got off to a fast start, because more than any other national political figure, he actually had a policy blueprint of sorts, one that he had been promoting for years. And though agendas were commonly propounded by presidents, not Speakers, in this instance the real president had nothing to say. Even in the best of times, Clinton had not been able to lay out a coherent view of the nation and the world, and November's defeat had robbed him of his self-confidence and stunned him into silence.

Not knowing when Clinton would recover his voice and his will, Gingrich realized that he was operating on borrowed time. His pseudo–prime ministership became a race against an unknown deadline, when Clinton would recover and the gates of the constitutional system would close against him. His haste to exploit his temporary opportunity led Gingrich into excesses that far exceeded the grasp allowed him by the election returns and the realities of the political system.

He began paving the route to his own downfall when he was at the height of his glory, immediately after the November election, by claiming an almost limitless mandate. This election was a victory for "some fairly big ideas," Gingrich declared in his first postelection speech. He scornfully dismissed those who had dominated Washington in recent years by embracing "counterculture values, bigger government, redistributionist economics, and bureaucracies deciding how you should spend your money," reminding people that "they were on the losing end in virtually every part of the country." Reverting to the fears he had sought to exploit in his campaign allusion to the Susan Smith case, Gingrich linked crime to a breakdown of American society, blaming both on policies embraced by the Democrats. "When you hear gunshots in your nation's capital at night and you know that young Americans have died needlessly, then I would suggest to you that we have every reason to have the moral courage to confront every weakness of the current structure and to replace it," Gingrich said. "And if the first wave of experiments fail, to have the courage to say, 'Well, that one didn't work,' and have a second one and a third one and a fourth one." Further, Gingrich made clear he was not prepared to give any ground: "I want to draw a distinction between two words. I am very prepared to cooperate with the Clinton administration. But I am not prepared to compromise."

A month later, his first speech as Speaker was likened by his supporters in the House—who greeted him with a thunderous ovation and chants of "Newt, Newt, Newt"—to a presidential inaugural address, a similarity Gingrich did what he could to heighten. Besides quoting FDR's most celebrated aphorism—"The only thing we have to fear is fear itself"—he also reiterated the Rooseveltian deadline he had set back in September, pledging to push each of the ten substantive provisions of the Contract to a vote within 100 days. It was a timetable designed to evoke the fateful nature of the challenge that Gingrich wanted his party to confront.

Yet even at this moment of triumph, Gingrich provided new evidence of his habitual heavy-handedness in dealing with his opposition, a tendency that often caused him more injury than his foes. On a talk show a few days before his election to the speakership, Gingrich had claimed that an unidentified law enforcement official had told him that "in his judgment, up to a quarter of the White House staff, when they first came in, had used drugs in the last four or five years." No sooner were the words out of Gingrich's mouth than White House Chief of Staff Leon Panetta struck back. "The time has come when he has to understand that he has to stop behaving like an out-of-control radio talk-show host and begin behaving like the Speaker of the House of Representatives," Panetta told reporters summoned to the White House. "We cannot do business with a Speaker of the House who is going to engage in these kind of unfounded allegations; he's got to abide by a higher standard here."

It was just a tactical skirmish, a feint Gingrich offered while he embroiled himself in the grand strategy of the Contract with America. But Panetta's response showed that the White House, even while ideologically paralyzed, still knew how to exploit the politics of personality.

For the time being, however, Gingrich was in the driver's seat. At the House podium, wielding a new gavel given to him by a proud constituent who had carved it from the trunk of an ancient Georgian walnut tree, he ramrodded the 104th Congress down a precedent-shattering path. It started with the opening session. Normally, this day is given over to ceremony and little else, with the legislators waiting for the White House to call signals. But Gingrich's opening day was dramatically different. Within hours of the noon call to order, the new Republican majorities, operating with almost military discipline, voted to abolish twenty-eight congressional panels, to cut more than 600 staff members, and to require a three-fifths majority to raise tax rates, all measures that fell under the rubric of the Contract. Before they adjourned at 2 A.M., the lawmakers did something else unheard of on opening day: They actually passed a law. It was a measure that would make members of Congress abide by the same regulations for dealing with their employees on such matters as discrimination and safety that they had established for everyone else.

Abetted by the same party discipline and on occasion by substantial reinforcements from the ranks of complaisant Democrats, by the time Gingrich's self-imposed 100-day deadline rolled around, he could claim a significant list of accomplishments, including creation of a line-item veto for the president, restrictions on federal regulatory agencies, and revisions to the country's system of civil laws. With a climactic gesture just before the deadline for House approval and over the protests of outnumbered Democrats and a beleaguered president, the House passed a $189-billion package of tax cuts that included a $500-per-child family credit, expanded individual retirement accounts, and imposed a 50-percent reduction in the tax on capital gains.

"It's actually been quite a run," said the exultant Gingrich, who then spelled out his further plans for national economic revival in a prime-time television address, the first ever delivered by a congressional leader. Combining lofty rhetoric with a harsh denunciation of past Democratic policies as epitomizing a "moral and economic failure," Gingrich borrowed another phrase from FDR: "This is the year we rendezvous with our destiny to establish a clear plan to balance the budget," he declared. "It can no longer be put off."

Bolstering the analogy with Roosevelt in a talk with reporters, Gingrich likened his task of coalition building to FDR's success in forging a mighty alliance of disparate constituencies that held together through the Great Depression, World War II, and all the attendant social traumas these upheavals produced. "I think that the job of political leadership is to manage the dialogue in such a way that your coalition holds together," he said.

"What we have to do on our side is to continually manage the transition to a more conservative America within a framework that we don't break down our majority."

But that turned out to be a good deal easier said than done. In fact, even the hullabaloo over Gingrich's early achievements could not obscure the significance of the defeats already suffered by the two most far-reaching measures in the entire legislative Contract, and both of these setbacks threatened Gingrich's efforts to create a conservative majority.

The first, the balanced-budget constitutional amendment, the centerpiece of the conservative agenda for a quarter of a century, had been adopted by the House only to fail to gain the necessary two-thirds majority in the Senate. One lone holdout among the Senate's fifty-three Republicans, Oregon's Mark Hatfield, was enough to doom the proposal, though Hatfield also had the company of thirty-three of the Senate's forty-seven Democrats.

The main reason for defeat would be a key to the trouble lying ahead for the Republican revolution: the political potency of entitlements. By most estimates, the proposed amendment could have garnered seventy votes or more in the Senate, well in excess of the two-thirds needed for passage, if its backers had added language explicitly barring the use of the Social Security Trust Fund surplus to help reduce the federal budget deficit. But the amendment's sponsors refused and thus lost the votes of a handful of key Democrats, along with Republican Hatfield's support.

It was not hard to see why the amendment's backers refused to adopt the ban. For years, the huge surpluses of the Social Security Trust Fund had been helping to offset the federal deficit. For example, if trust fund revenues were subtracted from 1996 budget revenues, the deficit would be $66 billion higher than it was. Without Social Security in the equation, lawmakers would have to find at least another $558 billion to balance the budget over the next seven years—on top of the $1.2 trillion already estimated to be the total cost of achieving a balanced budget by the year 2002. That would increase the burden of balancing the budget by roughly 50 percent, and, in the final analysis, this was just too big a load to carry, even for the sake of achieving the Holy Grail of conservative fiscal policy.

House Republicans complained bitterly about the Senate's lack of backbone. In their indignation, they ignored the underlying lesson of the budget amendment's defeat—the significance of entitlements. It would turn out that what held true for one entitlement—Social Security, which Republicans had pledged not to tamper with—also held true for another, Medicare. If Republicans had learned that lesson from the balanced budget amendment's failure they might have been able to save their revolution.

If House Republicans could blame the Senate for the failure of the balanced budget, they had only themselves to blame for the defeat of the Contract measure that was second only to it: the constitutional term limit for federal lawmakers. As with the balanced-budget amendment, a rhetorically compelling idea was defeated by political reality. Just as the power of entitlements had blocked the balanced-budget amendment, so the power of self-interest defeated term limits. Legislators did not want the careers into which they had poured the best years of their lives cut short by what they regarded as harmful whim. Forty Republican members of Congress joined the vast majority of Democrats in opposing the amendment, a final count that fell far short of the necessary two-thirds, with 227 in favor and 204 against. Many of the members of the big Republican freshman class new to Washington had pledged to limit their service. However, Republican conservative stalwart Henry Hyde of Illinois delivered one of the most impassioned speeches in opposition. "I won't concede to the angry, pessimistic populism that drives this movement because it is just dead wrong," said Hyde, who had served in Congress for twenty years. "America needs leaders, it needs statesmen, and it needs giants—and you don't get them out of the phone book."

But these were only the most evident of the realities that the new Republican majorities on Capitol Hill overlooked, their minds clouded by the hubris that had seized them on election night. Imbued with certitude about the absolute correctness of their ideological commitment, a conviction reinforced by their insular relationship with the economic interests and social-issue partisans who shared their beliefs, the House Republicans lost perspective on what they were doing. They claimed a mandate that did not exist. Their gains in the House and Senate were based on the vote of a majority of a minority—less than one-half the electorate participated in the election. Moreover, as the polls showed, less than one-fourth of those who did participate had even heard of the Contract with America, the basis of the supposed mandate, which of course was not to say that even this portion supported it. And while the results were dramatic in terms of Democratic losses, the majorities gained by the Republicans in both Houses were narrow indeed—three seats in the Senate and twenty-six in the House, only about one-third the average Democratic majority in that body over the past two decades. Under the circumstances, Gingrich and his cohorts might well have recalled, as John Kennedy did after his narrow victory in 1960, Thomas Jefferson's admonition: "Great innovations should not be forced on slender majorities." But as the weeks wore on after the midterm election, it became increasingly clear that what Gingrich had in mind were innovations that were great by any standard.

As the onetime Nixon strategist Kevin Phillips observed, the Contract with America was based on the same hazy concept underlying Reaganomics when it had emerged fifteen years earlier: "Morning will come again in America if we go back to the principles that made this country great." The difference was that unlike Reagan, a benign figure mainly concerned with preserving his popularity and delivering stirring speeches, Gingrich was out to undo just about all that Franklin Roosevelt had accomplished, not to mention the legacies of Truman, Kennedy, and Johnson. In May, when the House Budget Committee approved the GOP draft budget, it called for eliminating 368 federal agencies, commissions, and programs, transferring dozens of responsibilities to the states, and imposing unprecedented limits on Medicare spending.

The Republicans laid out the blueprint for a federal government that would tell the poor to look to the states or to private charity for more of the help they needed; that would all but abandon its role as a patron of the arts and humanities and supporter of education and housing; that would retreat from some of its international commitments, spending far less on foreign aid; and that would abandon such long-established and widely praised programs as the New Deal's Tennessee Valley Authority and the Great Society's VISTA volunteer program.

Swept away by the fervor of their own antigovernment rhetoric, Republicans overlooked the great American contradiction between the lip service that voters paid to the attacks on government that Republicans like to make and their reliance on the benefits government brought them, which Democrats liked to remind them of since Roosevelt's years in the White House. To undo so much of what Roosevelt and his legatees had accomplished—and win that eternal national debate—would require, first of all, a man of the stature of Roosevelt himself, whose memory Gingrich was so fond of evoking.

Just as Gingrich was no Reagan, though, he was certainly, as he himself must have realized, no Roosevelt. Roosevelt was a man possessed of such élan and self-confidence that an admiring aide once remarked, "He must have been psychoanalyzed by God." By contrast, Gingrich was a man so ill at ease with himself that he often inflicted on himself and on the causes he advocated more injury than his enemies could ever contrive. Beyond that, Roosevelt happened to hold the presidency, an office that for all its limitations was expected to serve, in the time-honored phrase, as a pulpit for leading the sort of debate Gingrich had triggered from the rostrum of the House of Representatives. The fact that the current occupant of the White House was himself no match for Roosevelt increased Gingrich's potential for influence as Speaker, but it did not enlarge that position to match the task Gingrich had set for himself.

Finally, and most important of all, when Roosevelt took office, his leverage was vastly enhanced by the fact that the nation was caught in the worst economic cataclysm in its modern history. Like the prospect of hanging, such misfortune concentrates the mind wonderfully. In contrast, the circumstances that confronted Gingrich and his Republicans—and Clinton and his Democrats in 1995—were much less specific and therefore much harder to focus on.

If Gingrich had been nearly as good a historian as he professed to be, he would have been able to apply these lessons of the past to benefit himself and his party. But his ascendancy to power blurred his scholarly judgment. In fact, not only did he fail to profit from the lessons of the New Deal era, but he allowed his party to repeat a mistake Republicans had made much more recently, during the Reagan era. That error was to behave in ways that fit the image Democrats loved to construct of them—as the party committed to serving the interests of the wealthy and powerful, heedless of the concerns of the average American.

Thus, Reagan's cost cutters, in their zeal to trim outlays for the federal school-lunch program, perhaps the most popular single program in the entire federal budget, were inspired to label ketchup and pickle relish as substitutes for vegetables, thereby permitting them to avoid the expense of serving green beans or carrots to 26 million children in nearly 100,000 schools around the country. However many pennies that may have squeezed from the budget, once the Democrats got hold of it, that attempted switch touched off a national wave of indignation and ridicule from which the GOP never fully recovered. Even some Republicans joined in the attacks, notably then senator Henry Heinz III of Pennsylvania, heir to his family's food-processing enterprises, who took the floor of the Senate to offer his expert judgment that ketchup was not a vegetable: "This is one of the most ridiculous regulations I ever heard of, and I suppose I need not add that I do know something about ketchup and relish, or did at one time."

As if that had never happened, Gingrich's cohorts in the House took off after the school lunch program again twelve years later, this time proposing to eliminate the various federal nutrition programs and replace them with smaller block grants to the states. States would receive a set amount of money and establish their own programs to spend it, but when this money ran out, states would have to allocate more from their own coffers or deny the children the food they had been getting. This touched a nerve among middle-class parents, who benefited from the program along with the poor, and gave the Democrats fresh ammunition for their perennial complaint that the Republicans were heartless servants of the privileged—the counterpart of the GOP indictment that the Democrats were the party of taxers and spenders.

Republicans fought back with an argument based on semantics, claiming that their parsimony did not really cut spending on these and other social programs that benefited millions of Americans but merely slowed the growth of spending. This was, however, a distinction without much difference, as most people realized. The projections for spending growth, which the Republicans sought to slash on a wholesale basis, were based on anticipated inflation, growth in population, and, in many cases, expectations of increased demand. For a program to continue to meet its objectives in the future as it had in the past, it needed more money. Voters seemed to understand this in its application not only to school lunches but also to loans to college students, another target for Republican funding cuts.

The Republican assault on the government threatened middle-class voters, the sort that Gingrich conceived of as being bulwarks of his conservative revolution, not just with spending cuts but also with attempts to weaken government regulation, notably the Clean Air Act. By the time Gingrich had celebrated his first 100 days benchmark, public uneasiness was growing about the pace and direction of the Republican agenda. Asked in an April 1995 poll which danger they feared more—that Republicans would go too far in helping the rich and cutting needed services or that the Democrats would go too far in keeping costly and wasteful government programs—by a margin of nearly two to one, voters named the Republicans as the bigger threat.

Republican lawmakers felt this backlash when they returned home to canvass their constituents during the Easter recess, and some legislators began to have second thoughts themselves, particularly moderates like Delaware congressman Mike Castle, the former governor of his state. At a town meeting, Castle heard complaints that Republican tax cuts were selfish and irresponsible in the face of huge deficits and that regulatory reform bills would gut environmental protection. "This is a contract with some of America," Peter Wells, a Newark, Delaware, minister told Castle. "An awful lot of that budget is going to be balanced on the backs of those who can afford it least."

In the face of such anger, Castle backed off. "Your lack of ease with all this is well founded," he said to one citizen. "There are legitimate concerns out there," he replied to another. Castle hoped the tension with the voters would subside, now that House Republicans had kept their promise to act on the Contract, but a look at the simple arithmetic of the Republican program made clear that voter concern was bound to grow. Republican leaders had been told privately soon after the election that they would have to cut Medicare and Medicaid growth by nearly $500 billion to keep their campaign promise of tax cuts and a balanced budget in seven years, realizing that a legislative scenario juxtaposing huge entitlement cuts with big tax cuts made them vulnerable to Democratic counterattack. As the months advanced in their revolutionary year, Republicans wondered how the Democrats would respond, particularly the top Democrat, Bill Clinton.

For a time, the president had almost totally absented himself from the public scene, allowing the Republicans to dominate the debate and the action. Whether deliberate or not, Clinton's behavior served his interest to a limited degree, as it encouraged the public to focus on the full extent of the Republicans' intentions and made their revolution, rather than his own record, the dominant political issue. Nevertheless, the president's silence was so conspicuous it became embarrassing.

When Clinton called a news conference in April, only one of the three broadcast networks, CBS, chose to cover it, and the president spent most of the time fielding questions on the Republican congressional agenda. Almost inevitably, he was asked point-blank about his own shrunken role in the debate. "The president is relevant, especially an activist president," Clinton replied defensively. "The Constitution gives me relevance; the power of our ideas gives me relevance; the record we have built up over the last two years and the things we're trying to do give me relevance." But if, as Clinton pointed out, the presidency was still a potential powerhouse in the political system, the country was left to wonder how he intended to use that power—a point underlined when he made a murky attempt at self-definition in his opening statement at the press conference: "My philosophy is that we have to go beyond this kind of politics as usual, the old debate about whether there should be more government or less. I think we need a better and different government that helps people who are helping themselves. My job is to work with people of good faith in both parties, to do what is best for America."

As it happened, it was not a product of political strategy but rather an accident of fate that allowed the president to find his tongue and thrust himself back into national attention. That event was the April 19 car bombing of the Oklahoma City federal building that claimed more than 160 lives and stunned the nation. Here at last was a misfortune for which no one could blame Clinton and which he could address without having to reconcile the countless internal contradictions and inconsistencies that had tormented his presidency. It was an opportunity for Clinton to discover the power of the personalized presidency, to which all his predecessors had resorted in one way or another. In the aftermath of this emotional trauma, the country turned to the president for support and leadership, not as a Republican or a Democrat, new or old, not as a conservative or liberal, but as a unifying force. And Americans also turned to him as a human being who could express the nation's collective grief and anger.

Clinton threw himself into that role and played it faultlessly. At first he was content to serve as spokesman for the nation's sorrow, but as the public rallied to him more strongly and spontaneously than at any previous moment of his presidency, he then shrewdly exploited this support for his political advantage. Speaking not only to those attending a memorial service in Oklahoma City, a few days after the bombing, but to a national television audience on what he had declared to be a national day of mourning, he urged Americans to recognize the "duty to purge ourselves of the dark forces which give rise to this evil," and promised: "Justice will prevail." Meanwhile, in a reminder to the nation that he was its chief magistrate, he assumed an appropriately stern stance, letting it be known that he would act to strengthen the government's hand against terrorism.

On the very next day, as the involvement of right-wing militant groups in the tragedy became clearer, Clinton took a much tougher line, charging that many of the nation's political leaders have failed to combat "purveyors of hatred," by clear implication denouncing the radio talk-show hosts who had become the Greek chorus of conservatism. "We hear so many loud and angry voices in America today who leave the impression, by their very words, that violence is acceptable," Clinton declared. "Some of us have not discharged our responsibilities," he added. "It is time we all stood up and spoke against that kind of reckless speech and behavior."

It was clearly a shot fired across the right wing's bow, and the president's targets lost no time in striking back. "Liberals intend to use this tragedy for their own gain," charged the most prominent conservative broadcaster, Rush Limbaugh. "I am here to tell you that it is irresponsible and vacuous to suggest that conservative arguments caused this tragedy." And Gingrich, confronted by a reporter who asked whether his attacks on the federal government had encouraged extremism, denounced that notion as "grotesque and offensive."

White House officials sought to brush aside any talk of the political implications of the bombing. "This is not a campaign gambit that he's on," said Harold Ickes. "This is a matter of national concern." Of course it was. But the fact remains that the bombing had served to remind the country and the political world of the symbolic powers of the presidency. It served as the domestic equivalent of an international crisis, providing a climate in which Americans rallied around their chief executive.

In the aftermath of the explosion, no one questioned Clinton's "relevance." While the death toll climbed, the same television networks that had refused to broadcast the president's news conference now followed his every word about the bombing. And perhaps most important, his enemies, for the first time since the election, were on the defensive. "It's where the Gingrich revolution suddenly turned inside out," George Stephanopoulos said later.

However, Clinton was not prepared to leave his political future to fate and accident. Instead, he developed a new political strategy designed to help him navigate the post-midterm Republican-dominated shoals. For help, he turned to his erstwhile Arkansas adviser, Dick Morris, whom he still regarded as his savior for having helped him regain the governorship in Arkansas. Clinton could certainly have had little question about the kind of advice he would get from this consultant. Forsaking his roots as a liberal Democratic activist on the west side of Manhattan, Morris had moved ever closer to the Republican side—a shift illustrated by the fact that his chief congressional patron in recent times has been Senator Trent Lott of Mississippi, then the Republican Senate whip and a longtime conservative stalwart on Capitol Hill.

Under Morris, Clinton became wedded to a new strategy somewhat obscurely labeled "triangulation," which depended on Clinton playing the congressional Democrats against the congressional Republicans to protect his own interest. The premise for this schemata was that the 1994 election represented a rejection of liberal activism. Morris reasoned from this, and Clinton evidently agreed, that for the president to survive politically and gain reelection, he must turn his back not only on liberalism but also on the Democratic congressional leadership because of its reputed leftward leanings. This strategy ignored the fact that it was the conservatives among the congressional Democrats who had caused Clinton the most trouble in his first two years, by undercutting his economic program and his health-reform proposal. But that was not the way Morris looked at the political world.

At any rate, when House Democrats got wind of Morris's new political blueprint, some Democrats denounced his plan as a cynical sellout and betrayal. This prompted Morris to draft a defensively toned memorandum for White House press secretary Mike McCurry to disseminate publicly. "Triangulation is not another word for centrism, vacillation, or appeasement of each political camp," Morris wrote. "It is not merely a bland or inoffensive position in the middle, halving the difference between the parties. It is the dynamic end product of a national debate that produces a set of insights that borrows from the best parts of each party's agenda."

In reality, the genius of triangulation was that it updated the Madisonian approach to the Constitution for late-twentieth-century politics. "Ambition must be made to counteract ambition," Madison wrote of his formula for bolstering the separation of powers, and Morris's concept called for Clinton to pit the ambitions of the Republicans against those of the Democrats to promote himself.

Triangulation's first demonstration came in June 1995, when Clinton agreed to a meeting with Gingrich, who was barnstorming in New Hampshire, supposedly determined to see a moose, in actuality eager to test support for a possibly new chapter in his political life—a run for the Republican presidential nomination. On a sunny afternoon, Clinton and Gingrich cohosted a unique sort of television talk show in the old New Hampshire mill town of Claremont. Although their discussion covered many of the most controversial and divisive issues on the national agenda, the result amounted to a bipartisan love fest. The two men took every opportunity to find points of agreement and, even when they held opposing views, sought to give each other credit for good intentions and conscientious effort.

"We have a lot of differences, but we also have some areas in which we can work together," Clinton said in his brief opening remarks. Taking his cue from the burst of applause that greeted the president's tone-setting comments, Gingrich responded in kind. "I believe all Americans can be told the truth and can actually watch their leaders have honest open disagreement and talk things out and find common solutions," he said. "The president and I will now have a dialogue, and maybe the country can learn a little about working together and not just buying commercials and attacking each other."

Moments later, Gingrich urged the audience to applaud Clinton's measured response to a question about holding down Medicare costs and health-care reform. "The president put his finger on something here where I think we both analyze it slightly differently but we both have the same commitment." The session was not ten minutes old before the president and the Speaker had literally shaken hands on an agreement to establish a bipartisan commission to find a way to reform campaign financing and lobbying and to curb the power of special-interest groups. The idea had been suggested by one member of the audience who blamed the special interests for dooming Clinton's efforts at health-care reform.

Nothing ever came of this proposal, but just bringing it up and seeming to agree on it dramatized the meeting and helped both Gingrich and Clinton get across a message that must have pleased Dick Morris and would have delighted Madison, too—divided government works. After the Claremont summit, Gingrich declared: "It was good for the country and fine for both of us."

Both President Clinton and House Speaker Gingrich gained from their joint appearance, but there were also losers in both parties. The meeting was bad news for Republican presidential candidates, not only because they were overshadowed by Gingrich but also because his cordial tête-à-tête with Clinton made the ouster of the incumbent president a less urgent matter than they wanted it to seem. As for the Democrats, that same mellow atmosphere undermined their hopes of demonizing Gingrich in order to regain control of Congress in the next election.

Just a few days after his meeting with Gingrich, Clinton staged a new demonstration of triangulation—with a vengeance. He decided to match the Republican plan to balance the budget with a plan of his own, which would take ten years instead of the seven the Republicans had targeted. Until that moment, the White House and the House Democrats had been following a careful strategy that called for them to pound away at the seeming harshness of GOP spending plans, in hopes that the public would become aroused and that the shell-shocked Republicans would edge toward compromise. Now Clinton planned to shift to an entirely different approach—compromise and reconciliation.

Forewarned of the move, Democratic legislative leaders hastened to the White House to make one last desperate attempt to dissuade Clinton from abandoning a strategy they believed would soon set off an outpouring of public outrage with the GOP plans. In trying to get the president to hold the line, the lawmakers acknowledged that at some point, he would probably want to propose his own budget-balancing plan. They further argued that the longer he waited, the more willing the Republicans would be to give ground. Recalling the film *Braveheart*, Richard Gephardt urged that like the thirteenth-century Scottish rebel leader, Clinton needed to wait until the last moment to impale the onrushing host of enemy attackers.

Clinton, however, had no interest in such comparison. The following week, he went on national television to unveil his plan to save $1.1 trillion over ten years by slowing the growth of spending on Medicare and Medicaid, trimming social and farm programs, and closing a number of corporate tax loopholes while still retaining the package of targeted middle-class tax cuts he had proposed in mid-December. "It's time to clean up this mess," Clinton said. The president would protect some programs from the budget axe—principally Social Security and education and training. But he warned: "Make no mistake—in other areas, there will be big cuts, and they will hurt."

Congressional Democrats were furious. Clinton had shifted his ground— just as the offensive against the Republican budget cuts had begun to make headway. What particularly outraged them was Clinton's proposal to make cuts in Medicare. Although the Medicare savings amounted to only about one-half of the $270 billion the Republicans had in mind, the Democrats in Congress feared that it would blunt their main weapon against the Republicans.

"I think some of us learned some time ago that if you don't like the president's position on a particular issue, you simply need to wait a few weeks," remarked Wisconsin representative David R. Obey, former chairman of the Joint Economic Committee. Even the usually circumspect Gephardt publicly criticized the new budget plan. "Opening the door to deep Medicare cuts while the Republicans are struggling to pay for their huge tax breaks threatens to make Medicare a political football," he said.

Senate Minority Leader Tom Daschle of South Dakota begged Democratic senators at a lunch not to publicly criticize Clinton. However, one senator, usually a Clinton stalwart, upon being given anonymity by the press, contended that the new budget plan was a sign that Clinton had decided to campaign against his fellow Democrats in an effort to convince voters that he and the GOP leadership of Congress could govern without them. The new plan was "a self-seeking bid for reelection" to show that "a bifurcated government can work," he said.

For all the hullabaloo it created on Capitol Hill, the president's dramatic shift was scarcely noticed by most Americans. The concern of House Democrats about Clinton undercutting them turned out to be groundless, though that was not Clinton's fault. Polls taken by the Democratic leadership showed that the public was scarcely aware of Clinton's gambit. This was because attention was being dominated by the debate over the budget and

Medicare between Gingrich and company, on one side, and the House Democrats, on the other, and Gingrich was slowly but steadily losing this battle.

Nonetheless, the president's maneuver did have a lasting impact on relationships between the White House and the congressional Democrats, creating unease and suspicion on Capitol Hill. "You didn't send any flowers, you didn't write any letters, you didn't even blow a kiss—you just upped and left," Charles Rangel of New York reminded the president, as Clinton and his fellow Democratic members of the House Ways and Means Committee sipped coffee at a Cabinet Room get-together a few weeks after Clinton had unveiled his budget plan. "Mr. President," asked Michigan congressman Sander Levin, "are you sleeping with the enemy? And later, Rangel asked Clinton pointedly: "Are we all singing from the same sheet of music?"

Clinton's equivocal response—"We should stick together as long as we can, but the time may come when we disagree"—served mainly to underline the tensions and uncertainty clouding the relations between the president and congressional Democrats as the struggle with the Republicans over fiscal policy headed toward its climax. The Ways and Means Committee members who met with Clinton in the White House Cabinet Room left there wanting to accept Clinton's qualified professions of support. Yet some brooded about the influence of Morris, whom they considered the author of the triangulation strategy. "I worry that this political consultant has told him, 'Cut the House Democrats loose and let them sink in deep water,'" admitted Washington representative Jim McDermott. "I don't know whether the president has really bought that as a plan or not, but all through the budget machinations, there have been moments of concern."

Congressional Democrats were mindful that the current partisan order of battle on Capitol Hill represented a role reversal of the last great budget clash in 1990. Then, leaders of the Democratic majority in Congress had cut a deal with Republican president Bush, which included a controversial tax increase; and that agreement had touched off a rebellion by outraged House Republicans, led by then GOP whip Gingrich against Bush, which many felt not only contributed to Bush's defeat in 1992 but also led to the GOP congressional triumph of 1994. "I don't think people understand that we have leverage, too," said California's Bob Matsui, recalling Gingrich's 1990 mutiny. "Look what Newt did to Bush 1990 when he hit him on the tax issue. He really did him big damage."

Yet it was far from clear that Democrats in the House were unified enough and bold enough to wage such an intramural battle. Sharp ideological cleavages divided Democratic House members. "There are a couple of hundred Democrats here, and we are all different," said Sam Gibbons of Florida, the senior Democrat on Ways and Means. And in many ways, they had not yet recovered from the previous November's defeat. "The reality is that the Democrats in the House are still going through some kind of catharsis," said Representative Pete Stark of California, then in his twelfth term. "We don't know what it's like to be in a minority."

Moreover, despite their uneasy relationship with Clinton, most saw advantages in their party's retaining control of the White House. "If we can't control the Congress, we need somebody in the White House to veto stuff and work with us to get a better break with Republicans," said McDermott of Washington. "And even if we take control again we still need a Democratic president to get anything done. Under Bush we passed things but he vetoed them. But what Democrats on Capitol Hill wondered about was how much Clinton felt he needed them. "I really think there is some sharp division among his advisers," said New York's Rangel. "It's the old question of whether he erodes his base with people who have stuck with him over the years or whether trying to walk like a Republican will pick up anything for him."

Such ambiguity was a far cry from the clear partisan and ideological battle lines drawn by Harry Truman, who, nearly half a century ago, was the last Democratic president to face a Congress dominated by the GOP. Truman laid the groundwork for his historic "give-'em-hell" reelection campaign in 1948 by challenging the Republicans on Capitol Hill at every opportunity on issues such as progressive taxation and protecting labor unions, an effort that Gingrich had vainly sought to persuade George Bush to use as a model for his own campaign in 1992. Not only did Truman win back the White House, but he led the Democrats to gain more than 70 seats in the House of Representatives.

Much had changed since 1948. Both parties had lost strength, and the Democrats in particular had seen their coalition erode. However, the factors that had contributed to Truman's victory and had made it seem almost inevitable became much clearer after the election than beforehand. Truman was the first Democrat to run for president since FDR's death. He could not be sure that the New Deal coalition that Roosevelt had created during the Great Depression would rally behind a new leader under dramatically different economic conditions. Truman took a chance, followed his own convictions, and made history.

Clinton's way was very different. Even though polls showed that his side was getting the better of the battle of the budget with the public, under Morris's prodding, he continued to give ground. In October, with the end of the fiscal year and the deadline for a budget agreement fast approaching, Clinton, who had previously wanted to take ten years to balance the budget, said he might accept a budget agreement that eliminated the federal deficit in seven years—if the GOP would accept some of his basic requirements, such as maintaining the Medicare and Medicaid programs at sufficient levels and spending enough on the environment and new technology. The president, however, issued a warning that he intended to veto legislation that contained the current Republican plans for Medicare reform and tax cuts. The White House argued that Republicans wanted to cut too much from Medicare and that they proposed too large a tax cut.

But the Republicans pushed ahead, adopting a revolutionary budget plan that would provide for a $245-billion tax cut at the same time that it sharply curbed federal spending and social programs. The GOP plan would end Americans' entitlement to federal assistance when they fall into poverty, while transferring enormous power to states to weave the social safety net as they saw fit. It would make deep cuts in farm subsidies that had been politically sacrosanct since the Great Depression.

"This will be a radical change in the way this government is operated," said Senator Dole, as Gingrich called adoption of the plan "the most decisive vote on the direction of government since 1933." Ways and Means chairman Bill Archer of Texas said, "The great social experiment of the last thirty years has led to an unprecedented expansion of the federal government and yet, sadly, it has failed to solve our nation's most difficult problems. The time has come to admit that tax and spend has failed."

The Democrats avoided making such sweeping ideological claims and instead focused on what they knew to be the weak link in the Republican armor—the Medicare cuts that frightened not only senior citizens, but also their offspring. The war of words between the White House and the Republicans turned especially bitter when Clinton's press secretary McCurry joined Democrats in contending that GOP leaders wanted Medicare to die. "You know, that's probably what they'd like to see happen to seniors, too, if you think about it," McCurry added sardonically. The Republicans would have been well advised to ignore McCurry's wisecrack. Instead, Gingrich and Dole issued a joint statement, called the comment "reprehensible, divisive, un-American," and urged Clinton to fire McCurry. But all they accomplished was to focus public attention on the issue that was steadily eroding their support.

Actually, if they had so chosen, the Republicans could have ended the battle by compromising and then claiming victory. For all his veto threats, Clinton had signaled a willingness to accept key elements of the Republican plan, amounting to a sea change in national fiscal policy. He had endorsed the goal of balancing the budget, even accepting the GOP's seven-year time line, had accepted the idea of ending poor Americans' entitlement to welfare, and had proposed his own reductions in Medicare spending. But Republicans were so convinced of the rightness of their beliefs that they refused to give ground and instead, like so many lemmings, plunged ahead to their political debacle.

Underlying their determination was the likelihood that unless Clinton signed their plan into law, the government would be forced to shut down. The Republicans reasoned that this would be politically unacceptable to Clinton, but the president looked at it differently. He had, after all, gone out of his way to depict himself as the voice of reasonableness by his willingness to compromise. If that made him seem weak in the eyes of Republicans, so much the better, because it would incline them to force him to the wall, thereby damaging themselves in the eyes of the public.

Thus, having backed himself against a wall, Clinton at long last stood firm and staked out the political high ground for himself. He labeled the GOP threat to close the government nothing less than blackmail and insisted he would not yield to it. And for good measure, he made patriotism an issue, accusing the GOP leaders of "playing political games with the full faith and credit of the United States of America," because the budget-balancing bills were tied to a required increase in federal borrowing power, without which a shadow would be cast over the government's credit.

On November 14, the long-threatened train wreck, as the impending government shutdown was called, was transformed into reality when Clinton vetoed a stopgap funding measure, which would have provided the money to keep the government going for two weeks but which would have raised Medicare premiums and made deep cuts in education and public health. Some 800,000 federal, supposedly nonessential workers streamed home, and the shutdown was on. The verdict came in quickly. Two days into the shutdown, a CNN/USA Today poll found that the public blamed the Republicans for the deadlock more than Clinton, by a wide margin of 49 percent to 26 percent. The Republicans had overplayed their hand. They had convinced the country that they were in charge in Washington—and now they were paying the consequences.

Indeed, the Republican burden grew with each day of the shutdown; despite the supposedly nonessential duties of the laid-off workers, the impact on the public increased. By the second day of the shutdown, processing of FHA, Veterans Administration, and other government-subsidized real estate loans had ground to a halt, causing anxiety among thousands of home buyers nationwide and prompting the real estate industry to scramble for makeshift solutions. The next day, Yosemite National Park was barred to visitors for only the second time in half a century—the only other shutdown having been forced by wildfires. With the Grand Canyon barred to tourists in Arizona, GOP governor Fife Symington beseeched the White House to permit National Guard troops to open the gates and provide services. "We have tourists in from all over the world. The Grand Canyon was the center point of their vacation, and they're being turned away. That's a horrible image for Arizona to be spread across the country," said the governor's spokesman, Doug Cole. All in all, the shutdown created a bad image for the GOP.

Meanwhile, Gingrich found a way to make the bad situation for Republicans worse. At a time when the leaders of his party professed to be taking a stand based on high principles, the Speaker blurted out to reporters that the GOP position had hardened in part because he and Dole felt they had been snubbed by the White House during their trip the previous week to Israel for the funeral of the assassinated Israeli prime minister Yitzhak Rabin. Gingrich claimed the president had not spoken to him and had treated him and Dole discourteously by showing them out the rear entrance of the airplane. "That's part of why you ended up with us sending down a tougher continuing resolution," he said. "This is petty, but I think it's human. You travel twenty-five hours with somebody, and nobody has talked to you, and they ask you to get off a back ramp so the media won't get a picture of the Senate majority leader and the Speaker of the House returning from Israel. Where is their sense of manners? Where is their sense of courtesy?"

The next day, Democrats in the House could scarcely restrain themselves. Representative Rosa DeLauro of Connecticut said that Gingrich's complaint "gives new meaning to the phrase 'whine and dine.'" Colorado Democratic representative Patricia Schroeder, holding up an Oscar statue, said Gingrich had "sewn up the category of best performance by a child actor this year." And several Democratic representatives displayed a blown-up cover of that day's edition of the *New York Daily News*. Twenty years earlier, that newspaper, famed for its irreverence, had made political history when it headlined President Ford's refusal to help bail out financially beleaguered New York City: "Ford to City: Drop Dead." Now, the tabloid topped itself with a front-page cartoon depicting Gingrich as a sobbing baby in diapers next to the headline: "Crybaby. Newt's tantrum: He closed down the government because Clinton made him sit at back of plane." The best the Republicans could do was adopt a resolution stopping Democrats from bringing the enlarged cover of the newspaper into the chamber.

Three days later, on Sunday, November 19, the Republicans began to retreat, and the longest shutdown of the government in the nation's history came to an end. GOP leaders agreed to pass short-term funding to keep the government running until December 15. All they got in return was the president's commitment to the goal of a balanced budget by 2002—a pledge that was nonetheless qualified by a promise to guarantee adequate funding for Medicaid, education, and other programs. Leaders from both parties said they hoped to have enacted by the December 15 date all the regular spending bills for the 1996 fiscal year, which began October 1; but when that deadline arrived, no new agreement had been reached, and the government shut down again. This time, fewer workers were involved, but the shutdown lasted for three weeks, until January 6, when the Republicans, divided and humiliated once again, backed down after receiving a presidential promise to submit a new balanced-budget plan based on Congress's own financial projections. But Clinton's plan would not pass muster with the Republican high command—and budget talks collapsed again. Three weeks later, the GOP approved, and Congress signed, a temporary truce to keep the entire government operating through March 15. In April, both sides would agree to a compromise, and a budget would finally be approved. But the battle had ended long before that with the disastrous Republican defeat.

"We thought that Clinton would cave," one Republican strategist told me later. Indeed, he *had* caved—first by agreeing to balance the budget by a certain date, then by moving that date up from ten years to seven, then on making significant cuts in social spending and in Medicare. But the Republicans, obsessed with what they believed to be the rightness of their cause, pushed ahead and transformed what could have been a partial victory into a debacle.

In the end, it was fittingly left to New Gingrich to write the epitaph on the abortive Republican effort. "It takes two elections to make a revolution real," he told Republican fund-raising audiences around the country. "It may just be that we need one more election." One thing was clear: Needed or not, another election was on the way.

8

The Lawmaker

For Republicans, it was a night to remember, and to build on. With each passing hour on election night 1980, the returns added new dimensions to their triumph. Not only had Ronald Reagan won the White House, but his party had seized control of the Senate, long a citadel of Democratic power. The victory was all the sweeter because it followed by only a few years the devastation of Watergate, which had called into question the very survival of the Grand Old Party. Suddenly, the door of opportunity was open for Republicans and for a fair number of Democrats who shared the faith in Reagan's conservative creed. But for no one was the vista brighter than for Bob Dole, Phil Gramm, Lamar Alexander, and Patrick J. Buchanan, men who, fifteen years later, would emerge as the dominant figures in the early stages of the 1996 campaign for the Republican presidential nomination.

As rich a prize as that nomination was, even more was at stake in the competition among these four than the chance to lead the Republicans into battle against Bill Clinton. By exploiting the opportunities the Reagan era had created, each in his own way would help to chart the direction of the Republican party over the next decade and half—and each had come to represent one of the principal tributaries of Republican belief. In the course of the struggle for the presidency, each man would also contend for the opportunity to redefine the party in keeping with the distinctive political identity he himself had established over the years since the Reagan era dawned.

Using his Senate leadership posts as stepping-stones, Bob Dole would become the chief tribune for Midwestern Republicanism, the stolid but enduring faith in a marriage of convenience between the rewards of the free market and the obligations of government. By contrast, erstwhile Democrat Gramm, who transferred his partisan allegiance to the GOP soon after Reagan's ascension, became his new party's most aggressive apostle of the take-no-prisoners conservatism spawned by his Sun Belt base. Alexander, relying mainly on his skills as a merchandiser of his ideas and personality, along with his experience as a state chief executive, would ultimately emerge as the leading spokesman for the born-again doctrine of federalism, laboring to transfer power from Washington to the states. Finally, as a journalist and critic, Buchanan would ride the rising tide of conservative ideology produced by the Reagan revolution to its crest, then plunge directly into the battle for the electorate, championing his own hard-edged brand of populism along the way.

Enlarging the potential impact for these various creeds was the historic opening that loomed before the Republican party—the chance to become the nation's majority party, a dominance the GOP had not enjoyed since before the Great Depression. It was a moment made even more precious because it had slipped away in the previous decade in the wake of the Democratic party's decline. Richard Nixon had taken advantage of the apparent end of the New Deal coalition and had thrust himself and his "silent majority" of white middle-class supporters into the void and to the forefront of the political arena. But the echoes of Nixon's victory speech on the night of his 1972 landslide reelection had hardly died down before he was in retreat and on his way out as a result of the self-inflicted wound of Watergate. As Pat Buchanan, the disgraced president's loyal aide, remarked in the midst of the darkening scandal, "We rolled the rock right up the hill, only to see it roll right down on top of us."

Even in the midst of their celebrations, most Republicans recognized their comeback victory was incomplete. Reagan's victory was marred by the awareness that his success owed more to the ineptness of the Democratic stewardship under President Jimmy Carter than to public confidence in the GOP. The Republican party would still need a strong new system of beliefs to construct a new majority. In trying to lay the foundation for such a creed, these four Republicans who hungered for the presidency shared many of the basic goals and enthusiasms that had fired Newt Gingrich in his drive to create a Republican majority in the Congress. Yet under the impediments imposed by the Constitution, Gingrich and his cohorts on Capitol Hill—and the party's presidential contenders—operated in separate and often opposing political worlds, an arrangement that undercut the significance of the policy goals they advocated. The result transformed the competition for the nomination from a battle of ideas into a struggle that would be decided by the power of money and the preferences of the party hierarchy.

At the moment of Reagan's triumph, though, ambitious politicians looked past such problems and instead focused on exploiting the potential of the new regime. For Bob Dole of Kansas, the Reagan victory carried special significance in light of the personal reverses he had previously suffered as he sought to gain national influence. After being cashiered as Republican

National chairman by Nixon's high-handed political operatives following the 1972 campaign, Dole next showed up on the national scene as Gerald Ford's vice presidential running mate in 1976, when he was instructed to beat up on the Democrats, a mission he carried out too well for his own political good. "They told me to go for the jugular," Dole later remarked. "Nobody told me it was my jugular."

Nevertheless, Dole got enough national exposure, and enough of a taste for national politics, to become emboldened to seek the presidency himself in 1980. His candidacy died early in New Hampshire, in a contest that gave him only 0.04 percent in the primary vote. Still, Dole exited the presidential stage in plenty of time to redeem himself with a huge reelection victory in Kansas.

It was another example of Dole's ability to overcome adversity, a skill he had honed since childhood. In Russell, Kansas, where Dole hailed from, the soil was as good as any place in the Great Plains, but the rainfall, or the lack of it, was a constant peril. During Dole's boyhood, a terrible drought coinciding with the Great Depression turned the surrounding region into the Dust Bowl. That meant hard times for Bob Dole, then in his teens, and his family. Dole's grandfather, Robert Dole, who lost the farmland he had owned, toiled for years as a tenant farmer and ended up on welfare; Dole often told the story of signing grandfather Bob's welfare checks when he was county attorney in the 1950s.

After the failure of his restaurant, Dole's father, Doran, managed a milk-and-egg station, then tried his hand at running the local grain elevator. Dole's mother, Bina, roamed the countryside selling Singer sewing machines and vacuum cleaners. "Six of us grew up living in a basement apartment," Dole would later tell campaign audiences. "That was Bob Dole's early life. And I'm proud of it because we learned a lot about values—about honesty and decency and responsibility and integrity and self-reliance, and loving your God and your family and your church and your community."

Later, he would learn about war. In 1945, Second Lieutenant Dole was shipped to Italy as an infantry replacement. In April, a month before the war ended, while leading his platoon against a German machine-gun nest, enemy shell fragments smashed his right shoulder and left him paralyzed from the neck down. Soon after he arrived in an army hospital in Topeka, encased in plaster from chin to hips, battling a severe infection that soon led to the removal of one of his kidneys. Despite medical predictions to the contrary, Dole learned to walk again, though his right arm remained paralyzed. Becoming a casualty did nothing to diminish his natural ambition, but the experience left him with dour suspicions about what life held for him. It was an outlook that defined his political style.

Dole entered politics at the bottom rung, as a Republican, winning a seat in the Kansas legislature in 1950, then moving up to county attorney. His explanation of his choice of the GOP reflected the prevailing disdain for the significance of both parties, an attitude that would intensify in the postwar era. As Dole later told the story, the leading Democrat in town came to his house soon after he returned from the war and told him that he ought to consider going into politics.

"But I don't know anything about politics," Dole protested.

"It's not necessary," came the reply. "You got shot. I think we can get you elected."

His next visitor was the leading Republican in town. He, too, told Bob Dole he should run for office—but as a Republican.

"Why a Republican?"

"Because there are twice as many Republicans as Democrats in Russell County."

Thus, as Dole would later tell voters in one campaign after another, "I made a great philosophical decision right there on the spot. I'd learned how to count in the army."

By 1960, the same year John Kennedy won the presidency, Dole had won enough favor among Republicans in Russell and its environs to be elected to the U.S. Congress. There, he at once established himself as a young man to be watched by forcing the Billy Sol Estes grain speculation scandal onto the front pages—this, much to the discomfiture of John F. Kennedy and his vice president, Lyndon Johnson, who was said to be a patron of the Texas swindler.

Dole's essential pragmatism led him to support programs that helped the farming country that elected him—rural electrification, soil conservation subsidies, and assorted federal aid for agribusiness. On some issues, notably those having to do with race, he took a more moderate stance than that of his party's hard-line conservatives, voting for the Civil Rights Act of 1964 and the Voting Rights Act of 1965, and arguing that Republicans should do more to open their ranks to minorities, not just out of fairness but for reasons of political self-interest. But by and large, his legislative career was based on his faith in fiscal conservatism, a candle that still burned brightly when he joined the Senate in 1969. His devotion to reducing the deficit was so constant that it once led him to offer to accept cutbacks in farm programs if other senators would swallow reductions in programs dear to their own constituents.

Through his fierce partisanship and his loyalty to his party's chief executive, Dole seemed dedicated to surmounting the long-standing intitutional barriers to party unity. In the polarized climate of the late 1960s, Democrats knew that whenever they attacked Nixon, whether it was on Vietnam or on his choices for the Supreme Court, they would have to answer to razor-tongued Bob Dole on the Senate floor. And Republicans knew that when Nixon needed their vote on one roll call or another, Dole, heedless of his lack of seniority, would be on their case, wheedling and nagging. "He's the first fellow we've had around here in a long time who can grab 'em by the hair and pull 'em down the aisle at the same time," said an admiring Barry Goldwater of his new colleague.

The president duly rewarded Dole's militancy by selecting him as chairman of the Republican National Committee, thus elevating him to the top echelon of GOP leadership. Dole went at the job as if he were still storming enemy positions at the head of his infantry platoon. With Nixon seemingly assured of reelection by George McGovern's hapless Democratic candidacy, Dole sought an all-out effort from the White House to boost Republican candidates to victory in House and Senate races. But Nixon, interested mainly in increasing the size of his own anticipated landslide, would have none of it, and Dole did not disguise his irritation, grumbling to John Mitchell, the head of Nixon's reelection campaign, about the failure to put the president's popularity to use in the congressional campaigns. Dole finally gave up after he was denied permission to make a public presentation to the First Lady of a sweater with an elephant on it.

"We have to appeal to donkeys," a Nixon aide told him.

"I'll give her a donkey sweater next week," Dole promised, but to no avail.

Nixon had the last word, ousting Dole from his party post right after the election in favor of George Bush. Despite his differences with the White House, Dole held enough chits with the Senate GOP leadership to wangle a seat on the Senate Finance Committee in 1973 and promptly steeped himself in what are among the most sensitive and far-reaching decisions made by the government: the writing and rewriting of tax laws. Probably nowhere else in government does so much money hang on the smallest change of word or phrase.

Dole ate it up. He became an authority—and the ranking minority member on the committee. And when the same tide that had swept Reagan into office brought the Republicans control of the Senate, the fifty-seven-year-old Dole, starting his third Senate term, found himself in the legislative majority for the first time since he had left Kansas and in possession of one of the richest prizes on Capitol Hill, chairmanship of the Senate Finance Committee. Dole made no bones about what he wanted to do. He intended to use the momentum of the Reagan presidency "to attack the sins of the past," particularly the federal deficit, his former press secretary Walt Riker recalled. "What was always atop his agenda was deficit and deficit reduction," recalled Riker. "I can tell you that in every speech and in every town meeting, in every thing he ever did, the deficit was talked about over and over again."

For the first months of the Reagan presidency, Dole bided his time, while the supply-side tax cutters had their day. But as interest rates climbed and red ink mounted, he became increasingly skeptical about the underlying theory of Reaganomics—that deep cuts in tax rates would somehow generate more tax revenue. "The good news is that a busload of supply-siders went over a cliff," Dole regularly wisecracked at GOP functions. "The bad news is that there were some empty seats."

As the federal deficit burgeoned rapidly in the wake of the tax cuts enacted in 1981, Dole stopped joking, and his Midwestern heritage of fiscal prudence came fully to the fore. For most of the past half century, the Republicans regularly played their expected role as budget balancers in the Midwest. "The long-established pattern was that Democrats would get elected, do a lot of things, go into debt," said David Keene, a longtime Dole adviser. "So people would elect a Republican, and he would raise taxes and balance the budget. And then people would throw him out and bring back a Democrat."

Dole created and pushed through Congress what by some measurements was the largest tax increase in history, totaling more than $98 billion, even getting Republican colleague Jesse Helms of North Carolina, the heart of tobacco land, to vote for a hike in the cigarette tax. But his insistence on raising taxes when supply-side theory was still riding high did him no good with conservatives in his own party. Over on the House side, ardent supply-sider Newt Gingrich, with typical brashness, labeled Dole with a phrase that would be remembered and repeated as long as Dole remained in public life: "the tax collector for the welfare state."

Although this verbal abuse from his own party surely complicated Dole's future, he did not show concern. "If you are in the minority, you can put out a lot of newsletters and say, 'I'm for lower taxes,'" he remarked of the carping from Gingrich and other House members. "We have a little different view in the Senate, because we're in the majority. We have to be totally responsible from time to time."

Meanwhile, Dole pressed his onslaught against public debt. Having taken over as Senate Republican leader after Reagan's reelection in 1984, he used his new prominence to push a deficit-reduction plan that focused on spending cuts, including postponement of Social Security cost-of-living increases. Once again, some in his own party rebelled, as they had in 1982. This time, Reagan broke with Dole, and the proposal died.

The episode served as a reality check. Even though the Senate Republicans had given Dole the title of leader, his authority in the Senate and the party would not go unchallenged, particularly in the area of economics and particularly if the new Republican senator from Texas, Phil Gramm, had anything to say about it. And he almost always did.

A lanky figure whose facial features inspired comparisons to various birds and amphibians, Gramm's conduct in the Senate was shaped by a combination of boundless intellectual energy that impressed many of his colleagues and overbearing self-certitude that antagonized a good many others. "In terms of IQ, he's in a different class than most members," recalled an admiring Jim Miller, who served as Reagan's budget director and years before that had been a fellow student of Gramm's at the University of Georgia, then taught with him at Texas A&M. "But he doesn't hide his light under a bushel."

Gramm was still on the Texas A&M faculty when his light began to shine on the national scene. The first important glow came in November 1973 from an article on the then-current energy crisis published in the *Wall Street Journal*. In the article, Gramm set forth the free-market principles he has lived by and voted for ever since. Dismissing the notion that energy resources should be conserved and production and distribution regulated by the government, Gramm drew an analogy to the high prices for whale oil due to the shortage of that fuel in the mid-nineteenth century, when it was the chief fuel source for artificial light. Arguing that the high prices provided a profit incentive for the development of efficient refining processes for petroleum and kerosene, Gramm concluded: "We owe the benefits and comforts of the present era to free enterprise and the scarcity of whales."

This essay established Gramm, then only thirty-one, as a leading advocate for the anticonservation forces in the national debate over energy, led to more appearances in print and on lecture stages, and, ultimately, to his entry into politics. Reminding Gramm that he had moved to Texas from his native Georgia only a few years before, his friend Miller asked how he proposed to avoid being depicted as a carpetbagger when he sought elective office in his adopted state.

"Jimmy," Gramm told him, "two Georgians died at the Alamo and they bought my birthright."

Running as a Democrat challenging entrenched incumbent Democratic senator Lloyd Bentsen for renomination in 1976, Gramm was predictably crushed. But the attention he got from this statewide contest helped him win a seat in Congress two years later. His career as a Texas lawmaker would reflect the same shifts in party alignment that were rumbling through the South and that had shaped Gingrich's destiny in Georgia.

Starting out in politics, it had never occurred to Gramm to pursue his ambitions outside the Democratic party. "I was born a Democrat," he told me. "My grandmother thought of Republicans as those Yankees from New Hampshire who burned down her grandmother's barn. I never met a Republican until I was grown."

Once in Washington, Gramm got to meet numerous Republicans, notably a young GOP congressman from Michigan named David Stockman, who in two years would become Reagan's budget director and the point man for the supply-side economic revolution. Gramm and Stockman turned out to be kindred spirits. "Gramm knew the entire supply-side catechism backwards and forwards," Stockman later wrote. Even better, Stockman found, Gramm was no mere theoretician. "He was steeped in detailed knowledge of basic federal programs" and could "rip through the alleged facts and mythical rationalizations which support little sinkholes of waste" throughout the bureaucracy.

By 1981, Reagan was in the White House, and Stockman, his right-hand man, turned to his ideological bedfellow Gramm to rally the "Boll Weevil Democrats," whose votes were needed in the House, to carry to passage Reagan's first budget, replete with supply-side tax cuts. The crucial moment came when Gramm, addressing a Boll Weevil caucus, once again invoked the memory of the Alamo, as he had done with Jim Miller, recalling the heroes who had crossed the celebrated line drawn in the sand by Colonel William Barrett Travis. One faint-hearted lawmaker pointed out that everyone who had crossed the line had died, and others murmured in agreement.

"Yes," said Gramm, "but the ones who didn't cross the line died, too. And no one remembered their names."

That settled it. The backing of the Boll Weevils, many from the Alamo state of Texas, ensured the passage of Gramm's budget, which in turn paved the way for adoption of the huge multiyear tax cut that reshaped the economic course of the Republican party. But Gramm did more to help the so-called Reagan revolution, then at its crest, than simply muster Democratic support for Republican policies. From his privileged post on the House Budget Committee, he reported to his ally Stockman about Democratic grand strategy. When the Democrats learned of this at their caucus following the 1982 midterm elections, they expelled Gramm from his committee position. He promptly expelled himself from the Democratic party. Not only that, he quit his House seat and announced he would run for re-election as a Republican.

The late Lee Atwater—future Republican National chairman and at the time a White House political operative—warned Gramm he was taking an unnecessary risk. He urged him to serve out the term to which he had been elected. But Gramm understood better than Atwater how much party allegiance had crumbled in America in the postwar era. Indeed, in Texas, Gramm's constituents held parties in such low repute that he was able to transform his betrayal of the Democrats into an act of conscience and courage.

"I had to choose between Tip O'Neill and y'all," he told his constituents, who had little use for the Massachusetts Speaker of the House, "and I decided to stand with y'all."

Gramm not only won easily in the special election, but he made himself into something of a folk hero in Texas, a status that helped him move on to the Senate in 1984—and to keep on climbing. Only six months into his term, Gramm called into his office Charles Black, the veteran Republican consultant who had managed his Senate campaign, and showed him a yellow legal pad on which he had sketched the outline of a balanced-budget scheme, amounting to a fiscal Procrustean bed for Congress.

The plan called for elimination of the deficit by meeting a series of targeted spending reductions over five years or, failing that, having the cuts made automatically. For fiscal conservatives, it was a moment in history: Gramm was providing the first hint of a document that would seek to change the way the U.S. government had been managing fiscal policy for nearly two hundred years. Far from being awestruck, Black performed the tactician's role he was assigned and kept his mind on the nitty-gritty.

"Get a moderate Republican to sign on," he advised his client.

Two weeks later, Gramm called Black in to report his progress. "I think I got the right guy," he said. "He's known as a moderate and he's a deficit cutter—Warren Rudman of New Hampshire." Gramm grinned. "New Hampshire, get it?" he said. Black got it.

The reference to New Hampshire, with its first-in-the-nation presidential primary, was a none-too-subtle hint of Gramm's White House ambitions, and the ballyhooed enactment of Gramm-Rudman, as the plan came to be known, markedly boosted those ambitions.

Nonetheless, even if this legislation was a personal triumph for Gramm, it was a worrisome sign for his party, making clear the limitations of the theories underpinning Reagan's economic policy. Problems abounded, including the swelling deficit and hard times in the Farm Belt of the Midwest and the energy-producing states of the Southwest, both bulwarks of the Republican political base. Thus, the midterm election of 1986, far from consolidating Republican strength, tilted Congress back to the Democrats, who recaptured the Senate, consigning both Bob Dole and Phil Gramm to the minority. Dusk was now falling on the Reagan revolution, and Republicans searched for a new prophet and a strengthened faith.

Even before the 1986 vote, the search for new answers was under way among some Republicans, and no one in this group was more active than Lamar Alexander, the governor of Tennessee. To those who believed the party needed a more constructive response to the times than the antigovernment creed that had informed the Reagan revolution, Alexander presented himself as the man with the answer. "Focused and disciplined" were the words used most often to describe him. Only forty-six years old as his gubernatorial tenure was ending in 1986, Alexander had a smooth face with bland features and exuded a carefully cultivated folksiness. He owed his advancement in politics not so much to his convictions, which were fuzzy at best, as to his intense devotion to his own advancement. "From the time he graduated from law school and served his stint as clerk to a federal judge, his ambition in life was to get elected to statewide office in Tennessee," Lee Smith, a classmate of Alexander's at Vanderbilt University, recalled. "And he didn't do anything at all without carefully calculating how it might impact that ambition."

While earning his law degree at New York University, Alexander had served a summer clerkship at the Department of Justice, then headed by Attorney General Robert F. Kennedy. "Washington was a boiling pot of political action," he later wrote in *Steps Along the Way*, a memoir of his political career. "Everyone played touch football. This was the age of the young, government can-do-something, coat-thrown-over-the-shoulder crowd." Alexander was impressed enough by the "Kennedy movement," to briefly consider becoming a Democrat. But like Bob Dole at a similar stage in his career, he made his ultimate choice for reasons that are reflected both in his own practicality and in the insignificance of the differences between the parties. "To get ahead in the Democratic party, you had to stand in a long line," Alexander explained. "The Republican party was wide open."

His first chance to move ahead loomed in 1970 when Alexander, then a junior aide in the Nixon White House, considered running for the Senate. Party leaders talked him out of it, and he settled for managing the gubernatorial campaign of Winfield Dunn, the first Republican to win the Tennessee statehouse in fifty years. Thus did opportunity shape the destiny of Alexander. Instead of marching in the footsteps of former Senate Republican leader Howard H. Baker, an early mentor on Capitol Hill, he would ultimately dedicate himself to the cause of dismantling the federal government and turning its power back to the states and cities. When Alexander tried to succeed to the governorship himself in 1974, he failed dismally, hurt by the Watergate scandal and his own uninspired campaign style. "He ran as a three-piece suit," Vanderbilt University political scientist Richard Pride recalled.

On his second try in 1978, however, Alexander's advisers persuaded him to humanize himself by opening his campaign with a walk across the state. Wearing a red-and-black plaid lumberjack shirt, he trudged more than 1,000 miles, shook countless hands, suffered a badly sprained left ankle when he was front-ended by a pickup truck, and gained the attention that helped him to victory. Alexander's carefully contrived pathway to the top reflected the forces that defined American politics in the third quarter of the twentieth century: energy, ambition, and the ability to present a pleasing personality, all blended together under the supervision of a "hired-gun" political consultant. Of minimal importance in this equation was content—anything having to do with substance and belief. And almost invisible was the element of accountability: the acknowledgment by the candidate that he owed it to the electorate to fulfill any promises tendered.

For all his efforts over eight years to capture the governor's office, Alexander never took the time to figure out what he wanted to do when he got there. "When my walk across Tennessee ended, I honestly still couldn't have expressed just in so many words why I wanted to be governor or what I hoped to accomplish," he later admitted with remarkable candor. "I hoped it would articulate itself along the way."

Not until his second term did Alexander find the cause that would define his governorship and help him get started as a national figure: education reform. It was by no small coincidence that this was exactly the same issue the governor of a neighboring state, Bill Clinton of Arkansas, was promoting at the same time. For an ambitious young governor, education had a certain magic, something both Clinton and Alexander perceived. Not only did it address a major problem in their states, but trying to deal with it was also bound to win national attention, thanks in good measure to the just-released report of the National Commission on Excellence in Education, which had deplored "the rising tide of mediocrity" in schools across the land.

Alexander's proposals bore a striking resemblance to Clinton's and included a controversial plan to award "merit-pay increases" to teachers who could claim to be better qualified. He rammed the scheme through the legislature only after a furious battle with the state teachers' union. The struggle left such scars that Alexander later singled out "not finding a way to work better with the Tennessee Education Association" as his "greatest failure" in office.

In the midst of his endeavors in Nashville, Alexander, like Clinton, carved out a conspicuous role for himself among his fellow governors. In particular, he became a proponent of the Reagan-era New Federalism doctrines, which, prefiguring a trend that was to gain momentum after the 1994 elections under the fancier name "devolution," sought to shift responsibility for welfare and other federal programs back to the states. Mindful that despite Reagan's landslide reelection, the 1984 returns left the Democrats controlling two-thirds of the governorships and a majority of the legislatures, Alexander sought to energize Republicans at the local level. National issues are "tremendously important and so fascinating," he told the 1,500 delegates to a Southern Republican leadership conference in the spring of 1986. "But when we get together, that's all we talk about, and the Democratic governors are running down the street proposing programs to improve the schools, clean up the garbage, fix the roads, and make the children more healthy—and they get elected."

Alexander had put his finger on the bifurcated outlook of voters, which had fostered the new era of divided government just beginning to take hold across the country. To take charge of the "tremendously important" issues of managing the nation's economy and its national security, Americans wanted Republicans in the White House. But when it came to getting the government to deliver the goods, Americans counted on Democrats. In effect, the electorate had built a wall right through the middle of the political system, a barrier against which both parties would bang their heads in frustration for years to come.

Whatever merits Alexander's practical counsel might hold for Republican strivings on the state and local level, it offered little appeal for the conservative activists who provided the party with much of its passion and intellectual energy, more and more of whom, as the Reagan era drew to an end, were turning to Patrick J. Buchanan as their principal spokesman. Buchanan certainly came by his convictions honestly. They were shaped by his father, William Baldwin Buchanan, a blustery, hulking figure whose outlook was defined by his hatred of communism and all things tainted by it, his devotion to the rules of the Roman Catholic Church, and his three political icons: Joe McCarthy, General Douglas MacArthur, and Fascist Spain's Generalissimo Francisco Franco. "Unfortunately, in disciplining his son," Patrick Buchanan later wrote, "it was General Franco that my father chose as the role model."

Coming of age in such a household, Pat Buchanan regarded Lamar Alexander's talk about picking up garbage and fixing streets as trivializing on a shameful scale. For Buchanan, the name of the game in politics was seizing the White House and all that went with it. "If conservatives would turn the nation around," Buchanan wrote in his 1976 book *Conservative Votes, Liberal Victories*, "they must set as their central political objective the capture of the presidency."

In rallying conservatives to his side, Buchanan could call upon loyalties forged during his years in the Nixon presidency. In addition to being an influential in-house lobbyist for conservative causes, his speechwriting for Nixon's vice president, Spiro Agnew, provided a megaphone for conservatives' deep-rooted resentment of what they regarded as liberal domination of the press. It seemed only fitting that when Buchanan, then thirty-five, left Nixon's service in 1974, he reentered newspaper work, where he had begun his career and where he could now carry on, face-to-face and hand to hand, his battle against "the political power of America's media monopolies," which he targeted as "the most formidable obstacle" in the path of conservatives.

Buchanan, who had been an editorial writer for the *St. Louis Globe Democrat* before he joined up with Nixon, had no easy time getting reestablished in the Fourth Estate. Although he himself was untarnished by Watergate, his connection with Nixon dragged on his attempts to market his syndicated column. "He only got paid for the columns they printed, and it wasn't much," recalled Angela "Bay" Buchanan, his sister and, later, his campaign manager. Initially, he considered himself strictly a print journalist. When he filled in as a guest commentator on TV and watched his own performance, he told his sister, "I rolled off the bed laughing I was so bad." Nevertheless, further opportunity came his way, and in the Milquetoast world of electronic journalism, Buchanan's bare-knuckles style made him a star, first on radio, then on television. However, he was so harsh in expression and unyielding in belief that he sometimes embarrassed even his conservative allies, as when he dubbed AIDS nature's "awful retribution" against homosexuals and questioned whether the bombing of abortion clinics was any worse an offense than the act of abortion itself.

Reagan's reelection brought Buchanan back to the White House, where he plunged headlong into the fight to fund the Contras in Nicaragua and the Star Wars missile defense program. As Reagan's influence ebbed with the Iran-Contra scandal and the imminent end of his tenure, many of Buchanan's old allies urged him to run for president himself, claiming, as Buchanan later put it, that only his candidacy could prevent the Republican nomination from being yielded to "the Republican establishment," represented by Reagan's vice president, George Bush, the heavy favorite in the race. But conservative leaders warned, and Buchanan himself admitted, that his candidacy would only assure Bush's nomination by dividing the right wing between himself and Jack Kemp, then a New York congressman whose own candidacy was well under way. Buchanan ultimately heeded this cautious counsel.

Afterward, reflecting on the contrast between himself and Kemp, who was absorbed with such economic esoterica as tax rates and monetary reform, Buchanan wrote: "Economics is not the science that sends men to the barricades. Whether the choice of weapons is words or guns, men fight to preserve the most beautiful of the pictures in their minds."

With Buchanan on the sidelines, a vision of some sort was much in demand among Republicans as the 1988 campaign approached. In the eyes of many Republican activists, the underlying purpose of that competition, more than just filling Reagan's vacancy, was to find a replacement for his ideology. Neither George Bush, the front-runner in the race, nor his chief rival, Bob Dole, had much to offer in that regard. But this was a bigger handicap for Dole, who had to catch up to the vice president.

Yet Dole refused to take this deficiency seriously. Meeting with his board of strategy, Dole "was very contemptuous of all the talk about vision," recalled Tom Rath, a ranking member of the Dole brain trust. "His answer to the vision talk seemed to be, 'Give me a picture of the in-basket in the Oval Office and you can put anything in it you want and I can handle it.'"

As his frustrated campaign advisers came to realize, Dole did not seem to hold to any beliefs that went beyond the particular circumstances of a particular piece of legislation. Although his command of the inner workings of government was unrivaled, he had a hard time impressing the significance of this on the electorate. When a debate moderator in Iowa asked what his goals for the country were, Dole rambled on at length about his skills as a lawmaker. "But what are the goals?" the moderator insisted. "And that's where I want to go," Dole retorted. The truth was Dole had not said anything about going anywhere.

Dole's difficulties were compounded by the transformation in the GOP economic orthodoxy that had taken place during the Reagan regime. "For Dole, the traditional budget balancer and deficit hawk, it was as if the party's economic theories had flipped," said David Keene, Dole's longtime adviser. "And Dole, who had always been an economic right-winger, now found himself on the other side of the divide from a lot of people in the right wing."

This economic form reversal proved to be Dole's undoing in the 1988 New Hampshire primary, where the momentum had appeared to be running his way following his victory in the Iowa caucus. The Bush campaign let the air out of Dole's balloon in the final hours of the New Hampshire campaign with a television commercial that warned the tax-hating citizens of the Granite State that when it came to raising taxes, Dole "can't say no." This strategy turned out to have fateful consequences for Bush as well as Dole, for while the gambit assured Dole's defeat, it also led Bush into the read-my-lips no-tax pledge that would undermine his presidency.

Dole, however, was the one to suffer first. By the afternoon of primary day in New Hampshire, Tom Rath recalled, "I could see from the way Dole acted that he felt it had slipped away." Rath had arranged for an elegant luncheon to be catered at campaign headquarters. "Forget that," Dole said, and he put in an order for Kentucky Fried Chicken and Carvel ice cream.

Returning to the Senate once again as the leader of the minority, Dole put whatever resentments he felt behind him and became George Bush's newest best friend. The acid test came in fall 1990, when Bush, desperate to head off a recession that he feared would end his presidency, cut his deal with the Democrats to raise taxes. Even while Gingrich and the House Republicans rebelled, Dole held the line in the Senate and helped ultimately to get the budget through.

As difficult as this deal was for Dole to swallow, it was an even more bitter pill for Gramm. The agreement nullified the Gramm-Rudman law, which had been his pride and joy. Confronted with a choice between his president and his convictions against raising taxes, the wily Gramm opted for both. As a member of the Senate negotiating team, Gramm supported the original arrangement with the Democrats, which called for more than $100 billion in new taxes. But when the House turned that down, Gramm opposed the new budget proposal, which not only had a bigger total of new taxes but also raised tax rates on wealthier Americans.

Frustrated on the legislative front, Gramm began making long-range preparations for the presidential candidacy that everyone expected him to launch at the first opportunity. He consolidated his base in Texas, gaining reelection with a record 60 percent of the vote, and, just as important, raised enough money so that he emerged with a $4-million surplus to help finance his drive for the White House.

For Lamar Alexander, the Bush presidency also meant frustration. Based on the reputation he had gained in Tennessee, Bush named him secretary of education in 1991, but the new secretary and the Democratic Congress wrestled each other to the ground. The lawmakers stymied Alexander's efforts to cut back on the federal role in education, while Alexander blocked congressional efforts to aid the schools. With Bush's defeat, Alexander saw new opportunity. "I thought President Bush's defeat signaled a generational change in our politics," he recalled. "Basically, we were replacing one of the most respected veterans of World War II with two guys in their forties. I thought our party would be going through the same sort of change, and I wanted to be part of it."

If Alexander regarded the 1992 election as a portent of generational change, Pat Buchanan viewed the outcome in stark ideological terms, as a repudiation of the centrist approach to governing. Bush had claimed to be Reagan's legatee, but he had turned out to be—or so Buchanan and many conservatives believed—a closet centrist, not much different from the self-styled centrist governor of Arkansas who had led the Democrats to victory. What the election showed, Buchanan and other conservatives believed, was that centrism was not the answer for the GOP.

Buchanan was in a better position than anyone to make that argument, having spearheaded the conservative challenge to Bush in the 1992 contest for the GOP nomination, while Dole, Gramm, and Alexander had all collaborated with the incumbent. Buchanan's candidacy was doubly divisive. It pitted conservatives against the GOP establishment, whose leaders rallied around Bush, and it also divided the conservative movement itself, particularly because Buchanan's "new nationalism" led him to repudiate the free-trade principles to which most conservatives were committed and to which Buchanan himself had previously paid allegiance. What drove him to this apostasy, Buchanan claimed, was the emotional experience of campaigning in recession-ridden New Hampshire, where the sorry condition of the state's working families mocked the claims made for the much-revered free-trade system. "I knew times were tough up there, but I didn't know how deep it was," he said later. "I didn't know the degree of anger and alienation and bitterness."

After a strong showing in New Hampshire, Buchanan's campaign petered out. But he saved his harshest blast for last. During his address at the national convention in Houston, he proclaimed, "There is a religious war going on in our country for the soul of America," imploring his listeners to "take back our cities, take back our culture and take back our country." When some Republicans claimed Buchanan's speech contributed to Bush's defeat, Buchanan, since returned to his role as columnist, shot back: "Republicans did not lose in 1992 because Pat Buchanan gave a blazing speech in Houston. They lost because Big Government conservatives . . . spent four years in an orgy of spending, raised taxes, and aborted a seven-year recovery." Whatever impact the speech had on the electorate, it was clear that candidate Buchanan meant it as a calling card, signaling that his first campaign would not be his last.

But in 1996, he would have plenty of company. Bob Dole signaled his intentions only hours after Bill Clinton's victory in the three-cornered race with Bush and independent Ross Perot was assured. In the midst of the talk about a mandate for the new president, Dole reminded one and all that "57 percent of the Americans who voted in the presidential election voted against Bill Clinton. . . . I intend to represent that majority on the floor of the U.S. Senate," he declared.

Dole's colleague from Texas, Phil Gramm, was hard on his heels, vying with Dole for the title of Republican who had tried hardest to keep Clinton from succeeding. He selected as his main target the health-care reform proposal, which was the centerpiece of Clinton's domestic program. After successfully campaigning against it, Gramm jibed at his old rival Dole: "I was conservative before conservative was cool."

As for Alexander, he spent two months in the summer of 1994 driving across the country, meeting people, gathering material for campaign speeches, and developing his campaign slogan: "Cut their pay and send them home." The slogan anticipated the 1994 election returns, which sent enough Democrats home to put the Republicans in charge. Those dramatic results robbed Alexander's battle cry of much of its punch, but it also created a more fundamental problem for his rivals for the nomination—indeed, for the whole party. Republicans could no longer concentrate simply on denouncing Democrat Bill Clinton's administration. Suddenly, they themselves had become responsible for a large share of the government.

In the immediate aftermath of the midterm elections, such long-range problems hardly concerned the contenders for the Republican presidential nomination. They were riding the wave of euphoria from the huge midterm victory, which had shocked the political world. To hear some of the talk in Washington from so-called political insiders in both parties, the presidential election in 1996 was all but over. If Clinton had any sense of reality or decency, he would step aside in favor of Al Gore; that way, the Democrats might have a chance—not to win, but to avoid an outright disaster.

But seasoned strategists in Republican ranks took a more sober view of the portent of the midterm election for the presidential campaign. Whatever forces were responsible for the Republican triumph on Capitol Hill, the country's divided system of politics and government made it uncertain whether Republican prospects for the presidency could benefit either from these forces or from the result they had achieved. It was one thing to mount a campaign against a Democratic Congress by exploiting dissatisfaction with a Democratic president, but it would be quite another, and more difficult, task to develop a constructive alternative to challenge that president directly for control of the White House.

Moreover, as they looked ahead to the next two years, Republican presidential strategists found themselves in uncharted waters. For the better part of the past half century, GOP presidential candidates, incumbent or otherwise, had the relatively simple task of running not only against their Democratic opponent but also against the Democratic majority in charge of Congress. But in 1996, whoever the GOP standard-bearer turned out to be, he would have to run in close harmony with the Republican-controlled Congress—a prospect that set off alarms among party leaders such as Eddie Mahe, Gingrich's collaborator in the GOPAC planning a few years earlier. "The merging of our congressional agenda, which is going to be aggressive, with our presidential campaign message could create some opportunities for real pain," Mahe told me at the time.

Republicans would have to find a way to contend with the inherent conflict between the glowing promises of the presidential campaign trail, where White House contenders deal in sweeping generalizations, and the unpleasant reality of Congress, where legislators make deals that inevitably alienate some group of constituents. Heightening the potential for grief was the ambitious agenda promoted by congressional Republicans under their Contract with America rubric—and by Bob Dole, who seemed determined to maintain his position as majority leader while he pursued his quest for the White House.

The last votes had scarcely been counted before Dole, with his customary concern for holding down the deficit, made plain his limited enthusiasm for the Contract's proposals sponsored by Speaker Gingrich, particularly its sweeping package of tax cuts. Asked if he believed Congress could cut taxes, increase defense spending, and still manage to balance the budget within five years, as the House Republican Contract with America promised, Dole replied: "It would be difficult."

Nor did the glow of victory erase Dole's recollections of his past disagreements with Gingrich, the man in charge of enforcing the Contract. Dole observed that Gingrich had reportedly described him as "maturing," and, recalling Gingrich's famous jeer after Dole had pushed through the 1982 tax hike, the Senator remarked: "So, I guess that makes me a matured tax collector for the welfare state."

The Contract also presented ample opportunity for clashes between Dole and Phil Gramm, the latter being Dole's chief competitor on budget policy in the Senate and his rival for the nomination. All through the early stages of the campaign year, Gramm had tried to use Dole's occasional deviations from strict adherence to some of the Contract's hard-edged proposals as evidence that the front-runner was insufficiently committed to the conservative cause.

Just as touchy and potentially divisive were the so-called social issues, particularly school prayer and abortion. Although these issues had been left out of the Contract precisely to avoid conflict, their omission caused unrest among the party's potent cohort of Christian conservatives, whom Gingrich sought to placate within a month of the midterm elections by announcing that he wanted to push for congressional adoption of a school-prayer amendment. Gingrich's initiative provoked an immediate protest from Republican governors, who argued that congressional Republicans should concentrate instead on the economic discontent that they believed had produced the Republican landslide. This sort of intraparty friction was bad news for GOP hopes of assembling a united front against Clinton in the fall of 1996. "If we don't deal with economic issues," warned Michigan governor John Engler, "we'll need more than prayer to solve our problems."

Along with such ideological tensions, the contenders for the presidency confronted more prosaic, but nonetheless vexing problems arising from the schedule of contests for the convention delegates. The candidates found themselves at the mercy of a primary and caucus calendar that had been condensed to an unprecedented degree. The compressed calendar of delegate contests was, in turn, a product of deeper problems in the political system. For the past two decades, since the primaries had taken on transcendent importance in the presidential nominating competition, the timing and sequence of the primary contests had become another factor distorting the political process. During a series of quadrennial struggles, the leaders of both parties had lost control of the system for selecting their standard-bearers, a process that was now dominated by a combination of tradition, local and regional chauvinism, and whim and caprice.

The Democrats had been much more active than the Republicans in trying to regulate and manipulate the schedule, though their efforts often contradicted each other. On the national level, Democratic officials sought to maintain stability by banning states from shifting their place on the calendar in a way that might threaten the status of other states, particularly New Hampshire, which jealously guarded its role as home of the nation's first primary, and Iowa, which just as obsessively cherished its position as the site of the first official delegate competition of any kind, the Iowa precinct caucuses. Yet on the regional level, Southern Democratic leaders undermined the status quo by creating the Super Tuesday conglomeration of primaries, intended to promote the choice of a presidential candidate suited to Southern tastes.

The Republicans, however, following the pattern of their laissez-faire approach to public policy, generally avoided meddling with the primary schedule, leaving such decisions to local officials. But this hands-off approach backfired in 1996, when, in hopes of stealing the glory and influence reaped by Iowa and New Hampshire, California, New York, and a number of other big states crammed their primaries into the early weeks of the campaign. Thus, in contrast with 1992, when only fourteen states with 631 delegates had cast their ballots for president by mid-March, by the same time in 1996 under the new calendar, twenty-three states were scheduled to choose nearly 1,100 delegates, more than enough for a majority at the party's August convention in San Diego.

This front-loading raised to astronomic levels the cost of running for president, which had been climbing steadily in any case. In past campaigns, little-known candidates with limited financial resources could hope that a victory in the early contests in Iowa and New Hampshire would boost their prestige and allow them to raise enough funds to compete effectively in the later primary contests, which ground on until mid-June. To have any chance of success now, however, a candidate needed to ante up a huge sum at the start of the competition. The rule of thumb among Republican strategists, as they surveyed this calendar in early 1995, was that to compete effectively, a candidate would need to raise at least $20 million by the end of January 1996— more money for one candidate than the combined total raised by Bill Clinton and his rivals in all the Democratic candidacies by that date in 1992.

By raising the stakes of running for president, the front-loaded calendar limited the Republican field, eliminating candidates who spoke for important elements of the Republican electorate. Most prominent among these was Jack Kemp, not only the prophet of supply-side economics but also one of the few Republican leaders who argued for broadening the party's horizons to reach minority groups. William J. Bennett, the former education secretary, an eloquent advocate of moral and cultural values, and Richard Cheney, former House whip and secretary of defense, a man respected for his intellect and integrity even by those who disagreed with him, were other casualties of the new calendar.

Boosting the cost of getting nominated also boosted the chances of the person able to raise the most money—namely, Dole—thereby creating another advantage for the candidate who already had more advantages than anyone else. When it came to picking its presidential nominees, a royalist tradition governed the Republican party, leading to the selection of whichever candidate the party's hierarchy favored. This tendency had become even more explicit in the past twenty years, during which there had been an informal line of succession, with each nominee followed by the man who had been his chief rival for the nomination. Thus, Reagan followed Ford, Bush succeeded Reagan, and now it seemed to be Dole's turn. This tendency was so strong that it took on the force of a self-fulfilling prophecy.

"One thing we have to face here is the humongous lead that Dole has among Republicans, and the fact that Republicans nominate whoever their front-runner is a year out from the election," Fred Steeper, who served in the Bush and Ronald Reagan campaigns, told me early in 1995. No Republican front-runner had been upset since 1952, when Ohio senator Robert

Taft, known as "Mr. Republican," lost out to Dwight D. Eisenhower, the proximate mid-twentieth-century equivalent of George Washington—a role none of Dole's rivals came close to approaching. Back in the pack, the other candidates might take comfort in stories of obscure candidates who, in the past, had rocketed to the top after catching fire in Iowa or New Hampshire. But that sort of thinking had a fundamental flaw for Republicans, as Steeper noted: "These guys who come from asterisks in the polls to getting nominated were all in the Democratic party."

Not that Republicans were unmindful of Dole's weaknesses. "If you were to ask for a résumé of the right candidate to run in 1996, you probably wouldn't come up with somebody who had never had a job outside of government and who has been in Washington thirty-five years, and would be seventy-three when he is inaugurated," his longtime adviser David Keene acknowledged. But Dole's candidacy, after two previous failures, raised more fundamental concern, shared even by the party leaders who backed him. "Their worst fear," Keene said, "is that after all these years, he still won't be able to come up with some kind of message."

That concern was shared by Dole's campaign staff—and by the candidate himself. "In a presidential campaign, voters look at three things," Bill Lacey, Dole's chief strategist told me. "Character, leadership experience, and message. No one can quarrel with Dole's character and experience. Our only vulnerability would be if we don't have a viable message."

Desperate to avoid another defeat in his third try for the presidency, nagged by his supporters and handlers, Dole would try for two years to find that magic formula for a "message" or "vision," or whatever the buzzword of the day happened to be. But his heart and mind were never in this exercise. Dole was a lawmaker, a legislator first and foremost, and he was practiced at the wheedling and cajolery that prevailed in the cloakrooms of the Capitol, where the lofty language expected on the presidential stump would have seemed like posturing. As Dole saw it, he was obligated—to the people of Kansas who had sent him to the Senate, and to his Republican colleagues who had made him their leader—to deliver the goods, to give them what they wanted, or, at least, as much as he could. His success in carrying out that task for three decades should be sufficient proof of his fitness for the presidency. Anything more was beyond his ken.

His appeal for votes rested more on his long seasoning in Washington than on any set of core beliefs. "I think I have made a lot of tough decisions," he told his campaign rallies. "I don't say they've all been right. But most have been difficult. . . . The tough ones are tough. If you want somebody who's been tested and somebody who can make it work, then I want to apply for the job."

9

The Pitchfork Rebellion

SINCE DOLE HIMSELF could not create a message, his handlers sought to graft one onto his announcement speech when he officially declared his candidacy in April 1995. The result was something dubbed the "three R's," which read like the output of a paint-by-the-numbers kit but which Dole manfully articulated first in Kansas and then in the seven other states he visited during his announcement tour: "My mandate as president would be to rein in the federal government, to reconnect our government in Washington with the commonsense values of our citizens, and to reassert American interests around the world."

As awkward as this recitation was for him, the candidate retained his humor and perspective. "You know you have a big stake in my candidacy," he told me onboard his campaign charter plane on announcement day.

"What would that be?" I asked.

"If I'm elected," he said grinning, "I'll be the first president named Bob."

That notion might have served him as well as the "three R's," a slogan whose minimal appeal soon became all too apparent. Far from being a unifying theme for his campaign, it seemed merely a mélange of standard ideas from the conservative catechism that failed to serve the main purpose of a message—to provide justification for Dole's candidacy, to give voters a reason to make him their president.

Part of the problem was that Dole found it hard to indulge in the government bashing that was all the fashion among Republicans in the wake of their 1995 triumph. "I don't stand here and say the government is terrible," he told his audiences. "That's not true. Government has done a lot of good things," and to illustrate, he would mention how the GI Bill helped him get through college and law school.

"You have to say our government does a lot of good things, and then go on and make your case for shrinking it," Dole explained to me. "If you get out there with a sledgehammer and say, 'I'm going to destroy this,' people may clap a little. But on the way home they'll say, 'What is that guy going to do if he gets elected?'"

Still and all, Dole kept searching for the chord to arouse the passions or at least spark the enthusiasm of the electorate. A few weeks after announcing his candidacy, he flew to Los Angeles, heart of the entertainment industry, to condemn Hollywood for debasing the nation's culture with movies, music, and television programs that he said had produced "nightmares of depravity" drenched in violence and sex. "A line has been crossed—not just of taste but of human dignity and decency," Dole claimed. That speech got Dole a flurry of headlines, a round of praise from conservatives, and a barrage of abuse from liberals who accused him of impinging on the First Amendment. Still, it did not fill the empty space in Dole's candidacy. As the primary contests would show, voters were looking for a political leader who would address their problems, not a movie critic or a preacher.

Searching for a more relevant issue, Dole, late that summer, unveiled an outline of his new economic doctrine. In essence, Dole, who for years had been telling his joke about a busload of supply-side economists driving over a cliff, got onboard the supply-side bus himself—sort of. Demonstrating his adherence to his new faith, he intoned its scripture before the Economic Club of Chicago. "High marginal rates discourage work, reduce the rewards of entrepreneurship, and encourage tax avoidance," Dole declared dutifully, never letting the phrase "budget deficit" escape his lips. And he embraced the other major tenets of the supply-side policy—a "flatter tax system," abolition of the Internal Revenue Service, and a constitutional amendment requiring a three-fifths vote in Congress to raise taxes.

But once again, Dole had fallen short in his effort to fire up his candidacy. Supply-siders complained that Dole lagged behind the supply-side curve, the leading edge of which now reached to the flat tax. Whereas Dole had only alluded vaguely to a "flatter tax," his rival Phil Gramm had pledged without qualification or caveat that if elected to the White House, he would see to it that a flat tax would be fully in place before his first term ended. Mostly, what Dole had accomplished by his economic speech and his denunciation of Hollywood was to reduce the incentive for the party's die-hard conservatives to oppose him—and to make it easier for them to accept what he hoped they would think of as the inevitability of his nomination.

Indeed, it was this idea—that he could not be stopped—that became the main engine driving Dole's candidacy. Although presidential candidates generally shy away from the front-runner designation lest they build expectations they cannot meet, Dole and his advisers had no such compunctions. In nearly every press release, they referred to him as the "Republican presidential front-runner," relying on a sort of Calvinist syllogism that suggested that Dole had been anointed by the party establishment because he was destined to win the nomination and that he was destined to win because he had been anointed.

To reinforce that point, within a few weeks of Dole's formal announcement of candidacy, his staff proudly released a twelve-page list of their candidate's Republican VIP backers, topped by eight governors and sixteen senators. And in keeping with the notion of inevitability, the endorsers offered their own backing as evidence of Dole's qualifications. Announcing that Dole had the collective blessing of the Speaker of the South Carolina Assembly, the president pro tem of the Senate, the governor and lieutenant governor, and all the Republican committee chairs in the General Assembly, the former governor of that state, Carroll Campbell, claimed: "A man who can appeal that broadly has something special."

What Dole had that was particularly special was money. Collecting funds was at least as high on the Dole campaign's priority list as collecting endorsements. By the end of summer, he had taken in nearly $15 million, far more than any of his competitors, and he was well along the road to the $20-million target for the beginning of the primary season.

Along with his money and endorsements, as the campaign ground on, the level of Dole's opposition was one of his most important assets. In the main, Dole's rivals seemed to be relying more on Dole doing some damage to himself—either by losing his famous temper in public or committing some other blunder that would give them an opening they could not create for themselves. In campaign debates, they sniped away at him, hoping to provoke an outburst. At one gathering in Denver, for example, Gramm, reiterating his oft-repeated claim that he deserved much of the credit for defeating Clinton's health-care reform proposal, then sharpened his point by contending that he had staked out a hard-line position in opposition "when the pollsters in Bob Dole's office said it was political suicide to take on health care." But Dole just let such brickbats fly by, with little more than a derisive grimace in response.

"It's very hard to force a professional like Dole to make a mistake," House Speaker Newt Gingrich told me at the time. "He may make a mistake, but it won't be because somebody forced him to do it. And in the effort to try to force it, the others may actually chew themselves up."

If they could not get Dole's goat, his rivals hoped that Dole's ingrained tendency to bargain and compromise on legislation could prove to be his undoing, causing him to make pragmatic sacrifices of portions of the GOP Contract with America, cherished by conservatives. "To me, he's the Contract killer," said Earl Ehrhart, the Republican whip of the Georgia House of Representatives and a Gramm supporter. "Everything Gingrich sends over, Dole cuts in half and then says: 'OK, and now we'll compromise on the other half.'" But despite such carping from his foes, on most matters of consequence, Dole stuck closely to the party line, as set by Gingrich, in large part because he feared that to do otherwise would turn Republican conservatives against his candidacy.

Still others among Dole's opposition contended that his senior-citizen status would ultimately hurt him. "People are going to want somebody from a younger generation to lead the country into the next century," said Mike Murphy, chief strategist for Alexander. But the sticking point was who would that somebody be?

None of the candidates in the field seemed up to playing that role. Although most Republicans, including Dole, rated Phil Gramm as Dole's most dangerous foe because of Gramm's reputation as a fund-raiser and his prominence in the Senate, Gramm's arrogance hindered his ambitions as much as Dole's inarticulateness hurt his candidacy. "He's like the kid you knew in grade school who was smarter than you and every day found a way to remind you of it," Senator Trent Lott once remarked.

The heart of Gramm's appeal to conservatives was a pledge stark in its simplicity, particularly by comparison with Dole's often hazy and convoluted rhetoric. Nearly everywhere he went, he promised "to finish the Reagan revolution" by taking power from Washington and turning it over to the middle-class families "who do the work and pay the taxes and pull the wagon in America." Judging from their rhetoric on a host of issues, Dole and Gramm would wind up in the same place. But conservatives liked the idea that Gramm seemed determined to get there sooner. "I'm going to get the government out of your cash register," Gramm promised the owner of Hubba's Coffee Shop, as he bounded into the premises on a brief handshaking stop in New Hampshire.

Yet nearly everywhere he went along the road that he hoped would carry him to the nomination, Gramm seemed to get in his own way. Recalling a bitter public argument with the late Democratic representative Claude Pepper of Florida over Social Security, he told an audience in Manchester, New Hampshire's biggest city, that afterward, his mother phoned him to take the side of Pepper, a longtime champion of the elderly. She said, according to Gramm, "When that sweet Claude Pepper is speaking, you shut up and listen to him." At that point, Gramm had the audience in his pocket, disarmed by his apparent confession of error. Gramm's vanity, though, would not allow him to let the matter rest there. "If we had listened to Claude Pepper," he went on, "Social Security would have gone broke. That was a case where I was right, and we won, and where the country benefited." But whatever the country might have gained, Gramm's candidacy had just suffered a self-inflicted wound.

While Gramm waged a losing battle against his own ego, Lamar Alexander struggled to recover from the unusual political sin of being right too soon. Although he had been quicker than any of his rivals to sense the resentiment of Washington that pervaded the country the year before with his "cut their pay and send them home" slogan, his outsider's agenda had been in effect co-opted by the new Republican-run 104th Congress, which included his two prime rivals for the nomination—Dole and Gramm. Striving to update his message in the wake of the election, Alexander began telling voters that the heinous legacy of Democratic congressional rule—the swollen federal bureaucracy and the moral decay undermining the nation's spirit—could not be cleared away without a Republican president to work alongside the Republican Congress.

What the country needed, Alexander argued, was a president like himself, trained in state government, "committed not just to fixing things in Washington but . . . to moving responsibility out of Washington back to where it belongs and to leading a spiritual revival."

But Alexander's background as a former Nixon White House aide and Bush cabinet member contradicted his claim to be an outsider. So also did the fact that the connections he had made in public life helped him, through a series of investments, to increase his net worth tenfold since he won his first term as governor in 1978. Alexander claimed he had taken great care to scrutinize the opportunities offered him to avoid ethical problems. But when I asked him if he could recall any opportunities he had turned down, he could not name a single one.

Another contradiction in Alexander's candidacy was his claim to want to take over the federal government mostly to turn its responsibilities back to the states. Why did he not just run for governor? "Because it will take a president to reverse the past fifty years of Washington taking power away from the states and neighborhoods," he told me. Besides, he pointed out, he had already been a governor.

It was revealing of the nature of the Republican campaign that of the four most prominent candidates, the only one generating any degree of enthusiasm on the hustings was the one given the least chance of gaining the nomination—Patrick J. Buchanan. Even his conservative fans discounted Buchanan's prospects. After dismissing a Bob Dole stump speech in Greenville, South Carolina, as "long on fluff," David Gossett, a local attorney, told me that by contrast, Buchanan inspired him. "I would support Pat in a minute if I thought he had a gnat's hair's chance of success."

Buchanan had a rare chance to reach a broader audience in August 1995 when Ross Perot staged a sort of bipartisan jamboree in his hometown of Dallas, which he billed as nothing less than "the political event of the century." But whatever one called it, as the event unfolded, it served to demonstrate the defects of the political system and the failings of the two major parties. Perot claimed that his conference, which drew more than thirty prominent politicians from both parties, including the White House counselor Thomas F. (Mack) McLarty III, as personal representative of the pres-

ident of the United States, would uplift American politics. "We'd like to get
the American people fully informed so that they are not manipulated by
propaganda, sound bites, and negative politics, which is what it's pretty
well deteriorated to now," Perot said. But whatever uplifting took place
was limited to Perot's own ego, which hardly needed a boost. Although describing himself as just a "bit player" at the proceedings, Perot actually cast
himself in a starring role that included welcoming and closing speeches at
the conclave, as well as introductions of each and every speaker.

A totally synthetic and disembodied event that had no connection with
the political process, the conference's only justification for existence was
the presence of hundreds of journalists who made it into the media event of
the political year. Why did the politicians come? They were afraid not to.

A recent survey by Republican and Democratic pollsters had showed that
despite the claimed successes of the new GOP majorities on Capitol Hill,
three out of five Americans thought the country was on the wrong track
and that three out of four mistrusted government leaders, an all-time high.
The poll's findings indicated an opening for a third-party candidate. Yet
Perot scarcely seemed the ideal man for the job. His negative ratings were
too high. Wishful thinkers often mentioned the former Joint Chiefs of Staff
chairman Colin Powell as a possible independent presidential candidate.
But Powell maintained his self-imposed silence on his political ambitions, if
any, until the publication of his memoirs, scheduled for the month after
Perot's conference. And the suspicion gathered strength among political
professionals that the Gulf War hero was more interested in promoting his
book than running the risk of political combat.

In this environment, Republican leaders, who feared a Perot candidacy
would draw voters from their ultimate nominee, hastened to Dallas hoping
they could persuade Perot not to run—and also hoping to win over some of
Perot's followers. Democrats shared that goal, and they also wanted to stay
on Perot's good side, fearing that he could turn a White House bid into an
all-out assault on Clinton.

Unlike the other candidates who were drawn to Dallas by fear and anxiety, Buchanan was impelled by opportunity, and he took full advantage of
it. With an impassioned attack on internationalism, he repeatedly brought
the crowd of Perot supporters to their feet—and threw front-runner Bob
Dole on the defensive. "What are we doing to our own people; what are we
doing to our own country?" Buchanan asked as he denounced NAFTA, the
General Agreement on Tariffs and Trade (GATT), and the Mexican bailout.
"I want to say today to all the globalists, when I raise my hand to take oath
of office, your new world order comes crashing down."

To broaden his assault on the establishment beyond his America First
theme, Buchanan redeclared the "cultural war" he had launched in his
memorable 1992 GOP convention speech, decrying assorted erosion of the

social tradition, which he attributed to the overreaching of the federal government. "They turn Easter into Earth Day and worship dirt," he said. "They took Washington's name off Washington's Birthday," he said. "It's now Presidents' Day. So we can all pay homage to Millard Fillmore, Franklin Pierce, and Bill Clinton."

When it was Dole's turn to speak, he seemed distinctly out of place as he confronted an audience whose resentment of the Washington establishment had been whipped to a fever pitch by Buchanan's rhetoric. The best Dole could do was to offer a limp defense of America's leadership in the world, which he traced back to his own role as a World War II combat hero. "I know we are all here to try to figure out how to fix America," he said. But then he recalled welcoming the leaders of the new democracies in Eastern Europe to the United States. "They didn't want foreign aid," he said. "What they really wanted was to be like America. America is the greatest place on earth," Dole said. "That's where I come from."

"This was a tough audience for Dole," his campaign manager Scott Reed conceded. "But he wasn't going to spread the red meat out for this audience," Reed added. "That's not the way Dole is, and that's why people are going to elect him president."

But as autumn approached, that was far from clear. The Republican presidential campaign, which had gone on for most of the year, had left a huge vacuum that begged for a leader to fill it. In late summer, Colin Powell had finally identified himself as a Republican and as a possible candidate for the party's nomination. But that idea stirred a storm of protest from conservatives irate about the general's support for abortion and affirmative action. Powell decided that the game was not worth the candle and pulled out of the race he had never officially entered.

Meanwhile, another voice was making itself heard with increasing force on the hustings. This belonged to Malcolm S. Forbes Jr., the multimillionaire publishing magnate and ardent advocate of supply-side economic theory, known to his friends, of whom he seemed to be acquiring more every day, as Steve.

Success in presidential politics requires two ingredients above all others—message and money. In the 1996 contest for the Republican nomination, front-runner Bob Dole had enough of the latter but little of the former. Long-shot Pat Buchanan was in the opposite circumstance—with a powerful message but not enough money to get it across. Their two principal rivals, Alexander and Gramm, had neither. Steve Forbes had both—and thus, despite the fact that he had no political experience and little more personal appeal than a waxen image, he was able to wreak havoc on the Republican campaign.

Forbes's message reflected his membership in a new generation of the rich. In the past, in keeping with this country's egalitarian ethic, wealthy Americans who entered politics seemed self-conscious, if not downright guilty, about their affluence. But following the dawn of the Reagan era and his success in rededicating the government to the promotion of materialism, the wealthy shed their embarrassment. Rather than conceal or make amends for their wealth, they seemed determined to protect and enlarge their holdings, an attitude illustrated by the advertising slogan "Capitalist Tool," sported by *Forbes* magazine, flagship of the family's publishing empire.

Just as Pat Buchanan had acquired his outlook on the world from his father, so Steve Forbes Jr. had learned from Malcolm Forbes Sr., who succeeded in vastly expanding the eponymous business magazine founded by *his* father from a marginal venture into what its competitor, *Fortune,* referred to as "one of the most profitable publications in America." For Malcolm Sr., or Super Malcolm, as he was called, business was literally a pleasure. To create a personality for himself that would make his magazine irresistible to the superrich and other advertisers, Steve Forbes's father collected Fabergé eggs, dated Elizabeth Taylor, taxied friendly tycoons around town in the company helicopter, and entertained them in his Normandy chateau or his own island in the Fijis. He achieved the ultimate in conspicuous consumption in 1989 by hosting a $2-million fete in Tangiers to celebrate his seventieth birthday, replete with 200 Berber horsemen and 600 belly dancers. In the face of widespread complaints about this unseemly extravagance, the birthday boy promised not to deduct the cost from his income-tax return, though as *Fortune* tartly noted, "If he kept that promise it would be a departure from his usual practice."

Although Forbes the younger lacked his father's panache, he developed an intellectual rationale for the elder Forbes's acquisitive behavior by drawing on his contacts with supply-side enthusiasts in New York and Washington, who viewed individual wealth as the chief catalyst for prosperity. And soon Forbes edged his way into the public-policy arena—first, as chairman of Empower America, a conservative advocacy group, cofounded by supply-side champion Jack Kemp, whose presidential ambitions he encouraged, and next as adviser to Republican New Jersey gubernatorial candidate Christine Todd Whitman, for whom he crafted the tax-cut proposal that was the mainstay of her victorious candidacy.

Now in 1995, with Kemp on the sidelines, the supply-siders, who had been such a major part of the Republic ascendancy in the 1980s, found themselves without a horse in the race for the Republican nomination, which, in view of Dole's early performance, they viewed as potentially winnable. After much persuasion by Jude Wanniski, an economic consultant who had been a longtime Kemp adviser, Forbes agreed to run in Kemp's stead as the "candidate of growth and opportunity."

No one had to ask where his money was coming from—he would spend his own million, he made clear from the beginning. And because, unlike his opponents, he had passed up federal matching funds, he was free to spend as much as he wanted anywhere he wanted, whereas the other candidates were tied into ceilings in respective states.

Just as important, no one had to ask what his candidacy was about. He answered that question on the September day he announced his proposal for a flat tax of 17 percent. Along with generous personal exemptions, he claimed, his proposal would do away with taxes on the poor and provide modest savings for the middle class. It would also, though Forbes naturally did not dwell on this point, eliminate taxes for wealthy individuals who live off interest from their investments and thus save Forbes himself a small fortune.

"High taxes and high mortgage rates have put families on a treadmill, and the treadmill is winning," Forbes said. What he did not say was that his proposal, if enacted, would add $200 billion or more to the deficit. In order to cut down on the red ink, exemptions would have to be scaled back or the 17-percent rate boosted. The net effect would be to *raise* not lower taxes for the lower-middle and middle classes. But for the time being, those wrinkles were buried underneath the wave of ballyhoo generated by Forbes's commercial touting the virtues of his flat tax.

Moreover, as an important corollary to the flat tax, Forbes offered himself as a political outsider. This was, of course, the same role Lamar Alexander had been trying to fill, but Forbes, as someone who had never held or even sought elective office, was better suited to the part. "I am running because I believe this nation needs someone in the White House who can unlock the stranglehold that the political class has on American life," Forbes declared.

Even with his flat-tax plan and his financial resources, Forbes still needed a manager to direct his campaign. Lacking experience, Forbes's choice, Bill Dal Col, a former Kemp aide, picked two consultants, Tom Ellis and Carter Wrenn, both former lieutenants of Senator Jesse Helms, to whom he turned over the day-to-day management of Forbes's candidacy. Their role would turn out to have far more impact on the course of his candidacy than he expected, a reflection of the rising importance of political consultants in filling the role once played by political party leaders. Motivated not by personal loyalty or principled belief but by their own ambitions, they render their services to whichever candidate offers the most in remuneration or in prestige. These hired guns are another of the distortions created by the decline of parties and the transformation of politics into a pseudo-science devoted to the exploitation of emotions and the confusion of thinking.

By the time Ellis and Wrenn signed on with Forbes, both men had a well-earned reputation for political thuggery. During Reagan's 1976 challenge to incumbent Gerald Ford, Ellis had distributed handbills in North Carolina warning voters that Ford was considering Massachusetts senator Edward Brooke, a black, as his running mate. In the 1990 North Carolina Senate campaign, when a black Democrat, Harvey Gantt, was challenging Helms, Ellis and Wrenn collaborated on their most notorious commercial creation. Known as "Hands," the ad depicts a pair of white hands crumpling a job-rejection letter while a voice-over explains that the job went to a black because of "quotas."

And so when Forbes's campaign got under way in the fall of 1995, while the candidate stumped around the land trumpeting his theme of "hope, growth, and opportunity," his massive television blitz, betraying the stewardship of Ellis and Wrenn, sounded a much harsher and uglier note. Of course, some of Forbes's commercials simply plugged his flat tax. "I say scrap the tax code," Forbes intoned in one ad. "Put in a low flat tax. It's simple, it's honest—and that's a big change for Washington." Or: "I'm Steve Forbes. If you take away the tax code, you take away the power of the Washington politicians."

A large segment of the Forbes video barrage, though, was made up of attacks on his rivals. Some of the material was borrowed directly from the North Carolina campaign against Gantt. Thus, a 1990 Helms ad with the punch line "Harvey Gantt—liberal values, Jesse Helms—North Carolina values" had been transformed into a 1996 Forbes ad with the tag line "Bob Dole—Washington values, Steve Forbes—conservative values."

The standard Forbes campaign technique was to take a grain of truth and expand it into a mountain of calumny. One commercial claimed that Gramm had helped "engineer" Bush's infamous 1990 tax increase, though he had only been a member of the negotiating team that had initially backed the tax increase and had ultimately voted against the boost in revised form. Another denounced Dole for putting off a Senate vote on the term-limit amendment, when the Republican leader had done so at the request of term-limit proponents.

Heightening the impact was the sheer volume of the commercials as Forbes far outspent his rivals, particularly in the key states of Iowa and New Hampshire. In the last three months of 1995, Forbes spent in excess of $15 million on television, nearly as much as Dole had spent during the entire year on all the expenses of his campaign. And as the new year began, Forbes was buying television time at a rate about double that of his chief rivals. "Forbes is on the tube more than Dionne Warwick," complained Tom Rath, who, following his stint as a Dole adviser in 1988, had switched to Lamar Alexander. "It's kind of like being stalked."

Within less than three months, polls showed that Forbes had blown past Dole's other rivals and was closing in on the front-runner himself. Dole's advisers professed to be pleased with this state of affairs, contending that Forbes himself could not be nominated because his flat tax would not stand close scrutiny. And some of his other views, notably his reluctance to support a total ban on abortion, could cause him trouble among GOP conservatives. Therefore, or so Dole's people said, Forbes was performing a service for Dole by blocking the path of the more plausible candidates.

In reality, Dole's advisers were worried sick—and not just about Forbes. The publisher's rise had been so swift and unexpected that they could not be sure what, if anything, could be done to stop him. At the same time, and of more fundamental concern, the entire national political climate once so favorable to the Republican cause had deteriorated as a result of Clinton's success in outmaneuvering the Republican congressional leadership in the battle over the budget.

That was bad news for all the Republican candidates, but it was particularly ominous for Dole, who, as Republican Senate leader, was more closely linked than any others to what was fast becoming a Republican debacle in Washington. Privately, Dole and his advisers at times feared the House Republicans were on a kamikaze course with the White House, but Dole decided he could do nothing to persuade Gingrich and his cohorts to moderate their position because it would be interpreted as a betrayal on his part of the conservative cause. "There was no point in time when we were going to allow a shaft of light to show between us and the House leadership," Sheila Burke, Dole's Senate chief of staff, said later. "If that had happened, we would have been savaged by the right."

These were the dangers to Dole's presidential hopes faced by those in the so-called V-8 group (V for victory, eight for the number of participants), the high command of Bob Dole's presidential campaign, when they convened on a raw Washington day in December in Dole's Capitol Hill headquarters, only two months before the Iowa caucuses began the formal competition for delegates. Their mood was uncommonly tense and anxious, and it was easy to see why. The lead item on their agenda was to approve the first series of Dole commercials to be shown in New Hampshire in the new year. But those commercials were intended to be part of a broader message— which the candidate was still struggling to develop after nearly a year of pursuing the nomination. And his board of strategy was in such disarray that the first ads in the sequence had not yet been produced.

Don Sipple, a former adviser to California governor Pete Wilson during his short-lived presidential candidacy, sought to provide a context for the discussion. "The public has not been engaged in this race at all," he told his colleagues. All that Americans really had noticed about politics was the collapse of budget talks and the government shutdown, a dismal situation in which Dole's prominent role could hardly be concealed. "This budget thing has sent a signal to the American people that something is really wrong in Washington," Sipple pointed out.

But how should Dole respond? As the majority leader of the U.S. Senate, he could hardly transform himself into an outside critic of Washington, à la Forbes. "We need to tell people that Dole is fighting for a balanced budget, and fighting for tax cuts," someone suggested. "Well, he may be fighting for those things, but he's not getting them," Sipple responded.

The meeting broke up without reaching any clear decision on strategy. Ultimately, Dole's advisers approved a hodgepodge of commercials that did little either to repair the damage done by Forbes's onslaught or to provide a convincing rationale for Dole's candidacy.

From then on, until the New Hampshire primary, the Dole candidacy struggled through what Dole's erstwhile pollster Bill McInturff later described as "eight weeks of terror," a period that resulted in McInturff's dismissal from the campaign. If Clinton himself had written the Republican campaign script, he could not have done a better job of undermining his GOP opposition—or so it seemed during the first two months of 1996, as Dole's decline seemed to accelerate and the rest of the field sank deeper into a swamp of negativism.

The tip-off on what was to happen came at the first major campaign event of the new year—a televised debate in Des Moines, Iowa. Forbes, the fastest-rising star on the Republican presidential horizon, paid the penalty for his recent campaign gains when his rivals pounded away at him. Alexander led the charge, ridiculing Forbes's flat-tax plan as "a truly nutty idea . . . in the Jerry Brown tradition." Adoption of Forbes's tax plan, Alexander warned, would produce calamitous results, including a real-estate crash and the end of hopes for a balanced budget.

Suddenly forced on the defensive, Forbes struck back at his opponents. "They can't stand the idea," he said of their attacks on the flat tax, "because I'm going to take away the principal source of their power."

For good measure, Dole and Gramm took turns deriding each other. Gramm accused Dole of "being on three sides of a two-sided issue" because of his recent equivocal statements on a proposed constitutional ban on abortion. But Dole gave back at least as good as he got. Accused by Gramm of cutting "a secret deal" with Clinton on the budget, Dole jibed: "Next time you're in town let's talk about it," an allusion to Gramm's freedom to campaign in the hustings while Majority Leader Dole had been stuck at his duty station on Capitol Hill.

The net result of such badinage, compounded by a torrent of negative commercials unleashed by all of the candidates who could afford to buy the time, was predictable: It blackened the reputation of the entire field. "It's everything that voters tell us they hate about politics and politicians," Dick Bennett, head of American Research Group, an independent polling firm in New Hampshire, told me then. "The Republicans have lost the high ground," said Drake University's Hugh Winebrenner, an analyst of the Iowa political scene and author of a book on the Iowa caucus. "If they were going to convince the people of Iowa and the people of America that Bill Clinton is an unethical person, someone they couldn't trust or put their faith in, they have damaged their own cause by the way they ripped into each other."

Reflecting the ferment in the race, the once-proud front-runner Dole had to endure the humiliation of finishing third in an Alaska GOP straw poll, behind both Forbes and the winner, Pat Buchanan, as well as the ignominy of slipping behind Forbes in some New Hampshire polls. "There is no doubt about the fact that at this point Bob Dole is in free fall," crowed Texas senator Phil Gramm, eager to divert attention from his own fifth-place finish in Alaska. "I think there is not a clear front-runner in this race."

But apart from overstating Dole's difficulties—polls elsewhere in the country suggested the Kansas senator had probably steadied himself at least for the moment—Gramm's assessment raised an embarrassing question about his own candidacy. If there was no new front-runner, what did that then say about Phil Gramm, after he had spent a year of his life and the better part of $20 million to be in a position to move to the head of the field if Dole should falter?

Once past the big talk, and the big money, which his campaign spent almost as fast as it came in, Gramm had trouble establishing a distinct identity for his candidacy. He had set out to corner the market on conservatives. But to the average voter, "Gramm was too much like Dole," as his campaign manager, Charles Black, conceded. "There were differences, but they were nuances and not clear differences."

Gramm certainly did not help his cause with his overbearing demeanor on the stump, a style that was particularly unsuited to the retail politics of New Hampshire. In January, on a visit to Robie's General Store, a campaign landmark in the town of Hookset, the senator agreed to a game of checkers with seventy-seven-year-old Dorothy Robie, the proprietress. TV cameras rolled, and onlookers crowded around for a better look at this charming vignette in front of the store's potbellied stove. It did not last long. On the second move, Gramm double-jumped his opponent. Ten minutes later, the senator walked off triumphant, as pleased as if he had just vanquished one of his presidential rivals.

"Senator, you *beat* her," Gramm's shocked New Hampshire coordinator, James Courtovich, pointed out as the campaign bus pulled away. "If someone wants to play checkers with me, I'm going to play checkers," Gramm replied.

For Pat Buchanan, whatever Phil Gramm's shortcomings were, the Texan's candidacy was a major obstacle. Like Gramm, Buchanan sought to capture the hearts of conservatives. But if Gramm lacked passion, Buchanan, because of his divisive rhetoric and because he had never held elective office, lacked credibility. To prove himself, Buchanan had to find a way to defeat Gramm. "Gramm's problem is Buchanan, and Buchanan's problem is Gramm," Buchanan told me in the spring of 1995. "Gramm's got to get me out of the way or he can't challenge Dole, and I have to get him out of the way. One of the two of us can beat Dole."

In politics, one distortion often leads to another. The front-loaded schedule and Forbes's high-rolling candidacy had stood the nominating process on its head, and as a result, the contest between Gramm and Buchanan was settled by a fluke—a relative handful of voters participating in a makeshift election.

Initially, Buchanan had hoped to get Gramm out of his way by finishing well ahead of him in the Iowa caucuses, but Steve Forbes's entry into the campaign in September had forced Buchanan to reconsider that plan. By late fall, it became apparent that the millions Forbes was pouring into television commercials in the early primary and caucus states had changed the context of the race, transforming Forbes into the chief threat to Dole. By overshadowing the rest of the Republican field, Forbes dimmed Buchanan's chances of making the strong showing in Iowa he needed to finish off Gramm.

But Buchanan had learned how to respond when backed into a corner at the feet of a master in the art, Richard Nixon. He found a new field of battle, Louisiana, and attacked. At Gramm's instigation, the state party had abruptly set up a delegate selection caucus and thrust itself onto the campaign calendar on February 6, only a week ahead of the Iowa caucuses and much over the protests of that state's GOP. Out of deference to Iowa's party leadership, most of the candidates had passed up Louisiana. But not Phil Gramm. He saw an easy chance, in a state next door to his own Texas, to win all twenty-one delegates at stake and gain momentum for Iowa. Early in the year, Gramm strummed the Cajun state's Republican hierarchy like a guitar, gaining the support of three members of the state's congressional delegation. But then, convinced that he had the state locked up, he left his Louisiana operation to fend for itself while he concentrated his resources elsewhere.

For the Buchanan campaign, the realization of the opportunity thus created was roughly comparable to the desperate excitement that swept the French general staff in August of 1914 when General Von Kluck made his fateful decision to turn his legions away from Paris and toward the Marne. "They offer us their flank!" the French cried out in exultation. No one recorded what Pat Buchanan said when he realized Gramm's blunder. His actions, though, were clear. He immediately alerted his local staff, shifted his schedule, and plunged headlong into a whirlwind round of campaigning.

This was a serious gamble for Buchanan. A poor showing in Louisiana would wreck his candidacy—and circumstances seemed arrayed against him. The Louisiana GOP provided only forty-two polling places scattered across the state, and voting was limited to only four hours, conditions that seemed made-to-order for Gramm's allies among the party higher-ups to manipulate the result. But it was a calculated risk, one that Buchanan believed his political mentor would have approved. "Nixon would have called it a big move and said: 'You got to do it,'" Buchanan told me.

And what better place to test Buchanan's indictment of the GOP's dominant corporate and political establishment than among the bayous, where Huey Long's fiery populism took root and where his impassioned rhetoric still reverberated? Like the legendary Kingfish, Buchanan talked not only of gaining high office but of reshaping the national political landscape, in particular the framework of the conservative movement that defined Buchanan's early career. "We conservatives believe in free enterprise; we believe in the values of family and community," Buchanan told his campaign rallies. "But when go-go global capitalism is uprooting entire communities and families, I ask conservatives to figure out what it is we're trying to conserve." At every stop along the way, he decried the damage inflicted on the state's textile industry by unfair foreign competition, citing as a prime example the closing of a Fruit of the Loom plant in the Acadiana region that had cost 300 jobs.

Far from being offended by his harsh rhetoric, his audiences warmed to Buchanan's passion. "I like the way he speaks his mind and tells it like it is," said Bob Fennett, a Baton Rouge lawyer, after listening to Buchanan pound away at trade deals that cost Americans jobs and mainly benefited huge corporations. "I think folks here are sick and tired of these mealymouthed politicians. And I think NAFTA has shipped a lot of jobs overseas."

On election night, February 6, James Carville, the Louisiana-bred Democratic consultant who had engineered Clinton's victory in 1992, was watching television in his Washington home when he was startled to see returns that showed Buchanan trouncing Gramm. Carville got on the phone to his Republican friend Bob Courtney in the GOP's headquarters in Baton Rouge.

"What the hell is going on there?" Carville asked.

"Just keep watching," Courtney told him.

Carville and other Democrats had good reason to be taken aback by Buchanan's success. It was the decline of living standards and wages for millions of blue-collar and white-collar workers, which had continued under Clinton's tenure in the White House, that had paved the way for Buchanan to emerge. "I think you judge the success of an economy not on whether your gross domestic product is $6 trillion or $7 trillion but on whether the real income of working men and women is rising each year," Buchanan told me as he stumped through Louisiana. "And that hasn't been happening." Instead, he said, "The real income of working men and women who work with their hands and tools and machines is down 20 percent in twenty years."

To hear such rhetoric from the lips of Republican Buchanan was a bitter pill for Democrats who put Clinton in the White House. "Clinton got elected by raising many of these same issues that Buchanan is raising," said Mark Levinson, chief economist for New York's 125,000-member District 37 of the American Federation of State, County, and Municipal Employees. But in office, Levinson complained, "Clinton has been more worried about cutting the deficit than raising incomes for working families."

Little more than 20,000 people voted in Louisiana, only 6 percent of the state's registered Republicans. But given the high expectations Gramm had created for himself, the symbolic impact of the results on his candidacy was devastating.

While Gramm was fading fast, Forbes also was slipping, the once-bright promise of his candidacy tarnished by the backlash created by his assaults on opponents and by their counterattacks on him. This left Buchanan free to concentrate on Dole when he moved on to Iowa. There, he hammered away at the same themes of economic nationalism that had gained him glory in Louisiana. "What we need is a president of the United States who's gonna tell the Europeans, 'Listen, fellas, you're going to play fair or we're going to play rough,'" Buchanan declared in tiny Creston, in western Iowa, where his touring Winnebago, dubbed the "Go-Pat-Go Express," paused for a press conference. "And that's what we're going to do to open up foreign markets to American products," he pledged.

Bob Dole won the Iowa precinct caucuses, but it was Buchanan, by finishing right on his heels, who came out of the state with momentum. By finishing third, ahead of Steve Forbes, Lamar Alexander managed to keep his candidacy alive, more than could be said for Phil Gramm, whose fifth-place finish sounded the death knell for his candidacy, as he formally acknowledged a few days later.

At Dole's headquarters in Washington, his advisers, who had concentrated only on defeating Gramm and had never taken Buchanan seriously, now verged on panic. At first they responded by launching attack ads at Buchanan, branding him an extremist. But then some of Dole's strategists argued that Buchanan was the wrong target. The real threat to Dole, these advisers contended, did not emanate from Buchanan, whose support for all its intensity was viewed as limited to fewer than one-third of the Republican primary electorate, but rather from Lamar Alexander, a more or less moderate conservative who had the advantage of being acceptable to most groups in the party. Two days after Iowa voted, Dole's chief strategist, Bill Lacey, whom he later dismissed, called in with the conclusion he had reached, which he based partly on talking to journalists: "Dole can afford to lose to Buchanan in New Hampshire," Lacey said, "but he can't afford a loss to Alexander."

Dole's handlers turned their big television guns around and took dead aim at Alexander, branding him as "more liberal than you think" and calling him a big taxer, based on his two-term record as governor of Tennessee.

Most New Hampshire Republicans thought Alexander was a conservative before Dole's attack, but afterward, by a margin of more than two to one, they considered him a "moderate liberal," a category that in the world of New Hampshire's conservative Republicans was only a trifle less despised than Bolshevik.

While the Dole forces concentrated on the negative tactics that had become the mainstay of the front-runner's candidacy, Buchanan set the frozen New England countryside ablaze. The environment was made-to-order for him. Although the pain of the 1992 recession had subsided, anxiety about economic insecurity hung like a cloud over middle-class families. "We did not get a single question about flag burning or school prayer," Tom Rath of the Alexander campaign told me after his candidate had staged an issues forum in Concord. "We got asked about tax policy and employment policy. Every question was about the economy."

Arriving in the state flush with his successes in Louisiana and Iowa and, as he told a welcoming throng of supporters, "brimming with hope and opportunity," Buchanan devoted himself to promoting his newly conceived conservatism of the heart. "This is a campaign that will stand for working men and women of this country whose jobs are threatened and will stand against unfair trade deals done for the benefit of huge corporations," he declared. "This is a campaign that stands up for middle-class American families who are under terrible stress because of high taxation and economic insecurity."

Dole reeled before the Buchanan onslaught. Everywhere he went in the closing hours of the New Hampshire campaign, thousands of balloons showered down upon him, banners waved, and rock bands blared. But all the jubilation and hoopla belied the sober demeanor of the candidate and the somber realities confronting his campaign. "All my life has been a preparation for this moment," the Republican Senate leader told his supporters. But with all that preparation, he had yet to find a satisfactory way to express the lessons learned from his years of seasoning in the Senate and whatever convictions he held about the foundations of American life into a credo simple and direct enough to command the allegiance of the citizenry. His handlers threw up their hands and tried to find excuses. "He's from Kansas," David Carney, Dole's chief, pointed out. "They are the salt of earth. But they just don't project."

While his television commercials carried the attack to Alexander, damning him as a liberal and double-damning him as a pseudo-conservative, Dole's staff tried to cobble together a new approach to economic policy to compete against Buchanan's powerful attacks on the arrogance of big corporations and the flaws in U.S. trade policy. But "Dolenomics," as the senator proudly called his manifesto, turned out to be little more than a sketchy rehash of ideas Dole had talked about previously, and the senator mentioned it only briefly afterward. It went the way of the "three R's."

When Dole did try to address the economic anxieties of the middle class in his own words, he made himself the target of jeers and ridicule. "I didn't realize that jobs and trade and what makes America work would become a big issue," Dole declared as he toured a factory on the eve of the vote, a statement in which his candor was too painfully obvious.

And while Dole brooded, Buchanan exulted and mocked his establishment foes. "This is too much fun," he told his supporters on the last weekend of the campaign. "We've got them all on the run. They're nervous and frightened. They're in terminal panic. They hear the shouts of the peasants from over the hill. All the knights and barons will be riding into the castle. pulling up the drawbridge. And all the peasants are coming with pitchforks after them."

The peasants turned out in force on primary day, enough to give Buchanan a narrow victory over Dole that stunned the political world. "We're going to give voice to the voiceless," Buchanan told his supporters, who were so numerous that fire marshals had to turn hundreds away from his election-night rally at Londonderry.

> We're going to reach out to the men and women of this country whose jobs have been sacrificed on the altars of trade deals done for the benefit of transnational corporations who have no loyalty to our country and no loyalty to anybody. We're going to recapture the lost sovereignty of our country; we're going to bring it home. We are taking back our party as a prelude to taking back our country. We do not apologize for the fact that we're going to take control of our national destiny.

It was well for Buchanan to savor the moment, because there would be no more triumphs to come. And for all his brave talk and despite his stunning success, his pitchfork rebellion had taken him as far and as high as he could go in Republican presidential politics in 1996. Dole, the loser in the most hallowed and time-honored of all presidential trial heats, the New Hampshire primary, held all the high cards for the rest of the game. He still had huge financial and organizational advantage over Buchanan and his other rivals, who, thanks to the calendar, would have precious little time to catch up.

Moreover, Dole had beaten the man he had to beat—Alexander—who could do no better than third place in New Hampshire, just behind Dole. As Dole's advisers had come to believe, Alexander was the only one of Dole's rivals who could appeal to a broad enough spectrum of voters and party leaders to make himself a credible alternative. As it turned out, Dole's assault on Alexander in New Hampshire, although it could not prevent Buchanan's victory, may have saved Dole's candidacy.

Now, with Alexander safely disposed of, Dole found in Buchanan's triumph the cause for his candidacy that had hitherto eluded him. He would fight to save the center from extremism. The battle from now on, Dole told his supporters on his night of anguish in New Hampshire, would be "a fight for the heart and soul of the Republican party." These were not the sort of matters with which Dole had previously exhibited much concern. Nevertheless, at this opportune moment, he instructed Republican primary voters that they must decide "if we are the party of fear or of hope. If we are angry about the present or optimistic about the future."

In some respects, Dole's defeat in New Hampshire seemed the latest jolt in a wave of turbulence that had been rocking the political landscape since the Bush presidency began to fall apart six years earlier. And Buchanan's victory sent shock waves not only through the Republican leadership, whose members rallied to Dole's side, but throughout the upper echelons of American politics and business. Indeed, in Washington, the Brookings Institution, the bulwark of the establishment, convened a conference to ponder whether the political center was undergoing a collapse.

And if Buchanan rhetoric on economic policy in general and trade in particular was seriously meant, then the nation's elite had reason for concern. As John Judis observed in a trenchant analysis in *New Republic*, Buchanan's attempts to curb the excesses of global capitalism brought to mind the efforts of the reformers of the late nineteenth century to counteract the social chaos wrought by massive industrialization. Whereas conservatives and even liberals had shied away from any restraint on market forces, Buchanan had proposed a series of government initiatives that placed him to the left not only of his Republican colleagues but also the Democratic president Bill Clinton and his economic advisers.

Although his incendiary oratory made him more adversaries than even a bellicose Irishman could handle, Buchanan at times behaved as if he were determined to be his own worst enemy. Bill Bennett, who made no secret of his distaste for Buchanan, claimed the columnist's conduct on the campaign trail in the wake of his New Hampshire triumph was a deliberate display of his contempt for the political process. "He was on top, and he could have had it all," Bennett told me. "But he really didn't want it, because he didn't want to give up all the money he made on television."

Whatever motivated Buchanan, his behavior was enough to shatter the hopes of his backers. "He got sort of bombastic," acknowledged his Louisiana media consultant Roy Fletcher, one of the architects of Buchanan's triumph in the state. Afterward, Buchanan's spokesman Greg Mueller suggested the candidate would have been better served by stressing his kinder, gentler themes, which Buchanan had labeled as "the conservatism of the heart."

Instead, with his harsh rhetoric and aggressive demeanor, he resembled a caricature of himself. In Arizona, which held its primary a week after New Hampshire, Buchanan stalked around in a black hat, at one point waving a shotgun over his head and declaring, "These aren't just for shooting ducks." The Sturm und Drang he generated drained his momentum from New Hampshire and left him in third place behind the winner, Forbes, and the second-place finisher, Dole—and for all intents and purposes, that finished his candidacy.

The implication of Buchanan's defeat in Arizona was not lost at the Brookings Institution, in the midst of its conference on the threat to the political center in Washington. "The center looks a lot better this morning than it did going into Arizona," remarked one of the conference panelists, Republican congressman Steven Gunderson of Wisconsin.

Forbes, who had revived his candidacy after finishing fourth in Iowa and New Hampshire, by winning in Delaware on the Saturday after New Hampshire, hoped to build on his Arizona victory. But when the publisher sounded his trumpet, no one answered. The party leaders who might have rallied to his side were too busy helping Dole save the party from the dragon Buchanan.

Alexander had a similar experience when he tried to compete against Dole in the South Carolina primary that followed the Arizona contest. "We didn't understand the level of fear that the Buchanan candidacy created in mainstream Republican leaders," Tom Rath said. "They felt that his success would be damaging to their position as ranking Republicans. And they also thought it would mean electoral disaster."

With the South Carolina primary that came four days after Arizona, the turmoil that had gripped Dole's candidacy and the entire party since the previous fall suddenly ended. A mere ten days after New Hampshire had given victory to Patrick J. Buchanan, Dole, with the considerable help of the Republican party leaders, whose backing he had obtained months before, won the March 2 primary in South Carolina. He did not lose again, and in mid-March, he clinched the GOP nomination by winning primaries in four big Midwestern states.

And so the center held. Dole had described his candidacy after New Hampshire as a crusade to save the party's heart and soul. But the survival of Dole, the symbol of the GOP center, came about more because of the strength of his campaign's resources than as a result of the power of his ideas to inspire the party's heart and soul. Thus, campaigning in New York, where he would make a huge haul of delegates against the badly outspent Buchanan and Forbes teams, Dole summed up his candidacy this way:

> I would say that if your faucet was leaking this morning when you left home, let's take that example, you'd probably want a plumber with some experience. Or if your car broke down you'd probably want a mechanic with experience. But sometimes when we talk about picking a president of the United States we overlook what I think is very important, experience. Experience. I think that's what this is all about.

Dole may have talked about fighting for the GOP's heart and soul. But like a good plumber, he relied mainly on nuts and bolts. "We got campaigns going in every state that votes this week," said senior Dole adviser Dave Carney, explaining the Dole advantage in the mass Super Tuesday primary. "These other guys don't. They are just not prepared to compete with us." Dole won all nine states and the 241 delegates that were at stake.

The tempestuous course of the Republican campaign demonstrated that neither Buchanan's melding of social conservatism with economic national-ism nor the supply-side theories preached by Steve Forbes were yet strong enough to gain a majority within the GOP. But it also raised doubts about whether the principal themes of Dole's brand of traditional Republican-ism—free trade and budget balancing—could win an election, unless the candidate could find a more compelling means of expressing those beliefs. Looking back on the trials and tribulations of the past three months, Dole's campaign manager Scott Reed said, "We are a better campaign and Senator Dole is a stronger candidate having gone through it." But whether he was strong enough to win the White House remained very much in question.

10

The Return of the Comeback Kid

WHEN THE TWO MOST POTENT figures in national politics met at a Washington dinner in the spring of 1996, it was inevitable that their conversation turned to the 1996 presidential election. Given their relative circumstances, it was also probably inevitable that when House Speaker Gingrich and President Clinton chatted during the predinner reception, it was Gingrich who had the most to say.

"You've done some things very well since we took over the Congress," the Speaker told the president. "But now you have to face how hard this campaign is going to be. Right now, if I had to guess," Gingrich added, "I'd say your chances of winning are about one in three."

The president did not take umbrage at this gratuitous observation, or so it seemed to Gingrich when he later told me about the conversation. "We were just two professionals talking business," the Speaker explained. But Clinton did not argue the point, either. Indeed, at that particular moment in political time, not many in Washington, including leaders of Clinton's own party, would have had much ground for disagreeing with the Speaker's assessment.

True, the tragic bombing in Oklahoma City had worked to Clinton's advantage, allowing him to emerge from the shadows of public discourse and score a point or two against the leaders of the conservative tide that had engulfed the nation. But it was by no means clear that this recovery represented anything more than a temporary relief for the beleaguered chief executive.

Even as the overblown reaction to the Republican midterm triumph subsided, Clinton still faced a fundamental problem: He lacked any compelling rationale for his presidency, let alone for winning reelection to a second term. During the course of his first two years in the White House, he had retreated from his program for economic revival and had botched his effort to enact health-care reform—the two central planks of his challenge to the Republican regime. In both cases, his handling of these proposals had been governed by the fear of antagonizing the political center, an ill-defined segment of the ideological spectrum where he imagined the majority of voters to be. But this rationale had been destroyed by the electorate, which, viewing his professed moderation as temporizing, brought about the downfall of the president's party and Clinton's own humiliation.

Now Clinton was adrift, as his own advisers acknowledged, and had lost the energy and focus that his candidacy possessed or seemed to possess. "In 1992 you knew what he stood for; he stood for change and economic revival," Harold Ickes, the president's deputy chief of staff and longtime political adviser, told me in the spring of 1995. "But if you look back at what Clinton was talking about in 1994, there was so much coming out that you couldn't get a grip on what he stood for."

Ickes claimed Clinton's lack of focus reflected the overall decline of his party. "Since Walter Mondale lost in 1984, the party has been waiting for emerging new leadership and no one has emerged yet. Now the country is going through a real change, and the party is going through a period in which it's going to take another five or ten years for new leadership to emerge."

But in this bleak reality lay Clinton's salvation—or at least his lifeline for political survival. Just as the distortions of the political system had paved Clinton's path to the White House and had led to the morass into which his presidency had been submerged, so these same circumstances had drained his party and its leaders, Clinton's potential rivals, of the conviction, energy, and nerve required for a challenge to his nomination, which could have ended his political career. Thus, the first key to Clinton's comeback in 1996—what would be one of the most dramatic political rebirths in American history—was something that did not happen: No Democrat contested his renomination.

This nonevent was all the more remarkable given the weaknesses in Clinton's own position, to which his critics readily attested. "He has no core constituency, no base of support," pointed out Ted Van Dyk, an adviser to Democratic presidents and would-be presidents, going back to Hubert Humphrey. "You could say he is in the middle. But you could also say that at any given time, he is anywhere and nowhere."

To Van Dyk and others, Clinton seemed ripe for a challenge to his renomination, which would mobilize all the discontent in the Democratic party and unseat him. After all, such insurrections were part of the Democratic tradition: Since Franklin D. Roosevelt, every sitting Democratic president had been dogged by an impassioned challenge of one sort or another. Just before the 1948 Democratic convention, Southern conservatives, rebelling against President Truman's civil-rights program, joined forces with Northern liberals who were convinced that Truman was doomed to defeat in the fall, in a futile effort to draft Dwight Eisenhower as Democratic standard-bearer. In 1964, Alabama governor George Wallace ran against Lyndon Johnson in protest against his civil-rights policies in particular, and the reach of federal power in general, garnering impressive vote totals in three Northern primaries and stirring up the so-called white backlash, which in one form or another had haunted the party ever since. In 1968, four years after Johnson's landslide victory over Barry Goldwater, Eugene McCarthy led an antiwar insurrection that forced Johnson to forsake his plans to win another term in the White House. And in 1980, Ted Kennedy marched at the head of an army of discontented liberals in a vain attempt to seize control of the party from incumbent Jimmy Carter. In fact, Carter would seem to have been better positioned than Clinton against such a challenge, since he had won election in 1976 with a popular majority, whereas Clinton had earned only 43 percent of the vote in 1992. Moreover, polls showed a healthy majority of Democratic voters wanted to see Clinton's renomination challenged.

But in truth, there was more discontent among Democratic voters than there was willingness among party leaders to exploit their feelings and run against Clinton. "There is not at present any ideological focus to the Democratic party," said Carl Wagner, a veteran of the 1968 rebellion against Johnson and the 1980 insurgency against Carter. "What would the rationale for a candidacy against Clinton be?" he asked sarcastically. "Would you claim 'I can reinvent government better'?"

Those who failed to take up the cudgels against Clinton made excuses for their inaction. "I think part of it is practical politics," said Don Sweitzer, political director of the Democratic National Committee and platoon leader in the liberal legion that rose against Carter. "The last time we had a Democratic president we ran against him on principle, and we helped weaken him and helped him lose." In reality, of course, Carter's loss to Reagan stemmed not from the intraparty mutiny but from the incumbent president's own failure in dealing with skyrocketing inflation and the Iran hostage crisis.

The truth was that the men who had the prominence and status to be considered as potential challengers had no clearer sense of the country's direction or their own individual destinies than Clinton himself did. For example, Bill Bradley, the New Jersey senator and erstwhile New York Knicks basketball star, sounded as if he was fast losing interest in politics altogether. From the start, Bradley seemed out of place in the Democratic party, though Democrats were happy to count him as one of their own because of his premanufactured all-American fame. Most celebrities from the world of sports or entertainment who entered politics gravitated to the Republican party, as had Ronald Reagan and Jack Kemp. Bradley, though, told me he had rejected the GOP because "there's no policy to embrace change in the Republican party."

But it was never very clear what sort of change Bradley wanted to carry out as a leader in the Democratic party. A wealthy and remote figure and an ardent champion of the economic and political establishment, he had an antiseptic conception of the political process, viewing it as a benign mechanism that would surely provide justice and equity for all, provided it could be shielded from the selfish demands of partisanship. During one of the intermittent efforts he had made over the years to test his presidential ambitions, I heard him give much the same speech to the New Jersey Democratic Party State Convention in Atlantic City that he had not long before given to the New Jersey Chamber of Commerce.

"You know," an aide told him afterward, "you didn't deliver a real political convention speech."

"I'll take the rap for not throwing out red meat to the audience and for not bashing Reagan," Bradley replied. "I know what I'm doing."

What Bradley thought he was doing was trying to establish his own agenda for the future, which would combine Democratic compassion with Republican materialism. "The long-term future of the party," Bradley told me, "is not served by an endless parade of satisfied constituencies as much as by an overall message that is in the general interest." But the appeals to the so-called general interest that Bradley tried to fashion were so disconnected from the concerns of the electorate that they failed to register outside the regional parameters, where his past athletic prowess had helped him gain a following.

And even in his own state, the Bradley magic was fading fast. The senator who had won reelection with 65 percent of the vote in 1984 had barely edged out his Republican foe, the then-unknown Christine Todd Whitman, in 1990. "Hey, Bill," one longtime Knicks fan shouted at Bradley as he campaigned against Whitman. "How about one more jump shot for us?" "Sorry," Bradley replied. "The heart is willing but the knees are weak." And after that election, Bradley's will and ambition seemed to weaken, too.

By the time I talked to him in 1995, not only had Bradley ruled out running for the presidency, but he was in the process of making up his mind not to seek another term in the Senate. He cast his own frustrations as part of a broader debilitation of American politics and society. "The parties generally have gone the way of other institutions," he said. "We have to stop thinking that the only focus of power and leadership in our society comes from elected political leaders and particularly from the president." Whether Bradley sincerely believed that political leadership had dwindled in importance or was trying to rationalize his own unwillingness to run risks as a politician made no difference. He was not going to challenge Clinton.

Neither was Bob Kerrey, another Democrat who did not really fit into the party, or into politics. Kerrey was particularly valued by other Democrats because he was a war hero, having lost his leg and won the Medal of Honor in Vietnam. Although war heroes are welcome in both parties, as Bob Dole had found out years before, they are particularly cherished by Democrats. Ever since Yalta, Democrats, unlike Republicans, have been denied the presumption of patriotism. Kerrey's medal and his artificial limb both served as proof of his own patriotism and, by inference and association, helped his party.

Kerrey had another credential much esteemed by Democrats. He had made a huge success in the restaurant business back in Nebraska. This served as evidence of his faith in the free-enterprise system, an issue on which Democrats lacked credibility. But when he ran for president in 1992, Kerrey turned out to be a dud. He had no coherent framework for his ideas. And even though he was one of the first presidential candidates to come up with a plan for national health insurance, he had a hard time explaining the plan in terms voters could understand and support.

Kerrey seemed primarily interested in cutting government rather than in using it effectively, as Democrats had always tried to do in order to survive. During his ill-fated presidential campaign, he proposed slashing the number of cabinet agencies in half, from fourteen to seven. And after the election, he set his sights on cutting the costs of entitlements, persuading Clinton to put him in charge of a commission in which recommendations made to drastically overhaul Social Security went nowhere.

In the wake of the 1994 Democratic debacle, Kerrey seemed overwhelmed by contrition and remorse. "There was a great defeat in November, and we still have not regrouped," he told me, explaining his disinterest in running. "And had we not lost the House and Senate, there might be a challenge. We in Congress have to accept our share of blame. Many thought it was a repudiation of the things Clinton was doing. But it was also a repudiation of us."

Kerrey made plain that the task of rebuilding the Democratic party was a challenge beyond his aptitude and interests. "I'd have to go into suburban America where 80 percent of the people own their own homes and say, 'This is why you should be concerned about what's going on in the inner city.' I'd have to tell people who perceive no benefits from government why there are things government has to get done," said Kerrey. "I don't have that answer."

If any Democrat seemed to have good reason to challenge the incumbent president it was Richard Gephardt, the leader of the House Democrats and a far more traditional party leader than either Kerrey or Bradley. Gephardt had fought the president tooth and nail on NAFTA, which was, along with Clinton's economic program, the major legislative accomplishment of his first two years. And barely a month after the midterm election, Gephardt made a point of unveiling his own proposal for a middle-class tax cut. In announcing his tax plan, which was more intended to benefit lower-income groups than the plans of either Clinton or Gingrich, Gephardt promised to cooperate with the president, but added pointedly: "Our agenda will come from America's houses, not the White House." And Gephardt delved into thematic areas normally reserved for presidents—or presidential candidates. "At the ballot boxes, we may have lost the majority," Gephardt contended, "but in the hearts and mind of working America, the values we stand for, the policies we fight for are still in the majority."

Yet Gephardt, too, backed away from a challenge to Clinton's nomination. "The president has been and is now taking Republicans on full force on the Contract with America," he told me. "He is carrying a mainline Democratic message. I think he deserves to be reelected." Yes, Gephardt conceded he and Clinton had their differences. "But they haven't been disagreements on the fundamental issues that the party represents," he claimed.

This, of course, was false. Trade policy, and its impact on working people, on which they had sharply differed, went to the heart of what the Democratic party stood for, or used to stand for. The truth of the matter was that Gephardt was too comfortable where he was to put his position as the party's House leader at risk by making a run for the presidency. That would force House members to choose between Gephardt and the incumbent president, with all the power he possessed to help or hurt their political careers. That was not a choice Gephardt wanted to force people to make. When I asked Gephardt whether other Democrats shared his view of Clinton, he said: "You'll have to ask them. But I don't see anybody running."

Of all the potential candidates for the Democratic nomination, by far the most candid was Jerry Brown, Clinton's most tenacious adversary in the contest for the 1992 nomination. Brown said he opted out of 1996 because he saw no way to overcome what he called "the money domination" of politics. Brown had been widely ridiculed as an unreliable flake, a reputation he had partially earned. Yet at least he was willing to publicly confront the dim condition into which the Democratic party had descended. "The Democratic party is moribund," said Brown, who had put his energies into a new nonpartisan group called "We the People," which aimed at achieving social and political reform. "There is no vitality anymore. Fear of Gingrich stifled dissent within the party and worked to Clinton's advantage," he said. Potentially powerful constituent groups such as organized labor and black Americans had been afraid to wage full-scale campaigns against Clinton policies with which they disagreed, such as NAFTA and the crime bill, because they feared it would make the president more vulnerable than he already was. "Thus, each outrageous departure from Democratic tradition is embraced as the only way to save Clinton," Brown said.

"I don't see anybody running," Gephardt had said. Neither did the White House. But taking the party's history into account, "we are working from the assumption that we will have a challenge," presidential press secretary Michael McCurry told me in March. "We have to think equally of the possibility of something from the left or something from the right."

Something from the left was more dangerous, McCurry said, because it would drain resources more quickly, since the structure of the nominating process is more attuned to interests on the left. In practical terms, in the spring of 1995, a challenge from the left would come from only one politician, and that was Jesse Louis Jackson, ordained minister, civil-rights agitator, and two-time presidential contender.

With Cuomo's career shattered by defeat, Kennedy transformed into an establishment figure, and Brown broke and discredited, only Jackson could rally what remained of the party's left—if, in fact, anyone could. And unlike anyone else on the scene, Jackson had already established a premise for challenging Clinton—the president's failure to fulfill the promises of his campaign.

Speaking out even before the 1994 election, on behalf of "the vast body of workers, blacks, Hispanics, and urban America" that had helped elect Clinton in 1992, Jackson said: "Those of us who voted for racial equality and workers' rights and economic stimulus and education equity as keys to reduce pain and hardship are sadly disappointed. The option of running is open, and the option of running in a general election deserves as much attention as running in the primary."

By choosing either of these courses, Jackson could make Clinton's road back to the White House much rougher. If he contested Clinton for the Democratic nomination, Jackson's appeal to blacks and other liberal constituencies could force Clinton to pay more attention to the left, at a time when the "New Democrat" president would probably want to move to the center. But Clinton would certainly win such a contest and might even help himself with white Southern voters in the process of suppressing a Jackson challenge. Much more to be feared was an independent Jackson candidacy, which might well siphon off enough black voters to ensure Clinton's defeat.

By the spring of 1995, Jackson's two options were still open, and he was still unhappy with Clinton's performance. He referred scornfully to his own party as "Demopublicans," sounding as if he were leaning toward making a run as an independent, if he ran at all. "We are finding it increasingly difficult to get people whose legitimate interests are not being addressed to register and vote for Demopublicans," he said. Adding an edge to this implied threat of an independent candidacy was Jackson's claim that he had a computer database of 500,000 supporters built up over the past decade. Moreover, his Rainbow Coalition could serve as the skeletal basis for a third-party organization.

In reality, for reasons of his own, Jackson did not want to run. He knew that a challenge for the nomination would be hopeless. Howard University political scientist Ron Walters, who had been an adviser to Jackson in his 1988 campaign, said, "I think he probably has had enough of running in primaries and losing." As for an independent candidacy, "Jackson did not want to be the person who was blamed for giving Newt Gingrich control of the whole federal government," Steve Cobble, who was Jackson's chief delegate hunter in 1988, told me.

But Clinton had made it hard for Jackson to stay out of the race, by promising in the aftermath of the midterm election to conduct a review of the federal affirmative-action programs. If Clinton undercut affirmative action and Jackson did *not* run against him in protest, then Jackson would lose whatever credibility he had as a liberal paladin. Jackson therefore sought to pressure Clinton to give him a way out of running.

In the summer of 1995, when Jackson's aide Cobble, who is based in New Mexico, happened to be in Washington, Jackson invited George Stephanopoulos and Harold Ickes from the White House to a meeting in his eighth-floor headquarters on K Street to discuss the president's course on affirmative action. He made sure Cobble was on hand, too.

"I was there as a prop," Cobble told me later. For an hour, Jackson lectured the two White House emissaries on the importance of preserving affirmative action. It was good politics, and good government, Jackson argued, because the business establishment favored affirmative action as a way to avoid racial conflict. Moreover, Jackson suggested how affirmative action could be retained, with minimum political risk, by taking advantage of the support for the programs in the business communities.

"You've got to be creative," Jackson argued. "Let the corporate executives get out front on this, and they will give you political cover."

Cobble said not a word, except when Ickes, who had worked side by side with him in Jackson's 1988 campaign, asked: "What are you doing in town?"

"I'm just here to help Jesse, any way I can," Cobble replied.

Ickes grinned. The meeting broke up with no commitment on either side, and Ickes and Stephanopoulos returned to the White House to report to the president. But it did not escape their attention that Jackson was serious about affirmative action, serious enough to be conferring with his top political operative.

Clinton got the point. A few weeks later, he announced that his administration intended "to mend, not end" affirmative action. Jackson also kept his part of the bargain. The threat of his independent candidacy died aborning. Clinton was home free.

With the possibility of any challenge to his nomination ended, Clinton was now able to concentrate on preparing for the general-election campaign against the Republicans. This was a multifaceted challenge, but the president and his aides carried forward one part of the task with more urgency than all the rest—the raising of money.

By the time voters cast their ballots in November 1996, the Clinton campaign and the Democratic National Committee, which became little more than an appurtenance of the campaign, raised and spent more money than any presidential campaign in political history. In the process, the president and his aides and allies, weaving a tangled web of sham and chicanery, committed wholesale violations of the spirit of the federal campaign laws and came close enough to breaking the letter of those laws so that congressional and Justice Department investigations were called down upon their heads. They helped to produce what former Common Cause president Fred Wertheimer called the worst election in modern times, "worse even than the illegal contributions gathered by Richard Nixon's men during the Watergate era," a benchmark of corruption previously unmatched in this century.

More fundamentally, their activities exposed the federal campaign finance structure as yet another distortion in the political system. Unlike most of the other systemic defects that stem from the inherent rivalry between the presidency and the Congress, this malfunction resulted in part from the intervention in the political process by the judiciary, in fulfillment of the watchdog role it had been assigned in the earliest days of the republic.

The courts did not create the problems connected with campaign financing, but by undermining the efforts of the legislative branch to correct these problems, they turned these remedies into a cure that was in some ways worse than the initial disease. All through the history of the republic, the influence of big money has corrupted the political process. But not until the Watergate scandal rocked the Nixon presidency did Congress make a serious effort to curb this venal force. The post-Watergate reforms were flawed at the outset. One weakness was that enforcement of the new regulations was delegated to the Federal Election Commission, a toothless puppet of the lawmakers it was supposed to police. Another was the establishment of political action committees as conduits for corporate political giving, in effect legitimizing and systematizing what corporations had been doing much less efficiently under the table for years.

Illustrating the miscreant and misguided impulses that generate such so-called reforms, the authorization for the PACs gained approval from a Democratic-controlled Congress, even though big business is popularly believed to side with Republicans, and because labor unions, which traditionally side with the Democrats, were also allowed to have PACs. In fact, the unions were among the most eager proponents of the law, believing that it would enhance their influence in the political marketplace.

Although the unions made good use of PACs, their contributions and influence had been far overshadowed by the giving of the corporate world. The saving grace for the Democrats was that their incumbents benefited from the corporate PACs at least as much as Republican officeholders, because business, striving to serve the interest of its stockholders, tended to give money first not to proponents of ideological abstractions but rather to those who held power and controlled access.

Still and all, whatever their defects, the Watergate reforms did establish the first enforceable limits on political spending and giving, as well as providing for federal subsidies to level the playing field for candidates dependent on smaller contributions. But the ink on the new statutes was barely dry before they were eviscerated by the Supreme Court, which construed the limits on spending as a violation of the First Amendment, thus equating money with speech. In effect, as New York University law professor Burt Newborne has pointed out, the high court supplanted the constitutional doctrine of one man, one vote with a new dictum: "One dollar, one vote."

By refusing to limit the power of the rich to promote their political interests, except if they accepted government subsidies, the court opened the way for Ross Perot's bankrolling his independent candidacy in 1992 and for Steve Forbes's assault on the Republican nomination in 1996. Another and broader consequence of the court's decision was to encourage politicians of all shades and beliefs to get around the ceilings on contributions, which remained firmly in place, by hook or by crook, in order to meet the unlimited and insatiable demand for money to spend.

Given the frantic search to circumvent the restrictions on campaign giving, Congress inevitably carved out a loophole as wide as a bank vault door. Initially justified as a "reform" to strengthen the enfeebled parties, this exception to the regulations allowed fund-raising for such innocent-sounding "party-building" activities as ringing doorbells and printing up bumper stickers. In theory, the funds given for these purposes—called "soft money," as contrasted with "hard money," and given directly to candidates—would only benefit the party, not the individual office seeker. But this soon turned out to be a distinction without a difference, as lavish use of soft money for party building rebounded to the benefit of everyone connected with the party. And by the time Clinton's strategists began planning for the 1996 campaign, both parties were raising and spending soft money contributed by corporations, unions, and wealthy individuals alike, without any ceiling on either income or outgo, in sums that overshadowed the federal subsidies and hard-money transactions provided for by the original laws.

In the early months of 1995, Clinton and his advisers, still in a state of shock from the 1994 Republican avalanche, convinced that their backs were against the wall, were desperate to do anything that might help them recover. The whims and moods of the electorate were nebulous and difficult to predict. Money, however, was a tangible factor subject to influences within the control of the White House.

That same year, on the eve of his official announcement of his candidacy for the Republican presidential nomination, Texas senator Phil Gramm presided over a fund-raising dinner at the Dallas Convention Center that took in $4.1 million, the largest sum ever raised at a single event for any candidate for federal office, including sitting presidents. In an exultant mood, Gramm declared, in a comment that betrayed his inclination to gaucherie and which would before long demolish his hopes for the presidency: "I have the most reliable friend you can have in American politics: ready money."

Although neither Clinton nor any of his strategists was boneheaded enough to utter such a statement in public, the Clinton White House would have enthusiastically endorsed Gramm's judgment on the value of money. Moreover, with the power and prestige of the Oval Office presidency on their side, Clinton's fund-raisers were in a position to make Gramm and his contingent of Texas millionaires look like pikers.

Part of the allure of the presidency was simple avarice: There were businessmen and lobbyists willing to pay almost any price for the access they hoped would help advance their interests. But another part was simply the prestige that went with being the celebrity in chief. Clinton hosted a monthly White House coffee klatch for contributors. Donors of $10,000 or more were invited to dinner with the president and $100,000-givers got to sit at the same table with the chief executive, sometimes as many as thirty of them. History had its appeal, too. The Clinton campaign saw to it, the *Washington Post* reported, that its top givers and fund-raisers got to spend a night in the hallowed Lincoln Bedroom. Indeed, the White House put up so many fat cats during the two-year drive for funds that one campaign official compared the premises at 1600 Pennsylvania Avenue to an upscale branch of Motel Six.

By the end of June 1995, fully a year before the Democratic convention, Clinton's reelection campaign had already taken in $9 million, toward an ultimate limit of $30 million allowed by the FEC. This meant that after adding in $15 million revenue from federal matching funds and then subtracting legal expenses and the cost of fund-raising itself, the campaign would have more than $35 million to spend on getting President Clinton renominated.

"We are raising money as if we are going to have a hard-fought primary campaign for the nomination," Ickes told me in late spring of 1995. But no opponent was yet in sight, and even then, it was highly unlikely that anyone of consequence would challenge the president.

How would the money be spent? "That's a good question," Ickes acknowledged. But he added: "I am confident that we will find a way to spend the money." And he was right about that.

Dick Morris, a rival of Ickes for influence, was an important catalyst in energizing the Clinton fund-raising and spending apparatus. In June, Morris successfully lobbied the president to approve a television ad campaign reminding voters of Clinton's success in getting the previous Congress to approve his crime bill banning assault weapons and putting more police on the streets. "Deadly assault weapons off our streets," Clinton intoned in one such commercial. "One hundred thousand more police on the streets. Expand the death penalty. That's how we'll protect America."

Ickes derided the $2-million project as a waste of money, coming far too soon before the election to have any impact on voters. But Morris had other reasons for pushing the project, as one source familiar with Clinton's strategy session told me. "Simply because he had instigated the ad campaign, Morris would become more involved and more important in the president's reelection effort," this source pointed out. Besides, it was already plain that the president had sunk to such a low level in popular esteem right after the midterm election that his standings would rise, and Morris could take the credit for that. And just as Morris's prestige was bound to go up, so was his bank balance. As chief consultant to the Clinton campaign, he stood to make a tidy sum from the millions being spent on commercials.

No sooner had Clinton approved the June wave of commercials than Morris was back with a blueprint for another advertising drive, this one targeted on the Republican efforts to curb Medicare spending. Once again, Morris got his way. But this time, the funds to pay for the ads came not from the president's reelection campaign, which would have to expend some of its limited supply of hard money, but from the soft-money resources of the Democratic National Committee, on which there was no ceiling.

Under the law, only the president's reelection committee, not the national committee, could pay for his campaign commercials. But thanks to one of the various soft-money loopholes created by an obliging Congress and supported by the courts, the national committee could spend all the soft money it could raise by taking a position on "issues"—and Medicare was certainly an issue.

It remained only to raise the money, and that turned out to be no problem, given the intense participation of Clinton and Vice President Gore, both of whom served as magnets for the political fat cats. In September, the two men agreed to take on seven big DNC fund-raising events, to help pay for a ten-week $12-million ad campaign attacking the Republicans on Medicare and, in general, denouncing them as extremists. Although the campaign and the DNC maintained the legal fiction that this enterprise was a separate endeavor from the Clinton reelection campaign, in reality, behind closed doors at the White House, the president himself helped write the scripts for the DNC's "issues" commercials.

Meanwhile, to meet the unabating pressure from Morris and his cohorts for more money to fuel the campaign engine, the DNC turned to another, and relatively untapped, source of funds: foreign contributions. Given the globalization of the American economy, foreign corporations had acquired a huge stake in the myriad decisions made within the U.S. political system by both the executive and legislative branches on a range of issues from trade and labor to finance and the environment. As a result, more and more foreign businesses had been aggressively seeking to advance and protect their interests, just as American companies have always done—with campaign contributions.

Technically, it was illegal for foreign governments, corporations, or citizens to contribute money to American political campaigns. But just as there are loopholes in the laws governing giving by Americans, so huge gaps exist in the prohibitions on foreign giving. The laws allow exceptions for the U.S. subsidiaries of foreign businesses, so long as their giving does not exceed what they have earned in this country. Also exempt from the ban are foreign citizens legally residing in the United States, so long as the money is their own and they are not conduits for foreign funds. But as a practical matter, these rules are extremely difficult to enforce. It is possible to determine whether a company is a subsidiary of a foreign firm and whether a foreigner is living here legally. But it is next to impossible to figure out the real source of the money donated by the individual or the company, to deduce whether it came from the American earnings of foreign subsidiaries and the American holdings of foreign citizens, as the law requires, or whether the gift really originated in the treasury of a foreign corporation or in the bank account of a foreign investor.

And it just so happened that at this moment of need, the Democrats had, right in their official family, in the upper echelons of the Commerce Department, an operative highly skilled at finding and exploiting whatever loopholes existed in the laws governing foreign contributions. This was John Huang, a longtime Clinton friend, already something of a legend for his ability to open the doors to the halls of power in Washington to the Asian-American community and to powerful Asian business interests like the gigantic Indonesian Lippo conglomerate. So valuable was Huang to Lippo that when he joined the Commerce Department as deputy assistant secretary and became its highest-ranking Asian American, Lippo rewarded his past efforts with an $879,000 bonus.

But now his president needed him to serve elsewhere. At Huang's own suggestion, Clinton relieved him from his duties at Commerce and sent him to the Democratic National Committee. There, he set up shop as a full-time fund-raiser with the title of finance vice chairman, succeeding over the next few months in raising millions.

"I'd like to thank my longtime friend John Huang for being so effective," Clinton would later tell a $1,000-per-plate gathering in Los Angeles that would bring in half a million dollars, adding a comment that in its own way matched the tastelessness of Phil Gramm's adulation of "ready money": "Frankly, he's been so effective I was amazed you were all cheering for him tonight."

The money came in so fast, and was so badly needed, that no one thought to ask at the time whether Huang had crossed all the T's and dotted all the I's in his observance of the arcane laws governing foreign contributions. Only after it was too late did Clinton realize that Huang's efforts would hurt his candidacy and cast a shadow over his presidency.

Given the intensive coverage by "free media"—the electronic and print sources from which Americans get their news—of the same issues on which the Democrats had focused their commercials, it would be impossible to calculate how much influence, if any, those commercials had on the attitudes of the electorate. It is worth noting, though, that other Democratic pollsters reported that their soundings showed no significant difference in attitudes toward the president and toward the GOP between voters in states reached by the Democratic commercials and voters who lived outside the target zone. In other words, all the fund-raising and spending and law breaking may not have made a particle of difference on the outcome of the campaign.

Whether the commercials had anything to do with it or not, it was clear by the time the new year of 1996 had dawned that the president had won a great victory. By standing firm against the GOP assault on government, he had not only regained much of the public approval he had squandered during the first two years of the presidency, but more important, he had discovered what he had hitherto lacked—a purpose for his presidency and for his reelection campaign: the obstruction of the Republican counterrevolution. Just as Bob Dole, who would become the Republican standard-bearer, would salvage his candidacy for the nomination by defining himself as the anti-Buchanan force, Clinton now restored his mantle of presidential leadership by defining himself as the anti-Gingrich force.

In a year's time, the order of partisan battle had dramatically reversed itself. The Republicans were in full retreat from their bold revolutionary slogans, bitterly divided over who was to blame for their defeat. And worst of all, the front-runner for their presidential nomination, Bob Dole, was himself trapped by the debacle.

At this moment of triumph, Clinton was well positioned to launch a counteroffensive, able to marshal the populist rhetoric and ideas of his 1992 campaign while drawing on the lessons of his first two years in the White House and the Republican defeat. But that was not the course he followed. Instead of exploiting his victory in the battle of the budget, he followed a strategy shaped by the Democratic defeat in 1994.

This was not hard to understand. As he had demonstrated early in his tenure, Clinton had no real commitment to the populist doctrines he had mouthed in the campaign. And he was more uncomfortable with the Democrats who might have been his allies in a renewed populist crusade than with the Republicans with whom he now set about negotiating a truce on Capitol Hill.

Clinton set the tone for his retreat from victory in his State of the Union address to the nation in January 1996, in which he declared, to the loud applause of Republicans, that "the era of big government is over." On its face, this was a dubious assessment. The argument that had raged in the first year of the 104th Congress was not over the existence of big government but, first, over how fast—or to put it in Republican terms—how slowly big government would grow and, second, over how much of the burden and authority of the federal government could be shifted to the governments of the states. Indeed, Clinton had defeated the Republicans by resisting their efforts to slow big government. Of course, Clinton typically blunted the point of his claim about big government by adding the phrase "but we cannot go back to the time when our citizens were left to fend for themselves," a caveat that gave the Democrats their chance to applaud but left the country as confused as before about what the president actually believed.

Still, the unmistakable thrust of Clinton's speech was to starboard. To begin with, he set up a straw man to knock down: "We know big government does not have all the answers," he said, though he never identified who had ever claimed anything to the contrary. In a similar vein, he then added, "There is not a program for every problem." The president avoided having to deal with the continued economic anxiety that haunted millions of Americans by simply denying any reason for the existence of such feelings. Ignoring the continued stagnation of wages and living standards, he declared: "Our economy is the healthiest it has been in three decades."

Having disposed of the economy, the issue on which he had gained election in the first place, Clinton was free to dwell on the need for strengthening the nation's social fabric, and here he sounded much like the Republican opposition he had battled and defeated all year, repeatedly appropriating themes and gimmicks Republicans liked to call their own.

"Our first challenge is to cherish our children and strengthen America's families," Clinton declared. "Family is the foundation of American life. If we have stronger families, we will have a stronger America." He instructed the media to make movies and television programs "you'd want your own children to enjoy." He called upon the Congress to make V-chips a requirement in new television sets, giving parents greater control over what their children could watch. And he challenged the schools to do a better job of instilling character and education in their students, even endorsing the idea of making uniforms mandatory for public-school students "if it means that teenagers will stop killing each other over designer jackets."

The underlying strategy of the speech was for the president to focus on problems that few people believed were the responsibility of the govern-

The Return of the Comeback Kid

ment—like the moral behavior of their children—thus avoiding having to confront the sort of problems that citizens *did* look to their government to solve, problems that Clinton himself had promised to address in order to win the office he now held. The speech was well received that evening, particularly in comparison to Dole's rebuttal, which was narrowly drawn to appeal to Republican conservative primary voters. But the longer-range significance of the State of the Union speech was as a paradigm for the strategy of the forthcoming campaign, which differed from the 1992 battle plan as much as the rhetoric of the State of the Union address contrasted with Clinton's 1992 stump rhetoric.

The shift was symbolized by the replacement of James Carville, the self-described Redneck Rasputin of the 1992 campaign, who brought to that enterprise his populist fervor and values, with Dick Morris, Clinton's adviser from his early days in Arkansas, who had relearned his trade in the inner councils of the GOP. Gone was the "putting people first" battle plan of 1992, targeted at lower-middle-class workers who had been betrayed by the Reagan revolution. Clinton was still putting people first, but this time he was aiming at people higher on the socioeconomic scale—relatively comfortable suburban voters more concerned with the overall direction of society and the cost of government than with where their next paycheck was coming from. That explained his emphasis in the State of the Union address on "values"—violence on television, school uniforms, and the like—rather than the bread-and-butter issues that had been the mainstay of Democrats since FDR and, indeed, had been the key to Clinton's own success in 1992.

This strategy shift reflected not only Clinton's own inclinations but the defining impact of his struggle with the 104th Congress. Clinton was able to bid for the Yuppies, who would ordinarily vote Republican, because he did not have to worry about solidifying his own base, usually the first task of a candidate. Clinton did not have to do that in 1996; Gingrich had already done it for him.

Despite the president's claim that the economy was in better shape than at any time in the past thirty years, working Americans knew better. Although the president boasted about the 8 million new jobs he had created, the fact was that job creation lagged behind the record of previous recessions. And the new jobs left much to be desired when it came to wages, forcing workers to moonlight and both spouses in a family to work to make ends meet. "Some of our people say, 'I know there are 8 million new jobs—I got three of them,'" Andy Stern, president of the Service Employees Union, told me.

The sluggishness in wage gains was mirrored by the lack of improvement in the living standards of the average American. Median household income at the end of 1994 was still 6.6 percent below what it had been in 1989, at the peak of the business cycle, and had made no gain at all during Clinton's first two years in the White House. Although median household income climbed a bit in 1995, the median earnings of full-time workers were still declining. The rise in household incomes came about because many workers, like the members of Andy Stern's union, were filling two or three jobs. Even so, the median income of non-college-educated households was still 5 percent below its 1989 levels. The fact was, the recovery had been weak and average workers were not much better off than they were at the start—and, in some ways, maybe worse off.

These figures help explain the dreary view of the economy and of the national condition in general that was reflected in polls in early 1996. In a Gallup poll taken in March, two months after the State of the Union speech, 66 percent of those interviewed rated the economy as only fair or poor, twice as many as those who called it good or excellent. Moreover, though most voters were telling pollsters that they believed the country was on the wrong track, an evaluation that reflected discontent with the economy, in a striking contradiction of the normal rules of politics, it was incumbent Clinton, not challenger Dole, who won the largest share of these glum voters.

The explanation for that came from union members I talked to at the Service Employees Union annual convention in Chicago in the spring of 1996. For example, Carl Rocconi voted for Bill Clinton in 1992, hoping he would cure the nation's sick economy. Since then, Rocconi, a business agent for Chicago's Local 1 of the Service Employees Union, had found little to cheer about. "For working people, the economy has been just stagnant," he told me. "Real wages have laid flat. It's getting tougher and tougher to negotiate pay increases." Republican strategists had been counting on such discontent with the economy as a key to unseating Clinton in the election. But Rocconi had no hesitation in telling me who would get his vote in November: Clinton. He was equally clear about his reasons. "If Dole gets in, he will only make it worse," said Rocconi, who is married with two young children. "Look what the Republicans tried to do in the Congress."

"The Republicans want to cut Medicare and Medicaid where the Clinton administration wants to hold things where they are," said another delegate to the convention, Janet McNeely, a bus driver in Taylor, Michigan. McNeely, who could not remember the last time she got a raise, hoped for better days. But she said: "It takes time for the government to do things. And the Democrats have their hands full fighting the Republicans in Congress."

In the 1994 election, a good many union members had deserted their traditional home in the Democratic party in droves to vote for Republicans. But John Sweeney, the new president of the AFL-CIO, called this a mistake they were not likely to make again.

"In 1994, our members voted out of their own frustration and against the establishment," Sweeney told me. "What they got was the shock of their lives. They didn't vote to see Medicare and Social Security attacked."

And Democrats took every opportunity to warn them that they had even more at stake in the 1996 election. "We are not just fighting for a job here and a little better wages here and there," David Bonior, the House Democratic whip, told the Service Employees convention delegates in Chicago. "We are in a big historic fight in this country today. The people on the other side would like to destroy labor completely. They would like to take away the right to organize."

The bad news for Dole was that the misgivings about Republicans were not just limited to union members like the audience for Bonior's speech, who had long been the allies of Democrats. Broader polling measurements that covered more conservative voters who were also struggling to make ends meet and were haunted by fears of downsizing showed that most, nevertheless, planned to back Clinton. In 1994, fewer than 40 percent of all non-college-educated white males, of whom only about one in four come from union households, voted for Democratic congressional candidates, after a narrow plurality of them had favored President Bush in the three-way 1992 presidential balloting. But in the spring of 1996, polls showed these normally Republican voters favored Clinton.

What created these defections was the 104th Republican Congress and its heavy-handed efforts to slash social programs to balance the budget and cut taxes. Some Republicans complained that the GOP lawmakers had gotten a bad rap. "The Democratic establishment and their union allies have done a good job of defining the GOP Congress as a threat to people's well-being," complained former Bush campaign pollster and current Dole adviser, Fred Steeper. "People now have a caricature in their minds of the Republican Congress, which needs to be undone with lots of money and every communication device known to man."

But other Republicans grudgingly conceded that Gingrich and company were themselves at least partly to blame. "It's like Fidel Castro, right after he took over Cuba," said Illinois Republican leader Rich Williamson, a former Reagan White House aide. "One of his problems was that when he came in from the hills, he didn't take off his fatigues. And our problem is that some of the people who were critical to our success in 1994 didn't take off their fatigues when they took over in Congress. And that hurt us."

Republicans now found themselves paying a price for Gingrich's big talk and his domination of the Washington scene after the midterm elections. By a hefty margin, polls showed that it was the Republicans in Congress, not the Democratic president, whom they viewed as responsible for setting the national agenda in Washington. This judgment in effect allowed Clinton to escape from the responsibility incumbents normally bear for the condition of the country.

Some Democrats complained to me that Clinton relied too much on fear of Gingrich to mobilize his base. They wanted him to be more aggressive, particularly in taking big business to task for hogging the economic pie. "I'd like to see the president jawbone these corporate heads about sharing their profits with workers," said David Bonior of Michigan. "And I'd like to see him be tougher on trade." Clinton could have found significant support for such arguments, according to Guy Molyneux, a Democratic pollster who had been conducting focus-group interviews on voter attitudes on economic issues for the AFL-CIO. "People do blame government for what's happening economically," Molyneux said. "But it's not strictly the conservative interpretation that government takes too much of their income in taxes. A lot of people say that government hasn't done a good enough job of protecting working people by not clamping down on mergers and acquisitions and buyouts."

But for Clinton to follow the course advocated by Bonior and Molyneux would mean breaking with the efforts to strengthen his relationships with big business, which had become the heart and soul of his economic policy. By wooing corporate chief executives in 1992—winning more business support than any Democratic nominee since Lyndon Johnson in 1964—Clinton had bolstered his credentials as a "New Democrat" who would not tax and spend like a traditional liberal. And the emphasis early in his presidency on cutting the deficit, rather than boosting the economy, helped solidify his support in the boardrooms and executive suites. He was determined to reinforce and broaden his big-business base in the 1996 campaign. No less an authority than business friend and Clinton adviser Tony Coelho believed that the president would keep most business leaders from returning to their normal home in the GOP. "Executives are not out to defeat him," Coelho said. "They think Republicans will lose, and it's not worth it for them to try to make a difference."

Typically, Clinton had not allowed his left flank to be entirely unprotected. In the face of increasing evidence of corporate greed and mounting public indignation at the excesses of business, Clinton had addressed the issue of what he called "corporate responsibility"—but in terms so guarded that his rhetoric would scarcely give Coelho cause to revise his prediction. Businesses should give workers better health care, training, family benefits, pensions, and a greater say in the workplace, Clinton told an audience at Ohio's Xavier University in early spring. But turning aside the advice of some of his more liberal advisers, he failed to propose any new federal regulations, tax incentives, or other measures to advance these goals.

Instead, he praised American business as the "engine of prosperity and the envy of the world" and made plain he would oppose any regulatory efforts that could hold it back. "Business has a role to play, too, if we want people to have better lives," he said. Indeed, he pointed out that many businesses have shown that they can "do well by doing right"—prospering by investing in their employees' welfare. But he quickly added: "Let me be clear: The most fundamental responsibility for any business is to make a profit. We can't do anything that will try to freeze the dynamism of the economy, otherwise we won't be able to create jobs."

Despite the favorable indicators and his own maneuvering, the economy remained shaky ground for Clinton. In fact, when a *Los Angeles Times* poll conducted in spring of the election year asked about Clinton's handling of the economy, only 45 percent of respondents approved, while 46 percent disapproved. These figures added up to an opportunity for Dole—perhaps the only chance the Republican now had of winning the election.

But opinions differed sharply among Republicans as to how to exploit this opening. Some agreed with Whitney Ayres, who had polled for Lamar Alexander, that the best answer was the traditional Republican strategy: Blame the tax-and-spend Democrats. "He has to identify the causes of slow economic growth and tie these causes back to Democratic policies," Ayres told me, adding, "One of the primary economic burdens on middle-class families today are rising tax rates which take an increasing portion of their paychecks."

But senior Dole strategist Don Sipple believed that rhetoric had grown stale. Most voters realized that Republicans as well as Democrats were responsible for rising taxes and also understood that easing that burden would be difficult without cutting government benefits in ways that would hurt the middle class. "I think we have to reframe the economic issue so that it relates to people in their daily lives," Sipple said. "Because people are having trouble getting ahead, in a majority of two-parent families— both parents work. That limits their ability to be as active in their schools as they'd like to be and as active in their churches as they'd like to be. If we can reframe the issue that way, it will be a huge advantage for Bob Dole."

Dole's most formidable adversary in the contest for the GOP nomination, Pat Buchanan, argued that the GOP needed to sever its ties with giant corporations, particularly those with international interests, to deal effectively with the economic issues. "What is good for the corporate economy is no longer good for working Americans," Buchanan said.

But the suggestions of Sipple and Buchanan would each in their own way represent a dramatic departure from traditional GOP doctrine. And there was no sign that Dole was ready to make such a break. Indeed, Dole's critics within the party felt that he had yet to demonstrate an awareness of the urgency of the economic difficulties besetting millions of Americans. "Republicans have failed to show they understand the legitimate anxiety that's out there," said Richard Williamson. "It's not only people who have lost their jobs. Everybody has a neighbor without a job, or a brother, and Republicans have to say they understand that's happening."

Apart from Dole's own repeatedly demonstrated limitations in communicating such ideas on the stump, the party had a built-in problem because of its ties to the business community. Many corporations had enjoyed handsome profits during the Clinton years, wanted to continue making them, and took offense at any talk of hard times that could threaten their black ink. Thus, in the spring, when the Clinton White House put out a report boasting that the new jobs opening up in the economy paid better than average jobs, Republican National chairman Haley Barbour accused the administration of trying "to paint over the bleak picture that is today's economy with rosy hues." But that same day, Jerry Jasinowski, president of the National Association of Manufacturers, historically a bulwark of the GOP, hailed the report for undercutting "the excessive hype about corporate anxiety." Jasinowski added: "Maybe publication of this study signals an end to the unfortunate trend toward corporate bashing."

Just as the GOP's ties to the corporate world made Dole reluctant to confront the electorate's concerns with the economy, so Clinton was equally tongue-tied; as the incumbent president, he was unwilling to admit how much things had not improved. The net result, or the bottom line, to use the idiom of the marketplace, was that the nature of the political system and the makeup of both parties dictated that neither side would address the issue that mattered most to the voters.

Even as Dole groped for a way to turn the economic issue against Clinton, another opportunity presented itself to strike at a presidential area of vulnerability—his character. But this issue, too, would produce its own frustrations.

Doubts about Clinton's character had surrounded him since he had entered national politics, and Republicans did not lack for material to reinforce these misgivings. Early in the election year, the Republicans dug up a 1995 *Esquire* interview with Bob Kerrey in which the Nebraska senator remarked about his party's president: "Clinton's an unusually good liar, unusually good." They put the quote at the top of a fund-raising letter from Republican National chairman Haley Barbour that charged: "Bill Clinton is systematically sacrificing America's future for your children and grandchildren in order to preserve his position in the polls."

Then, in late spring, the Republicans got fresh ammunition when a federal jury in Little Rock convicted the president's business partners in the Whitewater venture, James and Susan McDougal, and his successor as governor of Arkansas on charges of fraud and conspiracy. The convictions served to bring Whitewater back to life after it appeared to have faded from public consciousness—and to give new spark to Republican attempts to use doubts about Clinton's character to undermine his candidacy and change the course of the election.

Although Republicans avoided commenting directly on the verdict, their allusions were unmistakable. "I want to be president because I want to return integrity to our government—a mission that's more important this week than even a week ago," Dole declared in a speech to the Republican National Committee a few days after the Whitewater verdicts were turned in. Echoing Dole's attack, Iowa congressman Jim Leach, chairman of the House Banking Committee and a leader in the Republican probe of the Whitewater affair, declared pointedly that "public officials have a special obligation to tell the truth and conduct themselves and their affairs, be they public or private, in a manner above all reproach."

In pursuing the character issue during the course of the campaign, Republicans followed two main lines of attack. In the broadest terms, Dole, in part by stressing the rigors that he had overcome during his own life, sought to define the office of president as the setter of moral standards for the nation—an office to be occupied by a man whom Americans could hold up as an example for their children. A sixty-second Dole commercial, shown around the country on his behalf by the Republican National Committee, leaned heavily on his upbringing in small-town Middle America, where "he learned the value of hard work, honesty, and responsibility," and on his heroism in World War II combat. "Like many Americans, his life experience and values serve as a strong moral compass," the narrator said.

Dole himself spelled out the implications of his background for his candidacy and for his service in the presidency, when in an address to the Catholic Press Association he called the election "a referendum on the basic values of the country." "Americans look to the White House for moral leadership," he declared. But he described the Clinton White House as "fundamentally adrift, without direction or moral vision."

More explicitly, Dole and his surrogates contended that because Clinton spoke with a forked tongue, he could not be relied on to fulfill his promises to promulgate policies that Republicans claimed he had lifted right out of their own agenda in the first place. "Every time Bill Clinton says one thing and does another, every time he talks like a conservative but governs like a liberal, he puts his character and credibility on the table," Dole declared. Another Republican National Committee commercial brought the character offensive to bear directly on Clinton, using film clips to depict the president as taking six different positions on balancing the budget. "Talk is cheap," the announcer concluded, but "double-talk is expensive."

Republicans took heart from national polls that showed that almost without exception, and by substantial margins, voters thought Dole was more honest than Clinton and more likely to stand by his convictions. "I want some morality in government, so that when you look at somebody and he tells you something you can believe it," Seth Harter—a tractor dealer and Dole backer from Englishtown, New Jersey, who came out to cheer Dole on a visit to the Garden State—told me in May.

Everett Carll Ladd, director of the Roper Center for Public Opinion Research, concluded that the character issue was keeping Clinton's approval rating from going much above 50 percent. "He works incredibly hard at the job, he is bright and pretty centrist, at least in his rhetoric, and he has great communications skills," Ladd pointed out. "But at the same time, his numbers are mediocre. So I have to believe that the character issue has held him down, though it hasn't been enough to put him down."

There was the rub for the Republicans. Much as the character issue had weighed Clinton down throughout his presidency, it lacked the heft to hurt him decisively. The same polls that demonstrated the doubts about Clinton's character also showed that most voters, unlike Seth Harter of Englishtown, still preferred Clinton to Dole in the White House for the next four years.

One reason the Republican indictment of Clinton's character had not won over the electorate was that Americans had heard much of it before. "And most of them decided that whatever Clinton did, it probably was not important, and it was a long time ago," Democratic pollster Mark Mellman contended. Indeed, Republicans were inhibited in their character crusade because they ran the risk of giving the character issue a bad name; that is, they could use it so much that their tactics would rob questions about honesty and trust of much of their meaning and provoke suspicion of their own motives and even, among some voters, sympathy for Clinton.

"I think they [Republicans] are trying very hard to malign the man and to hold the things over him that happened years ago, and I think they're giving the man a raw deal," said Ethelyn Slifko, an office manager from La Plata, Maryland, who voted for Clinton in 1992 and intended to do so again. "And he's held his head high and done a good job of it."

But the more fundamental problem for the Republicans was the need to demonstrate to voters how and why Clinton's personal behavior and mores affected his performance in office and why that should influence their decision at the voting booth.

"There is a lot of drip-drip-drip that there is something wrong with him [Clinton]," said Dole adviser Don Sipple. "But it is hard to get a handle on it. Voters have to see a consequence for them before it becomes a relevant, salient issue." In a sense, Dole and the Republicans were battling the political system and the deeply rooted cynicism it inspired. "What we're trying to do is convince voters that Clinton changes his stripes from day to day," said Fred Steeper. "But it's going to be a tough case to make," he conceded, "because people are going to think that all he's doing is being a politician."

By the spring, Dole had raised and spent just about all the money he was entitled to raise and spend under the Federal Election Law—more than $37.2 million. But this was not as big a problem as it seemed, because of the plenitude of loopholes in the law. The biggest was that the Republican National Committee could pay for Dole campaign appearances so long as what he said and did was limited to so-called party-building activities rather than promoting his own candidacy. This distinction was just as meaningless as the sham the Democrats had been using to hide behind commercials that took positions on issues, notably Medicare, but which, of course, were intended to boost Clinton's candidacy. That did not keep the Democrats from complaining bitterly about Dole's evasion of the law. "We're watching closely with some slight amazement at the brazenness of their campaign spending," said Clinton campaign press secretary Joe Lockhart. But there was no danger to Dole any more than to the Democrats, because the Federal Election Commission had explained that it would not rule on any complaints until after the November 5 election. "We don't want to interfere with the political process," said FEC spokeswoman Sharon Snyder. In sum, except for adding to the stockpile of voter cynicism, the fund limit meant little.

The real problem for Dole remained that he still had nothing to say that would make voters care about his candidacy. And this point was underlined in mid-May when Dole startled the country by announcing he was leaving the Senate in order to concentrate full time on running for the White House. "The very least a presidential candidate owes America is his full attention," Dole declared. To dramatize the change, Dole, on his first day on the campaign trail after he quit, doffed his habitual banker's gray three-piece suit and donned a light blue blazer and an open-neck shirt and chinos.

Despite the fresh appearance, the candidate had no new message to offer. In his first postresignation announcement, Dole lapsed into his familiar cryptic ways, leaving his listeners with the burden of filling in the gaps. "I want to be president because I want to restore an instinct for decency to our national life and culture," he said, without elaborating. And he concluded by urging his listeners to "tell your friends what Bob Dole is all about. I'm not really complicated. I come from the commonsense Midwest," once again failing to even attempt to explain what that meant, or why voters should care.

But where Dole fell down most of all was in not separating himself from the 104th Congress. "Clinton has been convincing the American people he is protecting them from the Republicans in Congress," said GOP consultant Jude Wanniski, an adviser to Jack Kemp and Steve Forbes. "Dole is going to have to do the equivalent of a read-my-lips pledge and say to voters that 'I will protect you against the Republican congress.'"

Given Dole's own sense of loyalty and kinship with his colleagues on Capitol Hill, it would have been hard for him to go that far. Instead, though, he seemed determined to tie himself into the biggest obstacle to his political success. "But let me remind you—this Congress was elected by the American people to reform, and reform we did. We kept our promises." Then he ticked off examples of legislation enacted, from welfare reform to tax cuts, which Clinton had vetoed. And Dole sought to turn the Democratic indictment of extremism lodged against the GOP lawmakers on its head by declaring, "Just think where Bill Clinton would have taken America without a Republican Congress."

Dole claimed on his charter plane back to Washington after the speech that "it will take more than one day" to accomplish the transformation to which he had committed himself. But why a man who had been running for president on and off for sixteen years needed more time to explain his candidacy remained a mystery.

Not surprisingly, a month later, Dole seemed to have made no progress as I traveled with him in New Jersey, where the state party had imported him to serve as the star attraction at a party fund-raiser. The visit was remarkable for how little use Dole made of it. Although this state was considered a battleground vital to his steadily dwindling election chances, he said nothing in public beyond a few sentences, bantering with reporters who appeared to monitor the photo opportunities arranged by the campaign staff. "We're not in any hurry to start putting out our agenda," he declared at one stop. "If we did it now, there wouldn't be anything left for the convention or afterward." But in reality, time was running out on his candidacy. Privately, Dole strategists conceded that by the time the summer political conventions opened—in about two months—they would have to succeed in moving their candidate from his current standing, about fifteen points or more behind President Clinton in public opinion polls, to a position right on the president's heels. Historically, whichever candidate leads on Labor Day has almost invariably won the presidency. Mindful of that lesson from the past, Dole's aides groped for ways to get their candidate ahead, or at least even, by the time the Republican convention ended on August 16.

11

Divided They Ran

BEFORE DOLE COULD PROPERLY PREPARE for the convention and for the fall campaign against Clinton, he first had to deal with a problem within his own party that threatened to undermine the slim chance he had of success in the fall. This was the struggle over abortion. The importance of this issue in the politics of the Republican party testified to the shallowness of American political parties. The constitutional impediments to the healthy growth of parties made it possible for factions, the very forces that Madison and his colleagues despised, to wield influence far out of proportion to their numbers. In the case of abortion, the so-called pro-life proponents who bitterly opposed abortion swept into control of the party machinery in 1980 as part of the Reagan takeover and had remained there ever since. Opinion polls showed that Republicans held widely divergent views on the right of women to control their reproductive processes. Yet the foes of abortion allowed for no dissent from their unrelenting opposition to abortion in the party platform.

The strength of the antiabortion forces derived from their single-mindedness and willingness to expend vast amounts of time and energy fighting for their cause in a political system in which the majority of citizens barely summoned up enough interest to vote. Although polls showed that a majority of Americans favored some right to abortion, in the only poll that really counted—on election day—it was only those who regarded abortion as a sin against God who could be counted on to vote for or against a candidate solely dependent on the candidate's stand on that issue. Thus, for convention after convention, the antiabortion forces prevailed, keeping their plank in the platform because they cared more than anyone else.

But in 1996, that dominance was threatened by the weakness of Dole's position as a challenger to Clinton, whom he trailed by margins well into the double digits throughout the spring. Months before the August Repub-

265

lican convention in San Diego, some of Dole's advisers counseled that the candidate make some change in the party's stance on abortion, not just for the sake of winning over pro-choice voters but, more important, to give new life and greater breadth to Dole's candidacy. Don Sipple, for one, proposed going beyond a change in the platform and selecting a pro-choice vice presidential candidate, notably Colin Powell. "We need a symbol of tolerance," Sipple told me. "Right now we look like intolerant, judgmental assholes. We look very rigid, inflexible. We need something big to change that image."

Sipple was no political naïf. He knew that for Dole to even think of asking Powell to be his running mate, Dole had to be competitive with Clinton—not fifteen or more points behind, as he was at the moment. "Otherwise it looks like a desperate and weak move," Sipple said. "Frankly, Powell would be a fool to get on the ticket this way."

Powell was no fool. By June, with Dole still lagging far behind Clinton, Dole's advisers realized that their candidate would have to deal with the abortion issue directly rather than relying on the symbolism of his vice presidential choice. But Dole's efforts to resolve the abortion dilemma took him down a road strewn with misadventures, which led to a debacle as surely as if he had planned that outcome. The pattern demonstrated Dole's weak hold on his own party, reflecting the fact that his nomination had resulted from his money and his resources rather than his convictions. Dole's abortion ordeal also stemmed from his inability to recognize the difference between the symbolism of presidential politics and the literalism of the legislative sausage factory, of which he was an acknowledged master. In legislation, it was only the end result that counted. In presidential politics, by contrast, perception and style often mattered most, particularly when it came to such an emotional issue as abortion, where the opponents of abortion rights insisted on being called "pro-life" and their adversaries styled themselves "pro-choice."

The fiasco over abortion began unfolding on June 6, when Dole issued a statement calling for "a declaration of tolerance" in the Republican platform. This would acknowledge that the GOP officially recognized that many Americans, indeed many Republicans, held differing views on abortion. The *New York Times* called it Dole's "first unequivocal statement on abortion." But in fact, the statement was clouded with ambiguity. The most important unanswered question was over the placement of the tolerance declaration in the platform. The antiabortion forces indicated from the start that they would accept such a statement only if it were contained in the preamble and could be interpreted to apply generally to every other issue in the platform. But such placement would not make for the dramatic statement Dole wanted, so the nominee-to-be indicated, in his fashion, that the preamble would not do. On June 10, Dole said of the tolerance plank,

"It's *probably* going to be in the abortion plank, not in the preamble" (emphasis added). Dole's resolve seemed to harden a few days later when he was confronted by a banner borne by an antiabortion activist that declared: "Tolerance belongs in the preamble." Dole responded, "But then it doesn't mean anything; the Bible says we ought to be tolerant."

Even the authority of the gospel had little impact on Ralph Reed, head of the vehemently antiabortion Christian Coalition, and Illinois congressman Henry Hyde, whose opposition to abortion was so staunch that Dole had named him chairman of the convention platform committee to reassure pro-life forces. Although both were sincere in their opposition to abortion rights, each was motivated by his own particular concerns, typical of the factionalized condition of both political parties—and these factors took precedence over Dole's attempt to broaden the reach of his candidacy. Reed knew that his position in the competitive world of the Christian conservative movement depended on the vigor of his opposition to abortion. For his part, Hyde realized that his prestige and status as a leader of the House Republicans was at stake.

Neither would be trifled with, as each made plain after they met to discuss Dole's maneuvering. Reed warned of "strong opposition" to any attempt to put a tolerance declaration in the abortion plank itself. And Hyde let it be known that he was considering stepping down from his platform post in protest if Dole bulled ahead with his tolerance crusade.

Dole backed down. A month after he had set off the controversy, he tried to put an end to it by announcing that the suddenly offensive word "tolerance" would not appear in the abortion plank itself but would instead be relegated to a plank all its own, where abortion supporters now bragged, and Dole himself had earlier conceded, it would mean nothing.

About all Dole had accomplished was to trigger a public debate on the last issue the party wanted to focus attention on—its disagreement over abortion. Although the argument seemed absorbed with semantic differences, these differences took on political potency in the context of the abortion issue. It could be argued, as some politicians did, that abortion did not really belong in the political arena because it dealt with highly personal questions. But it was precisely because the abortion issue touched directly on people's well-being and values, often literally in life-and-death terms, that it assumed salience in a political world where most debate seems abstract, remote, and trivial.

And now partisans on both sides seized upon Dole's public hemming and hawing on the platform as an invitation to sound off on the issue. Some supporters of abortion rights, like Massachusetts governor William Weld, argued that the Republican party, with its commitment to opposing the reach of government, had no business endorsing the power of government to reach into a woman's womb. "I think it's very important for the party to send a message that we are inclusive, that we are welcoming, that there is room for a range of opinion on abortion and other issues," Weld said. "And I think the easiest and best way to do that is by taking the plank right out of the platform."

Such a move might be expected to help Weld in November in liberal Massachusetts, where he was running for the U.S. Senate against incumbent Democrat John F. Kerry. And it might also help Dole achieve the broadening of his candidacy some of his advisers sought. But many Republicans feared that the benefits of such a change for Dole in the presidential race would be outweighed by the risk he would run of alienating his hard-line conservative base, which was almost unanimously opposed to abortion. And this threat was compounded by the continued candidacy of Buchanan, who had been unrelenting in his opposition to any change in the platform. "Anyone who wants to change the abortion plank is going to come over Pat Buchanan," the columnist had declared early in the campaign, and he had not retreated an inch from that position. Indeed, just before the convention platform committee was due to meet in San Diego, Buchanan sounded a warning of the trouble he might make for Dole in San Diego, rejecting even the watered-down compromise that Dole had recommended.

Buchanan announced that he deemed the so-called tolerance plank that Dole had proposed "not acceptable." His main objection was the compromise plank's description of abortion as an issue of "personal conscience." Not so, cried Buchanan. "Abortion is a matter of right and wrong; it's a matter of life and death," Buchanan said. He proposed his own version of a tolerance plank and threatened a floor fight at the convention, which Dole's advisers were orchestrating as a display of unity, unless his language was accepted.

As if all this was not troublesome enough, Dole compounded the problem for himself by making yet another change in his abortion position, which was made known to the world when formal drafting of the platform began in San Diego a week before the convention opened. The working draft of the document submitted by Dole's aides to the platform committee placed a "declaration of tolerance" in close proximity to the plank calling for a ban on abortion, where it would indeed "mean" something, to use Dole's terminology. The draft specifically cited abortion as one of the issues on which dissent was acceptable and softened the tone of the plank calling for a ban on abortion. Infuriated, the foes of abortion, who thought they had already won the platform battle, rebelled by throwing the committee into confusion.

The issue now extended beyond abortion to Dole's credibility as a candidate and his control over his own party. Officials tried to minimize the damage by putting off action on the abortion issue until the end of its workday—after the deadlines for major newspapers and television networks in the East had passed. The conflict, though, was impossible to conceal. In desperation, the Dole campaign sent its top aides to lobby balky committee members. Reluctant delegates were offered the chance to talk to Dole himself, in hopes they could be won over.

But all this was of little avail. A poll of convention delegates showed they were split into several camps on the issue. One in five supported a constitutional ban, without any statement about tolerating differing views; one in four supported the ban but preferred it be accompanied by a statement on tolerance; and about one in three favored rescinding the party's support for a constitutional amendment prohibiting abortion. But whatever the polls showed about differences of opinion, the foes of abortion controlled the platform committee—and unlike Dole, they seemed to know exactly what they did and did not want.

What they did not want was any change in the platform's long-standing opposition to abortion. In June, when Dole had first called for adding the tolerance language, he said, "I have been chosen the Republican nominee, and I intend to run on a platform that reflects my views." And he declared that the wording of the party platform would be his decision. Now he discovered otherwise. In a stinging rebuke to the man the convention would nominate a few days later, the committee shredded Dole's proposed "declaration of tolerance" on abortion—dramatically underscoring his lack of control over his party on the eve of his nominating convention. Even the phrase "tolerance is a virtue" was stripped from the document Dole's aides had written. Antiabortion activists cheered. "This is a big win for the pro-family movement," declared Ralph Reed, head of the Christian Coalition. It seemed scarcely to matter to Reed and the other foes of abortion that it was a big defeat for Dole.

And it could not have come at a worse time. Dole aides had hoped to spend the week leading up to the convention focusing attention on Dole's newly announced economic plan calling for an across-the-board reduction in income-tax rates. Whatever the pros and cons of the long-delayed plan, Dole's advisers believed it represented his only chance of overtaking Clinton. But the time spent grappling with the emotionally charged abortion issue diverted attention away the tax plan. By the time the convention officially opened, Dole had managed to get favorable reviews for his surprise choice of Jack Kemp as a running mate. And, determined to offset the damage done by the public squabble over abortion, Dole's managers presented a convention show redolent of the themes of harmony and open-mindedness.

Colin Powell, whose potential entrance into the presidential competition had set off alarms among party conservatives, led off by preaching civility in public debate, help for the downtrodden, and a welcome for all Americans in the Republican party. Even Pat Buchanan did his bit for unity by backing the Dole-Kemp ticket, though his endorsement was notably lacking in the passion and conviction that had sparked his own candidacy. And in a bid to close the gender gap, which now yawned wider than ever, the Republicans presented as their keynote speaker Susan Molinari, a thirty-eight-year-old member of Congress from Staten Island, and, like Powell, a supporter of the right to abortion.

Indeed, the convention program exuded so much moderation that it irritated some conservative delegates. "There's a disconnect between the platform and the image projected at the convention," said Karen Johnson, an Arizona delegate who was especially angry that Molinari had given the keynote address on Tuesday night. "This is the image the hierarchy of the party wants to project to reach out to more voters." The best proof of where the party really stood, conservatives argued, was in the platform, which, besides retaining its outright opposition to abortion, called for a constitutional amendment to remove automatic citizenship for children born in America to some noncitizens, the denial of government benefits for U.S.-born children of illegal immigrants, and an end to affirmative action.

Dole's acceptance speech was just as schizoid as the rest of the convention and the party he now led. At one moment, seeking to make an asset of his septuagenarian status, he summoned up the time-honored virtues of the national past. "Let me be the bridge to a time of tranquillity, faith, and confidence in action," he asked. "And to those who say it was never so, that America has not been better, I say, you're wrong, and I know, because I was there. I have seen it. I remember."

But in almost the next breath, he was off on a harsh and derisive tirade. "It is demeaning to the nation that within the Clinton administration a corps of the elite who never grew up, never did anything real, never sacrificed, never suffered and never learned, should have the power to fund, with your earnings, their dubious and self-serving schemes," he said, without offering even a word to identify either the corps of culprits or their purportedly misbegotten undertakings.

One thing Dole did not do in the speech was to utter a word about the abortion issue, or anything else in the platform. That document, he claimed, he had somehow not found time to read, an oversight it was evident he had no plans to rectify.

The fundamental problem with the Republican convention was that Dole's aides had placed upon it an unrealistically heavy burden—establishing Dole as a plausible challenger to Clinton, which, in four days, would mean undoing the impressions created by the 104th Congress and Dole's own inadequacies as a candidate. Even without the abortion controversy, Republicans knew that task was probably beyond their doing. "I think we can get a jump start out of the convention," Clarke Reed, a longtime Mississippi GOP leader, told me before the conclave opened. "Though, actually, what we need is more of a pole vault."

Before they could start hammering away at Clinton in a bid to win over the swing voters now leaning the president's way, Dole strategists conceded that they would first need to use the convention to nail down the backing of the normally Republican voters who lacked enthusiasm for Dole. "The problem with Republicans right now is they don't really know who their nominee is," Paul Manafort, Dole's convention manager, said at the outset of the San Diego conclave. "They know basic things about him, but that's it." But the blur that had emerged from the abortion fight and the divergence between the hard-right substance of the platform and the moderate sheen of the convention did nothing to define Dole's own image.

In the aftermath of Dole's platform debacle over abortion, Speaker Gingrich sought to comfort his fellow Republicans by calling attention to the plight of the Democrats, who, Gingrich pointed out, were deeply divided over the welfare-reform bill Clinton was about to sign. Gingrich was about half right. It was true that welfare reform had split the Democrats, pitting liberal against conservative and the White House against Congress. In fact, however, the Republicans were also factionalized by this very same issue. Republican lawmakers wanted welfare reform enacted so they could brag about it to their constituents, whereas the Dole campaign did not want a new law but a campaign issue that could be sustained only if no new law had passed and Clinton failed to keep his campaign promise "to end welfare as we know it."

Welfare thus became the defining issue of the campaign and a compelling example of the Madisonian system operating at the peak of efficiency: Within each of the parties, the self-interest of the legislative branch was in clear contradiction with the political welfare of the party's presidential candidate. Both sides had foreseen the significance of welfare reform early on.

"The only legislation that is really going to count this year is welfare," Harold Ickes had told me the previous December. "The rest pales by comparison. People want to have a safety net for the poor," Ickes said. "But they don't think the system is working well. They want it changed." And apart from public dissatisfaction with the existing structure of the welfare system, Clinton had given the issue a life of its own by his campaign promise to carry out far-reaching change. What it all boiled down to was that the president, in his effort to portray himself as a New Democrat, had raised the stakes on welfare reform. Now the center of the debate was not on the merits of reform but on the president's credibility.

The Republicans knew that and they sought to push Clinton into a corner, forcing him to choose between breaking his promise and hurting the Democratic core constituencies. Nor did the Republicans ever lose sight of the fact that Clinton had already twice vetoed welfare measures the Republican Congress had passed. Did he really want reform, Gingrich asked, or was welfare another broken promise, like the middle-class tax cut? It was time to put up or shut up.

As the time for a decision neared, Gingrich sought to raise the stakes beyond even what Clinton had done. Another presidential veto of welfare reform, Gingrich said, "would send a signal that basically until there is a presidential election, there is no point in trying to pass reform with this White House vetoing everything that is commonsense reform."

The legislation that moved through Congress was severe—far too severe, in the judgment of many Democrats. The bill would eliminate the sixty-one-year-old federal guarantee of cash assistance for the nation's poorest children, leaving their fate in the hands of the states, which had vast new authority to run their own welfare programs according to their own dictates. That was tough enough. But Gingrich wanted to make it tougher yet—too tough in fact for Clinton to sign—by including provisions to give the states authority to cut Medicaid spending and impose more stringent eligibility requirements on Medicaid for children.

To sign such a bill would mean that the president would retreat from the stand he had taken during the battle of the budget in defense of Medicare and Medicaid. Clinton might want to be a New Democrat, but he could hardly claim to be any sort of Democrat if he approved of those Medicaid cuts on the poor.

Forcing Clinton to veto the welfare bill made good sense to ideologue Gingrich. And it also made sense to the Dole campaign. "We always felt that the most important part of our issue cluster on values was going to be on welfare," Scott Reed, Dole's campaign manager, told me. "Clinton had made statements that he would end welfare as we know it. He was very vulnerable on that issue. Our point to the House and the Senate was: Why let him off the hook? We wanted them to stick it to Clinton, and put the failure of welfare reform on his ticket."

But nearly 100 Republican House members, determined to pass a measure that stood some chance of becoming law, signed a letter calling on GOP leaders to reverse field and move a separate welfare bill that Clinton could sign. "The House and Senate were in a survival stage," Reed said. "They were both concerned that there was going to be a Democratic sweep. So they put their selfish interests ahead of the nominee."

"Bob Dole's running his race," was the way Republican representative Jim Bunn, a freshman from Oregon, put it. "I'm running mine."

Dole had little choice. He sent word to Senate Republicans urging them to "pass a sweeping welfare-reform bill," without making any mention of Medicaid. "Dole saw what was coming down and what was going to happen," explained one Republican Senate staffer involved in the welfare negotiations. "And rather than have it happen to him, he decided to take the initiative."

Still, the president seemed dissatisfied, warning that Republicans would have to "make this bill even better," without specifying how, before he would sign it. That was too much for Dole. He urged Republicans to hold firm. "I hope Congress will pass a tough welfare-reform bill, not just any welfare-reform bill," he said. "And I challenge the president to finally sign a welfare bill." But the pressure to pass a bill was too great. The lawmakers gave enough ground so that Clinton got a bill he could sign.

Largely because of this compromise, Clinton turned the week following the Republican convention into a triumph for his campaign—and a disaster for Dole—by signing welfare reform and two other new laws on which Republican lawmakers, desperate to save their jobs, had no alternative but to share credit with him in order to impress their own constituents.

Day after day, the White House celebrated Clinton's achievements. On Tuesday, August 20, it was a raise in the minimum wage, which the president called "pro-work, pro-business and pro-family," adding, "This bill says to working people of America: If you're willing to go to work, your work will be honored."

The next day it was a health-reform measure that would protect Americans who changed jobs from losing their health insurance. No mention was made that the law offered no protection against insurers charging the job changers with exorbitant rates or of the new reform's failure to address the plight of the growing number of Americans who lacked any sort of health insurance and who had been left out in the cold by the defeat of Clinton's earlier health-reform package.

Thursday marked the signing of welfare reform, which the president delicately described as intended to "re-create the nation's social bargain with the poor." Even as he signed the law, Clinton acknowledged its faults and promised to correct them. "We can change what is wrong," Clinton claimed. "We should not have passed up this historic chance to do what is right."

All in all, said Scott Reed in disgust, "it was Clinton's best week"—and, he might have added, one of Dole's worst.

But the enactment of welfare reform was not favorable news for all Democrats. Half the Democrats in the House and Senate, including the party leaders in both bodies, voted against the welfare bill the president signed, amid charges that Clinton was playing election-year politics. No issue so dramatized the divisions among Democrats in their year of supposed unity. Al From, president of the Democratic Leadership Council, the ideological womb of the New Democrat movement, hailed the legislation as establishing a system "that creates opportunity and promotes responsibility," which he contended "reflects the values most Americans share." But Andrew Stern, president of the Service Employees Union, whose members made up the backbone of what was left of the traditional Democratic party, warned that the new law would "devastate the lives of welfare recipients and hardworking people around the country." He added, "This is a sad day for workers across the country."

Whatever the merits of the legislation—and the drastic changes it encompassed raised questions that would take years to resolve—the political significance of Clinton's signing the measure was clear. It was bad news for Democratic challengers who were hoping to unseat Republican incumbents by branding the 104th Congress as extremist. The credibility of that argument was badly damaged when the Democratic president literally gave his stamp of approval to what was arguably the most extreme accomplishment of the 104th Congress.

Clinton's defenders argued that he had no other choice but to sign a bill in which the faults were so grievous that he pledged to rectify them before the ink was even dry on his signature. Yet, as some of Clinton's own advisers counseled, the president was in an excellent position to veto the bill.

First off, Clinton held such a commanding lead over a candidate whom Walter Dean Burnham described as "probably the most intrinsically inarticulate presidential candidate since Alton J. Parker," the 1904 Democratic party standard-bearer, that his prospects could scarcely have been seriously damaged by his signing or vetoing any single piece of legislation. Beyond that, as Harold Ickes, the most seasoned and soundest of Clinton's political advisers pointed out to him, in a memo that he later showed to his former boss, Jesse Jackson, Clinton could actually benefit politically from a veto. Ickes, a liberal but also a realist, had learned his trade in the jungles of Manhattan's Democratic politics and had been involved in half a dozen previous presidential campaigns. By seeming to sacrifice what most people presumed to be his political interest for the cause of the millions of children threatened by the new law's drastic cuts in benefits, Ickes argued, the president would be perceived to be acting out of conviction. This is an impression that would greatly benefit any politician, but particularly one who, like Clinton, was widely suspected of having no convictions at all.

Moreover, as the liberal economic analyst Robert Kuttner suggested, Clinton could have converted the Republican bill into an initiative of his own. He could easily have challenged the Republicans to channel the $50 billion they claimed the bill would save into establishing a jobs program for the poor. The Republicans almost certainly would have passed up the challenge, giving Clinton additional justification for vetoing the measure and also providing him with a campaign battle cry that could have rallied the traditional Democratic base to the polls on November. That would have given a huge boost to Democratic hopes of recapturing the House, an effort Clinton all but doomed to failure with his decision to sign the bill.

But that was not the kind of campaign that Clinton wanted to run. It would have contradicted his strategy of triangulation, which emphatically did not include a Democratic-controlled Congress. Clinton had made his lack of interest in promoting Democratic chances of recapturing the Hill clear from the beginning. In December 1995, in a talk in the Roosevelt Room of the White House, I had asked the president if he was going to go all-out to elect a Democratic Congress in 1996. Clinton seemed to sidestep the question. "Well, the historical experience is that the best thing a president can do to help elect a Congress of his own party is to persuade the American people that the vision he has and the program he has is the right one."

A few weeks later in an interview with the *Washington Post,* Clinton was even more explicit in defining his reluctance. "The American people don't think it's the president's business to tell them what ought to happen in congressional elections," Clinton said. Besides, he argued, it would not work. "The evidence that presidents have been successful in making that kind of argument to the American people is not very heavy."

But the truth of the matter was that the evidence went in the other direction. Few presidents had made a vigorous argument to vote for their party's candidates for Congress. In fact, other Republican leaders had criticized Reagan and Nixon, the two most recent presidents to be reelected, because they did so little to urge the election of Republican members of Congress. And their party made only modest gains in the Congress in the ensuing election.

But President Truman, whose circumstances were most analogous to Clinton's as a Democrat facing a Republican-controlled Congress, had helped his party to gain seventy-six seats in the House and nine in the Senate and to retake control of both Houses by focusing his own candidacy around the struggle for Congress. Right after his acceptance speech, Truman began his campaign by announcing he would summon "this last, worst 80th Congress" back into a special session to "pass the laws people need on matters of . . . importance and urgency." As Truman expected, the special session accomplished little. But it gave him more evidence to back up his indictment of the "do-nothing" Congress.

In his celebrated whistle-stop tours across the country, Truman did not plead for support. He demanded it—or else. If the Republicans retained power in Congress, he warned on Labor Day in Detroit's Cadillac Square, "You men of labor can expect to be hit by a steady barrage of blows. And if you stay at home . . . and keep these reactionaries in power, you will deserve every blow you get."

Given the public perception of the 104th Congress, it would have made at least as rewarding a target for Clinton as the 80th Congress had been for Truman. However, Truman attacked the 80th Congress because he wanted the election of a Democratic Congress to help him carry out what he wanted to do as president. By contrast, Clinton had no such program, as his reelection campaign would demonstrate. And he had no real purpose in the election beyond winning another term for himself.

In fact, the election of a Democratic Congress would have returned him to the same predicament he had found himself in during his first two years as president. He had done much better with a Republican Congress, as the polls testified, and he stood to do even better now that the aggressive conservatism that had infused the 104th Congress at its outset had been tempered and diluted.

As a practical matter, Clinton could not campaign for a Republican Congress. And at any rate, he did not want the Republicans to add to their strength in the legislature, which might cause a return to their aggressiveness. For appearances' sake, he had been supportive of the Democrats in Congress. He did help raise money for them, though some Democrats privately grumbled about the limited extent of the presidential largesse, particularly in view of the vast sums the Democratic National Committee was taking in. "The hard-money transfers to the Democratic Congressional Campaign Committee were more *de minimis* than in 1994," Mark Gersh, director of the National Committee for an Effective Congress, an organization dedicated to the support of Democratic House candidates, told me.

As to rhetoric, Clinton said as little about the Congress as he could without causing embarrassment to himself. Typical was his convention acceptance speech, in which, after mentioning the Republican effort to "blackmail" him into making concessions during the budget showdown of the previous winter, he said: "Of course there is a better answer to this dilemma. We could have the right kind of a balanced budget with a new Congress—a Democratic Congress." In an address that took the better part of an hour, this one sentence was the solitary reference to the congressional elections.

Electing a Democratic Congress did not fit in with the grand strategy that had emerged from the State of the Union address: a campaign focused not on mobilizing the Democratic base, which would have meant more votes for Democratic congressional candidates, but on wooing upscale suburbanites who, even if they did vote for Clinton, were likely to stick with Republican congressional candidates for Congress. And Dick Morris designed the Democratic convention, which convened in Chicago a week after the GOP convention ended, to reiterate and expand on the values and themes that would supposedly make the hearts of suburbanites beat faster.

The old liberal stalwarts such as the Reverend Jesse Jackson and Mario M. Cuomo were on hand but were relegated to supporting roles during the hours when the television networks were not airing the show. "Before nine P.M., we're running the 1984 convention," one convention planner told Ronald Brownstein of the *Los Angeles Times*, recalling the convention that had nominated Walter Mondale for president. "After nine P.M., we're running the Clinton convention."

During prime time, the Clinton arrangers brought on the stars of the convention, some of whose connection with the Democratic party, or with politics in general, was tenuous at most but all of whom sought to reinforce the bipartisan appeal that Clinton's strategists were counting on to energize his candidacy. They led off with two prominent Republicans, Jim Brady, Reagan's former press secretary, who had been wounded by gunshots in the 1981 attempt on Reagan's life, and his wife, Sarah, who praised Clinton for signing the Brady Bill, imposing a five-day waiting period on gun purchases. Then came Christopher Reeve, the cinematic impersonator in *Superman*, bound to a wheelchair by a horseback-riding accident, who appealed for more medical research in words that Clinton himself might have used during his battles over the budget. "Sure, we've got to balance the budget, and we will," Reeves said. "But we've also got to take care of our family and not slash programs people need."

Even the customarily provocative Hillary Clinton adopted an above-the-battle stance during her convention speech, in which she dwelled on the concerns of the average American family, repeatedly referring to her duties, and her husband's, concerning parenting their sixteen-year-old daughter, Chelsea. "For Bill and me, family has been the center of our lives," the First Lady said. "For Bill and me, there has been no experience more challenging, more rewarding, and more humbling than raising our daughter." Only once did she mention the opposition party—and that time favorably, when she noted that a Democrat and a Republican together had sponsored the health-care reform bill the president had signed into law earlier in the month.

All this laid a foundation for the president's own appearance, in which the man who had proclaimed the end of the big-government era deluged his audience with a flood of small governmental tasks that he claimed to have already accomplished or pledged soon would be completed, some so diminutive they seemed barely worth presidential effort: He would create a core of specialists to improve the reading ability of third-graders, enable every twelve-year-old to log on to the Internet, require chemical markers in gunpowder to ward off terrorists, and provide more information about neighborhood toxic waste to curb pollution. Clinton emphasized his initiatives to help parents—from the V-chip to family leave—declaring "no parent can do it alone, and no parent should have to." But he admonished mothers and fathers that they would have to lead the way. "Every tired night you spend reading a book to your child will be worth it many times over," he declared. "I know that Hillary and I still talk about the books we read to Chelsea when we were so tired we could hardly stay awake."

Some of the glow from Clinton's climactic moment was diminished by the overnight resignation from his campaign entourage of consultant Dick Morris, following disclosure that Morris had consorted with a high-priced Washington prostitute as recently as the week preceding the convention and had shared with her his sensitive conversations with the president.

Outwardly, though, the president seemed undismayed as he appropriated the hapless Dole's metaphor about a bridge to the past; and converting it to his own purpose, he reiterated it endlessly to dramatize what he wanted

Americans to believe was the meaning of the election. "The real choice is whether we will build a bridge to the future or a bridge to the past," Clinton declared in his peroration, "about whether we believe our best days are still out there or our best days are behind us, about whether we want a country of people all working together or one where you're on your own."

The close of the Democratic convention found Dole still lagging far behind Clinton, with few prospects for improvement. New York and California, both Clinton strongholds in 1992, were out of reach. Moreover, in the Big Five, states that cut a swath across the nation from Northeast to Midwest—New Jersey, Pennsylvania, Ohio, Michigan, and Illinois—Dole was almost as far behind as in the Big Two. In the three presidential elections of the 1980s, all five had lined up behind Ronald Reagan and George Bush. But in 1992, all reversed themselves and wound up in Clinton's corner, and now they seemed headed in his direction again.

Republicans saw the target of choice for their candidate in these states as the economy, with his chief weapon being his proposal for sweeping cuts in tax rates. "This is the weakest of five postwar recoveries, and two-thirds of workers have anxiety about their jobs," said Rich Williamson, a former Reagan White House aide and campaign strategist and 1992 GOP candidate for the U.S. Senate from Illinois. "Bob Dole has to say staying the course isn't good enough."

But to make that point, Dole would have to convince people "that the tax cut is real and that it will work," Michigan independent pollster Ed Sarpolus said. "There is a lot of skepticism that it won't happen, and also people worry that it will add to the deficit." Still another difficulty that Dole and the GOP would face in the Big Five was the party's stress on social issues, particularly traditional family values. This emphasis, which had helped attract conservative Christians in the 1980s and which Clinton and the Democrats were trying to mimic, seemed to have boomeranged in the 1990s, creating a perception of narrowness and intolerance. "To win Illinois," said Williamson, "Dole first would have to say: 'I am not a captive of the intolerant religious right. I am not Ralph Reed, I am not Pat Buchanan.' The swing vote in Illinois doesn't want to vote for that perceived intolerance." But it would be hard for Dole to make that argument after the Religious Right had crushed his own effort to inject a note of tolerance into the platform on the abortion issue.

Clinton faced challenges of his own in the Big Five. Voters in all states were still troubled by economic insecurity. And core Democrats in the big cities resented the president for pushing through NAFTA and signing the welfare bill, giving rise to concerns about low turnout among Democratic party leaders.

But here Clinton's ace in the hole was the Republican Congress. In Pennsylvania, "the 104th Congress was the difference between the public attitude in 1995 and now," said pollster Terry Madonna. "Pennsylvanians looked at what the Republicans were trying to do and just decided, 'This is not what we want.'" That record made it hard for Dole to take advantage of Clinton's potential weakness. In New Jersey, pollster Cliff Zukin told me then that the economic issue was hurting Dole. With memories of the 104th Congress in mind, "The same people who are gripped by economic uncertainty are the people who worry that when Dole talks about self-reliance, he means, 'We are not going to help you.'"

And then there were the problems Dole faced simply because he was Dole, which made him an unlikely choice for discontented voters. "If you want to bring about change, why would you go to somebody who has been part of the political establishment for thirty-four years?" asked Pennsylvania pollster Terry Madonna.

Against this opposition, Clinton had the freedom to conduct any sort of campaign he wanted. But like a football coach whose team was far ahead in the fourth quarter, he chose to sit on his lead, mounting a minimalist operation designed to protect his advantage over Dole but with no ambitions either to rally support for Democratic congressional candidates or to create a mandate for his second term. Typical was the forty-minute speech he delivered in Coraopolis, a college town outside Pittsburgh, in October, where Ed Sijowski, a seventy-seven-year-old retired locomotive engineer, came out to hear him speak. Sijowski worried about the future, particularly about paying medical bills for himself and his ailing wife, Grace. "I'd sure like to hear more about what's going to happen to Medicare," Sijowski told me before the talk. But Sijowski went away disappointed. Clinton had little to say about Medicare's future, except to warn that the election of his Republican challenger, Bob Dole, would mean "even bigger cuts" in the program than the ones he had vetoed during the previous winter's budget debate.

Rather, the focus of Clinton's speech, which closely tracked his convention acceptance speech, was a proposal for inflation-indexed treasury bonds—the latest in a series of small-bore proposals for the nation's problems that made up the foundation of his campaign for reelection.

Clinton senior adviser George Stephanopoulos, one of the president's chief image molders since the 1992 campaign, claimed that each of Clinton's proposals fell under the broad rubric of three fundamental principles—opportunity, responsibility, and community. The overall idea, Stephanopoulos explained, was to "provide opportunity for everyone by demanding responsibility from everyone," and so strengthen the community. But even Stephanopoulos admitted this bland and hazy rhetoric represented a comedown from the bold vision the president had painted in the 1992 campaign, when he called for spending $220 billion to revive the economy. "We couldn't do everything we wanted as quickly as we wanted," he said. "But they still are our goals. And we are doing as much as we can to reach them within the context of balancing the budget."

Yet the way the president was campaigning seemed likely to add to the problems he and his fellow citizens would face in his second term. "The president is using the entitlement issue to bolster his position by stressing the idea that Republicans would make unacceptably deep cuts in certain entitlement programs, particularly Medicare," said Robert Reischauer, former head of the Congressional Budget Office. "That puts him in a difficult position to then present the American people with some of the tough decisions that will have to be made in the next four years on entitlements. But it was clear that so far as the president was concerned, he would worry about such things after he had won a second term.

By early October, politicians on both sides were saying that the only chance Dole had of catching up with Clinton was to achieve some sort of miracle in the debates. But this notion, which was widely published and remarked upon, was fatuous on its face and typified the mythology that has grown up around campaign debates. These events have taken on the sanctity of motherhood in American politics. Candidates who agree to debate or challenge the other candidate to a debate are automatically presumed to hold the moral high ground. Candidates who refuse to debate are regarded automatically with suspicion. In fact, debates have become another distortion in a distorted system, and their shortcomings were clearly in evidence in the Clinton-Dole campaign.

These encounters are a pretext, a substitute for the sort of open and free exchange of views that would enliven campaigns and help voters to make informed judgments on the candidates. A number of circumstances have drained away the potential significance of these debates. First of all, with rare exceptions, these confrontations are not debates at all but merely joint appearances in which each of the candidates is protected by a moderator or a panel of questioners from being subjected to direct questioning by his or her opponent—or, just as risky, from being obliged to ask a direct question posed by his or her opponent. Far from promoting voter understanding about the candidates, the debates have a stultifying effect, freezing movement in a campaign until the debates are staged, after which interest generally evaporates. Although so-called debates have dominated media and public attention in every presidential campaign since 1976, the focus is invariably on style rather than substance, and on otherwise relatively trivial slips of the tongue.

Since debates became a presidential campaign fixture in 1976, only one or two have had consequential impact on the election outcomes. In 1976, Gerald Ford embarrassed himself by denying that the Soviet Union dominated Eastern Europe, and advisers blamed this lapse for his failure to catch up with Democrat challenger Jimmy Carter. In 1980, most politicians concluded that Ronald Reagan's candidacy was boosted by his debate performance against Carter, although the benefit was reputed to have come more from Reagan's disarming personality rather than from any substantive difference between the two men.

As the debate negotiations between Clinton and Dole demonstrated, far from being a weapon for an underdog, allowing him to energize the electorate and transform opinions, the debates are the tools of front-runners, who use them to enhance their control of the campaign. Mindful of that reality, Tony Fabrizio, Dole's pollster, said, "We wanted to drag out the debates for as long as possible, knowing that once the debates had ended, the press and the public would give up on Dole's chances."

But the Dole forces were in a weak bargaining position in the negotiations because they were so far behind the president. In a political variation of *Catch 22*, Dole's disadvantage in the campaign hurt his chances of using the debate to reduce that disadvantage. In addition, the Clinton forces outsmarted the Dole campaign in the public discussion about the debate by professing to want Ross Perot to participate in the encounters. This made Clinton seem magnanimous and Dole appear selfish and mean-spirited.

Although he was once again running for president, after going to the trouble of founding a third party that held its own convention to nominate him, the polls made clear that the country had soured on Ross Perot after his remarkable showing in 1992. His support never exceeded single-digit levels. Still, Dole's strategists desperately wanted to keep him out of the debates, fearful that his appearance alongside the two major party candidates would boost his stock and Dole would suffer more than Clinton. Actually, most polls showed Perot drawing equally from both of the major party candidates.

At any rate, Clinton's advisers did not want Perot in the debates either, because they believed his presence increased the possibility that Clinton would lose his temper, the one circumstance they felt could seriously damage his candidacy. "We thought he could upset the president," said Stephanopoulos. "It was a question of personal dynamics."

But for the benefit of the world and the Dole campaign, the Clinton campaign took another position. On September 17, when the bipartisan commission arranging the debates announced that Perot would not be included in the sessions because he had no realistic chance of winning the election, Mickey Kantor, lead debate negotiator for the Clinton-Gore campaign, issued a statement that read: "We regret the commission's decision" not to allow Perot to debate. And on the day the commission made its decision known, a senior White House aide insisting on anonymity said, "Fair is fair, and we think Mr. Perot should have his chance."

But these professions of dismay were just posturing, intended to bolster Clinton's already strong bargaining position by making it seem that by agreeing to debate without Perot the president's side was making a concession. "The Dole people didn't have much leverage going into the negotiations," Stephanopoulos pointed out. "They needed to make sure that Perot wasn't going to be in the debate." Once the Clinton negotiators agreed to Perot's exclusion, they were better positioned to be insistent on the two points that really mattered to them: a limited timetable—the debates would start on October 6 and end on October 16—and the choice of moderator, to be public broadcasting's news anchor Jim Lehrer, whose bland style would promote the Clinton campaign's overall effort to make the entire confrontation as dull as possible. "We wanted the debates to be a non-event," Stephanopoulos said. "Our strategy was no news, no surprises, no nothing. No campaign."

Along with the unfavorable ground rules, the Dole campaign faced another major problem going into the debates. Dole's economic plan, built around the promise of a sweeping income-tax cut, intended to be the center of his candidacy, simply was not catching on. Designed to make it easier for middle-class Americans to get ahead, as Dole contended, the plan depended on a 15-percent cut in income-tax rates. But Dole did not say exactly how he would pay for these tax cuts, claiming that any losses in government revenue would be offset by economic growth. That caused a credibility problem for which Dole could in part blame his own past phobia about deficits, which made this proposal seem out of character. Ross Perot's 1992 campaign rhetoric also contributed to public skepticism about the Dole plan. "Perot sensitized people to the tax-cut issue," said pollster Terry Madonna. "They know they can't have a tax cut without pushing the deficit up."

Given these handicaps, Dole's advisers understandably had a hard time devising a coherent strategy for their candidate. On the one hand, they sought to exploit Dole's only apparent advantage, the low expectations for his performance, by encouraging him to present what pollster Fabrizio called "his human side." On the stump, Dole almost always sounded like what he had been all his life, a legislator. In the debate, his handlers wanted him to discard the buzzwords of Capitol Hill and give viewers a sense of his personality, which they hoped would be a more favorable impression than voters had anticipated.

On the other hand, some aides who believed that Clinton was winning the election by masquerading as a moderate wanted Dole to go on the attack and expose the president as a deep-down-inside liberal. "He's got to unmask Clinton," Fred Steeper told me beforehand. "A lot of voters don't yet think Clinton is a real liberal on some of the key issues such as taxing, spending, and welfare." And this attack strategy had a corollary, which was the hope that by needling Clinton, Dole could provoke the president into losing his temper. "We thought if we could push his button enough times, Clinton would respond," Fabrizio explained.

But Clinton's advisers were ready for this ploy. Scrawled in bold letters across the notes he carried to the debate podium was this message: "Don't take the bait." "We told him beforehand, no matter what happens, just give a clear straight answer," Stephanopoulos said. The Dole aides had another gambit aimed at unsettling Clinton. They arranged for Billy Dale, the former head of the White House travel office, whose dismissal by Clinton had been a continuing embarrassment to the president, to be given a conspicuous seat at the Hartford Civic Center, the arena for the debate. Asked later why Dale had been seated there, Fabrizio quipped: "Because we couldn't get Paula Jones." But the Billy Dale gambit failed because Clinton apparently did not recognize him.

Dole himself had no better luck at provoking Clinton during the course of the debate, though occasionally his aides believed he had come close. "There were a couple of times in the first debate where Clinton's face turned red and we thought if we could push that button enough times, we could get the response we wanted from Clinton," Fabrizio said. As part of the strategy to irk Clinton, Dole cited a flood of statistics about rising bankruptcies and stagnating wages to refute Clinton's claim of economic recovery. And he got off his best quip of the night when moderator Lehrer asked about Clinton's boast that Americans were better off now than in 1992. Nodding in Clinton's direction, Dole retorted: "Well *he's* better off than he was four years ago."

That got Dole a big laugh. But it did not seem to faze Clinton, who joined in the laughter and blithely agreed with his opponent, saying, "That's right."

Dole also zeroed in on a question about the difference between his view and the president's on the role of government. "I trust the people; he trusts the government," Dole said. But sixty seconds later, when it was his turn, Clinton simply said he trusted the people, too.

For the most part, Dole was too fixated on carrying out his instructions to be warm and human to do justice to his other set of instructions—to pound away at Clinton. That would explain why he took a pass when moderator Lehrer gave him a chance to raise the character issue, supposedly Clinton's most vulnerable point. Asked whether there were "significant differences in the more personal areas that are relevant to this election," Dole said: "I don't like to get into personal matters. As far as I'm concerned, this is a campaign about issues."

That disappointed many of his supporters, David Keene among them. "I think when Jim Lehrer served him up that character question, Dole had a professional obligation to knock it out of the park," said Keene. "He could have said, 'Every time voters go to the polls, character is a major part of what influences their vote. They are looking for someone they can trust.'" At any rate, all Dole got out of his at-bat in Hartford was a base on balls when he needed a home run.

For the second debate, ten days later in San Diego, Dole abandoned his compunctions about the character issue and went after Clinton head-on.

"There's no doubt about it that many American people have lost their faith in government," Dole said in response to a schoolteacher's question about the values public figures impart to the nation's children. "They see scandals almost on a daily basis; they see ethical problems in the White House today; they see 900 FBI files of private persons being gathered up by somebody in the White House. So there's a great deal of cynicism out there."

But then, abruptly, Dole shifted gears, uttering what amounted to a non sequitur. "But I've always tried, in whatever I've done, to bring people together," he declared. And though he returned to the character issue intermittently, his scattershot thrusts failed to develop a coherent theme that would answer for voters the threshold question of why Clinton's character flaws should matter to them.

Clinton barely deigned to respond to Dole's attacks, instead reminding the audience at the University of San Diego's Shiley Theater of Republican efforts to cut popular government programs and of the economic progress made during his tenure. "I don't want to respond in kind to all these things," Clinton said at one point halfway through the debate, sounding almost indulgent of his older opponent. "I could. I could answer a lot of these things tit for tat. But I hope we can talk about what we're going to do in the future. No attack ever created a job or educated a child or helped a family make ends meet. No insult ever cleaned up a toxic-waste dump or helped an elderly person."

Clinton's soft answer served the purpose of turning away Dole's wrath, such as it was. As the debate went on, Dole's fire grew less sustained—deterred as he was by Clinton's unwillingness to engage and his own inability to come to grips with the issue.

The upshot of the last debate was just what Dole's advisers had feared all along—the practical end of Dole's candidacy. Reporters now covered his campaign as if they were assigned to the death watch for a terminally ill patient. And Republicans began saying in public what they had been muttering to themselves privately: Their presidential standard-bearer was finished.

"He didn't make the case that Clinton isn't fit to be president," William Kristol, one of the architects of the GOP's 1994 midterm election triumph, concluded. "I think most Republicans feel the presidential campaign is basically over, absent an act of God."

Now they turned their attention to a cause that was not lost, the battle for Congress. And trying to make the best out of adversity, some Republicans saw Clinton's seemingly unassailable lead in the presidential race working to the advantage of their House candidates. "If Dole continues to have problems down to the last ten days of the campaign, Republicans running for Congress are going to have a message to voters that says, 'Don't give Clinton a blank check,'" said Glen Bolger, the GOP consultant whose firm, Public Opinion Strategies, served more than fifty GOP House candidates around the country. "And that's a message that will work very well," Bolger said, "because people don't want another Democratic Congress run by a bunch of liberals who would move Clinton further over to the left."

If the Democrats cupped their ears for an answer to this argument from the president, they listened in vain. He spent his time campaigning in states like Alabama, Florida, and Georgia, where the polls showed that a visit from him might make the difference in his total of electoral votes—but where he could not be of much help to Democratic congressional challengers. And the president pumped hard for such unobjectionable ideas as wiring schools to the Internet, encouraging telecommunication, producing faster supercomputers, and similar items from the grab bag of trivia that made up his presidential platform. But the names Gingrich and Dole, which might have helped energize voters to support Democratic congressional candidates, rarely escaped his lips.

Yet his aides claimed that at heart he hoped for a Democratic sweep that would restore his party to control on Capitol Hill—only he felt obliged to pursue this goal by extraordinarily subtle means. "Voters are suspicious of partisanship," a White House aide told R. W. Apple of the *New York Times*. "So he is not going to go out there and ask them to give him a Democratic Congress so he can push through a Democratic program. You can't throw it in people's faces that way, at least in his view, or you'll remind a lot of them that they'd rather not see a concentration of power in one party's hands."

Whatever the president really hoped to achieve through this indirection, his tactics could hardly have been more pleasing to the Republicans desperately trying to hold on to Congress. Candidates of the party that had seized control of Capitol Hill in 1994 by coalescing around national issues now did all they could to put distance between themselves and their party's Contract with America; their controversial House Speaker, Newt Gingrich; and their party's presidential standard-bearer. "This is 435 individual races, and everybody's got to do what they got to do to win," said Rich Galen, an adviser to Gingrich. "In the forty or fifty campaigns that are very close, they have to do whatever works for them."

For months now, ever since the budget showdown, President Clinton had dominated the campaign and, indeed, national political debate, helped by the public rejection of the 104th Congress and his own mastery of political communication. But then in the closing weeks of the fall, a development occurred that for the first time seriously threatened Clinton's control of the campaign. And this could be traced not to any achievement of Dole's but rather to one of the great success stories of the Clinton campaign: the vast sums of money raised to promote the president's reelection drive.

The story came out in dribs and drabs, as such stories usually do. It began in September, when the *Los Angeles Times* disclosed that a South Korean industrialist named John K. H. Lee, whom the redoubtable John Huang had lined up to contribute more than $250,000 in soft money to the DNC, was not a legal resident and that his American affiliate had not generated any revenue. Even under the rickety structure of laws governing foreign contributions, Lee's gift was illegal. That opened the gates to a flood of questions about whether the money Huang and his cohorts had collected was truly U.S. money and what the givers had expected in return. In a near panic, the Democrats began sending money back even faster than they had collected it.

But it was too late to prevent the Republicans from pouncing upon the disclosures. "I can imagine no greater danger than foreigners' trying to buy access to the government," Speaker Gingrich declared. Dole accused the Clinton administration of "taking money laundering to an art form" and added with biting sarcasm: "You hear the president, who often talks about a bridge to the future. It seems it's a bridge to wealthy political donors. It goes through a Laundromat first, then takes a left at the Democratic National Committee, and then goes all the way down to the Oval Office."

The White House responded to the allegations and charges by denying any knowledge or responsibility of any wrongdoing, while waiting for the campaign clock to run out. On Friday, November 2, four days before the election, in a much-heralded speech on campaign reform, the president insisted that he and his party had "played by the rules" in raising money. In the face of brewing controversy over the issue, he called for changing those rules— after Tuesday's election. Along with reiterating his support for a series of measures that were in a bill that had bogged down in Congress earlier in the year, Clinton called for a ban on contributions to federal campaigns by noncitizens and by domestic subsidiaries of foreign companies—the type of donations that have been at the center of the furor over fund-raising by the Democratic party. But he did not address any of the specific questions that had surfaced over his party's activities.

Campaign reform advocates scoffed at the president's eleventh-hour conversion to the cause, noting that he had promised reform for four years even as he fattened his campaign coffers with questionable contributions. "Why should we believe him?" asked Ellen Miller, director of the Center for Responsive Politics, a campaign-finance watchdog group in Washington. "He promised a thorough cleansing of the system four years ago, and then he stood by idly and raised more money and incurred more obligations [to contributors] than any candidate in history."

The fund-raising controversy was the only development in the final years of his first term that in any way slowed Clinton's path to reelection. For the first time, Clinton was on the defensive as the ethics issue that Dole had been trying to raise for weeks without much result took on new salience.

The issue had little impact on the Democratic base. Instead, it hurt the president most among the upscale suburban voters he was trying to win back from the Republicans in the Northwest, the South, and the Rocky Mountain West. But it turned out that the damage Clinton himself suffered was minimal. The furor came too late in the day and Clinton was too far ahead for Dole to benefit significantly. Besides, as the Democrats pointed out, he and his party were hardly without sin when it came to circumventing the campaign laws.

In the end, the president only lost votes that might have carried him above his target of 50 percent of the popular vote, a goal whose meaning was diminished by Clinton's failure during the campaign to outline a mandate that would require a popular majority for him to carry out. His party, however, suffered more substantial damage—the destruction of its hopes for winning back the House. Exit polls showed that Democrats had a 4-percent lead in the generic vote for House candidates up to the last week of the campaign, Mark Gersh of the National Committee for an Effective Congress told me later. Voters who decided in the last week voted Republican by a 13-percent margin. And the group of voters that believed Democrats raised money unethically jumped 15 percent in the closing days of the campaign.

But the balance of evidence suggests that anyway, Clinton did not want the Democrats to regain the House. This president, who, as the Democratic challenger in 1992, had run against the Republicans and cast himself as an agent of change, was now, as the incumbent Democratic president in 1996, running away from his own party and basing his campaign on his defense of the status quo. In that he succeeded.

In politics, as in the rest of life, though, change is the law of nature, and even the stalemate Clinton would preside over at the start of his second term was bound to be transformed in one way or another during the next four years. "Tonight we proclaim that the vital center is alive and well," Clinton declared on election night. "It is a common ground on which we have made our progress." But the center is not a fixed point in political time and space. And the challenge for the reelected president was whether, as the ground beneath him shifted, he could keep his footing.

12

The New
Political Order

THE REPUBLICAN PARTY'S 1996 Christmas card, sent out a few weeks after the presidential election returned Bill Clinton to the White House, displayed a joyful elephant seated in front of a Christmas tree, opening a gift-wrapped replica of the U.S. Capitol. "Oh boy!" the pachyderm exclaims. "Congress again!"

Indeed, divided government is back with us—but with a dramatic difference from its previous heyday, when, for a dozen years starting in 1980, the Republicans controlled the White House while the Democrats dominated the House of Representatives and, half the time, the Senate, too. The explanation commonly offered for that arrangement was that voters wanted Democrats in charge of Congress, where they could do what they did best: hand out the benefits of government. However, only a Republican president, so the theory went, could be trusted to preside over the Cold War, keep the economy on track, and stand up for the traditional values of the middle class.

"Voters felt that Congress would take care of people at home and the president would take care of the country abroad," Fred Steeper, the GOP pollster who worked for both the Reagan and Bush presidential campaigns, told me. Or, as political scientist Walter Dean Burnham more elegantly put it, "Americans tend to be operational liberals and ideological conservatives." Divided government thus seemed to accommodate and reflect the fundamental conflict underlying American politics: the tension between the resentment and suspicion of government enshrined in the American tradition and the citizenry's more recent but nonetheless profound dependence on government to help cope with the exigencies of life. As cynics contended, the partisan split in control of the Congress and the White House allowed voters to receive the bounty of government from the Democratic Congresses they had elected while the Republicans they installed in the presidency would shield them from having to pay the cost. This contradiction was vividly underlined by the fourfold increase in the national debt during the Reagan-Bush era.

It was the emergence of this deficit as one of the principal concerns of national politics that helped bring about the end of that era of divided government, most directly through the notorious budget deal of 1990 and Bush's abrogation of his promise not to raise taxes. But other circumstances also undermined the shaky structure of divided government, notable among them the end of the Cold War. This simultaneously relieved the Democrats of a principal vulnerability, the suspicion they were soft on communism, while robbing Republicans of the advantage they gained from the perception that they were unalterably opposed to the Red scourge.

The importance of this deprivation did not escape George Bush, on whose presidential watch it took place. Realizing that claiming credit for his party for the victory over Communist aggression was not sufficient, he tried with near desperation to sustain some of the old Cold War aura for himself and his party by his 1991 confrontation with Saddam Hussein in the Gulf. But the threat from that quarter could not measure up to Bush's overheated rhetoric about Saddam or to the perceived apocalyptic danger from the Kremlin at the height of Soviet power.

Finally, and perhaps most important of all, Bush and the GOP ran out of luck so far as the economy was concerned with the onset of the 1991 recession. In politics as in the rest of life, timing counts for a great deal, a reality to which Bush could certainly bear witness. In 1982, Bush was Reagan's vice president when that year's recession staggered the economy, and Republicans suffered a thrashing in the November midterm elections. Few politicians in either party doubt that had Reagan been forced to seek a second term in that election, with unemployment above 10 percent he—and Bush, too—would have had their tenures ended. As it turned out, though, by the time Reagan did run for a second term in 1984, the 1982 recession was naught but a bleak memory. The economy had regained its health, a condition that lasted until midway through Bush's term, when the slump finished off his presidency and that particular era of divided government.

Then came the elections of 1992 and 1994, each of which in its own way offered hope first to the Democrats, then to the Republicans, that they might use those votes and the power they were granted to construct enduring electoral majorities. Neither of the political parties, drained of strength and vitality by defects of the political structure, was up to such a challenge. The politics of rejection prevailed, in which success led to defeat; yet only defeat offered the possibility of salvation. Although the Democrats could not maintain their advantage when the 1992 election gave them full responsibility for the federal government, their congressional defeat in the 1994 election, rather than paving the way for the grand victory Republicans sought, sowed the seeds for Clinton's reelection in 1996.

The election of 1996 left the political world turned upside down, with the previous institutional order of battle in Washington reversed. As a result of this exchange of power bases—a situation at least expected to last out the century—the two parties have been obliged to modify their behavior, ushering in a new political order, marked by ideological cross-dressing.

Democratic president Clinton provided the most striking example of this conduct during his reelection campaign. He stormed the high ground on values previously staked out by Republican presidents Bush and Reagan with such purportedly pro-family proposals as the V-chip, school uniforms, and curfews for youngsters. Clinton combined such symbolic appeals with a dose of substance, touting his plans for balancing the budget and battling crime, both concerns that Republicans previously regarded as their exclusive domain.

Republicans then denounced Clinton as both a plagiarist and a hypocrite. Speaker Gingrich provoked a heartfelt roar of approval at a GOP fund-raiser when he derided Clinton as "the first Republican ever to be nominated by the Democratic party for president."

But it was not just what Clinton said that irked, it was also the way he said it. Mixing Southern-fried charm with wonkish erudition, he displayed communications gifts that rivaled those of Ronald Reagan, allowing him to exploit fully the president's potential for personally dominating political debate. And he did so more skillfully than any Democratic chief executive since John Kennedy, evoking grudging admiration even from the staunchest of conservative Republicans. "Clinton really does a very fine job of explaining issues in a way that brings you around, makes you think and understand and feel that he understands your concerns," Angela "Bay" Buchanan, chairman of her brother Pat's presidential candidacy, told me during the heat of the 1996 campaign.

Overshadowed by Clinton's ability to benefit from the lessons taught by his Republican predecessors, but of equal significance, was the tendency of Republican legislators to join with Democrats and set aside conservative principles for reasons of political self-interest. As the 1996 campaign entered its home stretch, enough Republicans went along with the opposition party to make possible the enactment of the minimum-wage boost and health-care reform proposals, thus cloaking traditional liberal objectives in the mantle of bipartisanship. Similarly, the compromise on welfare reform came at the expense not only of ideological purity but of Bob Dole's candidacy.

"We made up our minds we weren't interested in making a statement," Trent Lott, Dole's replacement as GOP Senate leader, told party leaders after the election. "We wanted results." Looking ahead, Lott vowed: "We want to be sure that this will be a Congress that produces results, not for us, but for the American people. And the American people will reward us if we do."

Nonetheless, it did not take long after the election to demonstrate to Republicans and Democrats alike that such simple maxims would not suffice to guide them over the shoals ahead. The new challenges of assuming different roles that both parties faced were made harder by old problems—internal dissension and the absence of a central purpose.

Because their president occupied the White House, it was the shortcomings of the Democrats that seemed most conspicuous. "No political party is of any use to the people nor is any politician if he does not stand for definite principles," John F. Kennedy declared as he campaigned for the presidency in 1960. "And the principles I stand for in this century are the same principles which Woodrow Wilson stood for in 1912, which Franklin Roosevelt stood for in 1932, and which President Truman campaigned on in 1948." But as the last Democratic president of the century was inaugurated on January 20, 1997, the leaders of the party could no longer define their principles as the principles for which their past icons had fought, and it was far harder to tell what their party stood for than it had been when JFK was urging Americans on to a New Frontier.

During the 1996 campaign, most Democratic leaders tried not to confront this ambiguity out of fear of marring the intraparty harmony deemed essential to victory in the fall. But even before the pomp and pageantry of Clinton's inauguration had faded, fissures in the facade of unity emerged, threatening a postelection outbreak of hostilities. Clinton himself sought to steer clear of the battle by repeating his mantra of centrism. "We have clearly created a new center, not the lukewarm midpoint between overheated liberalism and chilly conservatism, but instead a place where throughout our history, people of goodwill have tried to forge new approaches to new challenges," he told cheering members of the Democratic Leadership Council.

However, not all Democrats were as impressed by the obsession with centrism. "If what we mean by the center is having the majority of people vote for you, then we are all based in the center," declared Paul Wellstone. He had won reelection to his Minnesota Senate seat by violating most of the DLC's moderate catechism. He spoke before a forum of grassroots activists sponsored by the Progressive Caucus, a group of fifty-two liberal House members, as the Democratic minority on Capitol Hill sought to maneuver for position in the 105th Congress. "We won our race in Minnesota by making clear we were against cuts in Medicare and we were for universal health-care coverage, environmental protection, and living-wage jobs, and we were for environmental protection. And the good news is, that's what the center of the country is focused on."

The fault lines in the party reflect sharp disagreement over the meaning of the 1996 election. On one side of the argument is the Democratic Leadership Council, which, right after the election, hired Mark Penn, whom Dick Morris had brought into the Clinton camp as the president's chief pollster, to conduct a national survey analyzing Clinton's victory. Not surprisingly, Penn concluded that Clinton had won reelection primarily by attracting a relatively upscale constituency drawn to his fiscal and social moderation, and that finding dovetailed neatly with the DLC's plans for the party's future, though it involved some tortured reasoning to get there.

Clinton had won the election, Penn claimed, "by adopting strong, defensible centrist positions on the federal budget, welfare crime, and immigration." Penn dismissed the fact that even according to his own polling, most of the voters for whom these issues held the greatest importance voted Republican. What counted, Penn claimed, was that by stressing his so-called centrist views on these Republican issues, Clinton won enough support from certain critical voting blocks—women, suburbanites, Catholics, independents, the middle class, and married people—to win the election. But this is specious reasoning. Clinton gained support across the electoral board in 1996 mostly because, as the incumbent, he was credited with helping the economy improve and also because of the inept campaign run by his challenger. Penn had no data to back up his assertion that the key voting blocks, mostly upscale, had been swayed by centrist arguments.

"Voters sent a clear message last November," Penn declared. "They want the president and the Republican Congress to forge centrist solutions to our most vital problems." He added, as if to rub it in concerning the House Democrats, still nursing their disappointment about their continued minority status: "If congressional Democrats had followed Clinton's lead on most of these issues, the party would have retaken the House." This reasoning was analogous to the strategic blueprint that had led to the downfall of Clinton's health-insurance reform proposal: trying to placate your adversaries instead of mobilizing your supporters.

Liberals struck back with their own poll, taken by Clinton's pre-1994 pollster, Stan Greenberg, and backed by a liberal advocacy group that called itself the Campaign for America's Future. They pointed out that most of the 6 percent increase in Clinton's share of the popular vote, which moved up from 43 percent in 1992 to 49 percent in 1996, came as a result of increased support from non-college-educated voters, with incomes below that of the upscale voters whom the DLC and Penn cited as boosting the president's standing. The main reason for the improvement among these groups, they claimed, was not such New Democrat concerns as the balanced budget and welfare reform but issues emblematic of the traditional Democratic reliance on activist government, specifically, Clinton's defense of Medicare and Medicaid and his advocacy of aid to education and environmental protection, a cluster of issues reduced acrimoniously to M2E2.

So far as the House Democrats were concerned, Ruy Teixeira, a political analyst for the Economic Policy Institute, a liberal think tank, pointed out that they received the same 49 percent of the popular vote as Clinton had, which in their case, unlike his, was not good enough for victory, though they did gain ten seats. Moreover, in the closing days of the campaign, Republicans and their business allies poured most of their resources into closely contested House races, conceding the presidential competition where Dole never was able to get within striking distance of Clinton. The real problem for House Democrats, Teixeira argued, was their inability to restore the support they had received from key cohorts in 1992, when they retained their long-standing majority in the House; that support had fallen off badly in their 1994 debacle. The most important of these groups was made up of non-college-educated white men, a working-class rather than middle-class cohort, and included more than one-fourth of the voting electorate; these voters gave congressional Democrats 53 percent of their vote in 1992, but only 35 percent in 1994 and 43 percent in 1996. But following the centrist path blazed by New Democrat Clinton was not the road that would regain a majority of this group, liberals argued. After all, Clinton got only 38 percent of their vote in 1996, five points below the level of support for congressional Democrats.

With the party adrift in the mythical center, if liberals looked to Clinton's inaugural address for some sign of direction and hope, they were due for disappointment. "Today we can declare that government is not the problem, and that government is not the solution," President Clinton contended. "We the American people are the solution."

It was a quintessentially Clintonian effort to resolve what his erstwhile strategist Dick Morris called the "Hundred Years War" between the Democrats and Republicans over the role of government. The president's admirers hailed this well-calculated formulation as epitomizing the pragmatism that enabled him to become the first Democrat to win reelection to the presidency in more than fifty years, but his critics cited Clinton's words as just the sort of evasion that had allowed the Republicans to regain control of Congress for the first time in more than sixty years. All that was clear was that Clinton had done nothing to settle the conflict over his party's future, which took on increasing urgency as the Democrats shifted their attention from the contests of 1996 to the forthcoming battles of 1998 and 2000 and the task of governing during the quadrennial. "The 1996 election was just a stopping point. It was not a finish line," outgoing party chairman Don Fowler told Democratic National Committee members who assembled in Washington on the day after the inaugural to gird for the next lap in the second Clinton term. "This party is at a crossroads."

One fork, favored by the DLC and its ideological comrades, extends the self-described centrist course Clinton followed during his reelection campaign and concentrates on battling for the same electorate that has decided the elections of the 1990s, which adds up to only about one-half the voting-age population. The other path leads toward an expanded electorate, which would be reached by stressing issues that would appeal to low-income citizens who have been in the nonvoting half of the population and that also converge with the concerns of most of the party's current constituents.

The choice is crucial, because electorates define political parties. The second option involves the most obvious risk, because it would steer the party into relatively uncharted waters and conceivably jeopardize some of the party's present moderate support. But party liberals and their allies claim that sticking to Clinton's current course is also a gamble, because it makes the party hostage to forces it cannot control, namely, the vicissitudes of the economy and the strategy of the GOP opposition.

Predictably, members of the party hierarchy who gathered for the national committee meeting favored the status quo. "Clinton has set a tone of keeping the country together and giving everybody an opportunity to improve their lives," said Michael King, chairman of the state party in New Hampshire, where Democrats in 1996 not only carried the state for Clinton but elected their first governor in sixteen years, adding, "I think the Democratic party is doing fine." Gary LaPaille, Illinois chairman and head of the national association of state party chairs, views the low turnout rate in recent elections—in 1994 it reached a seventy-year nadir—not as a cause for alarm but as a reassuring signal. It needs to be understood that LaPaille, as a fixture of Chicago's Democratic politics, the nation's last effective urban machine, did not achieve and retain his prominent position without developing extraordinary dexterity in his actions and utterances. In 1992, when the Illinois primary was critical to Clinton's candidacy for the nomination, LaPaille caused great distress among supporters of the Arkansas governor when he was imprudent enough to express unease about the womanizing charges then clouding Clinton's campaign. Clinton's smashing victory in Illinois, which all but sewed up the nomination, was then a cause of embarrassment for LaPaille, and a lesser fellow might have had trouble recovering his balance. But LaPaille moved swiftly and decisively to make things right. When his first son was born, he saw to it that it got around that the baby's middle name was Clinton.

It should be no surprise that so resourceful a politician would have little trouble regarding with equanimity the fact that, once again, the United States had confirmed its title to the industrial nation with the world's lowest voter-turnout rate. "The vast majority of people like to come out and vote against something or someone," he explained to me. "If you can please them with what you are doing in your administration, be you a state representative or a president, then, for the most part, those people won't come out, but your supporters will."

The only surprising thing about LaPaille's lack of interest in raising voter turnout is that he would publicly acknowledge it. The vast majority of his fellow politicians, in both parties, are reluctant to support actions that would significantly boost turnout, because any such change would threaten their own positions.

As Frances Fox Piven and Richard A. Cloward wrote of the Democratic party's failure to mobilize potential supporters during the Reagan era: "A party constructed on a restricted electorate, and incumbent politicians elected by a restricted electorate, risked serious disturbances to leadership, to funding sources, and to existing constituencies, were they to turn seriously to mobilizing the have-nots." Moreover, the impact of this lack of interest in low-income groups is to reinforce itself. "Despite the potential stimulus of new grievances and uncertainties," Piven and Cloward pointed out, "turnout in 1984 remained at a historic low, and the issues of concern to poorer people scarcely emerged in national politics."

Even in the wake of the dismal 1996 turnout, not many Democrats are willing to commit to efforts that would boost voter participation on election day. One of the few officeholding agitators for raising the turnout, Representative Bernie Sanders from Vermont, is not even officially a Democrat. The Socialist Sanders votes with the Democratic caucus in the House and chairs the Progressive Caucus of the House, whose fifty-one other members include such senior members as House whip David Bonior of Michigan and such other prominent figures as Charles Rangel of New York, Barney Frank of Massachusetts, and George Brown and Henry Waxman of California.

"If, as a result of our efforts, we can over a ten-year period increase the voter turnout from 50 percent to 75 percent, the composition of Congress and the person who sits in the White House will be fundamentally different from what it is now," Sanders told me, continuing: "I understand who the president is and who the Speaker is, but I also understand if we can involve working people and low-income people in the political process, then we can have tax reform, a change in trade policy, creation of a national health-care system, and a change in national priorities."

But in the wake of the Clinton reelection, not many in the party are willing to bother. Al From, head of the triumphant Democratic Leadership Council, reflected the self-satisfaction and complacency rampant among party leaders when he said: "There is an ideological transformation taking place in this party. We changed from the party that supported big government programs for everything to the party that declared the era of big government is over. Now we stand for growth and opportunity."

That is also what the Republicans claim to stand for, point out the liberals on the other side of the Democratic debate. "Democrats don't stand for anything except being saner than Republicans," contends economic analyst

Ruy Teixeira. The party's message boils down to this: "Even if we can't solve your problems today, we won't make them worse."

In the midst of their own confusion, Democrats could take solace from the fact that the Republicans were at least as ill-prepared to play out their role in the new political order. The fundamental problem was that Republicans had devoted so much of their energy to denouncing government that they had little to offer the country in the way of constructive solutions to the problems that ordinary citizens faced.

"We have lots of ideas, we've turned the government around, but as a party, we're profoundly unready to be a governing party," Lamar Alexander declared early in 1997, as he was already preparing for another run at the presidency in the year 2000.

Such warnings have been heard before from party leaders. "If you are going to broaden the base of the Republican party, you've got to realize that millions of Americans look to government as a lifeline," Jack Kemp told me more than a decade ago, not long after Ronald Reagan's massive reelection victory. "It's true 'that government is best which governs least.' But it's equally true 'that government is best that does the most for people,' and you need a balance between what government does for people and what people should be able to do for themselves."

That sort of argument got Kemp exactly nowhere when he sought the presidential nomination in 1988—and his inability to convert others in his party to such views was a major reason that he did not run for the presidency in 1996. As Dole's running mate, Kemp kept such heretical beliefs to himself, if he still held them, but the negative reaction to the 104th Congress forced some Republicans to face the underlying dichotomy in American attitudes toward government.

Although middle-class voters may cheer the Republicans' antigovernment rhetoric, they have a stake in government, a point driven home to them—and to the GOP—by the 1995 battles over Medicare, Medicaid, education, and the environment. By the time the 1996 election results were in, some Republican leaders could see a clear lesson for the future. After studying exit polls that showed Clinton with a huge advantage over Dole with women voters— attributed in large part to unrelenting Republican attacks on the Department of Education—New Jersey governor Christine Todd Whitman (whose state, once considered a GOP stronghold, fell to Clinton by seventeen points) declared, "We can't be a national party if we're going to be a party of white males." It was not just leaders in the liberal Northeast who raised the alarm. "The Republican party must put a compassionate face on a conservative philosophy," Texas governor George W. Bush said. "The message to women . . . is we care about people. The message is: We care."

Nevertheless, as events soon demonstrated, that message conflicts with what remains the fundamental antigovernment creed and thrust of the

party. The first notable postelection collision of the new compassion with
the old resistance to government came over the 1996 welfare-reform law—
and compassion crumpled. Republican governors, who had given their all-
out support to the controversial welfare revisions that Congress enacted,
discovered soon after the election that the new law was easier to endorse
than to live with. Particularly onerous was the cutoff of food stamps and
cash assistance to legal immigrants. This caused several prominent Republican state chief executives, led by George Pataki of New York, to agitate for
changes that would restore some of these benefits. But that idea did not sit
well with Republican congressional leaders, who viewed welfare reform as
the crown jewel of their accomplishments and feared that any concession to
the governors might give President Clinton more ammunition to keep his
promise to take some of the sting out of the legislation. The upshot was
that when the governors came to Washington for the national governors'
conference three months after the election, the rebels backed off and, instead of the ringing manifesto for change they had talked of issuing, settled
for a watered-down plea for mercy from the Congress and the White
House.

Some other Republicans, led by Ohio representative John Kasich, the
chairman of the House Budget Committee, are trying to dispel the idea that
the GOP is primarily the party of business. They want to steal some of the
Democratic thunder by co-opting the issue of "corporate welfare." Republicans who complain about welfare cheats should show the same zeal in
cracking down on handouts to big companies, they say.

Temporarily obscured by the internal arguments over government and
economic policy, but potentially even more explosive and divisive, are deep
differences among Republicans over social or lifestyle issues. The party's
stress on so-called family values, particularly opposition to abortion, first
articulated by Reagan and then echoed by Bush and Dole, has helped gain
the loyalty of Catholics and Protestant fundamentalists, while at the same
time disturbing other Republicans, who find this stress rigid to the point of
bigotry. "Social conservatives seem to feel they will cheerfully give up the
Business and Professional Women, the League of Women Voters, and people of that sort to get a few Roman Catholic blue-collar wives whose children are beyond the age of accidental pregnancy," one prominent Eastern
Republican leader complained to me.

This sort of internal factiousness is a relatively new phenomenon for the
GOP. For most of its modern history, it has relied on a relatively homogenous base of business and professional people, mainly WASPs. "You always
used to be able to figure that 75 percent of Republicans were WASPs, and
75 percent of WASPs were Republicans," the veteran consultant Eddie
Mahe recalled. In general terms, these Republicans stressed fiscal prudence,
while accepting the idea that government had a necessary but limited role

to play in guiding the economy and promoting social welfare. They also held moderate views on social issues.

Although they had spent most of the years since the advent of the New Deal in the minority, the Republicans had the benefit of internal harmony, which periodically allowed them to capture the presidency, capitalizing on voter dissatisfaction with the Democrats. Then came the long period of dis-affection with the Democrats, culminating with the failure of Jimmy Carter's presidency, creating an opportunity for the GOP. Ronald Reagan, with his formidable personal appeal, was able to capitalize on this, winning over masses of discontented Democrats and giving Republicans greater hope than ever before of emerging as the majority party. Since Reagan's day, the traditional Republican base has been supplemented by a variety of other groups, notably Southern whites and Catholics, both of which hold conservative views on social issues. The new heterogeneous complexity of the party creates potential areas of conflict at every hand between the Southern whites and the more libertarian Northerners over cultural issues such as abortion, school prayer, and gay rights, clashes that could be even more serious than substantive quarrels. What's more, these cultural clashes, freighted with emotion and symbolism, are much harder to settle than ar-guments over economic policy and the like. John Petrocik, a UCLA politi-cal scientist and sometime consultant to Republican campaigns, has said, "You can always resolve a substantive policy dispute by cutting the damn thing in half. But the cultural differences have to do with primordial com-mitments that people have made and that capture a large part of their self-identification."

For all the cultural diversity thrust upon the party since the 1980s, the Republicans remain almost entirely homogenous when it comes to race. Their monochromatic makeup has been, and continues to be, a cause of much hand-wringing to party leaders, for two reasons. The lack of black participation and black leadership is an embarrassment, which hurts the party among middle-class white suburban voters uncomfortable with the suggestion of racism. White feelings aside, if Republicans could consistently win a significant minority of blacks votes, as some of their gubernatorial candidates have been able to do in Northeastern states, they could make it very difficult for Democrats, now so dependent on a huge majority of black supporters, to elect anybody.

"We are not going to truly have a chance to be the majority party as long as we are willing to write off large segments of the electorate at the outset," Lee Atwater told me in 1989, when, as Republican National chairman, he was commissioned by George Bush to launch a major effort to win black votes, in a project boldly titled Operation Outreach. Heartened by the fact that, in 1988, Bush had pulled 12 percent of the black vote, compared with only 9 percent for Reagan in 1984, Atwater dreamed of garnering 20 percent of the black vote—a figure that, other things being equal, would assure their presidential candidates of victory.

But Republicans had huge obstacles to overcome. For years, ever since they nominated Barry Goldwater in 1964, the GOP had exploited the racial fears of whites to win their votes. It was Atwater himself who had seized upon the issue of Michael Dukakis's weekend furlough of Willie Horton in Bush's 1988 campaign, incurring the intense and abiding resentment of blacks. Just as important, Republicans stood in firm opposition to the activism of the federal government, which most blacks had good reason to believe had changed their lives for the better. It has been clear all along that Republicans had no intention of giving up the opportunity to play the race card when it served their political advantage, nor did they intend to abandon their opposition to government activism. Indeed, they have never tried to do anything different at all to win black votes, except occasionally to campaign more in black communities and try harder to recruit black candidates.

"We're going to talk about the same issues we've been running on, which are growth, opportunity, and looking to the future," Atwater told me, setting the tone for Operation Outreach that Republicans have followed ever since. The chances of success of this solipsistic strategy relied on the ability of Atwater and his successors to capture the loyalty of upwardly mobile black voters.

Their dream African-American voter is embodied in Odysseus M. Lanier, a Houston management consultant whom I encountered at an Outreach rally in Houston. "I used to have a Republican lifestyle and vote Democratic," said Lanier, who, together with his accountant wife, earns more than $100,000 a year and keeps a Mercedes and a Mitsubishi in his townhouse garage in suburban Houston. "Now I vote like I live."

But the Republican problem was and is that there are not enough upper-income blacks in general, and black businessmen in particular, to give the GOP much of a boost. Only about 10 percent of black families earn more than $50,000 a year, out of little more than 20 percent who take in more than $35,000 a year, and a large portion of the middle-class black sector is composed of people whose success depends on government involvement, either because they are government workers or are employed by private groups funded by government.

The folly of the Republican strategy was demonstrated by the 1996 election results. Eight years after Lee Atwater launched Operation Outreach and despite continued similar efforts by the GOP, Bob Dole received 12 percent of the black vote—exactly what George Bush got in 1988.

Nevertheless, instead of trying to appeal to blacks with substantive policy proposals that offer the hope of economic improvement, Republicans continue to woo them with gimmicks and imagery. In the process, they sometimes succeed only in embarrassing themselves, as when party leaders selected their only black congressman, J. C. Watts of Oklahoma, to deliver the official GOP response to President Clinton's 1997 State of the Union speech. Watts got in trouble before he ever opened his mouth. On the morning of his speech, the *Washington Post* quoted him as labeling Jesse Jackson and Washington mayor Marion Barry "race-hustling poverty pimps" who made their way in the world chiefly by keeping blacks dependent on government.

Watts claimed that he was misquoted. Meanwhile, though, Speaker Gingrich, who had previously invited Jackson to sit in his box in the Capitol to watch the State of the Union address, felt obliged to apologize to Jackson for Watts's reported remarks. But that attempt at pacification stirred up even more trouble. Former education secretary William J. Bennett, a leading voice in conservative Republican circles, accused Gingrich, still reeling from the $300,000 fine and official reprimand he had suffered for ethical misconduct, of trying to appease the Democratic party's left wing to rehabilitate himself. "If you want to add up statements that need to be apologized for, there are a lot more in Jesse Jackson's record than in J.C.'s," Bennett said. He added: "Few people have done more to further racial polarization than Jesse Jackson."

As for Watts's speech, it offered little besides the standard putdown of government. "Government can't ease all pain," the former University of Oklahoma football star claimed. "In fact, government sometimes rubs the wound raw and makes the healing harder." As for the nation's racial problems, Watts said: "The Republicans know we must, individually, all of us, accept our share of responsibility," adding even more enigmatically, "We must decide, as we stand on the edge of a new age, if we will be a captive of the past." That left blacks just as puzzled about what Republicans might do to help them as they have been for the past generation.

With neither party able to fill a leadership role, it was no wonder that the idea of bipartisan consensus gained increasing attention, with President Clinton as its chief promoter. Nearly every chance he got, Clinton boosted the notion of the two parties working together in harmony. "The American people returned to office a president of one party and a Congress of another," Clinton declared in his inaugural address. "Surely, they did not do this to advance the politics of petty bickering and extreme partisanship they plainly deplore. No, they call all of us instead to be repairers of the breach." Two weeks later, in his State of the Union message, the president made the same point. "The people of this nation elected us all. They want us to be partners, not partisans. They put us all here in the same boat, they gave us all oars, they told us to row."

The consensus approach to politics and governing is not new. Its most devoted advocate among modern times was Lyndon Johnson, who, by relying on the strategy of consensus, achieved initial success for himself and, ultimately, disaster for the nation he led.

On its surface, the idea of bipartisan consensus seems as unobjectionable as motherhood. What could be wrong with politicians working together for the common good? But experience has shown that the advantages consensus offers are mainly to the political leaders who preach it. It gives them relief from controversy and criticism, freedom to go their own way. For the electorate, however, consensus is a threat—because it tends to smother disagreement and ignore differences. In this regard, the experience of the foremost practitioner of consensus, Lyndon Johnson, is instructive. Johnson grasped the art of consensus in his native Texas, which, when Johnson was coming of age, was, like most of the rest of the South, a one-party state. Johnson learned early in his career to minimize and overlook genuine political disagreements in the interests of keeping all sides within the Democratic party and keeping the Democratic party dominant. As the Senate leader of his party, Johnson continued to practice consensus, albeit in a different setting. First, he formed an alliance with conservative senators, many of them Republican, to assure backing for his favored initiatives. Then, when the 1952 election swept the Republicans into the presidency for the first time in twenty years, creating a divided government, Johnson worked hand-in-glove with Dwight Eisenhower, the GOP's chief executive, crafting compromises and shouldering aside disagreement within his own party.

"The more the two parties could agree, the smaller the area of conflict shown to the American public, and the less I worried about the public's tendency to go off on a jag, paralyzing itself in the endless debate or stampeding us in panic," he later said of his Senate experience. It would not be too long after LBJ left the Senate that the destructive potential of this arrogant view would become painfully obvious to the country and the world.

In the White House, Johnson stood at the head of a united government, with Democrats in control of both the presidency and the Congress, but he continued to preach and practice the strategy of consensus. Its chief objective was the escalation of the war in Vietnam. By demanding national unity in response to those who challenged his policy in Indochina, Johnson shielded himself from criticism until he had led America so far into that quagmire that he destroyed his presidency and caused his fellow citizens untold anguish.

President Clinton's attempt at bipartisan consensus is also doomed. It is based on a false premise: that the voters in the 1996 election wanted a divided government dedicated to compromise. "This is how history makes decisions—with debate, then with consensus, claims Dick Morris, the Clinton campaign strategist whose thinking continued to pervade the White House outlook even after he himself had been banished. "Voters didn't think either party had a majority on virtue. They felt that Democrats, if they had control of both branches, would abandon their commitment to the balanced budget and water down welfare reform. And the Republicans would emasculate medical care and cut down on the environment."

However, this is a myth that contradicts the exit-poll results. More than four out of five voters backed candidates of the same party for Congress and the president. In the case of Clinton, 84 percent of those who voted for him also voted for a Democrat for Congress. No one, of course, can read the minds of these voters, but it is reasonable to infer from their choice that they had hopes that the Democratic party in the Congress and the White House would act to deal with the nation's problems. Instead, as the early days of Clinton's second term suggested, the strategy of consensus would be used to sidestep the nation's major problems, avoid accountability, and protect Clinton's own self-interest.

As he began his renewed tenure in the White House, fundamental problems demanded urgent attention. From every quarter, laments were heard for the American dream, which had lost its credibility because most families had to struggle to maintain their own living standards and found it hard to believe that their children's lives would be better than their own.

In addition, as the political columnist David Broder pointed out, "All of the major systems in this country—from the Pentagon to the neighborhood public schools, from the hospitals and nursing homes to the border patrols, from job training to affirmative action to the tax code—cry out for reexamination."

Yet the president's first major public utterances, like his speeches during his victorious reelection campaign, offered little hint of how he proposed to deal with these problems. In his State of the Union address, Clinton skimmed over the agonizingly difficult issue of entitlements with the mere suggestion that "we must agree to a bipartisan process to preserve Social Security and reform Medicare in the long run." As for his budget, it put off most of the pain required to achieve his promise of eliminating the deficit until after Clinton's own term in the White House had ended.

A darker side of bipartisanship was evident earlier, when, in the midst of the raging debate over Speaker Gingrich's ethical lapses on Capitol Hill, Clinton called for a cease-fire: "I want it to be over," Clinton told reporters, breaking his long silence on the case. "The American people have given us larger responsibilities. Way too much time and energy and effort is spent on all these things." It was not hard to fathom the motive behind the president's remarks. He and Gingrich shared an interest in seeing the voters lose interest in such controversies. Facing GOP-led investigations of his own financial and political dealings, Clinton's self-interest directed him to try to tone down the rhetoric of the Capitol's ethics wars, lest he suffer from a Republican backlash.

As the decade of the 1990s has demonstrated, the limitations of our political and governing system are a constant source of frustration; but consensus politics, as propounded by Bill Clinton, is not the answer. The basic fallacy underlying the strategy of consensus is the theory that Americans, as

Lyndon Johnson once put it and as Bill Clinton seems to believe, "share a fundamental unity of interest and belief."

The trouble is that on only a very few public issues do Americans have common interests and beliefs. Ours is a pluralistic society, and in the political system, diverse interests compete for the favors of government. The task of political leadership is to mobilize enough groups representing these interests to forge a majority coalition. The near-unanimity connoted by consensus is not necessary, nor is it even feasible. Those citizens who find themselves in the minority need only wait for the next election for the chance to assemble their own coalition to advance their interests.

The idea of consensus as propounded by Clinton short-circuits this competition. Such a notion might make the president's job easier in the short run, but in the long run, the rest of us lose. Like most of the other ill-conceived solutions to the distortions of our political system that have been attempted over the years, consensus stands a good chance of making matters not better, but worse.

A case in point is the balanced-budget agreement reached amid much fanfare in the summer of 1997, which promised an end to the deficit five years hence. It was presented to the country by the chief architects of the new bipartisan consensus—President Clinton for the Democrats, and for the Republicans, Speaker Gingrich and Senate Leader Lott—as a major triumph.

Reviving memories of Ronald Reagan's "morning in America" theme, Clinton claimed that by pulling together to achieve a bargain, replete with tax cuts, both parties had ensured "that the sun is shining in America again." Gingrich sang much the same tune, praising Clinton and the Democrats and promising to work in harness to make "bipartisan progress" not only at home but also "across the planet." Other Republicans were equally exuberant. Lott hailed the agreement as nothing less than "the beginning of a new era of freedom," while House Budget chairman Kasich called it "a dream come true."

It was not hard to understand why the Republicans cheered. Clinton, as a handful of Democratic critics pointed out, had given away the store. In fact, this outcome was more or less preordained by the budget agreement of 1995, when Clinton accepted the fundamental Republican objective of achieving budget balance by a certain date, even though no economic or political imperative demanded a balanced budget. Indeed, throughout the postwar years, both parties ordinarily accepted moderate deficits as an economic fact of life.

To make matters worse for traditional Democrats, Clinton also bought into the Republican notion of a $500 child tax credit, one of the key provisions of the GOP's Contract with America. With budget balance and tax cuts the defining principle of the budget debate, an all-but-total Republican victory was inevitable. Along with cuts in the inheritance tax, and the child tax credit for families with incomes up to $110,000, the Republicans got the huge capital gains cut they had long sought and surrendered on only one point—the idea of indexing capital gains for inflation.

And even with this minor concession, the tax cuts were dramatically regressive. Only one-fourth of all the reductions benefited those making less than $100,000 a year, whereas over one-third of all the tax breaks went to the top 1 percent. Put another way, the deal would give a typical family in the mid-20 percent of income distribution a tax break of about $150 a year, whereas a family in the upper 1-percent income bracket would get an annual reduction more than ten times that amount, or about $16,000.

The net result then served only to sharpen the inequities of the already uneven economic boom. Despite this, so devitalized was the Democratic left that only a few voices were raised in protest, among them that of the party's leader in the House, Richard Gephardt, who complained that the pact "sacrifices tomorrow's hopes for today's headlines."

On the Republican side, dissenters were just as scarce. They included Texas senator Phil Gramm, who objected because Clinton had persuaded the Republicans to agree to soften some of the most stringent provisions of the new welfare-reform law. But most Republicans had the good sense to know when they were well off. "Tax reform," a term that conservatives equated with tax cuts, "is best achieved through bite-sized bits, easily digestible to voters and easily understood by popular opinion," said Representative Tom DeLay of Texas, the majority whip. "This is the first bite of a seven-course tax-cut meal."

Even as they licked their chops, most Republicans were shrewd enough to realize that the little ground they had given up to Clinton, such as easing of welfare reform and scrapping their plan to raise Medicare premiums, would serve them well by shielding them against the accusations of hardheartedness that had undercut their conservative revolution in 1995.

Ideology aside, despite the self-congratulatory tone of Clinton and the Republican leaders, the deal stacked up as a hollow accomplishment. Rather than speeding up the achievement of a balanced budget, that dubious but much-sought-after Holy Grail of national politics, the consensus pact actually postponed the reaching of that goal for several years. What was far more important in making deficit reduction possible than the complicated and questionable schemes advanced by both parties was the simple fact of rapid economic growth.

This had gone on apace since the end of the Bush recession in 1991, producing tens of billions in unanticipated federal revenue. And the continued boom would mean erasure of the deficit before the year 2000, well in advance of the 2002 deadline set by the budget pact, which the president had dubbed "historic." And as it turned out, six months after that agreement was reached in the summer of 1997, President Clinton proposed in February 1998 a plan to bring the budget into balance by fiscal 1999. The real challenge facing the Congress and the president was not whether they could get revenues to match outlays by a certain date but what would happen in the years to come when aging baby boomers reach retirement age, thus taking more in benefits out of the system than they would contribute in taxes.

This issue was not addressed in the budget deal because the president and the congressional leaders found it politically unpalatable. In point of fact, the tax cuts that shaped the budget agreement were bound to make the long-range fiscal problems harder to solve. As the *Washington Post* concluded in a critical assessment of the agreement: "So much for discipline."

The off-year national elections of 1997 provided another demonstration of the enfeeblement of both parties, and their distance from the realities shaping the lives of the citizenry. Republicans hailed the results as a triumph, and they certainly had more to cheer about than the Democrats. GOP candidates swept the three major contests of the day—retaining the governorships of New Jersey and Virginia and the mayoralty of New York.

But mixed with the good news for Republicans were some sobering lessons. In New Jersey, the incumbent GOP governor Whitman's hair's breadth victory over a little-known Democratic challenger demonstrated that tax cuts, which Republicans have made the cornerstone of their party's philosophy, do not build lasting gratitude. Whitman had cut taxes with a vengeance when she took over as governor, and her supporters had been counting on that, along with favorable economic winds, to carry her to a reelection victory big enough to boost her potential for the GOP's national ticket in 2000. But the tax cut was just a one-shot measure—and Whitman did not follow up by bringing fundamental economic benefits to the state.

Her failure to get a plan to reduce the state's astronomical automobile insurance rates through the GOP-controlled legislature made her vulnerable to attacks from Democrat challenger James McGreevey, who seized upon this issue as a way to focus populist themes reminiscent of traditional Democratic appeals. "His agenda is focused on pocketbook issues and urban revitalization," Steve DeMicco, McGreevey's campaign manager explained. "And we get our strongest support from cities and organized labor."

Meanwhile, whatever benefits Whitman gained from her tax cut were offset by the escalation of local property taxes, caused by the state government's cutback in school aid. "People are watching property taxes go up and some think it's all just a political shell game," said Cliff Zukin, a Rutgers University professor of public policy. And McGreevey went all-out to reinforce that suspicion with campaign commercials that declare: "As governor, Christie Whitman cut the state share to education. Now New Jersey has the highest property taxes in the nation."

Also disquieting news for Republicans from the New Jersey results was the troublesome divisiveness within party ranks over abortion. Considered a national role model for moderate Republicans because of her strong support for abortion rights, Whitman came under attack from party conservatives on that very issue. They backed an independent candidate who competed successfully for votes from pro-life Republicans and made no secret that their goal was to dim Whitman's luster, even at the risk of a Democratic victory in the state.

At first glance, Republican hopes for a revival in the nation's cities, where the party has struggled to find a footing since the New Deal, seemed to get a lift from New York mayor Rudolph Giuliani's big reelection victory coming on top of the previous spring's landslide reelection of Los Angeles mayor Richard Riordan, a Republican, in the second-largest city in the United States.

It seemed far-fetched, though, to assume that Giuliani's notable success could be translated into a victory formula for Republicans in other urban areas. Giuliani benefited from a dramatic reduction in crime during his first term, but the truth was that the crime rate had also been declining in most of the nation's other cities, where Democrats are generally in control. Even more important, Giuliani is persona non grata in his own party, where he is widely accused of incipient liberalism, a charge given added credence by his decision to endorse Mario Cuomo against Republican George Pataki in 1994. The Republican hierarchy reacted to that by abandoning the idea of holding their 1996 national convention in New York.

For Democrats, the day's defeats were made harder to take by the failure of the centrist political themes favored by Clinton to catch on even in conservative Virginia. Mimicking Clinton's New Democrat approach, Don Beyer, the party's gubernatorial candidate in the Old Dominion, styled himself "a business Democrat." "I worry about financial statements every day of my life," Beyer told me during the campaign. "I worry about job creation. I worry about profit. And it gives me a different perspective on education and the workforce and everything else."

But Beyer, who started out as better known than his Republican opponent, James Gilmore, could never reconcile that perspective with the demands of traditional Democratic constituencies, and he fell flat on his face. Gilmore's difficulties in following the Clinton approach became clear early in the game, when he proposed eliminating Virginia's personal property tax on autos and trucks, a much-resented levy that costs car owners up to $900 a year. Beyer at first denounced the idea as irresponsible, then, in a typical Clintonian move, countered with his own limited and more complicated version.

But not only did Beyer's proposal fail to win over voters, it also made him vulnerable to criticism from Doug Wilder, the state's former Democratic governor, the first black to hold that office in history. Wilder complained, "I have heard from any number of Democrats who are asking: 'What does Beyer's campaign stand for?'" Wilder then refused to endorse

Beyer. His snub dampened the turnout of black voters, who, in Virginia, as elsewhere, comprise the most reliable Democratic constituency, thus ending whatever hopes Beyer had of victory.

For both parties, the disturbing news was that a seemingly strong economy is not the guarantee of reelection that many incumbents thought it to be. Campaign polls and the election results made clear that voters are still haunted by memories of the job-threatening downsizing that stemmed from the recession earlier in the 1990s. "People say they are in good economic shape, but underneath there is an undercurrent of fear," said Janice Ballou, director of the Eagleton Institute poll in New Jersey. "People feel like, 'I'm fine today, but what's going to happen tomorrow; one more increase in my taxes and auto insurance, and I'm down the tubes.'"

The defects in the consensus approach to governing and in Clinton's New Democratic themes, illustrated by the off-year elections, were underlined that same autumn on Capitol Hill in Washington by the defeat of Clinton's bid for fast-track trade authority. It was the worst setback the president had suffered since the failure of his health-reform plan. This rebuff was no easier to take, since Clinton knew that most of the opposition was centered in his own party, particularly in the House of Representatives, where Democratic leader Richard Gephardt led the fight against fast-track trade authority and only about forty of the more than 200 Democratic members backed Clinton. In a sense, consensus backfired. Clinton did have the backing of a majority of Republicans, but finding common ground with the opposition cost him the allegiance of his own party.

In the debate in Congress and around the country, the president and his allies contended that fast-track authority, which would all but eliminate Congress's ability to amend trade agreements, would stimulate commerce with other countries, thus creating more jobs and profits for American workers and businesses. Underlying the drive for fast track was faith in the beneficence of the globalized economy, which was one of the cornerstones of the Clinton economic policies devised by Treasury Secretary Rubin and supported by Wall Street and corporate America.

Fueling the opposition to fast track was the growing conviction among labor and liberal leaders that so-called free-trade policies were in fact sapping the energy of the American economy and contributing to the growing inequities in income distribution. They felt that the potential dangers from trade agreements with less-developed countries outweighed the benefits and cited the impact of NAFTA as evidence of the damage that would be done to the environment and to safety standards for workers.

Unable to persuade his opponents, Clinton instead used tactics that inflamed them and thus hurt his own cause. By claiming that he would win on the issue if the vote was held in secret, he implied that his opponents were inspired by fear of retaliation from special interests. And his assertion that a vote for the bill was "a no-brainer," made it seem as if the opposition was totally without merit.

In sum, Clinton's defeat on trade demonstrated that his efforts to push his party to the center, in order to achieve consensus with the Republicans, had sharpened the rifts within his own party between probusiness New Democrats like himself and traditional Democrats, whose views were more weighted toward labor unions and consumers.

The fast-track outcome represented a political watershed of sorts, comparable to the GOP setback in the 1995 budget fight, which had paved the way for Clinton's reelection. "It brought down the curtain on the kind of bipartisan governance that has dominated this period," said Stanley Greenberg, Clinton's former pollster, who had lost favor at the White House. "And it says that for the president to succeed, he is going to have to advance a more Democratic agenda on trade and other issues."

Indeed, it was not only Clinton's bid for new trade-negotiating power that was in ruins. His proposal for education testing was on hold; his choice to fill the top civil rights post in the Justice Department was in limbo; Congress wouldn't even let him conduct the census the way he wanted to, by giving more weight to minorities; and the campaign finance proposal he had supported was dead, killed by dueling filibusters between Republicans resisting limits on soft money and Democrats opposed to limits on labor's political muscle. Nor had Republicans done much better with their own initiatives. Their much-ballyhooed school-vouchers plan died in the House while a bill banning affirmative action had been shunted onto the back burner. "The logjam was a sign not only of stalemate between the parties but of decomposition and disarray within them," reported Ronald Brownstein and Janet Hook in the *Los Angeles Times*. "New Democrats and old ones, moderate Republicans and conservatives, are all engaged in hand-to-hand combat." And largely because of defections from its own ranks, neither party could put together the kind of coalition that would allow it to implement any kind of clear agenda.

Spurred by that reality and heartened by their victory on fast track, Clinton's liberal opposition now planned the offensive. When Clinton withdrew his fast-track proposal without a vote because he knew he would lose the contest, many realized that his action had not only ended his experiment in consensus but had signaled the onset of the twilight of his presidency and opened the door on the struggle for the White House in the year 2000.

Armed with the veto and backed by substantial Democratic minorities on Capitol Hill, Clinton could still stand in the way of Republicans. But confronted with his lame-duck status, as a result of the constitution's two-term limit on presidential service, and with a rebellion within his own party, as a consequence of his own strategic choice of so-called triangulation and consensus, his chances for meaningful substantive accomplishment were fading fast.

Accordingly, liberals now began to make their case in the struggle to define the political future for the Democratic party and the country. Their first argument was based on the shrinkage of the federal budget deficit resulting from the surging economy.

This was not a time for retrenchment or tax cuts with relatively small effect on most people, liberals contended. Instead, they insisted it was a scenario that could allow the government to spend more for education, health care, and other programs without walking the political plank by seeking a tax increase. "Rather than people getting $100 back in their pockets from a tax cut, I think they'd feel better if the surplus was used to help guarantee their health care," said Andy Stern, president of the Service Employees Union, the fastest-growing and most politically aggressive union in the AFL-CIO.

By no means were liberals counting on creating a new political Jerusalem, along the lines of Lyndon B. Johnson's vision of a Great Society. Their more modest but nonetheless significant objective was to reverse the antigovernment trend that took root in the Reagan presidency and has continued to flower under Clinton's New Democrat regime. A key factor on their side, they believed, was that despite the current economic sunshine, polls and the election results showed that voters remain troubled by recollections of the dark days of the 1991 recession and uneasy about long-range job security.

Just as they were gearing up to take on new challenges, though, liberals suffered a shattering blow with the disclosure of an illegal money-laundering scheme, involving union officials and Democratic party operatives who had helped fund the 1996 election of Ron Carey, leader of so-called reform forces in the Teamsters Union. Under Carey, the Teamsters had become a potent force in the new aggressive political stance of the AFL-CIO, headed by Carey ally John Sweeney, and had played a major role in the victorious battle against fast track. But then Carey aides confessed to federal investigators that they had funneled hundreds of thousands of dollars from the Teamsters' treasury to liberal good-government groups, money that was then diverted to finance Carey's 1996 campaign for the union leadership. The rationalization for this scheme was that Carey was running against James Hoffa, who was striving to assume the mantle once worn by his father, a figure viewed as the personification of labor corruption by most of the country, though still much admired by the Teamsters' rank and file. The immediate impact of the scandal was the ouster of Carey from his Teamster post and the likely triumph of Hoffa. But of broader consequence, the revelation that the forces presumed to be battling for social and economic justice on the left had been so willing to put ends before means struck at the moral justification for liberalism. And the embezzlement plot carried out in the name of reform also provided renewed evidence that the distortions of the political system inevitably entrap those who seek to reform it.

Shaken by this setback to labor, liberals turned to the Democratic leader of the House, Richard Gephardt, whom they hoped would become their paladin in the next presidential campaign. It was a role to which Gephardt had laid claim by waging a series of legislative skirmishes against the White House during Clinton's first term and then by his opposition to the budget agreement and fast track in 1997.

Now, flush with the victory over Clinton on trade, Gephardt, taking advantage of a speech invitation from Harvard's John F. Kennedy School of Government, moved to exploit his opportunity. In the harshest language ever used by a Democrat against the Clinton administration, Gephardt denounced the New Democrats' leadership of the Democratic party for lacking "core values" and retreating from "the principles that give us purpose and direction in a time of rapid change." Stressing the expanding gap between rich and poor, Gephardt issued what amounted to an indictment of the economic policies that Clinton viewed as his own strongest claim on a favorable verdict from history—not to mention the electorate. "The current recovery has not narrowed but instead widened the gap between the wealthy and the working middle class," Gephardt said. "There are more jobs, but average income languishes. There is less health coverage, with lower benefits."

Although Gephardt did not mention either Clinton or Gore by name, no one doubted he had them in mind when he assailed "New Democrats who set their compass only off the direction of others" and "who talk about the political center but fail to understand that if it is only defined by others, it lacks core values." And in the unkindest cut of all, a scarcely veiled reference to the abuses of the campaign fund-raising laws by the Clinton-Gore campaign, Gephardt declared: "We need a Democratic party that is a movement for change—and not a money machine."

This impassioned rhetoric naturally made the hearts of liberals beat faster, unless they happened to remember Gephardt's well-earned reputation for exercising caution under pressure. And in this case, the fire was intense. The words were hardly out of Gephardt's mouth before White House hatchet man Rahm Emanuel warned that Gephardt's attack "can only harm our party and prospects" and then added a gibe that recalled Gephardt's change of position on such issues as abortion. "It sounds like politics over principle," said Emanuel, "especially given his flip-flops on multiple issues." Then to make sure that Gephardt knew they were serious, White House officials boycotted a long-scheduled meeting with congressional Democrats to devise a joint education agenda. "We paused to take a breath," explained Clinton's deputy chief of staff, John Podesta. "We were digesting the speech."

Gephardt got the point. It was not long before he was on the phone to Clinton, telling the president that he had called off a planned appearance on *Meet the Press*. And when Gephardt finally did appear on television, he sought to belittle the significance of his disagreement with the president. "I think the president has done a very good job," he said. "There are always debates within the party, debates within the White House, debates within the Congress about where the party should go."

In fact, of course, such debates are few and far between, at least so far as the public knows about them. And the reason for that is that established political leaders avoid calling attention to their differences, since public notice makes it harder for them to compromise. Gephardt's brief flare-up and abrupt retreat into silence is another demonstration of how the political system works to drain meaning out of the presidential nominating process. Gephardt's attack on Clinton captured attention because Gephardt was widely viewed as a potential contender for the Democratic presidential nomination in 2000.

However, for Gephardt to actually go ahead and run, as many of his supporters hope and expect he will do, would involve him in the sort of political risk he has been reluctant to take on in the past. The risk arises because many party leaders, certainly President Clinton among them, would like to see the competition for the nomination over before it starts. Most, again certainly including Clinton, have already made up their mind about who the candidate should be—and his name is Albert Gore.

The vice president would have an immense advantage in any contest with Gephardt, or any other candidate, because of the support of the party leadership and the president. And what motivates these supporters, more than Gore's merits as a candidate or his chances of winning the election, is the simple fact that Gore, as vice president and Clinton's junior partner, is better able to look after their individual political interests than is Gephardt or any of Gore's other potential rivals.

These are the realities of presidential politics, which govern the nominating process in both parties. They are the same rules that assured George Bush of the Republican nomination in 1988 when he was viewed as the successor to Ronald Reagan. And they also favored Bob Dole in 1996, because, as the unchallenged front-runner, he enjoyed the prestige and contacts that were almost as potent as if he had been part of an incumbent administration.

In a contest with Gore, Gephardt would operate under enormous handicaps. Not only would the vice president's candidacy be better financed and better supported by the party leadership, but many of those same leaders would regard a Gephardt challenge as divisive and damaging to their party's chances of regaining the White House. Apart from hurting Gephardt's chances of gaining the presidency, this disapproval would also damage Gephardt's chances of getting the job he wants in politics second only to the presidency itself, the speakership of the House.

After his first run for the presidency, in 1988, Gephardt has had two chances to run again—in 1992, when the path was open to the nomination, and in 1996, when Clinton was in office but badly hurt by the Republican victory in 1994. Each time there was risk involved, and each time Gephardt backed away. For him to run in 2000, he will need to muster more courage than he has displayed in the past.

But if challenging Gore would be risky for Gephardt, nominating the vice president would represent something of a gamble for Democrats. Until the campaign fund-raising scandal broke, Gore's great strength in presidential politics was his image as "Mr. Clean," a perception that gained strength through contrast with Clinton's own tawdry reputation. But the revelations of his role in the abuses of the fund-raising law have altered that perception in two ways. Not only has Gore's behavior raised concerns among the public about his integrity, a hitherto-unquestioned asset, but, more seriously, his response to the allegations against him has suggested that he was insensitive to those concerns.

Gore's conduct was forgivable, or so his supporters could argue. To err is human, they could say. But for Gore not to understand the error of his ways will be harder to excuse, and more potentially troublesome. The really serious damage done to Gore is not from the disclosures that he had stretched the campaign regulations by making phone calls from his White House office to raise funds and collected political money at a Buddhist temple. Rather his problems stem from his abortive attempt to explain his conduct at a televised press conference, where he repeated over and over again the hollow phrase that there was "no controlling legal authority" spelling out whether his phone calls were legal. That response left many to conclude that the vice president was looking for a legal loophole instead of an explanation that would satisfy the public. Nearly a year after that press conference, Attorney General Janet Reno ruled that no independent counsel will be named to investigate the legality of fund-raising calls he made from the White House.

"Now that there's been a full and independent review, we can put this issue of the phone calls behind us once and for all," Gore said. "I'm very pleased by it." While his conduct was under scrutiny Gore refused to comment on the charges, claiming that would be unseemly while the investigation went on. Yet even after Reno's inquiry had ended, he held his tongue.

"It's a different rationale now," Gore said. But he never explained what the new rationale was. All he had to say was that since the inquiry was over, "I think that we can put these phone calls in the past." In other words, Gore chose to stand pat on the "no controlling legal authority" formulation. And this left him sounding more like a suspect taking the Fifth Amendment than a candidate for the presidency, a point the Republicans will certainly not overlook if he should become the Democratic standard-bearer.

But if the Democratic contest for 2000 was put on hold because of Gore's legal embarrassments and Gephardt's caution, the Republicans have had no such hesitation. More than two years before the first votes would be cast for convention delegates, GOP presidential prospects were out in force in Iowa and New Hampshire, the two opening states in the delegate selection process, campaigning with unprecedented intensity.

In early fall, as Lamar Alexander stumped in Iowa with one eye on the battle for the GOP presidential nomination in the year 2000, some folks wondered if the former Tennessee governor had not gotten his calendar out of kilter.

"Isn't it early to be in Iowa?" Alexander was asked.

"No," he firmly replied. "In some ways, it's too late *not* to be in Iowa."

To the vast majority of Americans, many of whom could barely remember the last presidential campaign, let alone think seriously about the next, this attitude was bound to seem bizarre. But it is another distortion in the political system. In bygone days, when political bosses and their machines ruled the roost, questions about the choice of presidential nominees were resolved at a far more leisurely pace, often in the proverbial smoke-filled room. In 1968, Hubert Humphrey did not announce his candidacy until April of the election year and yet gained the Democratic nomination from a convention bitterly divided over the Vietnam War. That fractious campaign ushered in an era of reform, triggering the proliferation of party primaries.

This broke the rule of the bosses, who were losing power anyway. But following the pattern of political reform, the evil done under the boss-dominated system was replaced by the harm committed by a new breed of self-selected contenders. Rather than waiting for the blessing of party bosses, they set out to scramble for their own support, literally years before issues were ripe for discussion. In this harum-scarum process, where time is at a premium, candidates like Lamar Alexander, who had no other responsibility except to campaign, enjoyed an advantage over those who happened to hold office. A famous family name can help, too, as in the case of George W. Bush, the president's son, who, without lifting a finger on his own behalf, is the acknowledged early favorite for the nomination.

Of course, no candidacies will be formally announced until sometime after the 1998 elections. And of the dozen or so prospects roaming the hustings before that, a fair number will never even reach that stage. Still, their efforts to help their party's state and local candidates win in 1998, hoping to gain friends who will boost their own prospective candidacies in 2000, have been viewed by political professionals as an important preliminary to the more structured presidential competition.

"What is going on now is a shakeout process," Steve Grubbs, Iowa Republican chairman told me. "In order to make it to the starting line in a year and a half, you have to be there now."

In both parties, the competition for the grand prize in 2000 has been stimulated because the incumbent president cannot succeed himself, something that has not been true since 1988. Moreover, Republicans and Democrats alike are struggling to redefine themselves as they head into the next century.

But most of the activity in Iowa and elsewhere has been among Republicans, because for the first time since 1940, when dark horse Wendell Willkie came out of nowhere to capture the nomination, the GOP lacks a clear front-runner. "There is no Michael Jordan," said Ohio Republican representative John Kasich, chairman of the House Budget Committee and one of many ambitious Republicans trying to take advantage of that void.

The particularly early start could set the stage for a portentous shift. Kasich said hopefully, "We are in the midst of a significant generational change in our party," likening what lies ahead for the GOP to the change Democrats went through when they nominated Clinton and Gore. The important issue facing GOP leaders, the forty-five-year-old Kasich contends, is whether this shift will go beyond age to fundamentals, such as the party's willingness "to take on the political system in a pretty direct way, to shake things up."

Kasich, whose fiscal conservatism is tinged with populism, demonstrated what he means by shaking things up in a talk at the Des Moines Bull Moose Club, an organization for young Republicans, when he urged an end to special tax breaks for corporations. "Corporate welfare ought to go, and the Republican party ought to lead the way," he said. "Now if we can go as a party and eliminate welfare for poor people, we ought to eliminate it for rich people as well." But Kasich's novel ideas are unlikely to win him favor among the staunch conservatives who dominate the nominating process in the GOP and who are far less interested than he in "shaking things up." Besides, Kasich possesses neither the financial resources nor the celebrity that would help him gain a foothold.

While Kasich used his stumping in Iowa to test out his ideas, Lamar Alexander had a more mundane goal for the talks he gave at fund-raisers for county parties and state legislative candidates—lining up supporters who would help him organize for his anticipated presidential bid. "I learned that Iowa is cold," Alexander said, recalling his 1996 Iowa campaign, when he finished third. "It takes a very committed person to go out and support you when it's 30 degrees below zero in February." And under the current system, these are the factors that spell the difference between success and failure.

Although up to a dozen Republicans are mentioned as possibilities for the campaign in 2000, most party operatives expect that no more than five will be able to raise the money to become serious candidates. In alphabetical order, those who deserve to be taken most seriously are:

- Lamar Alexander. His biggest assets are the experience and support he gained running in 1996, his Southern roots, and his vaguely centrist views. But he has shown himself all too willing to tailor his beliefs to suit political convenience.
- George W. Bush. He enjoys a potent political and fund-raising base as governor of Texas and priceless name recognition as his birthright. But his experience on the national scene is limited to his work as an aide in his father's campaigns.
- Steve Forbes. The reputation he made for himself in 1996 and his willingness to spend his own fortune could gain him a spot in the top tier. But the flat tax, which is the foundation of his candidacy, could also be its undoing, because it will make an easy target for his foes.
- Jack Kemp. On paper, Bob Dole's vice presidential running mate should be the favorite. He still has strong ties to conservatives, and he has broader appeal to minorities than any other Republican leader. But his so-so performance as Dole's running mate in 1996 suggests that he still lacks the discipline needed to win.
- Dan Quayle. A hard worker in the hustings, he is the number one heart throb of many party rank and filers and conservative Christians, who revere him for the enemies he has made. His main obstacle, said one Republican professional, "is that he is still standing in the big hole he dug when he was vice president."

During 1997, while the Republicans thrashed about for the right to succeed him, Clinton, despite his setbacks in Congress, continued to define the political debate, such as it was. Although his own ability to achieve substantive goals was clearly limited, he was able to drown out other voices. In this he was aided by the power and prestige of his office and by his skill at devising bite-size programs that he presented as solutions to the nation's economic and social problems.

Girding up for the sixth year of his presidency, Clinton got off to a flying start, unveiling new policy notions on an almost daily basis. "The State of the Union is no longer one evening but a month," boasted White House aide Rahm Emanuel. The *Washington Post*'s David Broder labeled Clinton "the Great Preemptor," for his ability to "force the Republicans to play catch-up in an effort to stay competitive." The sports metaphor was appropriate because Clinton and his team of aides were far more concerned with gamesmanship—scoring points with the press and in the polls—than substance. Unwilling to challenge the Republicans to put up adequate funding that significant federal programs would require, they instead propounded remedies that were no match for the acute needs they were supposed to meet.

The targets at which Clinton claimed to aim—particularly health care, education, and housing—were important enough to command the attention of public and press. But the inadequacy of the remedies recalled the health reform enacted by Congress with Clinton's blessing during the 1996 campaign, which sought to protect people who had lost or changed their jobs to maintain their health insurance. It did that, but, as already noted, the new law failed to put a ceiling on what insurance companies could charge.

This was strikingly similar to Clinton's much-heralded 1998 proposal to allow millions of Americans between sixty-two and sixty-five without health insurance to buy into the Medicare program. However, the president, in accordance with his New Democratic faith, did not seek funding for the plan and instead proposed to make it self-financed. The trouble with that approach is that the cost, more than $400 a month, would be greater than about 90 percent of the potential eligible population could afford. Meanwhile, the harsh truth remained that the number of adult Americans without health insurance had increased from 37 million, when Clinton was elected in 1992 and was promising to expand health coverage, to more than 40 million by his sixth year in the White House.

But the grandest deception of all was reserved for his State of the Union speech, in which, after pledging to balance the budget in the coming fiscal year, Clinton proposed using the budget surplus expected to build up in future years "to save Social Security first." Those words won him an ovation from the joint session of Congress. But all the rhetoric really meant was that the surplus would be used to whittle away the federal debt, just as the payroll tax increases levied in the 1980s, supposedly to bolster Social Security, were used to check the skyrocketing deficits of that decade. As for the future of Social Security, that remained a question that would be answered only sometime in the future.

Although Clinton's programs did not actually remedy the country's problems, they helped him with his political problems by keeping the Republicans off balance. The visceral GOP response to Clinton's barrage of proposals was to denounce Clinton for promoting the revival of big government and big spending. But the programs, with their penny-pinching design, had all been crafted to withstand that charge and instead to fit in with Clinton's promise to somehow deliver government activism without cost or bureaucratic intrusion. Besides, by attacking popular programs, Republicans ran the risk of seeming to live up to the reputation for negativism they had earned during the 1995 budget crisis.

But if Clinton was able to handle the Republicans, it soon became clear that he still could not control his worst enemy—himself. Just before he delivered his 1998 State of the Union address, he was confronted by the gravest in a long series of scandals that had poisoned his presidency—

charges that he had carried on an affair with a young White House intern and then had sought to obstruct justice to cover up the dalliance.

Clinton immediately went into his "Comeback Kid" mode, denying any wrongdoing, while the First Lady castigated his critics as part of "a vast, right-wing conspiracy." In his struggle for survival, Clinton enjoyed a critical advantage over the rest of the political world: He was more determined to stay in office than anyone else is to get him out.

Yet even if Clinton's oft-demonstrated tenacity suggested he could survive this storm, the furor undercut his effectiveness. His potential for substantive achievement had already been debilitated by the unrelenting limits of the political system: his lame-duck status and the opposition control of Congress. Now, as a result of his own folly, Clinton had lost his grip on the dimension of the presidency at which he was best—the bully pulpit.

As the 1998 midterm elections approached, lassitude dominated the political system. "Voters' anger fading," the *Washington Post* headlined a story over the spring primary contests. But if the anger was fading it was because America's *fin-de-siècle* politics offered no outlet for indignation. Awash in the good fortune that brought low unemployment and low inflation, office holders saw no need to debate more fundamental concerns such as anxiety over job security, the inadequacies of health care, the uncertainties of retirement and the widening gulf between the well-off and the disadvantaged.

In their complacency, politicians regarded the prospect of continued turnout decline with equanimity, even claiming it to be evidence of public contentment. "It's not rocket science," claimed Kentucky Sen. Mitch McConnell, chairman of the Republican Senate campaign committee, echoing Gary LaPaille, the chairman of the Illinois Democratic Party. "The happier people are, the less likely they are to vote." In actuality, though, low turnout was part of a vicious cycle, rooted in voter apathy and cynicism, which yields more power to special interests and thus adds to voter apathy and cynicism.

Setting aside the shortcomings of current political leaders, it remains true that the burdens they face are much heavier, because of the structural defects in the political system. Since these flaws are rooted in the Constitution's separation of the executive and legislative branches, it stands to reason that only through changing the Constitution can these shortcomings be fully remedied. One possibility, much pondered by scholars over the years, would be to combine presidential and congressional elections, putting candidates for chief executive, representative, and senator on the same slot in the ballot and electing them all for the same four-year term. This would give legislators more incentive to cooperate with the president, when he or she happens to be of the same party, and would make it easier for voters to hold them accountable. Another change would be to allow intraterm elections, at the call of either the president or a majority of Congress, to occur once during the regular four-year term, as a means of resolving deadlocks in government leadership.

The fact that both the president and the legislators, by invoking this potent option, would risk losing their offices would discourage its abuse.

But whatever the merits of these similar approaches to constitutional change, implementing them would demand vast resources—financial backing, intellectual energy, grassroots organizing, and imaginative leadership—of which there is no evidence at present, and there is little reason to believe this prospect would change in the foreseeable future. Any such effort would mobilize intense and far-reaching opposition from the interest groups and officeholders who now dominate our political system. More fundamentally, any campaign for constitutional change of this sort would be foredoomed because it would threaten to overturn the precarious balance between what Americans want from government and what they are willing to give to government, which determines the success or failure of every political endeavor. Nevertheless, these proposals for change are worth studying because they help make clear the inadequacy of most of the half-measures that are proposed as reforms.

Absent a transformation in the Constitution, Americans can look for only marginal change in their political system. And even this, judging from experience, would probably require a coincident event of calamitous impact, the most likely possibility being an economic debacle near the scale of the Great Depression, occurring while one party or another controlled both the presidency and the Congress. Such circumstances might trigger a true partisan realignment, with the party that had the good fortune to be out of power emerging with a durable majority.

In the meantime, Americans can best serve their own interests and the common good by learning to live with the imperfections of the political system that they have inherited and by keeping a watchful eye on its practitioners. With two wobbly parties in charge of the government, each avoiding its portion of responsibility while grasping for more than its share of credit, cynicism is counterproductive, but a vigorous skepticism can be a constructive force.

In particular, members of the electorate should learn to be skeptical of the blandishments tendered in exchange for their support. They need to remember that politics is made up of choices and trade-offs, that everything of value carries a price, and that, in this democracy, the first obligation of citizenship is to guard against self-delusion.

A Note
on Sources

The main single source for this book is my own coverage of the events depicted here as national political correspondent for the *Los Angeles Times*. I have also drawn on the reportage of the daily press, chiefly the *New York Times*, the *Washington Post*, and the *Los Angeles Times*, and the weekly magazines *Time* and *Newsweek*. Among the books that I found helpful were David Maraniss's superb biography, *First in His Class* (New York: Simon and Schuster, 1993), for background on Clinton's years in Little Rock (chap. 3); Bob Woodward's *The Agenda* (New York: Simon and Schuster, 1994), for its fly-on-the-wall reporting of the early days of Clinton's White House, particularly the start of Clinton's relationship with Alan Greenspan (chap. 6); William Greider's *Secret of the Temple* (New York: Simon and Schuster, 1987) for its rare look into the workings of the Federal Reserve (chap. 6); Elizabeth Drew's *On the Edge* (New York: Simon and Schuster, 1994), for its insight into the tensions that led to the unraveling of Clinton's first two years in the White House (chap. 6); Theda Skocpol's *Boomerang* (New York: Norton, 1996) (chap. 6); Paul Starr's inside account, "What Happened to Health Care Reform?" *(American Prospect*, no. 20), for their analysis of the failure of the centerpiece program in Clinton's first-term agenda (chap. 6) and *Campaign for President* (Hollis, N.H.: Hollis Publishing) for the campaign managers' own views of the 1996 election, particularly their debate strategy (chap. 11).

Index